Managing Faecal Sludge and Septage in Urban India

Managing Faecal Sludge and Septage in Urban India

A Primary Non-Technical Guide

U.B. Singh

KALPAZ

ISBN : 978-93-5324-239-8

First Published, 2020

Published by

Kalpaz Publications
C-30, Satyawati Nagar,
Delhi – 110052
Ph.: 011-47034999, 9811692060
www.kalpazpublications.com
E-mail: kalpaz@hotmail.com

Printed at: G. Print Process, Delhi

Contents

Preface

Sanitation is an important in all aspects of human life—social, economical, health, hygiene, and environment. Bad sanitation adversely affects all. Keeping good sanitation thus becomes responsibility of government and citizens at large. Sanitation has many segments; but in this book focus is only on management of faecal sludge and septage.

India got independence some seven decades ago. It has gained importance as second most populous country in the world. About one-third of its population is found inhabiting in different size of its towns. However, even after seven decades of Independence, a good number of its urban households lack potable water in their premises; and majority of the households have no access to any kind of sanitary toilets. Unfortunately, about one among every five Indians is bound to adopt open defecation. None of our cities is wholly covered by sewer network. Even the partially covered cities have no proper facilities for managing the septage flowing out of sewer. This apathetic situation reflects on the image of the country.

It is a welcome move that since many five years the Government of India drew its attention to the prevailing insanitary conditions and launched in mission mode a Clean India Movement (*Swachh Bharat* Mission) to create awareness among its citizens and make the country open defecation free in a time bound manner. Crores of individual household toilets, community toilets and public toilets have been constructed across the country. It is not a new move of construction of toilets. Many low cost sanitation projects were launched earlier as well but all those efforts were not effective to accomplish their aims. This new community led initiative focused on behavioural change. The government just facilitates through incentive. This joint (Government of India, State Governments, Urban/Rural Local Governments, and the community, target group) initiative has been successful and effective in achieving its objectives. But this has raised the concern. After 2-3 years or so, what will happen to the human excreta (semi-solid) having accumulated in the pits (linking every single pit with the sewerage network which is capital intensive, time taking and land availability). This is high time the urban managers should start working on developing infrastructure for properly managing the faecal sludge. If the country fails, the havoc thus created will have a non-bearable pain.

The upcoming situation warrants a holistic approach. Sanitation being the State-Subject (as enshrined in the Constitution) the state governments should come out with a State Strategy and effective and enforceable legislations and guidelines. The urban local governments (sanitation function entrusted to local government) should frame their own bye-laws, make budget provision, and equip their human resource to meet this challenge. The community at large should show its willingness to pay and provide active participation, as they are the ultimate beneficiary/sufferer. The society and other stakeholders should give their fullest. The slackness or apathy by any partner may hamper the solution to this upcoming problem.

I myself having spent three decades of my professional academic career on training, teaching, research and consultancy in urban affairs; also as a curious student of public administration; having keen interest in urban governance; and above all being an awakened member of urban civil society, was not aware of seriousness and gravity of this social problem. Although throughout these years I have been skilling the urban officials/managers and local people's representatives on different aspects of urban low-cost sanitation, very scant attention was ever drawn to the final disposal and reuse of the human excreta. First time I studied the subject of faecal sludge and septage management in a holistic manner when I was engaged as an Expert Consultant by International Water Management Institute (IWMI), Colombo, Sri Lanka for advising on the proposed institutional arrangement under a Bill and Melinda Gates Foundation (BMGF) sponsored project on developing a decentralized system of sanitation in Delhi slums. My interest deepened further when I was selected for participating in the International Conference on (4th International Conference on Faecal Sludge Management) FSM-4 held at Chennai in Tamil Nadu whereat the subject was discussed threadbare by experts/academicians, and case studies of various countries were presented by urban administrators. This has an everlasting impact on me. Although I left the assignment in mid-way due to bad health of my octogenerian parents, the subject created an immense interest. At my farewell I assured my colleagues to serve the cause of sanitation even after my disassociation from the project. This little contribution is culmination to that assurance and my interest in the subject.

The present book is a preliminary one focusing on conceptualising the subject in non-technical manner. This is an attempt to create awareness among the policy makers, urban planners, urban managers, urban technocrats, urban researchers, the community, civil society, and all those having some stake and interest in urban sanitation. The book consists of five main chapters and two appendices. A few chapters are based and further developed on the draft chapters prepared and submitted under the project. The book aims to create an academic environment towards this burning and forthcoming problem of faecal sludge and its cost-effective solutions.

My sincere gratitude to all those who acted as catalyst in initiating and creating interest in this subject, in guiding, in providing literature and all sorts of enabling environment. I am thankful to all the authors/editors of the books/journals etc. whom I have quoted 'extensively' and referred to.

I am thankful to M/s Kalpaz Publications, New Delhi for publishing the book in a record time.

U.B. Singh

Makar Sankranti, 2020 Lucknow

List of Tables

List of Figures & Charts

Figures

Charts

Abbreviation

AMRUT	:	Atal Mission for Rejuvenation & Urban Transformation
BIS	:	Bureau of Indian Standards
BOD	:	Biochemical Oxygen Demand
CBO	:	Community Based Organization
CLTS	:	Community Led Total Sanitation
CPHEEO	:	Central Public Health and Environmental Engineering Organization
CPCB	:	Central Pollution Control Board
CSE	:	Centre for Science & Environment
CSR	:	Corporate Social Responsibility
CSTFs	:	City Sanitation Task Forces
CT	:	Census Towns
DEWATS	:	Decentralized Wastewater Treatment System
DLB	:	Directorate of Local Bodies
DPR	:	Detailed Project Report
Eco-san	:	Ecological Sanitation
FFD	:	Faecal Flow Diagram
FS	:	Faecal Sludge
FSM	:	Faecal Sludge Management
FSSM	:	Faecal Sludge and Septage Management
FSTF	:	Faecal Sludge Treatment Facility
FSTP	:	Faecal Sludge Treatment Plant
GIS	:	Geographical Information System
GPR	:	Ground Penetrating Radar
GoI	:	Government of India
GVMC	:	Greater Visakhapatnam Municipal Corporation

HRD	:	Human Resource Development
HRM	:	Human Resource Management
IEC	:	Information, Education and Communication
IHHT	:	Individual Household Toilet
ILCS	:	Integrated Local Cost Sanitation
IWM	:	Integrated Water Management
JnNNURM	:	Jawaharlal Nehru National Urban Renewal Mission
lpcd	:	liters per capita per day
LCS	:	Low Cost Sanitation
MDGs	:	Millennium Development Goals
M&E	:	Monitoring & Evaluation
MEF&CC	:	Ministry of Environment, Forests & Climate Change
MHM	:	Menstrual Hygiene Management
MH&UA	:	Ministry of Housing & Urban Affairs, Government of India
MIS	:	Management Information System
MLD	:	Million Liters per Day
MoHUPA	:	Ministry of Housing & Urban Poverty Alleviation
MoU	:	Memorandum of Understanding
MoUD	:	Ministry of Urban Development, Government of India
MSW	:	Municipal Solid Waste
MSWM	:	Municipal Solid Waste Management
NBC	:	National Building Code
NGO	:	Non-Government Organization
NIUA	:	National Institute of Urban Affairs
NUSP	:	National Urban Sanitation Policy, 2008
OD	:	Open Defecation
ODF	:	Open Defecation Free
ODF+/++	:	Open Discharge Free
O&M	:	Operation & Maintenance
OSS	:	On-Site Sanitation
OSSF	:	On-Site Sanitation Facility
PPCP	:	Public-Private-Community Participation

PPE	:	Personal Protective Equipment
PPP	:	Public Private Partnership
SBM (U)	:	Swachh Bharat Mission (Urban)
SDGs	:	Sustainable Development Goals
SFD	:	Sludge-flow Diagram
SHG	:	Self-help Group
SMS	:	Sending Message Services
SPCB	:	State Pollution Control Board
SS	:	Suspended Solids
ST	:	Statutory Town
STF	:	Septage Treatment Facility
STP	:	Sewage Treatment Plant
SWM	:	Solid Waste Management
SWOT	:	Strength Weakness Opportunity Threats
UDD	:	Urban Development Department
ULB	:	Urban Local Body
URIF	:	Urban Reform Incentive Fund
UN	:	United Nations
UNDP	:	United Nations Development Programme
UNEP	:	United Nations Environment Programme
UNICEF	:	United Nations Children's Education Fund
VGF	:	Viability Gap Fund
VIP	:	Ventilated Improved Pit (Latrine)
VTO	:	Vacuum Truck Operator
WHO	:	World Health Organization
WM	:	Water Management
WW	:	Waste Water
WWTP	:	Wastewater Treatment Plant

Glossary

Activated Sludge: An aerobic treatment process in which oxygen and micro-organism concentrations in wastewater are artificially elevated to facilitate rapid digestion of biodegradable organic matter

Aerated Pond or Lagoon: A natural or artificial wastewater treatment pond in which mechanical or diffused air aeration is used to supplement the natural re-oxygenation processes

Aerobic Treatment: Treatment of wastewater with the help of micro-organisms that rely on oxygen

Anaerobic Digestion: Decomposition of organic material by anaerobic bacteria in the absence of air

Anaerobic Lagoon: A system for treatment of high-strength wastewater and sludge that involves retention under anaerobic conditions allowing the liquid to infiltrate into the surrounding soil

Biochemical Oxygen Demand: A measure of the organic pollutant strength of waste water.

Bio-solids: This usually refers to treated faecal sludge or byproduct of the treatment of domestic sewage in a sewage treatment plant. Bio-solids consist primarily of digested organic matter and dead microbes and can be used as organic fertilizer or soil conditioner OR see Sewage Sludge

Black Water: Wastewater discharged from toilets

Bucket Latrine: A traditional but unhygienic form of sanitation in which faeces is deposited into a bucket which is collected regularly (usually at night) and taken away (usually by 'sweepers')

Composting Latrine: A latrine designed to receive both faeces and waste vegetable matter with the aim of reducing moisture content and achieving a carbon-to-nitrogen ratio that promotes rapid decomposition

Desludging: Removal of sludge or settled solid matter from treatment tanks such as septic/Imhoff tank, interceptor tank or sedimentation tanks OR This refers to the process of cleaning or removing the accumulated sludge/ septage from a septic tank, pit latrine or wastewater treatment facility

Digestion: Microbiological process that converts chemically complex organic sludge to methane, carbon dioxide, and inoffensive humus-like material

Disposal: Discharge, deposition or dumping of any liquid or solid waste onto land or water so that it may enter the environment

Domestic Sewage: All forms of wastewater derived from residential properties, as well as black water and grey water from commercial and institutions buildings OR Waste water composed of untreated human waste coming from residential and commercial sources; Domestic sewage does not include industrial and/or hazardous wastes

Dry Latrines: All forms of latrines that do not require water for flushing

Dry Sanitation: Disposal of human excreta without the use of water for flushing or anal cleansing

Ecological Sanitation (eco-san): A form of dry sanitation that involves separation of faeces and urine in order to facilitate recycling of nutrients in local agricultural systems

Effluent: The wastewater that flows out of a treatment system (in this case septic tank) or supernatant liquid discharged from the septic tank OR any form of wastewater or liquid waste that flows from an operation or activity OR The wastewater that flows out of a treatment system (in this case septic tank) or supernatant liquid discharged from the septic tank

Excreta: Faeces and urine

Faecal Sludge: Faecal sludge is the solid or settled contents of pit latrines and septic tanks; The undigested sludge that is collected from pit latrines and leach pits; It differs from sludge produced in municipal wastewater treatment plants; Faecal sludge characteristics can differ widely from household to household, from city to city, and from country to country; The physical, chemical and biological qualities of faecal sludge are influenced by the duration of storage, temperature, soil condition, and intrusion of groundwater or surface water in septic tanks or pits, performance of septic tanks, and tank emptying technology and pattern

Faecal Sludge Management (FSM): Also known as septage management, FSM includes the various technologies and mechanisms for collection, transportation, treatment and disposal of sludge produced by septic tanks, pit latrines, and wastewater treatment plants; OR Faecal Sludge Management (FSM) involves safely collecting, transporting, treating and disposing the faecal sludge from the on-site sanitation systems; A more commonly used term has been septage management, which is a historical term to define sludge removed from septic tanks

Faecal Sludge and Septage Management (FSSM): FSS Management (FSSM) deals with on-site sanitation systems, while wastewater management is concerned with sewered sanitation; FS may be treated in separate treatment works or co-treated with sludge produced in wastewater treatment plants

Grey-water (also known as Sullage): Wastewater produced by washing and bathing activities

Improved Sanitation: Connection to a public sewer or septic system, or access to a pour-flush latrine, a simple pit latrine or a ventilated improved pit latrine

Leach field: A trench filled with sand, soil, gravel and brickbats for disposal of septic tank overflow into the surrounding soil

Leach Pit (sometimes known as a Cesspit): An underground tank that is used where there is no sewer and household wastewaters are drained into them to permit leaching of the liquid into the surrounding soil

Night Soil: Human excreta, with or without anal cleansing material, which are deposited into a bucket or other receptacle for manual removal

On-plot Facilities: The components of a sanitation system located within a householder's plot

On-plot Sanitation: A sanitation system that is wholly contained within the plot occupied by a private dwelling and its immediate surroundings. Commonly, on-plot sanitation is equivalent to 'household latrine', but may also include facilities shared by several households living together on the same plot

Off-site Sanitation: A system of sanitation that involves collection and transportation of waste (wastewater either by sewerage or septage/faecal sludge by vacuum truck) to a location away from the immediate locality

On-site Sanitation System: Sanitation infrastructures that are designed to collect, store and dispose of human excreta at the household premises and include septic tank system and various types of pit latrines; OR On-site sanitation systems collect, contain and partially treat the faecal waste and wastewater. The sludge accumulated in these systems need to be periodically removed and treated before being disposed into the environment

Pathogens: Micro-organisms such as bacteria, viruses and protozoa that cause disease

Percolation Rate: The rate at which liquids move through soil

Pit Latrine: A form of on-plot sanitation with a pit for accumulation and decomposition of excreta from which liquid infiltrates into the surrounding soil

Pour Flush Toilet: A type of latrine where a water seal trap is used to prevent smells and to reduce insects

Sanitation: Interventions (usually construction of facilities such as latrines) that improve the management of excreta and promote sanitary (healthy) conditions

Scum: It is extraneous or impure matter like oil, hair, grease and other light material that floats at the surface of the liquid in the septic tank, while the digested sludge is stored at the bottom of the septic tank

Septage: The settled solid matter in semi-solid condition usually a mixture of solids and water settled at the bottom of septic tank. It has an offensive odour, appearance and is high in organics and pathogenic microorganisms. It is a mixture of wastewater and sludge removed from a septic tank during cleaning operations; OR Faecal sludge (settled solids, scum and liquid) that accumulates in septic tanks

Service Provider: A public or private entity, operator or water utility that is engaged in the collection, desludging, handling, transporting, treating, and disposing of sludge and septage from septic tanks, cesspools, sewage treatment plants, etc.

Septic Tank: An underground tank that treats wastewater by a combination of solids settling and anaerobic digestion. The effluents may be discharged into soak pits or small-bore sewers, and the solids have to be pumped out periodically or a form of on-plot sanitation for the anaerobic treatment of sewage/ black water; OR A watertight, multi-compartment, usually sub-surface receptacle that receives sewage from houses or other buildings and is designed to separate and store the solids and partially digest the organic matter in the sewage

Sewage: Sewage indicates the liquid waste from the community. It is extremely foul in nature. It is a mixture of wastewater from all urban activities from residential, commercial properties. It may also contain a component of industrial wastewater

Sewage Sludge (sometimes referred to as Bio-solids): A semisolid residue generated during the treatment of domestic sewage including both solids removed by sedimentation and biological sludge produced by biological treatment; OR sludge generated at the sewage treatment plants as a result of sewage digestion process is termed as sewage sludge. Sewage sludge is often more problematic than faecal sludge from household toilet facilities because it contains contaminants from industrial wastewaters

Sewer: It is an under-ground conduit or drain through which sewage is carried to a point of discharge or disposal or a conduit, usually a pipe, which is used to collect and convey wastewater away from its point of production to its point of disposal

Sewerage: The term sewerage means the structures, device, equipment and appurtenances intended for the collection, transportation and pumping of sewage and liquid wastes but excluding works for treatment of sewage. It is a network of interconnected sewers in an area, district or town

Sewerage system: A system of sewers that collects and conveys wastewater to a treatment plant for treatment prior to disposal point. It includes all infrastructures for collecting, transporting, and pumping sewage

Soak Pit: A porous-covered chamber that allows wastewater to soak into the ground. It is also known as a soak-away or leach pit

Soak Pit/Soakaway: A pit, typically after a septic tank from where wastewater slowly seeps into the ground through perforated sides and bottom

Stabilisation: Process of treating septage to reduce pathogen densities and vector attraction to produce an organic material that may be applied to the land as a soil conditioner

Suction Truck: A vehicle used for mechanized sludge removal from septic tanks and lined latrine pits

Sullage: Domestic dirty water not containing excreta. Sullage is also called grey water; OR Wastewater from bathing, laundry, preparation of food, cooking, and other personal and domestic activities

Superstructure: Screen or building enclosing a latrine to provide privacy and protection for users

Twin Pit Latrine: Twin-pits for pour-flush toilets are two underground leaching pits linked to one single pour-flush toilet by a Y-junction. The two pits are used alternately. The pits are lined either with a porous material or holes in the walls

Ventilated Improved Pit Latrine (VIP): A dry latrine system, with a dark interior and a screened vent pipe to reduce odour and fly problems

Vent Pipe: A pipe that facilitates the escape of gases and odours from a latrine or septic tank

Waste water: Liquid wastes from households or commercial or industrial operations, along with any surface water/storm water

Wastewater Treatment: A combination of physical, chemical, and biological processes to remove suspended solids, dissolved pollutants, and pathogens and render the water harmless to the environment

Water Closet: A pan, incorporating a water seal, in which excreta are deposited before being flushed away using water

Water Seal: Water held in a U-shaped pipe or hemispherical bowl connecting a pan to a pipe, channel or pit to prevent the escape of gases and insects from the sewer or pit

1

Urbanisation & Its Impact in India

Introduction

Urbanisation is an index of transformation from traditional rural economics to modern industrial one. It is a long term process. Kinsley Davis (1962) has explained urbanisation as a process of switch from spread out pattern of human settlements to one of concentration in urban centres. It is a finite process— cycles through which nations pass as they evolve from agrarian to industrial society. Urbanization is essential for socio-economic transformation, wealth generation, prosperity and development. The emerging future of cities largely depends on the way we plan and manage urbanization, and the way we leverage this transformative process to 'provide the setting, the underlying base and also the momentum for global change' (WCR Report: 2016). The onset of modern and universal process of urbanisation is about a century old phenomenon and is closely related with industrial revolution and associated economic development. Historical evidence suggests that urbanisation process is inevitable and universal. Currently developed countries are characterized by high level of urbanisation and some of them are in final stage of urbanisation process. Majority of the developing countries, on the other hand, started experiencing urbanisation only since the middle of 20th century.

Since 1990, the world has seen an increased gathering of its population in urban areas. This trend is not new, but relentless and has been marked by a remarkable increase in the absolute numbers of urban dwellers. Globally, more people live in urban areas than in rural areas. Sometime in 2008, human kind achieved a momentous milestone: for the first time in the history, half of the world's population lived in urban areas (UNFPA: 2009). In 2014, the proportion of the world's population residing in urban areas increased to 54 percent. In 1950, 30 percent of the world's population was urban; and by 2050, 66 percent of the world's population is projected to be urban (2014: Revision of World Urbanization Prospects).

Indian Urbanisation Pattern

The demographics of India are remarkably diverse. India is the second most populous country in the world with more than one -sixth of the world's population. At the moment, India is among the countries of low level of urbanization and it has been relatively slow compared to many developing countries. The annual exponential growth rates of urban population reveals that it grew at faster pace from the decade 1921-31 to until 1951. Thereafter it registered a sharp drop during the decade 1951-61. The decades 1961-71 and 1971-81 showed a significant improvement in the growth, which thereafter steadily dropped. This reflects a gradual zigzag increase in trend of urbanisation.

India shares most characteristic features of urbanization among the developing countries. Total population in the country recorded an increase from 23.84 crores, in 1901, to 102.7 crores (4.3 folds increase) in 2001, and 121.02 crores (five folds) in 2011; whereas urban population increased from 2.58 crores to 28.58 crores (11 folds increase) during the twentieth century and further to 37.71 crores in 2011(14 folds increase) in one hundred and ten years (1901-2011) (Table-1.1).

Table-1.1: Trend of Urbanisation in India: 1901-2011

Census Year	*Total Population (000's)*	*Total Urban Population (000,s)*	*Decadal Change in Percentage*		*Cumulative Increase against 1901 Population (per cent)*		*Percentage of urban Population to Total Population*
			Total	*Urban*	*Total*	*Urban*	
1901	238.40	25.8	—	—	-	-	10.8
1911	252.09	25.9	+5.7	+ 0.4	4.8	3.9	10.3
1921	251.32	28.1	(-) 0.3	(-) 8.5	5.4	8.9	11.2
1931	278.98	33.5	+ 11.0	+ 19.2	17.0	29.8	12.0
1941	318.66	44.2	+ 14.2	+ 31.9	33.7	71.3	13.9
1951	361.09	62.4	+ 13.3	+ 41.4	51.5 (1.5 fold)	141.9 (2.4 fold)	17.3
1961	439.23	78.9	+ 21.6	+ 26.4	84.2	205.8	18.0
1971	548.16	109.1	+ 24.8	+ 38.3	129.9	322.9	19.9
1981	683.33	159.3	+ 24.7	+ 46.0	186.6	517.4	23.7
1991	846.39	217.4	+ 23.9	+ 36.5	255..0	742.6	25.7
2001	1027.02	285.4	+ 21.3	+ 31.3	330.8 (4.3 fold)	1006.2 (11 fold)	27.8
2011	1210.2	377.1	+17.9	+32.1	407.6 (5 fold)	1361.6 (14.6 fold)	31.16

Source: Computed from data taken from Census Reports from 1901 to 2011, Rural Urban Distribution of population.

Figures in parentheses denote increase in comparison to 1901 population).

The urban content, however, has not shown the proportional increase. As per data available, urban ratio in the country in 1901 was 10.8; increased to 17.3 in 1951and 27.8 in 2001and has now reached to 31.16 in 2011, much below the projected level.

The process of urbanisation is a continuous one, which is not merely a concomitant of industrialization but a concomitant of the whole gamut of factors underlying the process of economic growth and social change. Surprisingly, increase in number of urban centres in the country has not been proportionate to urban population. Some fluctuations in number of towns in 1961 Census and after have been observed. It is because of some towns were declassified and some new ones were added at each census counts. Following the changes in the definition of urban areas and city size in 1961 Census (Bose 1978), 1971 Census later on adopted the same urban definition with slight modification of the term "town group" as urban agglomeration by merging several towns. The number of towns in the country grew from 1827, in 1901, to 5161, in 2001(2.8 times) and further to7935 in 2011 (4.3 times) (Table-1.2).

Table-1.2: Number of Towns from 1901 to 2011

Census Year	*Number of Towns/ UA's*	*Decadal Increase in number of Towns*	*Cumulative Increase in Towns in comparison to 1901*	*Urban Population (million)*	*Percentage Urban Population*
1901	1827	-	-	25.8	10.84
1911	1815	(-) 0.66	(-)0.004	25.9	10.29
1921	1949	7.38	6.7	28.1	11.18
1931	2072	6.31	13.4	33.5	11.99
1941	2250	8.59	23.2	44.2	13.86
1951	2843	26.36	55.61(1.6 fold)	62.4	17.29
1961	2365	(-) 16.81	29.4	78.9	17.97
1971	2590	9.51	41.76(1.4 fold)	109.1	19.91
1981	3378	30.42	84.89(1.8 fold)	159.3	23.34
1991	3768	11.54	106.24(2.1 fold)	217.4	25.72
2001	5161	36.97	182.48(2.8 fold)	285.4	27.78
2011	7935	53.75	334.32(4.3 fold)	377.1	31.16

Computed from data adapted from Kadi &Nelavigi (2015): Growth of Urbanisation in India; *The International Journal of Science & Technology; www.theijst.com*

Source: Census Data 1901-2011.

Figures in parentheses denote cumulative increase from 1901.

Urban areas in India are of three broad types: Statutory Towns (STs), Census Towns (CTs) and out-growths (OGs). Statutory towns are administratively declared urban areas by a state law which includes all manner of urban local bodies, such as municipalities, cantonment boards, and Industrial Township. Census towns are complete settlement units that are classified as urban areas by the Registrar General of India, as part of the census operations, if they cross the threshold on three specific urban characteristics, viz. size (population of at least 5,000), density (at least 400 persons per square kilometer) and non-farm nature of workforce (at least 75 percent of working male workforce earning their livelihood from non-agriculture sector). A major surprise from the data compiled by Census 2011 came with the number of census towns (CTs) rising from 1362 to 3894, while the number of statutory towns (STs) increased marginally from 3799 to 4041. Up to 2001, the focus on census towns was limited; as their share in the total urban population was low (7.4 percent in 2001) and their numbers were growing gradually. However, the sudden increase in the number of census towns has highlighted the need for more attention to this class of settlements. However, settlements declared as census towns continue to be administered as rural areas. Out-growths (OAs) are viable units which emerge adjacent to but outside the administrative limits of statutory towns. These are however not complete settlement units, like an entire village (Bhagat: 2011). Table-1.3 depicts the number of statutory and census towns state-wise in the country.

Table-1.3: Number of Census Towns from 2001 to 2011

Sl. No.	*States*	*2001*			*2011*			*Percentage Increase in Towns*
		Statutory Towns	*Census Towns*	*Total*	*Statutory Towns*	*Census Towns*	*Total*	
	INDIA	**3799**	**1362**	**5161**	**4041 (6.37)**	**3894 (185.90)**	**7935**	**53.7**
1.	Chandigarh	1	0	1	1	5	6	500.0
2.	Daman & Diu	2	0	2	2	6	8	300.0
3.	Kerala	60	99	159	59	461 (365.66)	520	227.0
4.	Dadar Nagar Haveli	0	2	2	1	5	6	200.0
5.	Nagaland	8	1	9	19	7	26	188.9
6.	West Bengal	123	252	375	129	780 (209.52)	909	142.4
7.	Lakshadweep	0	3	3	0	6	6	100.0
8.	Chhattisgarh	75	22	97	168	14	182	87.6
9.	Tripura	13	10	23	16	26	42	82.6
10.	NCT of Delhi	3	59	62	3	110 (86.44)	113	82.3
11.	Assam	80	45	125	88	126 (180.00	214	71.2
12.	Andhra Pradesh	117	93	210	125	228 (145.16)	353	68.1
13.	Puduchery	6	0	6	6	4	10	66.7
14.	Andman Nicobar Islands	1	2	3	1	4	5	66.7
15.	Jammu & Kashmir	72	3	75	86	36 (1100.0)	122	62.7

(Contd...)

16.	Odisha	107	31	138	107	116 (274.19)	223	61.6
17.	Goa	14	30	44	14	56	70	59.1
18.	Arunachal Pradesh	0	17	17	1	26	27	58.8
19.	Manipur	28	5	33	28	23	51	54.5
20.	Bihar	125	5	130	139	60 (1100.0)	199	53.1
21.	Jharkhand	44	108	152	40	188 (74.07)	228	50.0
22.	Haryana	84	22	106	80	74 (236.36)	154	45.3
23.	Gujarat	168	74	242	195	153 (106.76)	348	43.8
24.	Maharashtra	251	127	378	256	279 (119.69)	535	41.5
25.	Punjab	139	18	157	143	74 (311.11)	217	38.2
26.	Meghalaya	10	6	16	10	12	22	37.5
27.	Uttarakhand	74	12	86	74	42 (250.0)	116	34.9
28.	Rajasthan	184	38	222	185	112 (194.76)	297	33.8
29.	Tamil Nadu	721	111	832	721	376 (238.74)	1097	31.9
30.	Uttar Pradesh	638	66	704	648	267 (304.55)	915	30.0
31.	Karnataka	226	44	270	220	127 (400.0)	347	28.5
32.	Madhya Pradesh	339	55	394	364	112 (103.66)	476	20.8
33.	Mizoram	22	0	22	23	0	23	4.5
34.	Himachal Pradesh	56	1	57	56	3	59	3.5
35.	Sikkim	8	1	9	8	1	9	0.0

Computed from data adapted from Kadi &Nelavigi (2015): Growth of Urbanisation in India; The International Journal of Science & Technology (ISSN 2321 – 919X) ;www.theijst.com
Figures in parentheses denote percentage increase

Although urbanisation is a necessary condition for modernisation, the kind of urbanisation taking place in India is marked by the growth of a few large cities and metropolitan centres. Thus, the urbanization process in India has continued to be top-heavy, oriented towards large cities. This is because of higher demographic growth in larger cities, attributable to both natural increase in the resident population and higher net in-migration. In turn, this is consistent with the fact that larger cities are generally more efficient in generating growth and attracting investments, thus attracting more population (Kundu: 2011).

This has led to tremendous growth in million cities (cities with population of ten lakhs and more) in post-independence era. Their number increased from solitary metropolitan city in the beginning of the 20th century (Kolkata) to 5 in first half of the century (1901-1951), to 35 in the last five decades (1951-2001), and further to 53 in 2011. Interestingly, more than one-third of urban population is found inhabited in these metropolitan cities; and about two-thirds of urban content is concentrated in class-I towns (towns with population of one lakh and more), including metropolises. The total population of 12 million plus cities in 1981in the country was 42.1 million. The average population growth rate, of the million plus cities during 1971-1981 was nearly 40 percent. In 1981, 12 million plus cities contained over six percent of the Indian population. In 1991, 23 million cities with a total population of 70.7 million accounted for about 8 percent of the total population of India. This eight percent was equivalent to about 33 percent of the total urban population. It was revealed by the 2001 Census that there were now 35 million cities accounting for 107.9 million persons. The population of these 35 cities was about 38 percent of the total urban population. The overall decennial increase in population in 35 mega cities is about 68 percent during the 1991-2001 decade. In 2011, the number of metropolitan towns increased to 53, containing more than two-fifths of the total urban population. (Table-1.4)

Table-1.4: Growth of Million Cities in India, 1901 – 2011

Census Year	*No. of Million + Cities*	*Total population (Million)*	*Percent Increase*	*Percentage of urban Population*	*Percentage of Total population*
1901	1	1.51	-	5.84	0.6
1911	2	2.76	82.3	10.65	1.1
1921	2	3.13	13.4	11.14	1.3
1931	2	3.41	8.9	10.18	1.2
1941	2	5.31	5.7	12.23	1.7
1951	5	11.75	21.3	18.81	3.3
1961	7	18.10	54.0	22.93	4.1
1971	9	27.83	53.8	25.51	5.1
1981	12	42.12	51.3	26.41	6.2
1991	23	71.12	67.8	33.29	8.4
2001	35	107.9	52.8	38.1	10.5
2011	53	160.7	48.9	42.6	13.3

Source: 1. Computed from Census reports (1901 - 2001). Census of India, Occasional Paper I of 1986, "Study on Distribution of Infrastructural facilities in different Region and Levels and Trends of Urbanisation", Social Studies Division, Office of the Registrar General, New Delhi, p. 571.

2. Census of India, 1991. Part-II A (ii) – Towns and Urban Agglomerations classified by population in 1991 with variation since 1901.

3. Census of India, 2011: Provisional Population Totals.

The above analysis shows that the nature of India's urbanisation is quite different from the historical experience of the Western countries. Due to the high rate of natural increase in population, India has experienced urbanisation without labour absorption. Despite more than doubling of the percentage of urban population, the proportion of labour force engaged in the agricultural sector has not declined. It has slightly increased in a decade. The role of rural migration in India's urbanisation is less significant when compared to the experience of Western countries and even many of the developing countries. However, due to the high rate of natural increase in population, supplemented by the rural-urban migration, urban population is growing very fast. Further, the concentration of urban population in few larger cities (as number of towns has since not increased proportionately) has resulted into mushrooming of slums and shanties (un-served or under-served localities, and symbol of urban poverty), stress on infrastructure and basic civic services, informalisation of economy, pressure on city management, etc. Davis (1954) used the term 'over urbanisation' (for such a situation) wherein urban misery and rural poverty exist side by side, with the result that city can hardly be called dynamic and where inefficient, unproductive informal sector becomes increasingly apparent.

Demographic Profile of Uttar Pradesh

Uttar Pradesh is the most populous state in the country, accounting for 16.4 percent of the country's population. It is also the fourth largest state in geographical area covering 6.88 percent of the country's total geographical area, encompassing 2, 43,290 square kilometers. The pace of urbanization has been lower in the state. The level of urbanization has also been lower than most other states. The numbers of urban centres with more than one lakh population have grown slowly over the last thirty years. The growth of urban centres with population less than five thousand have, on the other hand, grown more significantly and these centres have grown in larger numbers in the western part of the state. Further, the tremendous increase in number of census towns (CTs) from 66 in 2001 to 267 in 2011 has added another but acknowledged management complexities. Demographic details of the state are compiled in Table-1.5.

Table 1.5: Uttar Pradesh: Demographic Profile (1901-2011)

Year	*Population (crore)*	*Decadal Growth (%)*	*Urban Population (crore)*	*Decadal Growth (%)*	*Level of Urbanisation (%)*
1901	4.86	-	0.54	-	11.09
1911	4.82	(-)0.97	0.49	(-)8.98	10.19
1921	4.67	(-)3.08	0.49	0.61	10.58
1931	4.98	6.66	0.56	12.81	11.19
1941	5.65	13.57	0.70	26.00	12.41

(Contd...)

1951	6.07	6.61	0.86	22.93	14.31
1961	7.38	22.37	0.95	9.90	12.85
1971	8.83	19.78	1.24	30.68	14.02
1981	11.09	25.49	1.99	60.54	17.94
1991	13.21	19.12	2.60	36.63	19.67
2001	16.69	25.85	3.45	26.82	20.78
2011	19.98	20.23	4.45	28.75	22.28

Source: Compiled from different Census reports; Population of Uttar Pradesh retrieved from Statistics Times.com on 29-8-2019.

As per 2011 census, Uttar Pradesh has 915 towns, consisting of 648 statutory towns (containing about 92 percent of the total urban population) and 267 census towns (inhabiting about 8 percent of the total urban population). The statutory towns consist of 630 municipal towns, 5 industrial townships (containing a meagre portion of 0.21 percent of the total urban population or 0.23 percent of the population contained by statutory towns) and 13 towns administered by Cantonment Board. (Number of municipal towns has since increased (July, 2019) to 652 as many new municipalities of different types have since been created. A number of proposals for constituting new lower level municipalities for transitional areas (certainly not confined to census towns only) are under consideration by the state government. Data presented in Table-1.6 depict the population content of different types of municipalities. The census, 2011 analysis shows that about 8 percent of urban population inhabiting in census towns in the state is beyond the purview of municipal laws and still governed by rural laws.

Table-1.6: Details of Municipal Network in Uttar Pradsh (July, 2019)

Municipality	*Number*	*Area (Km^2)**	*Population 2001 (crores)**	*Proportion to Total Municipal Area (%)*	*Proportion to total Municipal Population (%)*	*Proportion to total Urban Population (%)**
Nagar Nigam (Municipal Corporation)	17	2142.46	1.88	29.28	45.08	42.25
Nagar Palika Parishad (Municipal Council)	198	2406.06	1.54	32.89	36.93	34.61
Nagar Panchayat	437	2767.59	0.75	37.83	17.99	16.75
Total	**652**	**7316.11**	**4.17**	**100.00**	**100.00**	**93.61**

Source: Uttar Pradesh Nagar Vikas Vibhag ka Karya Vivaran (in Hindi):2018-2019).
Area and Population vary as number of Municipalities varies

Impact of Urbanisation

While urbanization is generally a positive given its strong correlation with economic prosperity, India's urbanization has been constrained by a combination of inadequate policy focus on cities, weak local governments, inadequate investments and widening gap in service delivery. Urban water supply and sanitation is a critical component of urban service delivery and provision of universally affordable and equitable access to water and sanitation is central to making India's cities liveable. So is the case with municipal solid and liquid wastes management. Our cities are full with filth and public agencies have miserably failed in collecting and disposing of solid waste and safe disposal of sewage and faecal sludge.

India's urbanisation is hence followed by some basic problems in the field of housing, slums, transport, water supply and sanitation, water pollution and air pollution and inadequate provision of social infrastructure. Most of the large cities using capital intensive technologies cannot generate employment for these distress rural poor. So there is transfer of rural poverty to urban poverty. Poverty induced migration of illiterate and unskilled labourer to large cities add urban involution and urban decay. Poverty induced migration occurs due to social push. Mega cities in the country have been growing in number and in urban population, not in urban prosperity and culture. Hence, it is urbanisation without urban functional characteristics. The mega cities are subject to extreme filthy slums and very cruel damaging shelter, drinking water, electricity, sanitation to the extremely poor and migrants, majority from generations.

Cities have since grown at such high and uncontrolled rates that a combination of factors now explains why informal settlements are the dominant land for major work-force in urban areas. Insufficient urban infrastructure especially housing and services, the poor vision of city planners, the inconsistency of urban land use management, inadequate planning scheme, clashes on land rights, and economic crisis are all further contributing to the slum expansion. The neo-liberal economic policies have also led to rapid proliferation of informal settlements, increase of social inequalities and spread of poverty.

The slum challenge continues to be one of the faces of poverty, inequality and deprivation in many cities in developing countries. Slums are the products of failed policies, poor governance, corruption, inappropriate regulation, dysfunctional land markets, unresponsive financial systems, and a lack of political will.

A lasting solution to the challenge of slums can only be achieved through concerted efforts of all stakeholders. It is important to create an inclusive environment that encourages the commitment of the authorities and the engagement of the concerned communities to enhance a better understanding of the slum challenge (WCR: 2016).

The rural-urban divide in the country has been a cause of major concern and not enough effort has been put in to build synergies between the urban and rural parts of the economy. The ability to manage urbanization and prepare cities for their new role is one of the biggest challenges facing India's planners. The growth momentum cannot be sustained if healthy urbanization is not accommodated and facilitated (Ahluwalia: 2011).

Closely linked to the issue of slums particularly in the fast growing cities is the challenge of providing adequate basic services and infrastructure. This challenge is central to the economic performance of cities, and their ability to provide a minimum quality of life to their citizens. The major services which cities provide include transport networks, water and sanitation connections, electricity, health, education, and a whole host of other ancillary services such as street cleaning, the maintenance of public spaces and parks, public lighting, archives, and cemeteries. When urban services are lacking or are severely strained – as in large areas in many poor cities with large informal settlements – the basic productivity of all citizens will be compromised.

Further, the country is benefitted by demographic dividend. As such, India is young today and will remain so until it becomes a country full of old population after 40-50 years. As a result, the young population labour force is expected to increase tremendously. This demographic dividend can add to growth potential, provided two conditions are fulfilled. First, much higher levels of health, education and skill development must be achieved. Second, an environment must be created in which the economy not only grows rapidly, but also expands good quality employment/ livelihood opportunities to meet the needs and aspirations of the youth (Twelfth Plan: 2012).

Although urbanization has the potential to make cities more prosperous and countries more developed, many cities all over the country are grossly unprepared for the multidimensional challenges associated with urbanization. Generally, urbanization has relied on a model that is unsustainable in many respects. Environmentally, the current model of urbanization engenders low-density suburbanization— largely steered by private, rather than public interest, and partly facilitated by dependence on car ownership; it is energy-intensive and contributes dangerously to climate change. Socially, the model of urbanization generates multiple forms of inequality, exclusion and deprivation, which creates spatial inequalities and divided cities, often characterized by gated communities and slum areas. Cities face growing difficulties in integrating migrants and refuges so that they equitably share in the human, social, cultural and intellectual assets of the city, and thus have a sense of belonging. From an economic perspective, the model of urbanization is unsustainable due to widespread unemployment especially among the youth and the existence of unstable and low-paying jobs and informal income-generating activities, which create economic hardship, unequal access to urban services and amenities and poor quality of life for many (WCR Report: 2016).

Summing Up

All these urban challenges are further exacerbated by the failure to create appropriate institutional and legal structures to promote sustainable urbanization. Indeed, poorly planned and managed urbanization – which translates into low densities, separation of land uses, mismatch between infrastructure provision and residential concentration, and inadequate public space and street networks, among others – diminishes the potential of leveraging economies of scale and agglomeration.

The Millennium Development Goals (MDGs) and the recently adopted Sustainable Development Goals (SDGs) place considerable emphasis on the improvement of basic services – in both urban and rural areas. Sustainable urbanization requires generating better income and employment opportunities in both urban and rural areas; expanding the necessary infrastructure for water and sanitation, energy, transportation, information and communications; ensuring equal access to services, like education and health care; developing sufficient quality housing and reducing the number of people living in slums; and preserving the natural assets within the city and surrounding areas (Urbanisation Prospects: 2014).

References

- *UNFPA (2009): State of the World Population: Unleasing the Potential of urban Growth, New york*
- *UN Population Div.2007*
- *UN Habitat (2008-9):State of the World Cities 2008/2009, Harmonious Cities, Earthen, London*
- *Davis, K. (1962): Urbanisation in India-Past and Future, in R. Turner (ed) India's Urban Future, University of California press, Berkley*
- *UN DEAS (2007): World Population Prospects: the 2006 revision highlights, New York*
- *Bhagat, R.B. (2005): Urban Growth by city and town size in India, paper presented at the annual meeting of Population Association of America, Philadelphia, PA*
- *Davis, K. and Golden, H.H. (1954) Urbanisation and Development in pre-industrial Areas, Economic Development and Cultural Change, Vol 3, No.1*

- *Government of India (2011): Report of the High Powered Committee for Estimating the Investment Requirements for Urban Infrastructure Services* (known as Ahluwalia Report)
- *Peter, Newman (2006): The Environmental Impact of Cities, Environment and Urbanization, 18(2), Oct, 275*
- *Government of India (2011): Faster, Sustainable and More Inclusive Growth (An Approach to the Twelfth Five Year Plan)*
- *S. Kadi, K. P. Nelavigi (2015): Growth of Urbanisation in India; The International Journal of Science & Technolodgy ; Vol 3 Issue 7; July;pp.30-38; www.theijst.com*
- *Distribution and Growth of Population in Million Cities; 11 Chapter 2:metro.pdf, accessed on 26-11-2017*
- *Kundu, A. 2011 Trends and Processes of Urbanisation in India. In Human Settlements Group, International Institute for Environment and Development (IIED) London & United Nations Population Fund (UNFPA) New York: Urbanisation and Emerging Population Issues- 6, 1-60. http://pubs.iied.org/pdfs/10597IIED.pdf*
- *United Nations Department of Economic and Social Affairs/Population Division; World Urbanization Prospects: The 2014 Revision*
- *Bhagat, R. B. (2011): "Emerging Pattern of Urbanisation in India", Economic and Political Weekly, 46 (34): 10-12 as quoted in Pradhan, K. C.(2012): Unacknowledged Urbanisation: The New Census Towns of India; Centre for Policy Research* **,** *New Delhi, accessed from www.cprindia.org on 19-11-2017*
- *U.N. (2015):World Urbanization Prospects- the 2014 Revision*
- *Bose, A.(1979):Studies in India's Urbanisation 1901-2001(Studies in demography);*
- *Government of India; Registrar General of Census Operations in India; Census Reports of various years*
- *Government of India; Twelfth Five Year Plan*
- *UNHABITAT : World Cities Report, 2016*

2

Sanitation in Urban India: Status & Challenges

Introduction

Sanitation refers to all conditions that affect health, especially with regard to dirt and infection, and specifically to the drainage and disposal of sewage and refuse from houses (The Concise Oxford Dictionary). A WHO Study Group (1986) formally adopted this meaning by defining sanitation as "the means of collecting and disposing of excreta and community liquid wastes in a hygienic way so as not to endanger the health of individuals and the community as a whole" (WHO: 1987).

Thus, sanitation is taken as a broad term which includes safe disposal of human waste, waste-water management, solid waste management, water supply, control of vectors of diseases, domestic and personal hygiene, and hygiene maintenance in food and housing. Sanitation and environmental sanitation converge in many aspects. Environmental sanitation is largely viewed as "the control of all those factors in man's physical environment which exercise a deleterious effect on his physical environment, health, alleviating poverty, enhancing quality of life, and raising productivity—all of which are essential for sustainable development" (WHO: 1992). For the limited purpose of this book, sanitation however has been confined only to the faecal sludge and septage management (sewage from latrines), more so unsewered one.

A hygienic household toilet is the most important aspect of sanitation. Besides restoration of dignity, privacy, safety and social status, sanitation has strong bearings on child mortality, maternal health, water quality, primary education, gender equity, reduction of hunger and food security, environmental sustainability, global partnerships and ultimately on poverty alleviation and improvement of overall quality of life.

Status of Urban Sanitation

India's urban population has sharply increased from 19.9 percent in 1971 to 31.2 percent in 2011. This unprecedented growth, along with high economic growth, has resulted in a severe challenge for Urban India, in terms of addressing the incremental infrastructural needs of a fast-growing urban population. One of the major challenges arising out of increased migration of the populace from rural areas to cities and towns in search of an improved quality of life has been the issue of access to sanitary facilities, and the attendant menace of open defecation, especially in areas housing economically weaker sections of society, where open defecation spots are more likely to be found (Triggering for Behavior Change towards Open Defecation Free status).

Even moderate urbanization (albeit with rapid growth in urban population) in the country has resulted into unplanned and haphazard growth of cities, especially larger urban centres. This has led to increasing problem of housing, overcrowding in small houses, steady growth of slums and unplanned settlements and severe deleterious effect on civic services in urban areas. Negative consequences of urban 'pull' (migration from small towns as well as villages) has resulted into housing shortage and critical infrastructure and civic services inadequacies. The large Indian cities, as discussed earlier, contain majority of the urban population, are grossly unprepared for the multidimensional challenges associated with urbanization, especially relating to sanitation.

Sanitation overall is generally considered one of India's biggest challenges. The National Sample Survey (65th Round: 2010) estimated that eight percent of the urban households were dependent on pit latrines, and 29 percent dependent on toilets connected to septic tanks, underlining the predominance of on-site arrangements – and it is not clear how the wastes are disposed from this majority of installations. The Census of India,2011 statistics reveal that only about one-third (32.7 percent) of urban households (HHs) are connected to a piped sewer system; less than two-fifths (38.2 percent) dispose of their wastes into septic tanks; seven percent have pit latrines; 50 lakh pit latrines are unsanitary (no slabs/open pits); 13 lakh are service latrines; out of which 9 lakh toilets dispose faeces directly into drains; 2 lakh latrines are serviced by humans (illegally), 1.8 lakh latrines serviced by animals. Finally, about 18.6 percent urban households still do not have access to individual toilets – about 6 percent use public/community toilets and 12.6 percent are forced the indignity of open defecation. The overall access to toilets is depicted in Figure-2.1. More than one-tenth of the population practice open defecation (Hawkins: 2016).

This pathetic situation not only deteriorates environment but also adversely affects human health.

The National Family Health Survey-3 (NFHS: 2005-06) reported that 17 percent urban households in India did not have access to any toilets at home, 24 percent households were sharing toilets (technologies not specified), about 19 percent had their toilets connected to sewers, the majority had on-site installations – about 27.6 percent households had septic tanks and 6.1 percent had pit latrines that were classified as "improved". Another 5 percent toilets were as "Flush/pour flush not linked to sewer/ septic tank/pit latrine" – in other words, human excreta from these installations were being let out untreated onto land and water bodies without any confinement or treatment. In other words, about 33 percent households had "improved" on-site systems and 5 percent of the households were on on-site unimproved toilets.

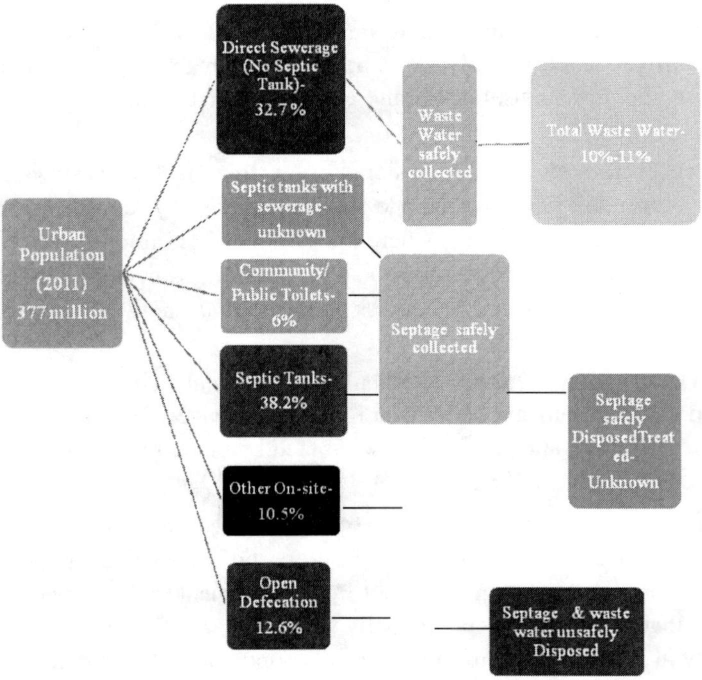

Source: Office of the Registrar General and Census Commissioner of India (2011) and Central Pollution Control Board (2009).

Figure 2.1: Access to Toilets

Official coverage figures do not, on their own, give the full picture regarding access to sanitation services (GoI: 2008). Existing arrangements can in fact be deficient in a number of ways, described as under:

(i) There may be a 'complete lack of facilities'. For example, there may be settlements with no toilets at all, while facilities for the safe emptying of septic tanks, and the treatment of septage, may be lacking across the entire town.

(ii) Sanitation facilities may be available but could be 'inconvenient, unpleasant or unhygienic'. This may be the result of inappropriate design or construction, or inadequate management arrangements. Poor management is often a problem with community toilet blocks.

(iii) Sanitation facilities may be available, but some people have 'limited access' to them. For example, people may not be able to afford to connect to an existing public sewer.

(iv) Sanitation facilities may be in place but are 'not operated or maintained properly'. Poor operation and maintenance of a facility shortens its useful life and could, at worst, result in rapid total failure.

(v) There may be no provision for the 'treatment of wastewater or excreta'. Local drains and sewers may simply relocate waste to another part of town where it causes local pollution. Households are primarily concerned about the cleanliness of their immediate surroundings and much less worried about the wider impact on the environment.

Whatever may be, as per data available, every tenth person is practicing open defecation, either voluntarily or for lack of services. We have to depend on data collected, analysed and disseminated by the Registrar General for Census Operations in the country.

India is not an exception. Many other countries experience insanitary conditions. Between 2000 and 2015, the proportion of the global population using improved sanitation increased from 59 percent to 68 percent. This means that 4.9 billion people globally were using an improved sanitation facility in 2015. One -third of the world's population (2.4 billion people) still does not have access to an improved sanitation facility, one that separates human waste from human contact. Almost a billion people (946 million) do not use any sanitation facility and defecate in the open. The unsafe management of faecal waste and wastewater continues to pose a major risk to public health and the environment (UN: 2015).

As articulated in the National Urban Sanitation Policy (NSUP), achieving totally sanitized cities requires going beyond building toilets towards adopting holistic city-wide and community-led approaches (GoI:2016).

The problem of sanitation in urban areas is also very serious since almost all our cities, including even the states capitals and major metros, have a large percentage of the population (45 percent in Delhi) not connected to the sewer system. Most of the urban India has still not been able to eliminate the scourge of open defecation, at census 2011, over 12.6 percent of urban households resorted to open defecation. While this is a sharp reduction from 18 percent in 2001, concerted efforts on a war footing are required to eliminate open defecation all-together (UNDP:2016). Such a serious situation has attracted the attention of the Indian Government which has launched a mega scheme '*Swachch Bharat*" (clean India) in a mission mode to make the country free from open defecation by October 2, 2019 (150th year of Mahatma Gandhi's Birth Anniversary).

Limited Access to Sanitation Services

It is amazing that even after about seven decades of getting independence and having less than one-third of the population inhabiting in urban centres, Urban India has still not been able to eliminate the scourge of open defecation, at census 2011, over 12.6 percent of urban households resorted to open defecation. While this is a sharp reduction from 18 percent in 2001, concerted efforts on a war footing are required to eliminate open defecation all-together (Government of India : XII Plan).

In addition to the above mentioned social menace, Indian cities are the victim of lack of improved sanitation services. The Census 2011 reveals that a little less than one-third (32.7 percent) urban population is covered under direct sewerage facility. Contrarily, more than that (38.2 percent) of the population has 'septic tanks with no sewerage' and another one-tenth (10.5 percent) has on-site-sanitation service. Thus majority of the urban population in the country is not covered under traditional safe underground sewerage system. Also to be noted is that many of the households that have toilets connected to underground sewers are in large metropolitan cities and especially, in better planned housing areas in these cities.

Ironically, even after seven decades of independence, the extent of access to toilet services by population is far away from satisfaction. The Census 2011 has compiled state-wise data on availability and type of latrine facility. The state-wise scenario has been depicted in Table: 2.1.

Table-2.1: Availability and Type of Latrine Facility: 2001-2011

States	***URBAN***									
	Total Households (lakhs)		***Percentage of Households having***							
			Water Closet		***Pit Latrine***		***Other Latrine***		***No Latrines***	
	2011	2001	2011	2001	2011	2001	2011	2001	2011	2001
INDIA	**788.66**	**536.92**	**72.6**	**46.1**	**7.1**	**14.6**	**1.7**	**13.0**	**18.6**	**26.3**
Andhra Pradesh	67.78	41.74	79.4	47.0	4.1	15.1	2.6	16.0	13.9	21.9
Bihar	20.14	13.23	63.4	43.4	4.6	11.4	1.0	14.9	31.0	30.3
Chhattisgarh	12.39	7.89	58.7	38.8	1.1	5.2	0.4	8.6	39.8	47.4
Gujarat	54.16	37.58	85.2	62.1	2.1	9.8	0.4	8.7	12.3	19.5
J& K	5.17	3.90	68.5	26.5	4.3	20.2	14.7	40.2	12.5	13.1
Jharkhand	14.96	10.60	64.7	41.2	1.8	7.4	0.6	18.0	32.8	33.3
Karnataka	53.16	35.57	71.6	44.9	12.0	20.7	1.4	9.7	15.1	24.8
Kerala	36.21	16.53	75.3	74.8	21.9	11.1	0.3	6.2	2.6	8.0
M.P.	38.45	27.95	71.5	41.1	1.7	11.9	1.0	14.7	25.8	32.3
Maharashtra	108.14	80.70	67.3	44.4	2.4	7.1	1.6	6.6	28.7	41.9
Odisha	15.17	10.87	58.8	43.1	4.2	9.5	1.8	7.2	35.2	40.3
Punjab	20.94	14.90	85.6	46.5	6.8	20.5	1.0	19.5	6.6	13.5
Rajasthan	30.91	21.86	73.7	40.6	5.4	18.2	2.9	17.3	18.0	23.9
Tamil Nadu	89.29	58.99	66.5	45.5	6.8	11.2	1.8	7.7	24.9	35.7
Uttar Pradesh	74.49	51.71	77.2	32.0	2.9	18.1	3.0	30.0	16.9	20.0
West Bengal	63.50	45.54	61.6	55.2	22.5	22.9	0.9	6.8	15.0	15.2
Haryana	17.51	10.75	80.5	31.0	7.7	26.5	1.7	23.2	10.1	19.3
Uttarakhand	5.92	3.90	85.9	40.8	6.5	26.7	1.1	19.3	6.4	13.1
Himachal Pradesh	1.66	1.43	87.0	49.7	0.8	12.0	1.3	15.5	10.9	22.8
NCTof Delhi	32.61	23.85	86.0	47.4	1.7	15.2	2.1	16.5	10.2	21.0
Chandigarh	2.28	1.81	87.0	70.8	0.5	1.0	0.1	8.3	12.4	19.9
Goa	1.98	1.38	80.6	38.9	3.5	18.7	1.1	11.6	14.7	30.8
Puducherry	2.06	1.36	81.1	59.4	0.6	2.2	0.3	3.4	18.0	35.0
Assam	9.93	7.15	71.0	58.9	21.0	26.4	1.7	9.3	6.3	5.4
Arunachal Pradesh	0.66	0.48	74.9	28.1	13.9	32.1	0.7	26.8	10.5	13.0
Nagaland	1.15	0.67	79.1	19.9	15.0	40.5	0.5	33,8	5.4	5.9
Manipur	1.71	1.01	63.7	20.5	23.3	67.0	8.8	7.8	4.2	4.7
Meghalaya	1.16	0.91	82.9	43.5	12.3	33.1	0.6	14.9	4.3	8.4
Mizoram	1.16	0.82	80.9	34.5	17.2	54.5	0.5	9.0	1.5	2.0
Sikkim	0.36	0.13	91.8	87.0	3.3	1.9	0.1	2.9	4.8	8.2
Tripura	2.35	1.22	50.0	43.1	47.0	44.8	0.9	9.0	2.1	3.0
A&N Islands	0.34	0.23	86.8	58.7	0.2	6.7	0.1	11.1	12.9	23.5
Daman& Diu	0.48	0.12	84.2	60.6	1.1	3.4	0.1	1.5	14.6	34.6
D&N Haveli	0.38	0.11	80.3	71.6	0.7	3.5	0.3	2.2	18.7	22.8
Lakshadweep	0.08	0.04	97.2	70.2	0.5	0.8	0.0	12.8	2.3	16.2

Source: Census of India, 2011: Houses, Household Amenities and Assets (Latrine Facility).

It is seen that open defecation is still in practice in all the states. It contaminates the environment affecting entire communities and results in serious social, health, economic and environmental problems. Openly lying human waste enables breeding and transmission of pathogens, which carry diseases and infections (UN: 2015). The analysis reveals the real challenges relating to sanitation. Urban development in the country thus must give top priority to planning for water, toilets and sewerage as an integrated whole taking into account the likely expansion of the urban population.

The Urban Sanitation Challenge

As discussed earlier, urban sanitation, globally, remains a significant challenge for most low-and middle-income countries. Around 53 percent of the urban population in the least developed countries are still using unimproved sanitation.

In India, over the years, the demand for toilets has increased in urban areas, from 68 percent of the population in urban areas accessing toilets in 1991 to 88 percent in 2011. People have been building their own toilets connected to on-site-sanitation systems – especially septic tanks – in the absence of underground sewerage systems. Therefore, encouraging a faecal sludge management system is the way the present policy leverages the investment already made by people – a genuine reflection of the '*Swachh Bharat'* Mission (launched in 2014) was conceived and presented not as a government scheme, but as a people's movement. Under the mission, focus is on construction of toilets--individual households, community, and public— with sole aim to make the urban areas open defecation free. Lakhs and lakhs of toilets have since been constructed on government incentive across the country. These latrines mostly pit based, lack planning for making the faecal sludge management.

More than 38 percent of the Census 2011 urban households used toilets which relied on their own on-site systems, while 32 percent reported that their toilets were connected to sewerage systems. According to a USAID study (2010), by 2017, the number of urban households with toilets connected to septic tank would increase to 148 million urban households. Therefore, on-site pit latrines and septic tanks account for a substantial proportion of toilets in urban India –48 percent of urban Indian households depend on onsite facilities (Census 2011), and this proportion is since increasing. It may be noted that sewerage systems only partially cover Indian cities – a NIUA (2005) study of 300 Class-I and Class-II cities noted that… "while all the metropolitan cities have a sewerage system, only a third of the Class-I cities and less than one-fifth of the smaller sized urban centers have a sewerage system. However, the coverage by sewerage systems is partial in all these urban centers".

The mass construction of toilets as a result of mission-scheme are bound to complicate the matter and increases reliance on on-site sanitation system as creating sewerage infrastructure is capital intensive.

Thus, the present generation is facing a great challenge in providing adequate sanitation to rapidly growing urban population. It is argued that although sanitation coverage is higher in urban areas, the huge projected increase in urban populations makes the provision of affordable urban sanitation is a significant challenge (UN HABITAT: 2010). The studies and census data reveal that in urban areas in the majority of houses are served by on-site-sanitation systems such as septic tanks, pit latrines and unsewered public toilets. The faecal sludge collected from these systems is usually discharged untreated into the environment thereby posing great risks to water resources and public health. Peter, Isabel and Chris (2013) report that the need to establish an enabling environment for progress in urban sanitation is widely recognised.

The Millennium Development Goals (MDGs) did not monitor where the toilet discharged to – whether this was to sewer, septic tank, pit, open ground or drain – nor what happened finally to the liquid and solid products. Under the post-2015 Sustainable Development Goals (SDGs), there is now a focus on the whole sanitation service chain from containment through to disposal (Figure-2.2). The challenge for urban sanitation under the SDGs is therefore not only to achieve universal access to toilets, but also that all excreta are safely managed along the whole sanitation service chain (UN: 2011). This service chain is actually a value chain, as every step has a certain value added to it.

Figure 2.2: Sanitaton Service Chain

The effects of untreated sludge are a great public health concern. Strande (2014) explains in the absence of faecal sludge management (FSM) structures, untreated faecal sludge ends up in the environment when the containment structures filled up. This results in invasive contamination of the environment by pathogens. Schonning and Stenstrom (2004) classify these pathogens in four groups: (i) bacteria which cause typhoid, paratyphoid fever, and cholera; (ii) viruses which cause enteritis, meningitis, encephalitis, paralysis, and hepatitis; (iii) parasitic protozoa which cause amoebiosis and giardiasis; and (iv) helminths which cause enteritis, anaemia etc. The effects of these ailments cannot overemphasized as some can even be fatal if left untreated.

Human excreta contains a full spectrum of pathogens that transfer from diseased to healthy individuals through several direct and indirect routes, causing infections and superimposed infections. Infections enters human body through fluids, fingers, flies, food, and fields (Figure-2.3). Most transmission of infections can be avoided through proper sanitation and washing of hands before eating meals, and after defecation.

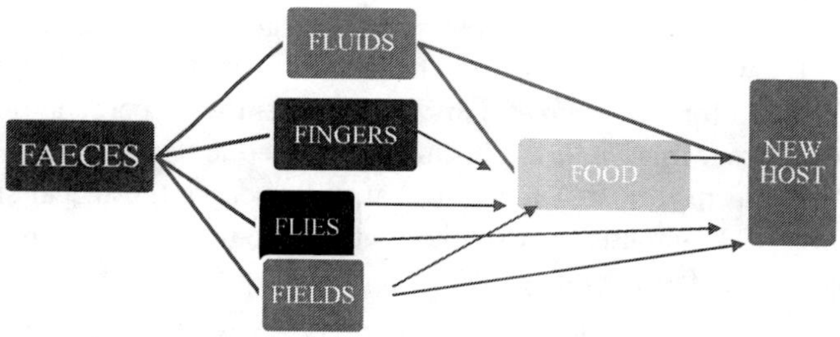

Source: Adapted from Wagner & Lanoix, 1958.

Figure-2.3: The F-diagram

Further, less than a third of the domestic wastewater undergoes to any form of treatment. Pollution impact and loss of fresh water owing to pollution is an area of concern. The National Urban Sanitation Policy (NUSP) reiterates the need for a combination of city-level sewerage systems complemented with on-site systems and effective septage management in smaller cities and in unserved areas to effectively address this situation (NIUA:2005). The sewerage system however needs proper treatment structure otherwise valuable components (manure) from faecal sludge are flown to rivers, thus polluting water sources (Joshi: 2017).

Summing Up

The sanitation planning and programme response will need to include improving the quality of on-site toilets and introducing faecal sludge management — at least in the short and medium term, before sewerage with proper effective treatment facilities becomes a realistic possibility. With this approach the faecal waste can be safely stored, removed and treated, reducing the public health hazard by protecting the neighbourhoods and the environment from faecal contamination. This will also have a city-wide effect by reducing infections carried into the rest of the city by workers living in the informal settlements. Sanitation and clean drinking water are critical determinants of health and are complementary to each other. Without proper sanitation, the incidence of diarrhoeal diseases due to contaminated drinking water will not come down, and without adequate water supply, improved sanitation is generally not possible. It is, therefore, necessary to adopt a habitation approach to sanitation and to institutionalize the integration of water supply with sanitation in each habitation. Provisioning of drinking water and sanitation services are constitutionally recognised as the responsibility of the states. Union Government programmes have played a significant role in increasing access to sanitation facilities (India &SDGs: 2016).

It is therefore, the Government of India's goal for all cities to have networked sewerage connections, which would send faecal sludge to a central location for treatment and disposal. Presently, 95 percent of towns do not have this infrastructure. This means that septic tanks or pits have to be emptied and moved to a location that will process the faecal sludge. Such a state of the situation warrants adoption of on-site-sanitation system for managing the faecal sludge.

Further, as households without toilets obtain facilities over the next few years, it is likely that many will acquire on-site arrangements like pit latrines and septic tanks in cities at locations where sewerage systems are not available. In contrast with the large proportion of on-site installations, limited attention has been accorded to proper construction, maintenance management and safe disposal of septage from septic tanks and pit latrines. While construction standards have been codified by Indian Standards Organization (ISO), the actual construction was largely left to households to manage – in practice, the installations are subject to local practices and considerable variations are observed. In many instances for example, soak-away outlets are not provided.

Those without privilege of having sewer facility are rarely connected at all and depend on their own on-site systems. Safely managing faecal waste is a particular challenge in unplanned settlements resulting from rapidly expanding cities. In these areas, faecal sludge is often allowed to accumulate in poorly designed and built pits, and then discharges directly into storm drain or dumped indiscriminately into water bodies or wasteland. As per a Central Pollution Control Board report (2015), only 263 out of the 4041 statutory towns in 2011, had or were building sewerage treatment capacity, leading most cities to discharge untreated wastewater into lakes, rivers and big drains (*nallas*) and polluting the environment (CPCB Report: 2015).

Limited capacities and resources with municipalities also resulted in little regulation of maintenance and cleaning of septic tanks and pits – in many cases, households do not report cleaning for a number of years. Some municipalities have desludging equipment or there are private players providing cleaning services but the supply of desludging services is far from adequate. In many instances, septage is dumped in drains and open areas posing considerable health and environmental risks.

Sanitary workers also work in hazardous conditions having to manually clean on-site pits and tanks without adequate protective gear and equipment. In fact, in most Indian cities, there is very limited disaggregated information on the types and numbers of on-site toilets and septage disposal systems and practices.

The National Rating of 423 Class-I, Indian Cities (covering 72 percent of Indian urban population) on Sanitation (MoH&UA, Govt. of India: May 2010) found that 65 percent (274) of these cities had unsatisfactory arrangements for safe collection of human excreta (whether on-site or sewerage).

Septage management should be an integral part of sanitation schemes. State should make adequate budgetary provision for effective septage management. State governments should enforce implementation of septage management and monitoring programme at the municipal level. There are considerable challenges in respect of treatment of sewage–treatment capacities in Indian cities are only 31 percent of the total waste generated. The 35 million-plus cities have 68 percent of the total installed wastewater treatment capacity but nearly 39 percent of these treatment plants did not conform to discharge standards into water bodies (Central Pollution Control Board: 2009). While conventional sewage treatment facilities are limited (that could potentially also treat septage), there is on the other hand, limited experience in India of developing and managing septage treatment facilities of different types.

Therefore, while considerable proportion of urban Indian households depend on on-site sanitation facilities, their construction, regular cleaning, and safe disposal of septage remain haphazard. Most of the septage is let out untreated posing considerable health and environmental risks. Hence, it is crucial that septage management is accorded urgent attention in Indian cities.

References

- *UNHABITAT (2010): State of the World's Cities, United Nations Human Settlement Programmes, Nairobi, Kenya.*

- *Schonning, C. and Stenostrom,T.A. (2004): Guidelines for the Safe use of urine and Faeces in Ecological Sanitation, Ecosanres SEI: Sweden.*
- *World Fecal Sludge Management: Diagnostics and Guidelines for Service Delivery in Poor Urban Areas Summary Report 6 May 2016 GWASP OTHER The World Bank, WSP.*
- *WHO (1992): A Guide to the Development of On-Site Sanitation.*
- *WHO(1987): The Ottawa Charter for Health Promotion, first International Conference on Health Promotion, 21st November,1987.*
- *National Institute of Urban Affairs (2005): PEARL Compendium of Good Practices.*
- *Government of India (2006): National Urban Sanitation Policy.*
- *The Concise Oxford Dictionary(2011); 12th edition, UK.*
- *United Nations (2015): Sustainable Development Goals- Guidelines.*
- *Government of India (Ministry of Urban Development) and WSP; (2008):Guide to Decision Making: Technology Options for Urban Sanitation in India.*
- *Government of India, Census of India, 2011: Houses, Household Amenities and Assets (Latrine Facility).*
- *Central Pollution Control Board, 2009.*
- *Wagner, E. G. and Lanoix, Jon (1958): Excreta disposal for rural areas and small communities; dHealth Organization, CHU211, Geneva.*
- *NITI Ayog, Government of India (2016): An Overview of the Sustainable Development Goals.*
- *Government of India(Ministry of Housing and Urban Affairs)(2014): Swachh Bharat Mission- Guidelines.*
- *UN HABITAT(2010): as quoted in Nyirendu,DC and Holm,R (2015): Faecal Sludge Management in peri-urban Malawi(investigating the policy gaps); 38th WECD International Coference, Loughborough University,UK.*
- *Strande, L., Routeltap, M. and Brdjanovic (eds)(2014): Faecal Sludge Management, IWA Publishing, London.*
- *Hawkins, Peter (2016): faecal Sludge management in India: finding Sustainable Solutions.*
- *WHO (1986): Report of a WHO Study Group on Young People's Health: A Challenge for Society.*
- *WHO (1987): Technology for water supply and sanitation in developing countries.*
- *WHO (1987): Report on Cost Recovery in community water supply and sanitation.*
- *UNDP (2016): India and Sustainable Development Goals : The Way Forward; www.in.undp.org/content/india/en/home/post-2015/sdg-overview.html; accessed on August 27, 2018.*
- *Hawkins (2016):Tomorrow's World: Today's Challenge, INOC, Wiesloch.*
- *U.N World Water Development Report, 2015.*
- *Central Pollution Control Board Report, 2015.*
- *Joshi, Sopan (2018): JAL, THAl, MAL (in Hindi);Baniyan Tree, Indore.*

- *Government of India, Ministry of Housing and Urban Affairs, USAID and WASH Institute: Triggering for Behavior Change towards Open Defecation Free status.*
- *Government of India, Ministry of Urban Development (2013): Advisory Note on Septage Management in Urban India.*
- *Government of India: Twelfth Five Year Plan.*

3

Legislative, Regulatory and Policy Frameworks

Introduction

As the world continues to urbanize, sustainable development challenges will be increasingly concentrated in cities, particularly in the developing countries. Nevertheless, rapid and unplanned urban growth threatens sustainable development when the necessary infrastructure is not developed or when laws are not implemented judiciously to ensure that the benefits of city life are equitably shared. An estimated, 863 million people representing nearly one third of urban residents in developing regions, lived in slums or informal settlements in 2012, characterized by housing that lacks access to improved water and sanitation (United Nations : 2014). Sustainable urbanization requires expanding the necessary infrastructure for water and sanitation. One -third of the world's population (2.4 billion people) still does not have access to an improved sanitation facility. Almost a billion people (946 million) do not use any sanitation facility and defecate in the open, though the right to adequate, affordable water and sanitation is implicit and acknowledged in various international declarations, covenants, conventions and statements (World Urbanisation Prospects: 2014).

India has been no exception to this global trend. It has witnessed a tremendous growth in urban population after Independence. But the increase in urban population has not been evenly spread throughout the country. Different regions have seen their urban populations grow more quickly, or less quickly. The rapid growth in number of metropolitan towns (having population of one million or more)from solitary one in 1901 to 35 in 2001 and further to 53 in 2011 is a glaring example of uneven urban growth in the country, especially after Independence. These metropolises contain about two-fifths of the urban population. The Indian urbanization thus shows a unique characteristic of concentration of urban population in larger urban centres, unlike western trend. This has led to unplanned and haphazard peripheral urban growth besides putting heavy pressure on existing urban infrastructure and civic services in the cities, especially in larger ones (having population of 1 lakh or more).

Effective and Enforceable Regulations for FSM

Faecal Sludge Management (FSM) is a relatively new field; however, it is currently rapidly developing and gaining acknowledgement. Over the last couple of years, the Government of India in the Ministry of Housing and Urban Affairs (its predecessor as well) has started telling the state and city governments that improving faecal sludge management is an important alternative to traditional sewerage systems and waste water treatment for urban sanitation (Shubhagato Dasgupta:2016). Faecal Sludge (FS) comes from on-site sanitation technologies, and has not been transported through a sewer. It is raw or partially digested, a slurry or semi-solid, and results from the collection, storage or treatment of combinations of human excreta and black water, with or without grey water. Examples of on-site technologies include pit latrines, un-sewered public ablution blocks, septic tanks, aqua privies, and dry toilets. FSM includes the storage, collection, transport, treatment and safe end use or disposal of faecal sludge.

In India, earlier laws dealt with sanitation in general and not faecal sludge management. Since early years of attaining Independence, the focus has been mainly on providing sanitation (latrines) on low cost and through total sanitation campaign. It is most recently the construction of different types of toilets under much ambitious scheme of '*Swachh Bharat*' (clean India) in a mission mode was launched in mass scale. Its main focus was to make the country open defecation free in a given time-frame.

In this backdrop, the chapter makes an attempt to study the Faecal Sludge Management (FSM) related direct and indirect laws (Acts, manuals, regulations, bye-laws, rules, notifications, ordinances, etc.), their relevance to different stages of FSM value chain, approaches adopted and enforceability. It will also identify the overlaps, duplication and gaps.

I-BASIC LAWS

The Constitution of India

The right to sanitation in India draws its legal basis mainly from the Fundamental Rights enshrined in the Constitution, and most importantly Fundamental Rights to Life (Article 21). Judicial decisions have interpreted fundamental rights to life to include right to sanitation/right to clean and wholesome healthy environment. The Directive Principles (Article 48-A) cast duty upon the government to create condition through legal and regulatory interventions to ensure right to sanitation by way of 'protecting and improving the environment'.

The supreme law of the land while dealing with the Fundamental Duties mentions that it is the duty of every citizen 'to protect and improve the natural environment' (Article 51-A(g)).

The Twelfth Schedule inserted to the Constitution as a result of the Constitution (seventy fourth) Amendment Act,1992 read with Article 243-W(ii) endows the Municipality to perform the functions of 'Public health, sanitation, conservancy and solid waste management' and 'Protection of the environment and promotion of ecological aspects' besides other local functions enlisted therein.

Further, the Constitution puts 'Public health and sanitation' (at Entry 7) in the List-II-State List in the Seventh Schedule.

Thus, the Constitution of the country while recognizing the importance of sanitation for a dignified and healthy human life has made the sanitation as a State Subject and thus has shouldered the responsibility of sanitation, public health and protecting the environment on the State Government, Urban Local Governments and the citizen at large.

The Environment (Protection) Act, 1986

In compliance to the United Nations Conference on the Human Environment held at Stockholm in June 1972 to take appropriate steps for the protection and improvement of the human environment, the Government of India enacted this law for implementing the decisions taken thereat and also for prevention of hazards to human beings. This generic enactment has a broad scope and encompasses protection of various variants of environment. Under this law the government has formulated a number of rules viz, Management & Handling of Bio-Medical Wastes/ Hazardous Wastes/ e-wastes/Solid Wastes/Construction and Demolition Wastes, etc.

None of the rules formulated so far, however, covers the faecal sludge. Hence there is a need to frame a dedicated Rules dealing with FSM in the country.

II- LAWS INDIRECTLY RELATED TO FSM

Water Acts

Going beyond the context of improving sanitation, Faecal Sludge Management (FSM) is an issue which sits naturally within the wider scope of Integrated Water Management (IWM) that recognizes the inter-linkages between water supply, sanitation, drainage and solid waste management, and the wider contextual issues of urban land use and water resources management. FSM affects or is affected by many of these factors. Hence, it is felt pertinent to review the various water related enactments.

The Water (Prevention and Control of Pollution) Act, 1974

The main objectives of this law include prevention, control and abatement of water pollution; restoration of wholesomeness of water; and assess pollution levels and punish the polluters. With these aims the Pollution Control Boards (PCBs) at the national and state levels have been constituted. The main functions of these Boards are to collect and analyse water samples, govern discharge of sewage and trade effluents for the purpose of monitoring the water pollution.

The National Water Framework, 2016

This Act mandates to make all efforts for appropriate treatment of waste water and its gainful utilization. It emphasizes on adopting all possible measures at the municipal level to synergise and integrate different development schemes for water conservation, drinking water, sanitation, watershed management and improvement of water quality.

Clear local regulations (bye-laws or ordinances), which are both enforceable and enforced are the logical and necessary extension of institutional responsibilities. Resulting institutional frameworks and bye-laws for FSM should ideally be incorporated into broader Integrated Urban Water Management (IUWM) approaches to achieve credibility and maximum results, but should be developed in any case. Regulations need not be overly complex to start with, especially when transitioning from informal services.

City- At the most basic level the regulations should ensure clean and safe operation (such as by ensuring correct designs and well-constructed containment infrastructure with regular and effective desludging by registered operators), that all faecal waste is safely disposed at designated treatment works, that sanctions are applied for disposal elsewhere, and that workers use protective clothing and undergo health checks. The responsible agency should be required to keep complete records and account for its operations and income, and manage the private sector operators in a fair and transparent manner.

III- LAWS DIRECTLY RELATED TO FSM

(A) Central Laws

(i) *Central Acts*

The Employment Of Manual Scavengers And Construction Of Dry Latrines (Prohibition) Act, 1993

This was the first legal instrument to prohibit the inhuman practice of manual scavenging in the states wherein the practice of manual scavenging was found prevalent. This Central Act focused on regulating the dry latrines and thus mandated to convert the dry latrines into pour flush latrines. This Act empowered the state governments to issue notification for protection and improvement of the environment or public health.

The Act, however, did not address the more insidious forms of manual scavenging, such as cleaning open gutters, manholes and septic tanks.

The Prohibition of Employment as Manual Scavengers and their Rehabilitation Act, 2013

This Act provides for the prohibition of employment as manual scavengers, rehabilitation of manual scavengers and their families. The main focus of this Central law is on: prohibiting construction of an insanitary latrine; prohibit employment as manual scavengers; rehabilitate manual scavengers and their families; and prohibit manual cleansing of sewers and septic tanks without protective equipment.

This Central law, though does not mention FSM (not too popular those days), aims at regulating two important segments of FSM service chain viz. containment and emptying/collection in a safe and sanitary way.

(ii) *Central Manuals, Codes & Rules*

The various Central organisations have issued from time to time Operational Manuals and Codes for regulating sanitary services in the country. A few important ones are discussed hereunder.

Code of Practice for Installation of Septic Tanks

These codes developed by Bureau of Indian Standards deal with methods of secondary treatment and disposal of septic effluents.

National Building Code, 2005

These codes provide guidelines for septic tank design, construction, installation, their operation and maintenance.

Manual On Sewerage and Sewage Treatment, 1993/2013

The earlier manual (1993) provided guidelines for construction of septic tanks. The revised version (2013) prescribes the scheduled desludging. The pit latrines and/or septic tanks are prevalently used in low-income settlements and also in new unplanned private colonies. There is lack of a suitable mechanism to ensure the compliance of norms prescribed. The states do have Building Regulation laws but their implementation is seldom monitored by house-building agencies--public or private.

Solid Waste Management (SWM) Rules, 2016

These rules framed under the Environment (Protection) Act replace the Municipal Solid Wastes (Management & Handling) Rules, 2000. The new rules have jurisdiction beyond municipal area. They apply to the final and safe disposal of post-processed residual faecal sludge and septage to prevent contamination of ground water, surface water and ambient air. Further, the SWM Rules 2016 apply to the final and safe disposal of post-processed residual faecal sludge and septage.

(iii) *Central Notifications*

The Government of India in the Ministry of Housing and Urban Affairs and its predecessor Ministry of Urban Development has issued from time to time guidelines for septage management. These are discussed as follows.

Advisory Note on Septage Management in Urban India, 2013

This recommends that septage management should be treated as an integral part of sanitation schemes. It mandates for scheduled desludging. The Advisory necessitates the Municipalities to formulate their own bye-laws and rules for management of septage. The rules should address the design of septic tanks, periodicity of emptying, licensing and reporting methods, and locations of transport, treatment and disposal.

Primer on Faecal Sludge and Septage Management, 2016

The Primer advises the states to frame a faecal sludge management policy for bridging the policy with practice and make FSM a reality. It mandates that responsibility of septage management lies with the Municipality which may encourage private sector participation.

(B) State Laws

Constitutionally, sanitation is a State Subject. It is therefore that the state governments have entrusted this important function to the urban local governments (Municipalities). In Uttar Pradesh, there are multiple agencies discharging the urban affairs in their specific jurisdiction. The statutory urban areas are governed by Municipal Corporations; Municipal Councils; *Nagar Panchayats*; Cantonment Boards; Development Authorities; Special Area Development Authorities; Housing & Development Board; *Jal Nigam* (Water Corporation) and Regional *Jal Sansthans* (Water Boards). However, management of sewerage and sewage in the state has been entrusted to *Uttar Pradesh Jal Nigam* (for installation of plants and machineries, and development of water and sewerage infrastructure including sewage (faecal) disposal) and Municipalities (for operation and maintenance); whereas solid waste and drainage management is the responsibility of respective municipal agencies.

The Uttar Pradesh Municipalities Act, 1916

This Act applies on *Nagar Palika Parishads* (Municipal Councils) and *Nagar Panchayats. Nagar Palika Parishad* (197) is constituted in smaller urban areas having a population of one lakh or more but less than three lakhs; whereas *Nagar Panchayad* (438) is constituted in transitional areas (nearer to rural areas). The Act clearly mandates the duty of Municipal Councils (*Nagar Palika Parishads*) and *Nagar Pachayats* to make reasonable provision for:

(i) Cleaning public streets, places and drains, removing noxious vegetation, and abating all public nuisances;

(ii) Constructing, altering and maintaining public streets , culverts, markets, latrines, privies, urinals, drains, drainage works and sewerage works;

(iii) Providing a sufficient supply of pure and wholesome water, guarding from pollution water used for human consumption and preventing polluted water from being used so;

(iv) Establishing and maintaining a farm or factory for the disposal of sewage;

(v) Making arrangements for preparation of compost manure from night soil and rubbish.

The Uttar Pradesh Municipal Corporation Act, 1959

This Act makes provisions for managing the cities having Municipal Corporation (*Nagar Nigam*). A *Nagar Nigam* (17) in the state is constituted in larger urban centre having a population of three lakhs and more. As per Act, it is incumbent on the Municipal Corporations (*Nagar Nigam*) to make reasonable and adequate provision for:

(i) The collection and removal of sewage, offensive mater and rubbish and treatment and disposal thereof including establishing and maintaining farm and factory;

(ii) The watering, scavenging and cleansing of all public streets and places and the removal of all sweepings there from;

(iii) The construction, maintenance and cleansing of drains and drainage works, and of public latrines, water-closets, urinals and similar conveniences;

(iv) Supplying, constructing and maintaining receptacles, fitting pipes and other appliances on or for the use of premises for receiving and conducting the sewage thereof into drains;

(v) Guarding from pollution water used for human consumption and preventing polluted water from being so used.

The Uttar Pradesh Urban Planning and Development Act,1973

The Act applies on Development Authorities (23), Special Area Development Authorities (9) and Town and Country Planning Organisation in the state. This Act provides for the preparation of town planning schemes in respect of all lands within the municipal area to ensure regulated development of towns to secure their present and future amenities and conditions.

The Uttar Pradesh Water Supply and Sewerage Act, 1975

This Act has jurisdiction over *Uttar Pradesh Jal Nigam* (Water Corporation) and Regional *Jal Sansthans* (Water Board) and erstwhile *Jal Sansthans* having brought into the administrative fold of respective municipal corporations. The *Jal Nigam* is responsible for developing infrastructure related to water supply and sewerage in whole state; *Jal Kal Vibhag* (department of water) caters the requirement of municipal corporation area; whereas two regional *Jal Sansthans* cater the requirements in their respective jurisdiction. The functions of the *Jal Nigam* are the following, namely:

(i) the preparation, execution, promotion and financing the schemes for the supply of water and for sewerage and sewage disposal;

(ii) to render all necessary services in regard to water supply and sewerage to the State Government and municipalities, on request to private institutions or individuals;

(iii) to prepare State plans for water supply, sewerage and drainage on the directions of the State Government;

(iv) to assess the requirement for materials and arrange for their procurement and utilisation;

(v) to establish State standards for water supply and sewerage services;

(vi) to review annually the technical, financial, economic and other aspects of water supply and sewerage system of every Jal Sansthan or municipalities;

(vii) to establish and maintain a facility to review and appraise the technical, financial, economic and other pertinent aspect of every water supply and sewerage scheme in the State;

(viii) to operate, run and maintain any waterworks and sewerage system, if and when directed by the State Government, on such terms and conditions and for such period as may be specified by the State Government;

(ix) to assess the requirements for manpower and training in relation to water supply and sewerage services in the State;

(x) to inspect all water supply and sewerage facilities in the State by whomsoever they are operated;

(xi) to obtain such periodic or specific information from any municipality and operating agency as it may deem necessary;

(xii) to prepare and carry out schemes for water supply and sewerage;

(xiii) to disburse loans to municipalities for their water supply and sewerage schemes.

As per Act, the responsibilities of a *Jal Sansthan* (Water Board) are as follows:

(i) to plan, promote and execute schemes of and operate an efficient system of water supply;

(ii) where feasible, to plan, promote and execute schemes of, and operate, sewerage, sewage treatment and disposal and treatment of trade effluents;

(iii) to manage all its affairs so as to provide the people of the area within its jurisdiction with wholesome water and where feasible, efficient sewerage service;

(iv) to exercise all powers and perform all the functions relating to water supply, sewerage and sewage disposal of the area which lies within its jurisdiction;

(v) to acquire, possess and hold lands and other property and to carry any water or sewerage works through, across, over or under any highway, road, street or place and, after reasonable notice, in writing to the owner or occupier, into, through, over or under any building or land;

(vi) *to abstract water from any natural source and dispose of waste water;*

(vii) *to examine the sewer or cesspool, the sewer or cesspool so examined is found to be defective, the Jal Sansthan may forthwith stop its functioning or disconnect it from the sewer of the Jal Sansthan, or require the owner or occupier to take remedial action as directed and within a time specified, by the Jal Sansthan and in any such event the Jal Sansthan may recover the cost incurred by it from the owner or occupier, as the case may be.*

In sum, clear local regulations, which are both enforceable and enforced, are necessary for successful and effective implementation of on-site-sanitation systems. It is found that the poorly constructed pits in most of the low-income settlement colonies in cities and towns are contributing to inadequate FSM, as well as to inadequate hygienic conditions for users. Typically, the CPHEEO Manuals, National Building Codes and the Building Regulations provide for only regulating the septic tanks by prescribing designs or parameters. However, in informal settlements, where only pits are prevalent, no such norm is enforced. It is therefore necessary that implementing agencies should shoulder the responsibility of regulating the construction of septic tanks as per norm. The improvement plan/scheme should consist of the provisions related to complete FSM service chain.

It is therefore mandatory that the State Government in the Department of Urban Development frame a State Sanitation Strategy/Plan in compliance to the National Policy on Faecal Sludge and Septage Management, 2017 incorporating the clear roles and responsibilities of all the public agencies (a State Septage Management Policy has been framed recently). Such a move will provide a legal base to agencies to formulate the plan for putting in place the complete on-site-sanitation service chain.

I- FSM Related Policies

On-site sanitation systems are the norm for both rich and poor in cities and towns, and are often the only form of sanitation available to poor people. However, they have been largely neglected by the institutions responsible for managing sanitation. The construction and servicing of on-site facilities is typically left to an unregulated informal sector. Faecal sludge management (FSM) has often been considered an inferior, stop-gap solution compared to conventional sewerage options, by governments, utilities and urban planners alike. However, they are increasingly recognizing that it will take many years, or may not be cost-effective, to achieve safely managed sanitation services via universal access to sewerage. Furthermore, FSM services are increasingly recognized as part of the solution in areas where sewerage is not technically feasible. Crucially, FSM services represent a feasible sanitation solution for many unplanned areas where it is hard to justify major public investments in underground infrastructure. However, till recently it was not a priority of the national and/or local government as part of its overall sanitation programme in the country.

A. Policies Creating Enabling Environment

In India, urban development was initially bracketed with public health. Hence, health related laws dealt with urban sanitation as well, as it was perceived, rightly so, that sanitation promotion is one of the most important roles the health sector can have in environmental health planning.

National Health Policy, 2002

This policy recognizes that sanitation impacts health of the community; and health status of citizenry is dependent on safe drinking water, basic sanitation, and a clean environment. It observes that even the meagre public health services which are available do not percolate to inhabitants of low-income settlements in cities.

The policy mentions that ambient environmental conditions are a significant determinant of the health risks to which a community is exposed. Unsafe drinking water, unhygienic sanitation and air pollution significantly contribute to the burden of disease, particularly in urban settings. The initiatives in respect of these environmental factors are conventionally undertaken by the other development sectors. In this backdrop, the policy initiatives, and the efficient implementation of the linked programmes in the health sector, would succeed only to the extent that they are complemented by appropriate policies and programmes in the other environment-related sectors.

It lays great emphasis upon the implementation of public health programmes through local self-government institutions. This Policy envisages that independently–the stated policies and programmes of the environment-related sectors be smoothly interfaced with the policies and the programmes of the health sector, in order to reduce the health risk to the citizens and the consequential disease burden.

The policy did focus on creating synergy among different environment-related policies and programmes with health programmes, but sanitation was treated peripheral in a limited way basically to hygiene.

National Environment Policy, 2006

The National Environment Policy is a response to our national commitment to a clean environment, mandated in the Constitution. It is recognized that maintaining a healthy environment is not the state's responsibility alone, but also that of every citizen. While the state must galvanize its efforts, there should also be recognition by each individual — natural or institutional, of its responsibility towards maintaining and enhancing the quality of the environment. It seeks to extend the coverage, and fill in gaps that still exist, in light of present knowledge and accumulated experience. It intends to mainstream environmental concerns in all developmental activities.

The principal objectives of the policy include: conservation of critical environmental resources; livelihood security for the poor; judicious and efficient use of environmental resources; integration of environmental concerns in economic and social development; application of principles of good governance to the management and regulation of use of environmental resources; and enhancement of resources for environmental conservation. The dominant theme of this policy is that while conservation of environmental resources is necessary to secure livelihoods and well-being of all, the most secure basis for conservation is to ensure that people dependent on particular resources obtain better livelihoods from the fact of conservation, than from degradation of the resource.

Environmental degradation is a major causal factor in enhancing and perpetuating poverty. It is increasingly evident that poor environmental quality has adversely affected human health. It has been shown that interventions such as reducing indoor air pollution, protecting sources of safe drinking water, protecting soil from contamination, improved sanitation measures, and better public health governance, offer tremendous opportunities in reducing the incidence of a number of critical health problems.

The policy envisages developing and implementing, initially on a pilot scale, public-private partnership models for setting up and operating effluent and sewage treatment plants. Once the models are validated, progressively used public resources, including external assistance, to catalyze such partnerships enhance the capacities of municipalities for recovery of user charges for water and sewerage systems. It prescribes to prepare and implement action plans for major cities for addressing water pollution, comprising regulatory systems relying on a appropriate combination of fiats and incentive based instruments, projects implemented through public agencies as well as public-private partnerships for treatment, reuse, and recycle of sewage and wastewater from municipal and industrial sources, before final discharge to water bodies.

The policy focuses mainly on protecting the forests, the principal resource of environment; and on conserving the forest resources/products for eliminating the poverty of populations dependent on forests. As regards sanitation, the policy concentrates on effluents from sewage treatment plants. To deal with the problem of effluents management, the policy advocates adopting public-private partnerships approach.

National Urban Housing and Habitat Policy, 2007

Urban areas in our country are characterized by severe shortage of basic services like potable water, well laid out drainage system, sewerage network, sanitation facilities, electricity, roads and appropriate solid waste disposal. This policy intends to promote sustainable development of habitat in the country with a view to ensuring equitable supply of land, shelter and services at affordable prices to all sections of society. Given the degraded habitat in low-income settlements and the frequent episodes of illness characterizing slum families, the policy feels that improved housing is of vital importance for improving the quality of life in urban areas, especially in low-income settlements. Further, the enhancement of housing stock must be accompanied with high quality provision of basic services.

The policy therefore envisages promoting action plans for creation of adequate infrastructure facilities relating to water, drainage, sanitation, sewerage and other services.

The policy focuses on the provision of basic civic services (including water supply and toilets) in the houses constructed for economically weaker sections of the society. It however does not deal with sanitation separately, but only as an integral part of a house.

National Water Policy, 2012

Water, a natural resource, is fundamental to life, livelihood, food security and sustainable development. Low consciousness about the scarcity of water and its life sustaining and economic value results in its mismanagement, wastage, and inefficient use, as also pollution. Growing pollution of water sources, especially through industrial and domestic effluents, is affecting the availability of safe water besides causing environmental and health hazards. Access to water for sanitation and hygiene is an even more serious problem. Inadequate sanitation and lack of sewage treatment are polluting the water sources.

The policy advocates incentivizing the least water intensive sanitation and sewerage systems with decentralized sewage treatment plan. It encourages the recycle and reuse of water after treatment to specified standards, and feels that incentive should be allowed through a properly planned tariff system. Efforts should be made to provide improved water supply with proper sewerage facilities. Least water intensive sanitation and sewerage systems with decentralized sewage treatment plants should be incentivized. The policy emphasizes that urban water supply and sewage treatment schemes should be integrated and executed simultaneously.

The policy advocates adopting an integrated approach for water supply and sewage treatment plan. It focuses on promoting recycle and reuse of treated water for non-potable purposes. The policy feels the need of adopting decentralized system for sewage treatment.

National Health Policy, 2017

The primary aim of the National Health Policy is to inform, clarify, strengthen and prioritize the role of the government in shaping health systems in all its dimensions— investments in health, organization of healthcare services, prevention of diseases and promotion of good health through cross sectoral actions, access to technologies, developing human resources, encouraging medical pluralism, building knowledge base, developing better financial protection strategies, strengthening regulation and health assurance. The policy envisages as its goal the attainment of the highest possible level of health and well-being for all at all ages, through a preventive and promotive health care orientation in all developmental policies, and universal access to good quality health care services without anyone having to face financial hardship as a consequence. This would be achieved through increasing access, improving quality and lowering the cost of healthcare delivery.

The policy emphasizes on reduction of air pollution, better waste management, water quality, housing, etc. It advocates the linkage of implementation of policy with the *Swachh Bharat* Mission programme, a campaign to clean India.

The policy concentrates on highlighting the relationship between sanitation (mainly pollution) and public health. It does not directly impact sanitation service chain.

The foregone discussion reveals that the above mentioned policies might not had any direct relations with urban sanitation or any of its segments, but they were instrumental in creating an environment where sanitation is recognized as an integral part of urban development and management. They succeeded in establishing importance of sanitation in human life.

B. Sanitation Related Policies

National Urban Sanitation Policy, 2008

In pursuance of the commitment envisaged under the Millennium Development Goals (MDGs) to extend access to improved sanitation to at least half of the urban population by 2015, and universal access by 2025, the Government of India formulated this maiden policy on urban sanitation. Thus the vision set of the policy is: "All Indian cities and towns become totally sanitized, healthy and liveable and ensure and sustain good public health and environmental outcomes for all their citizens with a special focus on hygienic and affordable sanitation facilities for the urban poor and women." In accordance, the goal is destined "to transform Urban India into community-driven, totally sanitized, healthy and liveable cities and towns." To bring clarity for achieving the set goal in sanitation is defined as safe management of human excreta, including its safe confinement, treatment, disposal and associated hygiene-related practices.

The policy recognizes a number of sanitation related issues and suggests ways to deal with them for achieving the goals. These issues include: sanitation is not a priority hence lack of adequate awareness about its linkage with public health; gaps and overlaps in institutional roles and responsibilities; ad hoc approach in managing the sanitation services; availability of limited technology; poor outreach to unserved settlements; and adopting the supply-driven approach rather than demand-driven. In view of sanitation being a State Subject and for adopting an integrated holistic approach, the Union Government advises to frame State Sanitation Policy and State/City Sanitation Strategy/Plan.

The policy focuses on generating awareness and bringing behavioural change among the masses. For making the cities open defecation free, universalization of sanitation facilities is given emphasis. It highlights the importance and need of reorienting and strengthening of institutional arrangements at national, state and city levels. The policy emphasizes on safe and sanitary disposal of human excreta and liquid wastes and therefore recommends encouraging recycle and reuse of treated waste water for non-potable applications; and promoting proper disposal and treatment of sludge from on-site installations (septic tanks and pit latrines).

The policy advises to ensure proper usage, regular upkeep and maintenance of household, community and public sanitation facilities; and strengthening of municipalities to provide sustainable sanitation services delivery.

This policy is the maiden dedicated initiative in the arena of urban sanitation. Although it does not make a mention of FSM, it provides a base for community-driven total sanitation in Urban India. The policy favours adopting an integrated approach, and hence feels need of formulating Sanitation Strategy/Policy/Plan by the states and cities.

The main focus of the policy is on proper disposal and treatment of sludge at the containment level only.

In compliance to these Central Notifications and also under advice of the National Urban Sanitation Policy, 2008, the state governments of Odisha, Tamil Nadu, Uttar Pradesh and Gujarat framed their own strategy/laws for faecal sludge management. The other states are still to follow the suit in compliance to the latest policy initiative by the Government of India and should formulate their State FSM Strategy/Plan and also to direct the municipalities to frame City FSM Strategy/Plan to manage this important service in a cost-effective manner.

C. State Policies Creating Enabling Environment

Uttar Pradesh State Water Policy, 1988

Uttar Pradesh, the most populous state in the country is endowed with bountiful water resources which were considered abundant but because of increasing demand for various purposes namely irrigation, drinking and domestic, power (thermal and hydro), industrial and other uses, its scarcity is becoming apparent which shall get more pronounced with increasing population. Water is a prime natural resource, a basic human need and a precious asset. Planning and development of water resources of the state are governed by this policy.

Water for drinking and domestic use has the highest priority while allocating the water resource of the state. The state has to provide adequate drinking water facilities (both for people and livestock) to the entire population in both urban and rural areas up to the year 2025. Sanitation facilities for entire population in urban areas and most of the rural areas should also be provided.

The main objectives of the policy include: preservation of the scarce water resources and to optimise the utilization of the available resources; bring about qualitative improvement in water resource management which should include users' participation and decentralization of authority;

maintain water quality, both surface and underground, to established norms and standards; promote formulation of projects as far as and whenever possible on the concept of basin or sub-basin, treating both surface and the ground water as a unitary resource, ensuring multipurpose use of the water resource; promote equity and social justice among individuals and groups of users in water resource allocation and management; ensure self-sustainability in water resource development; ensure flood management and drainage as integral part of water resource development; provide a substantive legal framework for management; provide a Management Information System (M.I.S.) for effective monitoring of policy implementation; and promote research and training facilities in the water resource sector.

In view of the vital importance of water for human and animal life, for maintaining ecological balance and for economic and developmental activities of all kinds, and considering its increasing scarcity, the planning and management of this resource and its optimal, economical and equitable use has become a matter of the utmost urgency. The success of the State Water Policy will depend entirely on the development and maintenance of general consensus and commitments to its underlying principles and objectives.

With the rapid increase in population the surface water sources as well as groundwater resources are coming under abstractive pressure. The rivers are slowly getting reduced to major drains with a trickle of a flow. The discharge of industrial effluents and domestic sewage through dozens of *nalas*/storm water drains has resulted into increasing the pollution level and thus worsening the status. A large volume of water supplied to urban inhabitants is converted into sewage (waste water), whose treatment would require huge capital costs. Demand would always outstrip infrastructure provision with the net result being pollution of river and water bodies.

Uttar Pradesh Health Policy

The state of Uttar Pradesh has formulated health policies which are made in order to give best health and hygienic services to its people. The main objectives of policy are to achieve an acceptable standard of good health amongst the general population of the country. This policy also defines the future vision and clearly recognizes the initiative aimed at stabilizing population and those for ensuring clear environment, minimum nutrition etc.

D. Directly Sanitation Related State Policy

Uttar Pradesh Urban Sanitation Policy (DRAFT), 2009

This draft policy in the state has been developed on the lines of National Urban Sanitation Policy, 2008. Like national policy it has vision to make all cities and towns in the state totally sanitized so that they become healthy and liveable. Its main twin focus is on spreading mass awareness about importance and need of sanitation, and also making urban areas open defecation free.

E. FSM in National Legislation

National Policy on Faecal Sludge and Septage Management, 2017

At present, the penetration of sewerage systems is low in the country and a little less than half of urban households are dependent on On-Site Sanitation (OSS) systems. This number is bound to increase as crores of individual toilets are being constructed under *Swachh Bharat* Mission (SBM). Thus, while the containment of human waste will be largely achieved under SBM, its treatment still poses a huge challenge. Further, only a little more than one-third of the sewage treatment plants in the country are found operational; and the treatment capacity that is available is only a little more than one-third of the total human waste generated in urban areas. Thus, till the time the Government's vision of complete universalization of sewerage system is achieved, it is felt that faecal sludge output needs to be managed in an environmentally safe and sustainable manner using complementary and alternative methods of treatment. In this backdrop, the erstwhile Ministry of Urban Development (presently Ministry of Housing and Urban Affairs) has launched this policy to facilitate nationwide implementation of faecal sludge and septage management in Urban India. The key objective of this dedicated initiative is to set the context, priorities and direction for states and cities in this regard. This policy is mainly a sequel and extension to National Urban Sanitation Policy, 2008, and recognizes the issues rose thereby.

This policy, in a nutshell, seeks to address the efficiency of systems in place for onsite sanitation and the faecal sludge output needs to be managed in an environmentally safe manner. This is a move on the path of mainstreaming Faecal Sludge and Septage Management (FSSM) in urban India, and ensures that all benefits of wide access to safe sanitation accrue to all citizens across the sanitation service/value chain.

It recommends the construction of septic tanks as per norms and standards, and their scheduled emptying. It feels that regular cleaning through a systematic extraction and collection procedure is essential to check environmental pollution. The policy cautions not to adopt manual cleaning, an illegal activity and a cognizable offence. It advocates promoting recycle and reuse of treated sewage for non-potable applications; and encouraging co-treatment of faecal sludge and septage at sewage treatment plants or co-treatment and management of faecal sludge and septage, and municipal solid wastes. The policy aims to establish synergy with all the initiatives dealing with sanitation in the country. The policy identifies key stakeholders and prescribes their roles and responsibilities.

As regards implementation strategy, the policy follows the approach suggested by the National Urban Sanitation Policy, 2008 and requires the states to develop an FSSM Implementation Strategy/Policy and Plan Guidelines providing an overall state level framework, objectives, timelines and implementation plans. The Operational Guidelines should include design of septic tanks/pits adapted to local conditions; delineation of various stakeholders—public and private, including the community; planning and implementation process for carrying out safe and sustainable management of all faecal sludge and septage; frequency of desludging; O&M of installations; licensing, record-keeping, monitoring and reporting arrangements for service providers; methods and locations of conveyance, treatment and safe disposal; levying and collection of tariffs or cess/tax etc. for septage management. The policy exhorts the states to facilitate the involvement of private sector through an easy and amenable PPP relationship framework, to ensure adequate financing and sustainability of projects.

The policy expects to yield significant benefits in terms of improved public health indicators, reduced pollution of water bodies and groundwater from human waste, and resource recovery leading to reuse of treated waste and other end products.

This is a maiden policy framework dedicated to faecal sludge and septage management (FSSM) in the country. It intends to cover all the statutory and non-statutory (including census towns) cities and towns. The policy highlights the importance of putting in place the institutional arrangement with clearly defined roles and responsibilities of all stakeholders (public and private, including community) at state, city and local levels; and unambiguous regulatory framework. The approach should be holistic and planned.

The non-statutory (census) towns, which are beyond the municipal boundary and control, would need to have in place an institutional framework with roles and responsibilities clearly defined.

F. State FSM Policies

In compliance to the national initiative, many state governments have formulated their FSSM strategies/policies. These national and state initiatives are compiled as *Annex-II.*

Uttar Pradesh State Septage Management Policy, 2019

According to the 3rd State Annual Action Plan (SAAP) for FY 2017-18 to FY 2019-20 submitted to the Ministry of Housing and Urban Affairs under Atal Mission for Rejuvenation and Urban Transformation (AMRUT), the status of sewerage and sanitation in Municipal Corporations and *Nagar Palika Parishads* indicates a substantial gap in demand and supply in sanitation infrastructure in state.

As per CPCB report 2015, Uttar Pradesh has 73 numbers of sewage treatment plants (STPs) having treatment capacity of 2646.84 MLD. Seven STPs of capacity 89.59 MLD are non-operational, three STPs of capacity 170 MLD are under construction and one STP of capacity 15 MLD is proposed. Lately, the state government has reserved amount out of their SFC grant for O&M of STPs as municipalities have no provision for the same.

Status of Sewer Connections and Septic Tanks

Across the urban parts of the state, 86 percent households have on-site sanitation, and their distribution among municipalities are 78 percent households in Municipal Corporations, 98 percent in *Nagar Panchayats*,and 90 percent in *Nagar Palika Parishads*. Assuming that there is one septic tank per household, there are 72 lakh septic tanks in state. The distribution among the different categories of municipalities is 30.2 lakhs in Municipal Corporations, 26.7 lakhs in *Nagar Palika* Parishads and 15 lakhs in *Nagar Panchayats*.

Status of Existing Wastewater Generation

As of 2018, it is estimated that 5558 MLD of wastewater is generated every day in the State.

Status of Existing and Proposed STPs

In the 652 municipal towns in the state, STPs are present in 29municipalitiess with established capacity of ~2646MLD through 99 STPs. An aspect that requires attention is the reported receipt of sewage at the STPs (currently at 71 percent) and there are pockets not covered by the sewerage network in the sewered cities. There is an opportunity for the cities with STPs to take advantage for septage management and co-treatment, subject to techno-economic feasibilities of collection and transport.

Across 18 municipalities, additional capacity has been created through new STPsto treat ~1948MLD (10 in new municipalities and 8in existing municipalities) under State schemes, AMRUT and *Namami Gange*. The total available treatment capacity will be 4594MLD upon completion in the urban parts of the State.

While on-site sanitation is prevalent across town and cities in the state, there are major gaps across sanitation service chain. Further as urban households without toilets obtain facilities over the next few years under *Swachh Bharat* Mission (SBM) across town and cities, it is likely that many will require on-site arrangement like pit latrines and septic tanks in cities at locations where sewerage systems are not available. While construction standards have been codified by Bureau of Indian Standards (BIS), the actual construction is largely with households to manage – in practice, the installations are subject to local practices and considerable variations. In many instances for example, soak-ways or drain fields are not provided.

While the gaps and consequences of lack of access to toilets are well reported, those relating to containment systems, faecal sludge and septage collection, conveyance and treatment remain largely unknown and unaddressed by most, if not all state agencies dealing with sanitation and the municipalities. Even in general discourse this major health hazard is not well understood or talked. This policy outlines the measures envisages for range of stakeholders towards preparedness to handle the entire sanitation value chain while addressing the following sectoral issues:

- Municipalities are of different sizes and morphology having different onsite sanitation treatment systems of varying size.
- Treatment gaps have implications on environmental safety.
- Varied capacity utilization of STPs has implications on septage addition and hence becomes a dynamic process to match unpredictable wastewater flows.
- The sector being in a nascent stage requires an integrated planning and life cycle approach for management.
- Fractured roles for agencies mandated for asset ownership, creation, operation and management (*Jal Nigam*, *Jal Kal*, municipalities, Private sector, non-profit organisations and citizens), requiring work coordination structures and role clarity.

- 92 percent of municipalities have no mechanism and require sustainable solutions. They need a dedicated focus and attention for septage management.
- Lack of understanding about containment and estimations have implications on system design for scheduled emptying.
- Service chain is largely dominated by private investments and is unorganized.
- Significant market opportunity to harness private sector efficiencies for emptying and treatment services.
- Occupational health & safety concerns for workers.
- Pricing for services and cost recovery.
- Low level of community awareness resulting in unscientific construction of OSS and cleaning practices.
- Weak capacities within municipal bodies.

The goal of the Policy is to improve water quality and protect public health in urban areas of the State by 2023. The objective is to enhance the ability of local implementers to build and operate septage treatment systems for urban centres and promote the behaviour change and supporting environment needed for systems to be effective and sustainable. The main strategy is to facilitate a bottom-up, demand-driven project development process by providing State Government support and incentives. On-site-sanitation systems in the state are based on septic tank, which is a simple structure and when designed, installed, and operated properly, can serve as the first step in the sewage treatment process, which transforms human waste into a manageable effluent. Effluent can be further treated, reused or disposed of, thus breaking a cycle of disease that is responsible for huge economic losses, countless lost lives, and immeasurable human suffering. The National Urban Sanitation Policy (NUSP) of 2008 provides a vision for healthy and liveable cities and outlines different elements that are needed to achieve the vision. Most recently, the National Faecal Sludge and Septage Management Policy (NFSSM) Policy (2017), *Swacch Bharat* Mission (SBM) (through ODF++ ratings) and Ministry of Housing and Urban Affairs (MoHUA), Government of India (GoI) through the Standard Operating Procedures (SOP), 2018 for cleaning of sewers and septic tanks has provided considerable impetus to this sector. NFFSM with an objective of fostering sustainable SM services in cities aims to create enabling environment, provide role clarity, align with existing Missions, comply with environmental discharge standards and negates gender insecurity. The Central Public Health and Environmental Engineering Organisation (CPHEEO) Manual of 2013 and The Prohibition of Employment as Manual Scavengers and their Rehabilitation Act, 2013, have provided key markers to further the technical, occupational and health support to personnel in this sector. Uttar Pradesh with 652 municipalities and urban population of 4.9 Crores (es. 2018) have been making significant efforts in improving the status of urban sanitation in its cities. Currently, wastewater treatment capacity of 3159 MLD is available and another 1281 MLD is under different stages of implementation. Nearly 9 lakh Individual Household latrines (IHHLs) constructed under SBM (U) over last 3 years also warrant immediate attention on FSM. Sanitation coverage in 610 municipalities is completely dependent on septic tanks. There are 72 lakh On-site Sanitation Systems (OSS) which generates approximately 5000 MLD of sewerage.

This highlights the magnitude of effort required for addressing environmental and public health safety on account of untreated sewage / septage. Given this context, Government of Uttar Pradesh proposes a holistic approach for septage management (integrated/standalone), as a way forward. It is with this view that this 5-year FSM policy (2019 – 2023) for Uttar Pradesh has been prepared. Government of Uttar Pradesh under this policy envisages a goal that "All ULBs commit to continually adopt sustainable septage management services, that is inclusive and equitable; for its citizens to live in an environment free of pollution and health hazards; with the support of the public and private sector, under a sector regulator".

The Policy articulates a three-pronged Septage Management (SM) Vision:

(a) by end of 2019, all preparatory activities of realizing SM target under a sector regulation is completed;

(b) by end of 2021, SM is mainstreamed in all municipalities and all *Nagar Nigams* (NNs) and *Nagar Palika Parishads* (NPPs) have significantly moved forward towards SM and;

(c) by end of 2023, all municipalities have implemented SM solutions in an inclusive manner empowering all stakeholders in the process.

The Service Levels and Charter for Key Stakeholders have been developed to streamline the processes. To facilitate impactful implementation, municipalities are categorized based on the availability of sewage treatment facilities. In the municipalities with existing operational STPs, co-treatment of septage will be promoted while Septage Treatment Plants will be taken up for large single cities or adopt a regional/cluster approach for group of cities with a view to achieving economies of scale. This policy also sets the direction for supportive actions to manage septage so as to deliver results on public health and environmental safety, occupational health and personnel safety issues, infrastructure, private sector engagement, financial sustainability and tariffs levels.A clear monitoring and evaluation of policy performance is desired annually for direction setting and alignment of the budgets.

The key outcomes envisaged are related to safe containment system, treatment of all generated wastes, safe working practices and reuse of all resources for a sustained circular sanitation economy. The policy shall bring about a paradigm shift in the management of septage with the active participation of citizens, private sector and Municipal bodies.

Inadequate Legal And Regulatory Basis

Most countries reveal a paucity of regulatory acts, ordinances and administrative rules on Faecal Sludge (FS) management. In some countries, where national acts stipulating the proper disposal of human waste exist, specific agencies are vested with the power to issue the necessary ordinances and exert control. Yet, the institutional responsibilities are often not perceived and/or performed, or else, responsibilities are assigned to several agencies and often overlap, thus leading to institutional interference and paralysis. Since formal attribution of responsibilities to the private sector is generally missing, clarity regarding the distribution of tasks between the public and private sector is also lacking. One of the consequences of the informal character of the private sector is the lack of rules regarding, for example, pit emptying, FS haulage and disposal (range of emptying fees, official discharge points, maximum number of trucks etc.). This can lead to abuse (e. g. cartelisation, increase in emptying fees etc.).

Rules and regulations must have a clear objective and sound coordination mechanisms. They must be adapted to any country's and city's specific needs, resources and capacities and be enacted according to specific circumstances. Rules and regulations must allow for evolution and adaptation over time, but with clear checks and balances to prevent elites and powerful interest groups capturing or using them for their own benefit.

In India, urban sanitation thus remains a significant challenge for urban policy makers and managers. The governments have been making attempts for extending the underground sewerage networks in cities (as was focused by JnNURM. and presently hammering on connecting the household toilets with sewer system (under AMRUT). That is the reason that most of the enactments dealing with urban management and services in the country have focused on sewerage system and septage management. In reality, this significant aspect has remained largely neglected and has been commonly addressed by a mostly unregulated informal sector. The governments--central as well as state-- are now beginning to recognize the fact that septic tanks are decentralized waste (human excreta) collection systems, which could be the way to achieve full sanitation solutions (SunitaNarain:2017).

Inadequate Containment and Building Regulations

In most of the cases, poorly constructed pits and septic tanks contribute to inadequate FSM, as well as to inadequate hygienic conditions for users. Typically, only septic tanks have regulated designs or design parameters, and in informal settlements, where the bulk of FSM services are typically though not only required, such regulations are, more or less by definition, not enforced. The question therefore arises as to how to persuade residents of informal settlements to adopt adequate sanitation infrastructure. The prevailing building regulations lack the link with the provisions of FSM service/value chain.

Summing Up

The National Policy on Faecal Sludge and Septage Management, 2017 has recognised Faecal Sludge Management (FSM) as an essential component of urban sanitation in the country. It thus provides basic comprehensive guidelines for faecal sludge and septage management practices to be adopted in urban India. However, this initiative must be complemented with state level sanitation strategy and city-level sanitation planning systems, and suitably formulated bye-laws/regulations that allow the public utilities/ authorities to oblige both households(community) and private service providers(desludgers/emptiers and entrepreneurs) to play their part in delivering a full FSM service/value chain.

The major laws including municipal laws and other policy documents should be reviewed and amended to make sure that they do not contradict each other. The rules and bye-laws on SWM should be used to link with FSM. The municipality should invest in treating and making sludge available to people in a form that is harmless to their health and harmless to the environment.

References

- *UNHABITAT: World Cities Report(2016): Urbanization and Development: Emerging Future.*
- *World Urbanisation Prospects, 2014.*
- *Government of India: Twelfth Five Year Plan.*
- *Report of Census, 2011.*
- *Shubhagato Dasgupta (2016):The Government Has Made a Welcome Shift in Sanitation Policy that Will Help Develop Indian Cities.*

- *Government of India: CPCB Report, 2015.*
- *Ministry of Urban Development (2005): Guidelines of JnNURM.*
- *Ministry of Urban Development (2015): Guidelines of AMRUT.*
- *WSP(2016):Fecal Sludge Management: Diagnostics for Service Delivery in Urban Areas (Summary Report).*
- *Sunita Narain(2017):Do it differently: Toilets are not enough to achieve sanitation, India must reinvent the waste business; Times of India, Edit page, February 11.*
- *The Constitution of India.*
- *The Environment (Protection) Act, 1986.*
- *The Employment of Manual Scavengers and Construction of Dry Latrines (Prohibition) Act, 1993.*
- *Prohibition of Employment as Manual Scavengers and Their Rehabilitation Act, 2013.*
- *The Water (Prevention and Control of Pollution) Act, 1974.*
- *The National Water Framework, 2016.*
- *U.P. Municipal Corporation Act, 1957.*
- *U.P. Municipalities Act, 1916.*
- *U.P. Water Supply and Sewerage Act,1975.*
- *Dodaneet al (2012): as quoted in A Guide to Development of On Site Sanitation., WHO.*
- *Hecht, Antony (2004): as quoted in ibid.*
- *National Health Policy, 2002 & 2017.*
- *National Urban Housing & Habitat Policy, 2007.*
- *National Urban Sanitation Policy, 2008.*
- *National Environment Policy, 2006.*
- *National Policy on Faecal Sludge and Septage Management, 2017.*
- *National Water Policy, 2012.*
- *Government of India (2014): Guidelines of SBM.*
- *Uttar Pradesh State Policy on Faecal Sludge and Septage Management, Draft (March 2019); prepared by CSE, New Delhi.*
- *Uttar Pradesh State Septage Management Policy, 2019.*

4

Institutional Mechanism for FSSM

Introduction

Sanitation in India owes its origin to the Constitution of the country, wherein it has been placed in List-II: State Subject. The Twelfth Schedule includes sanitation in Local Government functions. Sanitation thus remains in the complex web of national, state and local government responsibilities. It has further been compounded by the roles of parastatals.

Any work on sanitation improvement is carried out within a framework of household, community and governmental relationships, all of which affect the manner in which a programme is executed. Of major importance are the organizations or institutions that have been given responsibility for or have an interest in some aspect of sanitation improvement. Such bodies may be governmental ministries, departments of ministries, government organisations, municipalities, parastatals, non-governmental agencies or community-based organizations.

Although the 74thAmendment to the Constitution (1992) introduced water and sanitation as a local function to be devolved by the state governments to Municipalities, in many states, the governments continue to hold responsibility through parastatal agencies. Even in states, where urban water supply and sanitation function has technically been transferred to municipalities, municipalities are often inadequately equipped in terms of financial and organizational capacity. They tend to depend on state level departments and agencies for financing and execution of capital projects and their role is often limited to handling operation and maintenance (though they lack competence and finances for the same). As result, accountability for urban water supply and sanitation continues to be diffused across multiple tiers of government. It is pertinent to highlight that till recently the governments focused on universalization of conventional sewerage system.

The on-site-sanitation system was not given due recognition. It is in the recent past that the public authorities have realized the importance of on-site-sanitation system, as a feasible and cost-effective alternative to conventional sewerage system which is capital intensive.

In this backdrop, the chapter attempts to discuss the sanitation related roles and responsibilities of different government ministries, government departments and organisations at national, state, city and community (local) levels. The chapter has been divided into many parts. Part-I discusses the roles played by various Union Ministries as well as organisations at national level. Likewise, Part-II deals with the State Government Departments, and parastatals and organisations responsible for faecal sludge management system, directly or indirectly. Part-III discusses the organisatios at the field level viz. local government units. Part-IV mentions the importance of Community-Based Organisations (CBOs) and Non-Governmental Organisations (NGOs) and Part-V highlights the role and importance of other stakeholders playing in faecal sludge management process. The study is summed up with the observation that roles and responsibilities of institutions at different levels should be clearly defined for effective implementation of faecal sludge management programme in urban areas in Uttar Pradesh.

PART-I: NATIONAL LEVEL INSTITUTIONS

(A) Union Ministries

The study reveals that a host of Ministries of the Union Government play significant role in sanitation (including solid waste) and its related issues/aspects. These Ministries are discussed here under:

Ministry of Housing and Urban Affairs is the nodal ministry for sanitation in urban areas in the country. It is responsible for formulating policy guidelines, issue primers and advisories from time to time, and develop operational manuals. The Ministry has framed following policy guidelines:

- ***National Urban Sanitation Policy, 2008***: The policy, first of its kind in the country, promotes proper disposal and treatment of sludge from on-site installations; and makes provision for recycle and reuse of wastewater. The Policy mandated the state governments to frame their own policies keeping in view their local scenario. The urban local governments were directed to develop their City Sanitation Plan for accessing financial assistance from the Government of India. A net-work of Task Force and

Sanitation Committees to be constituted at state, city and community levels was also recommended. The states of Maharashtra, Odisha, Gujarat, Uttar Pradesh and Tamil Nadu are the pioneer to frame their own state specific sanitation strategy/plan. Many cities have developed their City Sanitation Plans and executed them with central assistance.

- ***Advisory Note on Septage Management in Urban India, 2013***: This initiative promotes scheduled and mechanical emptying of pits. It advises the states to associate the private sector in transportation of sludge. The Note suggests various methods of disposal including composting.
- ***Primer on Faecal Sludge and Septage Management, 2016*:** It was a maiden dedicated directive to states on implementing faecal sludge management programme.
- ***National Policy on Faecal Sludge and Septage Management, 2017:*** This is a dedicated National Policy on FSSM which recognizes the importance of implementing faecal sludge and septage management programmes in urban areas. The policy recommends ways and means for putting in place the effective mechanism for faecal sludge management systems by the states. It advises the states to develop their own state specific strategy/plan for managing faecal sludge by the municipalities in a scientific and safe way.

It is not that the Ministry's role has just been confined to framing certain laws, but it has launched a number of centrally sponsored programmes as well for providing better sanitation services to the people. Some of the central interventions directly focusing on sanitation services (earlier FSM was not duly recognized) are enumerated as under:

- *Integrated Development of Small & Medium Towns, 1979-80.*
- *Integrated Low Cost Sanitation Scheme, 1980:* A dedicated programme for construction of toilets.
- *Mega City Scheme,1993-94.*
- *Valmiki-AmbedkarAwasYojana* (VAMBAY), 2001
- *Jawaharlal Nehru National Urban Renewal Mission (JnNURM), 2005* (Urban Infrastructure Development in Small & Medium Towns (UIDSSMT)/ Basic Services to Urban Poor (BSUP)/ Integrated Housing and Slum Development Programme (IHSDP)
- *Scheme for Urban Infrastructure Development in Satellite Towns/ Counter Magnets of Million Plus Cities, 2007.*

- *Rajiv Avas Yojana (RAY), 2010.*
- *Swachh Bharat Mission (Urban), 2014*: A focused scheme on construction of toilets (individual household/community/public) and solid waste management in urban areas to ensure time-bound elimination of open defecation.
- *Atal Mission for Rejuvenation and Urban Transformation (AMRUT), 2015*: A mega scheme focusing on infrastructure creation that has a direct link to the provision of better services to people. It aims to ensure that every household in large towns (with a population of one lakh or more, as per 2011 census) has access to a tap with assured water supply and a sewerage connection.
- *Smart Cities Mission, 2015*: A scheme with focus on development of core infrastructure including sanitation and solid waste management in select cities.

The Ministry of Housing and Urban Affairs has recognized the importance of on-site-sanitation programmes and has accordingly framed the FSSM Policy, 2017 which facilitates the management of faecal sludge and septage in urban India. The current interventions in the form of SBM and AMRUT are accelerating the pace of construction of latrines with septic tanks, and also thus broaden the scope of FSSM.

Another important intervention (this was initiated by the erstwhile Ministry of Housing & Urban Poverty Alleviation which was merged with the Ministry and Urban Development which since rechristened as the present Ministry of Housing and Urban Affairs), though not directly related to FSSM, focuses through its National Urban Housing and Habitat Policy, 2007 (latest initiative which succeeded a number of policies issued earlier on Housing) promotes the creation of adequate infrastructure facilities relating to water, drainage, sanitation, sewerage, etc.

The Ministry should advise the states/municipalities for earmarking dedicated land for creation of Faecal Sludge Treatment Plant (FSTP) in every developed colony for low-income groups and economically weaker sections of the society.

Ministry of Environment, Forests and Climate Change is responsible for planning, promotion, coordination and overseeing the implementation of environment related policies and programmes. The Ministry has enacted ***The Environment (Protection) Act, 1986***, which empowers to take all necessary measures for protecting and improving the quality of environment, and preventing, controlling and abating environmental pollution. For carrying out the purposes of the Act, the Ministry has formulated a number of Rules for managing and handling Solid Wastes, Bio-Medical Wastes, e-Waste, Building Construction & Demolition Wastes, Hazardous Waste, etc. The ***Solid Waste Management Rules, 2016*** (replaced the earlier Municipal Solid Waste (Management & Handling) Rules, 2000) provides that treated sewage may be added to the solid waste for treatment and an integrated system for disposal may be developed.

There is a prime need for formulating a dedicated Rule on FSSM by the Ministry. Since FSSM is getting recognition and thus achieving momentum, the subject deserves a dedicated rule.

Ministry of Social Justice & Empowerment initiated and enacted ***The Employment of Manual Scavengers and Construction of Dry Latrines (Prohibition) Act, 1993*** which prohibited engaging in or employing for or permits to be engaged in or employed for manually carrying human excreta, an inhuman activity applied for cleaning the dry latrines. It also prohibited construction or maintaining a dry latrine, a prevalent practice in densely populated old localities and in low income settlements. However, this law does not cover the manual emptying of pits. The Ministry therefore subsequently revised the earlier law and enacted ***The Prohibition of Employment as Manual Scavengers and their Rehabilitation Act, 2013***. This new law focuses on prohibiting construction of an insanitary latrine; prohibits employment as manual scavengers; prohibits manual cleaning of sewers and septic tanks without protective equipment; and rehabilitation of manual scavengers. The law emphasizes on emptying of septic tanks by mechanical devices.

This Act covers two elements of FSM value chain, i.e. construction of proper septic tank for 'Containment' of faecal sludge, and 'Emptying' the tank mechanically.

Ministry of Chemical & Fertilisers plays a supportive role and has thus issued, from time to time, guidelines for sale of compost prepared along with other chemical fertilisers. This promotes the use of compost by farmers. This takes care of the 'Reuse' element of the FSSM value chain.

Ministry of Agriculture and Farmers Welfare acts as facilitator and has issued guidelines for granting subsidy for compost production, creating awareness among farmers for using organic manure (compost), and imparting training of personnel engaged in compost production, certification of compost quality, etc. This promotes use of compost, a prime product by disposal of sludge. The element of 'Reuse' in FSSM value chain is thus taken care of.

Ministry of Mines has issued guidelines for use of compost for rehabilitation of degraded land, mining spoil dumps, and abandoned mining areas, and for compensatory afforestation under the Mines and Minerals Act, 1987. This facilitates the 'Reuse' factor of the FSSM value chain.

Ministry of Power plays a facilitating role and has issued orders directing the thermal power plants to use wastewater, generated by the nearby Sewage Treatment Plant (STP), for cooling their machines. This order takes care of the 'Reuse' of treated wastewater.

Ministry of Industries has directed industries to use wastewater. This pertains to 'Reuse' element of FSSM value chain.

Ministry of *Jal Shakti* (the newly created ministry by merging Ministry of Water Resources, River Development and Ganga Rejuvenation with Ministry of Drinking Water & Sanitation) is responsible for the provision of drinking water and sanitary facilities in rural areas. It supervises and monitors the SBM-*Gramin* (Rural) programme. The Ministry is the nodal for the overall policy, planning, funding and coordination of programmes of drinking water and sanitation in the country. It provides inputs to other Departments/Ministries for formulation of policies impacting water and sanitation issues. It extends a helping hand in respect of policy formulation and planning of sanitation activities.

Ministry of Women and Child Welfare ensures gender mainstreaming of IEC material for FSSM across the country.

The above discussion reveals the supportive role of various Union Ministries. The Ministry of Housing and Urban Affairs should coordinate all the initiatives and converge at local level for effective implementation of complete FSSM value chain in urban areas.

(B) National Level Organisations

There are a number of organisations functioning under the control and supervision of certain Union Ministries. Such organisations are also destined to play important role in FSSM. The roles played by the relevant organisations are discussed here under:

Central Public Health and Environmental Engineering Organisation (CPHEEO), a technical wing of the Ministry of Housing and Urban Affairs deals with the matters related to urban water supply, and sanitation (including solid wastes management) in the country. The Organisation had developed ***Operational Manual on Sewerage and Sewage Treatment, 1993,*** which provided guidelines mainly on construction of septic tanks. Later on, it was revised and a new ***Manual on Sewerage and***

Sewage Treatment, 2013 has been issued. The revised manual mandates scheduled desludging as well.

The Manual makes provisions for two key elements of FSSM value chain. These are 'Containment' of faecal sludge in proper septic tank, and the scheduled 'Emptying' of pits.

Central Pollution Control Board (CPCB): This national organization has been created by the Ministry of Environment, Forests and Climate Change under the Water (Prevention and Control of Pollution) Act, 1974. It was further entrusted with the powers and functions under the Air (Prevention and Control of Pollution) Act, 1981. It serves as a field formation and also provides technical services to the Ministry on the provisions of the Environment (Protection) Act, 1986. Its principal functions are (i) to promote cleanliness of streams and wells in different areas of the states by prevention, control and abatement of water pollution, and (ii) to improve the quality of air and to prevent, control or abate air pollution in the country.

It is a monitoring body responsible (through its subordinate state units) for implementation of legislations relating to prevention and control of environmental pollution.

The guidelines issued by the Board provide monitoring mechanism to control environmental pollution (including the pollution emanating as a result of improper management of faecal sludge). The Board should develop indicators, if not exist, based on FSSM practices for better monitoring. The traditional indicators may not be suitable and applicable to FSSM services.

Bureau of Indian Standards is the National Standard Body of India established under the ***Bureau of Indian Standards Act, 1986*** for the harmonious development of the activities of standardization. It functions under the control and supervision of the Ministry of Consumer Affairs, Food and Public Distribution. The Bureau has issued following codes which are related to FSSM programme, may not be affecting directly:

- ***(Part 1: Code of Practice for Installation of Septic Tanks (Part 2: Secondary Treatment and Disposal of Septic Tank Effluents), 1985:*** prescribes three methods of disposal—Soil absorption system, Biological filters, and Up-flow anaerobic filters.
- ***National Building Code of India, 2005:*** provides guidelines for septic tank design, construction, installation, and their operations and maintenance.
- ***National Building Code of India, 2016***: is an updated, revised and expanded version of earlier Code, 2005. Some more chapters, including one on Solid Waste, have been added therein.

The Codes prescribe standards for design and construction of septic tanks; and the disposal methods. However, these Codes are applicable only to the new houses, where lay-out plan of a building is required to be approved by the Housing Agency. The agency responsible for approving the lay-out plan of a house/building ensures that prescribes norms have been followed (in lay-out plan); but seldom makes on-spot inspection to verify that approved lay-out plan is being fully complied with.

PART-II: STATE LEVEL INSTITUTIONS

(A) Government Department

Department of Urban Development of the state government is responsible for formulation of policy, providing funds, monitoring, coordinating and controlling the activities of the Municipalities, *Jal Nigam* and regional *Jal Sansthans*. The main objective of the Department is to plan for various infrastructure facilities and essential services related to water supply, sewage disposal, sanitation, urban poverty alleviation, and various municipal services. The Department formulates policies and programmes, provides grant for undertaking various developmental activities, issues directives and monitor the functioning of the organizations falling under its control.

Before Independence, the department was known as Public Health Department which was later on rechristened as Local Self Government Department. Later on it became Housing & Urban Development Department, which was divided into two separate departments known as Urban Development Department and Housing and Urban Planning Department.

The Department has neither developed any State Sanitation Strategy/ Plan nor got the City Sanitation Plan developed by its subordinate local government units (lately, the State Septage Managament Policy, 2019 has been notified). There is a prime need and high time that the Department should formulate State FSSM Strategy/Plan, clearly define the roles and responsibilities of every stakeholder, and develop a mechanism to coordinate and monitor the implementation of FSSM programme.

Department of Environment, Forest and Climate Change has been assigned the responsibility of improving the overall environmental quality in Uttar Pradesh. It is actively engaged in overall environmental assessment, monitoring, protection and awareness among the people of the state. It envisions conservation of natural resources like cultivable land, forests and water bodies. The state is committed to protecting, restoring and maintain sustainable use of ecosystems in the interst of inclusive growth and development. In order to achieve its mission, the state endeavours to: adopt world-class forest management practices for conservation of forests and bio-diversity; large scale plantation increasing the green cover; and sustainable harvesting of goods and services from biological resources.

Department of Housing & Urban Planning was established to ensure planned development of urban areas and create an enabling environment to provide affordable housing. The Department has taken a step to reach the citizens to make them aware of the laws, policies, programmes and procedural simplifications carried out. It controls, monitors and supervises functions of Development Authorities, Special Areas Development Authorities, Housing and Development Board and Town & Country Planning Organisation. Development Authorities are responsible for land management and developing housing colonies in areas of their jurisdiction, especially in larger towns. The main function of Housing and Development Board is constructing houses. Town and Country Planning wing is responsible for preparing master plans of cities and towns and regulating building bye-laws and building codes. Ensuring planned development of cities and effective implementation of housing schemes and creating healthy habitat is the main responsibilities of the department.

Department of Women and Child Development is responsible for ensuring gender equity in sanitation services.

(B) State Level Organisations

Uttar Pradesh *Jal Nigam* is the agency responsible for creating infrastructure for water supply, sewerage and drainage in this most populated state. *Jal Nigam* has jurisdiction over whole of the state (except Cantonment Area). Initially, Public Health Engineering Department (PHED) was created in 1927 to provide drinking water supply and sewerage facilities in Uttar Pradesh. In year 1946 it was rechristened as Local Self Government Engineering Department (LSGED). In 1975, it was converted to Uttar Pradesh *Jal Nigam* through Uttar Pradesh Water Supply and Sewerage Act, 1975. The basic objective of creating this corporation is development and regulation of water supply and sewerage services and for matters connected therewith. Its mission is: Safe Drinking Water and Clean Environment to all; and vision is technological intervention for Conservation of Water, Safe Water and Environment Management towards sustainable growth. It is a Design and Construction Organisation with powers to raise the loans and funds for implementation of water supply and sewerage projects in Uttar Pradesh.

The main functions of *Jal Nigam* include to provide all necessary services regarding water supply and sewerage to the state/local bodies; to provide services to other institutions private or government, on demand, as a construction and design agency; to establish standards for water supply and sewerage arrangements; to organise training required for development of technical manpower; and to advise the state government on tariff for water supply and sewerage in rural and urban areas. It is responsible for preparing and carrying out State Plan for Water Supply and Sewerage and to control river/lake pollution caused by domestic sewage as per directives of central/state governments.

Uttar Pradesh *Jal Nigam* is the principal implementing agency for River Pollution Control projects in the state. Its task is to prevent direct flow of waste water into important river bodies of the state, so as to maintain water quality of these rivers to a satisfactory level. This is being done by diverting waste water/domestic sewage flow to appropriate treatment sites before being allowed to drain out in river bodies. So for 15 major towns located on the banks of river Ganga, Yamuna and Gomti have been provided with waste water treatment facilities for cleaning about 42 percent of its domestic sewage flow.

The UP *Jal Nigam* has the mandate to manage water supply, sewerage system and septage in the state. It has got the technical personnel equipped with technique and the expertise in the subject. But its personnel may not be fully conversant and technically equipped for FSSM (a new subject for them). So may be the case with administrative procedures. For the purpose, extensive skill up-gradation programmes on FSSM value chain, and other non-technical areas of administration would be required.

Uttar Pradesh State Pollution Control Board is a statutory organisation entrusted to implement environmental laws and rules within the state. It was constituted in 1975, initially under the Water (Prevention and Control of Pollution) Act, 1974, in 1982 and consequently rechristened subsequent to the enactment of Air (Prevention and Control of Pollution) Act, 1981. The Board was also entrusted with the powers and functions under the Water (Prevention and Control of Pollution) Cess Act, 1977 along with other responsibilities under the Environment Protection Act, 1986.

Town and Country Planning Department is responsible for executing building regulations and preparing master plans. Hence in the master plan of a city land can be earmarked for setting up STPs.

Directorate of Urban Local Bodies was conceived in 1971 and became functional in 1973. This controls, supervises, guides and coordinates the functioning of municipalities in the state. It works under the control of the Department of Urban Development.

Directorate of Environment functions under the control and supervision of the Department of Environment, Forest and Climate Change. It monitors the environmental pollution and gives environmental clearance to industries.

PART-III: LOCAL UNITS

Municipalities are the units of local government. There are three types of municipalities in the state. Larger urban areas having a population of three lakhs and above have Municipal Corporation (*Nagar Nigam*); smaller urban areas with a population of one lakh and above have Municipal Council (*Nagar Palika Parishad*); and transitional areas have *Nagar Panchayat.* The Uttar Pradesh Municipal Corporation Act, 1959 applies on Municipal Corporation, and Uttar Pradesh Municipalities Ac, 1916 has jurisdiction over remaining two units of the local government. Presently, the state, having the second large municipal network, has 17 Municipal Corporations, 198 Municipal Councils and 437 *Nagar Panchayats.*

It is a statutory local government unit having people's representatives directly elected by the people. It is accountable to the people of the state through elected councillors. The Constitution of the country classifies water supply and sewerage as local functions (Twelfth Schedule) and advises the state governments to empower the municipality to undertake these functions. Further, the presence of people's representatives may be proved helpful in bringing the citizen nearer to municipal administration and increasing the people's participation in the provision of civic services.

The functions of water supply and sewerage was taken away from municipalities situated in the area under the jurisdiction of two regional *Jal Sansthans* falling under Bundelkhand region. But the smaller municipalities especially *Nagar Panchayats* have mandate but lack adequate expertise and finances for managing water supply and sewerage systems. FSSM is a new functional area for the existing municipal functionaries.

Development Authorities are responsible for undertaking housing construction. But water supply and sewerage in the areas developed by them is the sole responsibility of U.P. *Jal Nigam.*

Cantonment Board (LCB) is an autonomous body under the control of Government of India in the Ministry of Defence. The Cantonment Board is a regulatory body to manage and control the land/building activities as a whole or as a part in the Cantonment area in accordance with law, rules/ policies issued by the Ministry of Defence, which includes the maintenance of land records/details and boundary of Cantonment area. Cantonment Board also provides civic services and infrastructure facilities to the citizens living under it. At present, there are thirteen Cantonment Boards in the state.

Historically, cantonments were places where the army of colonial government had to be exclusively quartered in an effort to keep the armed forces totally insulated from the ruled. Cantonments meant quarters assigned for lodging troops, a permanent military station created by the British government in India for the location of military formation away from the civilian towns and insulated from the Indian nationalist influences. Housing was the core objective. Subsequently, housing itself attracted the civil population to reside in the cantonments and the economic spin-offs attracted other activities. The *bazaar* area was recognized and the anatomy of the cantonment got clearly defined with military, the bungalow and civil areas clearly defined. The cantonments as local self-government organizations have always remained a puzzle. The civilian population wants to be in it but is uncertain about their status and their future.

Due to repeated demand for reforms by the representatives of cantonment population, the Cantonments Act, 1924 was enacted to introduce local self-government in the cantonments, which contained substantial civil population. The Act was the first model municipal Act for cantonments, but in its implementation, decentralization and democratic norms were largely compromised because of the status of the citizen who occupied the property only as a licensee of the Government. It was later amended and the Cantonment Act, 2006 lays down both the mandatory and discretionary functions of the Board such as education, public health, sanitation, roads, street lighting, water supply and birth and death registration.

The vision of Cantonment Board is to provide to its citizens an environmental friendly and sustainable waste management system with complete safe disposal facilities by putting in place waste reduction and recovery mechanisms. Solid waste management is an obligatory function of cantonment boards in India. This service is an important aspect of maintaining the quality of life and environment of a town or city, but unfortunately it is poorly performed resulting in problems of health, sanitation and environmental degradation. Inadequate financial resources, institutional weakness, improper choice of technology and public apathy towards solid waste management have made this service far from satisfactory.

Cantonment Board aims to provide high quality services with universal access including the poor to make cantonment area slum free, citizen friendly, well-governed and environmental friendly.

PART-IV: BASTI (LOCAL) LEVEL INSTITUTIONS

(A) Public Authority

Ward Committee: It is a statutory unit constituted in compliance to the provisions of the 74th Constitution Amendment Act, 1992. The main objective of making provision of ward committee is to decentralize the municipal administration nearer to people and ensure citizen participation in local governance. This was expected to bring about closer interaction between the people and their elected representatives and thereby respond more effectively to the local needs. It was also hoped that it would lead to greater accountability of the councillors to their voters in constituency.

In Uttar Pradesh, as per municipal enactment a ward committee is constituted in every ward of a municipality having a population of three lakhs or more. It consists of ten representatives of Resident Welfare Associations and NGOs working in a particular ward.

Ward Committee is generally entrusted with sanitation services and cleanliness in the area, facilitation, collection of municipal tax, maintenance of parks, play grounds and other places of recreation, preparation of ward development plan, budget of the ward, facilitating in identifying the suitable beneficiaries to various government welfare schemes, etc.

Ward Committee is a statutory unit. Its objective is to deepen the democracy and ensure people's direct engagement in managing local governance (at ward level). For responsive, citizen-centric and accountable local governance, this constitutionally mandated committee plays important role in development of ward.

In Uttar Pradesh, though, the Acts were amended to this effect in 2009 and rules were framed in 2014, municipalities have shown no interest in constituting ward committees nor does the state government seem willing in administrative decentralisation of municipal administration. Thus an important provision of the Constitution has been belied.

(B) Community-based Organisations (CBOs)

For better appreciation of the people at large and also to associate the community in local governance, it is a pre-requisite to have community organized for a communal cause. In various government interventions ***Self-Help Groups (SHGs)***, ***Community Development Societies (CDSs)***, ***Resident Welfare Associations (RWAs)***, ***Resident Welfare Societies (RWSs)***, ***Area/Mohalla Samitis***, etc have been constituted. These community fora are registered under relevant state law (e.g. Society Act, Cooperative Society Act, Chit Fund Act, etc) and made legal entity. They are the prime mechanism to empower the community, and provide forum to remove their voicelessness. These community organisations play important role in creating awareness among the community, besides extending helping hands to public authorities in fulfilling the needs and aspirations of the people. This brings people nearer to public authorities. To be effective, government institutions must have regular contacts with the wider community that go beyond simply instructing the people what they must do. Community involvement is a tool to optimize the utilization of community (local) resources.

These community-based organisations can play an important role in developmental activities, if taken into confidence in right perspectives. They help in monitoring the project implementation and also in post-project maintenance and sustenance.

In many cities in the state, in some localities inhabited by effluent class of societies, especially in apartments, newly-built colonies, RWAs are playing active role in maintenance of civic services internally and redressing the grievances of inhabitants. These community-based organisations (CBOs) need to be popularized across the city for better and participatory governance.

(C) Non-government Organisations (NGOs)

These non-state actors have been playing appreciative role in various development sectors; e.g. women empowerment, livelihood creation and training, skills enhancement, community awareness, advocacy, training and capacity development, community development, school education, personal hygiene, mid-day-meal preparation and distribution, immunization programme, etc. However, they are not found actively involved in implementing faecal sludge management value chain. There is a need to associate and rope in NGOs in this process as well.

These NGOs can play an important role in creating awareness among the community, thus increasing the receptivity of faecal sludge management systems among community. They can advocate the people and create willingness-to-pay for faecal sludge services provided to them.

Most of these NGOs lack proper human resource. They claim to work on the principle of 'no profit, no loss', but the reality is found otherwise. They are not quality conscious. Most of them are engaged in women empowerment, livelihood generation programme, children education, immunization, advocacy, etc. The selected NGOs would need proper orientation towards FSSM.

PART-V: OTHER IMPORTANT STAKEHOLDERS

The governance and legislative reform vision of the Habitat Agenda are cogently reflected in the following paragraph:

> "Sustainable human settlements development requires the active engagement of civil society organizations, as well as the broad-based participation of all people. It equally requires responsive, transparent and accountable government at the local level. Civic engagement and responsible government both necessitate the establishment and strengthening of participatory mechanisms, including access to justice and community-based action planning, which will ensure that all voices are heard in identifying problems and priorities, setting goals, exercising legal rights, determining service standards, mobilizing resources and implementing policies, programmes and projects" (Habitat Agenda 1996: par. 181).

Households usually decide what type of on-site- sanitation system they build in their houses; use the toilet facilities; decide when they want their pits/tanks to be emptied and call for emptying services; and pay for the emptying services. At present, participation of the local population in the decision-making process of faecal sludge management is low, so is awareness of the need for adequate faecal sludge management. Willingness-to-pay for FS management is thus lower than for water supply (Bolomey: 2003). Knowledge on the need to empty the septic tanks/pits regularly is often lacking. (Klingel et al.: 2001). They are the primary stakeholders. Hence mass awareness programmes amongst households is must for their increasing willingness, as every household needs to play a pivotal role in FSSM service chain.

The Community: FSM requires collective actions reaching beyond households or individual initiatives pertaining to a latrine technology. In areas where latrines are already implemented and FS is not managed properly, the community or neighbourhood's willingness-to-improve (WTI) the current FSM situation may be assessed. The WTI is defined as a function of subjective costs (willingness-to-pay), expected benefits (return), convictions to change, concern, attitudes towards improvement, and social pressure by the neighbours. These driving elements can be as-sessed by a psycho-sociological survey.

Farmers, Farmers' Associations and Cooperatives: Farmers are the users or potential users of treated/un-treated faecal sludge. Their perception of the use of excreta as organic fertiliser, their demand for bio-solids (treated FS), their needs of bio-solid characteristics, their willingness and ability to pay for bio-solids are all factors influencing the planning of an improved

FS management (disposal or reuse, treatment type, financing mechanisms etc.). The demand is strongly governed by the availability of other fertilisers and their prices, as well as by the policy in place (e. g. promotion of organic farming).

Donors: In many countries, the sanitation and water sector is predominantly financed by ESA and supported by international consultancy. The external financial support is then predominantly geared towards the construction of infrastructure to provide access to sanitation to a large number of the population within a short period – a challenging task for the international sanitation community. However to sustain this trend of infrastructure provision, a strong capacity building programme is needed to provide local expertise for operation, maintenance and upgrading of these infrastructures.

Private Sector: Pit emptying services (small scale enterprises or individual manual de-sludgers); operation of faecal sludge treatment plants; and operation of public toilets generally is the responsibility of private sector. In the field of FS management, the private sector is mainly involved in pit emptying services and plays a demand-oriented role (full septic tanks or pits, farmers willing to reuse faecal sludge on their fields). Private manual pit emptiers are either small-scale enterprises (equipped with vacuum trucks or donkey/tractor-drawn collection vehicles) or individual de-sludgers. They mainly work independently from the public sector where public services are insufficiently ensured (Bolomey: 2003). They are also involved in operation and maintenance of public toilets and in faecal sludge treatment. Private players have a role to play in reuse of treated water. Their active participation must be ensured for sustainable faecal sludge management.

Community Leaders and Councillors: Community leaders (including religious leaders) have their own special interests, particularly where communal decisions have to be made about some aspects of a sanitation scheme or where leaders can set an example to other householders.

Artisans: In many cases there is a need for masons, bricklayers, drain-layers, carpenters, plumbers and other artisans to carry out part of the work. These workers often have experience in construction of houses and other buildings. Special skills may be required for the construction of latrines and associated works.

Local Contractors: Householders may require local contractors to carry out certain tasks for them, such as lining pits or constructing slabs. Where new techniques are being introduced or new forms of project support and funding used, contractors and subcontractors will require support.

Government Health Officials often play an essential part in sanitation improvement schemes, especially where the ministry of health is responsible for sanitation. Where a technical arm of government (such as a public works department) or an independent agency is responsible, management and supervision may be in the hands of technical officers. In some countries, health assistants, community and development officers and extension officers may be the link between an agency and the community. There is considerable variation in the terms used for different groups of workers and in the allocation of duties between these intermediate-level staff.

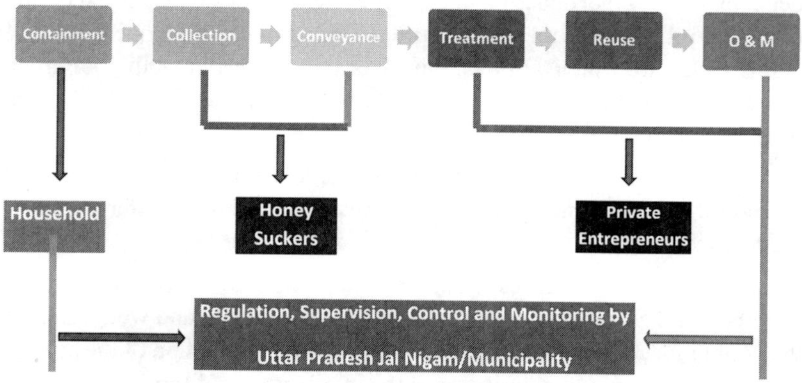

Figure 4.1: Role of Stakeholders in FSSM Service Chain

Summing Up

Governance is the double process of making and implementing decisions. Urban governance delivers sustainable development when it is environment friendly, participatory, citizen-centric, accountable, responsible and responsive, transparent, effective and efficient, equitable and inclusive. However, urban local government in many states fails on these counts. Urban governance in India is a victim of multiplicity of organisations and multiplicity of laws. The civic administration in Uttar Pradesh is too complex and segregated. It is very weak, lack suitable and sufficient personnel, with poor coordination amongst various local public agencies that must work together to create and maintain good functioning habitats in the state. This requires strong commitment by the government.

In Uttar Pradesh *Jal Nigam* has the mandate to manage water supply, sewerage system and sewage management. It has the technically equipped and qualified personnel, but they have gained experience of working in conventional sewerage and sepatage management systems. FSM may be a new area of functioning for most of the personnel—technical, administrative, financial. It is therefore necessary to enhance their skill and develop their capacity and capability in FSM for effective implementation of faecal sludge management in the state. Further, *Jal Nigam* needs to work in active collaboration with municipalities. The state government should be required to develop a proper coordinating mechanism to make FSM successful and effective.

Even in majority of the municipalities where urban water supply and sanitation is their responsibility, municipalities are often inadequately equipped in terms of financial and organizational capacity. They tend to depend on state level departments and agencies for financing and execution of capital projects and their role is often limited to handling operation and maintenance, for which they lack funds. As a result, accountability for urban water supply and sanitation continues to be diffused across multiple tiers of government.

Responsibilities of the different stake-holders are not clearly defined and coordination/communication mechanisms between the different actors are non-existent.

Local public authorities should be made aware of the key importance of improved FS management in attaining a better health and well-being of the population, of the economic benefits as well as protection of the natural resources. This would help increase the involvement of the authorities in FS management and the allocation of means for FS management to become an integral part of sanitation planning. Awareness raising campaigns should also aim at increasing the acceptance of improved FS management by the local population (e. g. by motivating them to call for emptying services frequently in order to avoid overflowing septic tanks) and their willingness to pay for the service. Technical capacity building alone is not sufficient to ensure sustainable FSM. Strengthening the municipal technical services and consulting firms with non-technical competence (financial, legal, institutional, socio-economic, urban planning) is urgently needed. Simultaneously, mechanical and manual emptying entrepreneurs, funding agencies and local stakeholders require capacity building in their fields of activity and responsibility. Universities and research institutes are the main potential providers of basic skills and continuing education for professionals. Target audiences or clients are the private sector (collection entrepreneurs, FSTP operators, consulting firms), officials, technical and social service staff at municipal level, technical staff, planners, and decision-makers/politicians at central and donor agency level all need proper orientation.

Municipalities are often faced with financial difficulties, which impair their ability to ensure services to the population. This is mainly due to a lack of management of the existing resources, and the non-allocation of financial resources to FS-related services. Personnel and institutional capabilities for urban management have to be developed on a massive scale across the state. Capabilities for planning locally are woefully inadequate, which is leading to projects not aligned with local priorities and poor coordination amongst separate initiatives.

There is little regulatory power to monitor whether faecal sludge is processed according to environmental and health standards. Most cities in the state lack the capacity to regulate treatment and dumping of waste. There is also a lack of approved sewage treatment plants (STPs) in the state to safely and effectively treat faecal sludge, if it is actually collected and able to be sent there. Twenty-seven Indian cities have only primary treatment facilities and 49 have primary and secondary treatment facilities. Hence, there is a need to set up sufficient number of FSTPs—at least one for every large city and one for a group of smaller towns.

This current generation is facing a great challenge in providing adequate sanitation to rapidly growing urban population. It is argued that although sanitation coverage is higher in urban areas, the huge projected increase in urban populations in developing countries makes the provision of affordable urban sanitation is a significant challenge (UN HABITAT:2010). The studies and census data reveal that in urban areas in developing countries the majority of houses are served by on-site-sanitation systems such as septic tanks, pit latrines and unsewered public toilets. The faecal sludge collected from these systems is usually discharged untreated into the environment thereby posing great risks to water resources and public health. Peter, Isabel and Chris (2013) report that the need to establish an enabling environment for progress in urban sanitation is widely recognized.

In a nutshell, the challenge and goal to be met is to ensure that all FS generated in the urban environment is discharged at designated storage or treatment sites, that illegally and indiscriminately dumped untreated FS is stopped and that FS is subjected to adequate treatment prior to agricultural use or land filling. An array of measures is required to achieving this (Montangero et al.: 2002). For the successful implementation of faecal sludge management (FSM) systems in the state, an institutional framework needs to be developed based on the specifics of the local situation. The focus should not be only on the physical infrastructure, but due attention should be given on the organizational and financial aspects. The selection of a faecal sludge management institutional framework must be driven by local socio-economic, climatic and environmental contexts, taking into account existing sanitation infrastructures, institutions and people's needs and aspirations.

State and non-State Stakeholder Agencies in Faecal Sludge Governance in Uttar Pradesh

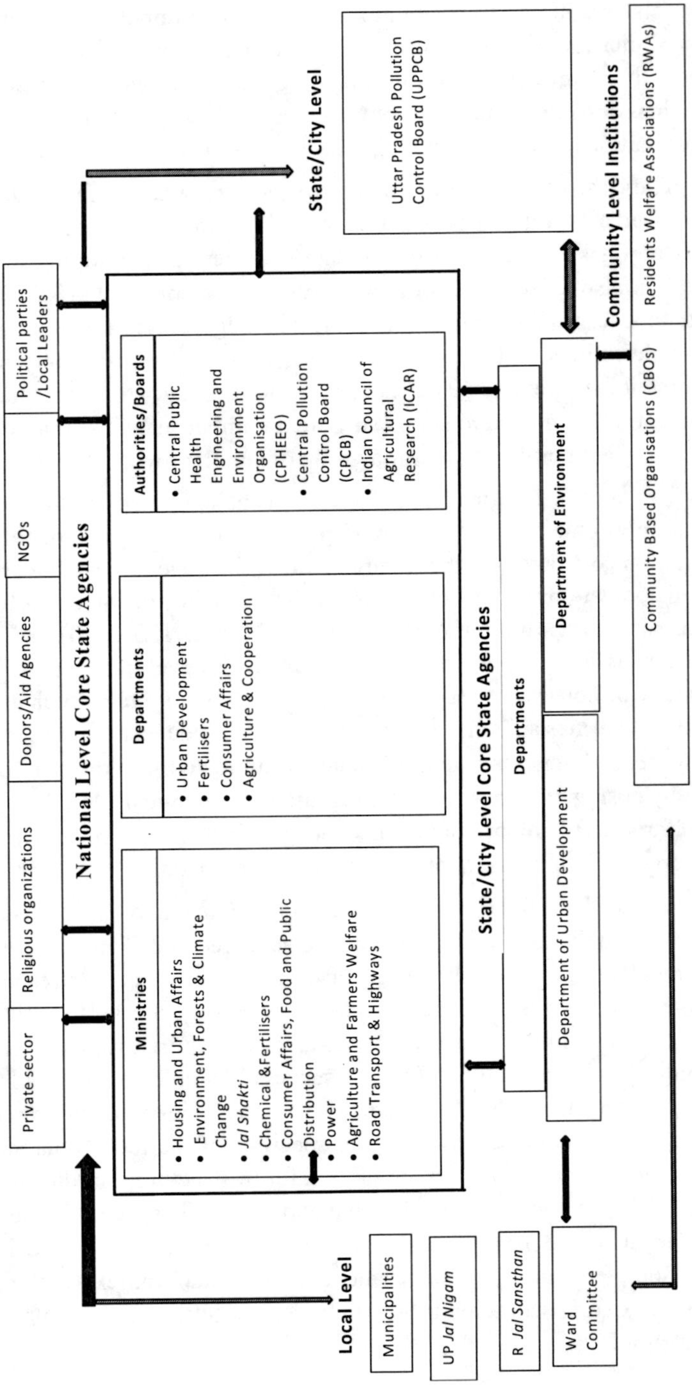

Chart-4.1: Stakeholders in FSSM.

References

- *cpcb.nic.in/introduction.phy. Retrieved on 3-5-2017.*
- *cpheeo.nic.in. Retrieved on 3-5-2017.*
- *bis.org.in/bis.overview.asp. Retrieved on 3-5-2017.*
- *www.mdws.gov.in/about_us. Retrieved on 4-5-2017.*
- *delhi.gov.in/wps/wcm/connect/environment/Environment/Home/About+Us. Retrieved on 4-5-2017.*
- *delhi.gov.in/wps/wcm/connect/doit_udd?Urban+Development/home. Retrieved on 4-5-2017.*
- *ndmc.gov.in/ndmc/history.aspx. Retrieved on 4-5-2017.*
- *http://djb.gov.in. Retrieved on 4-5-2017.*
- *delhi.gov.in/wps/wcm/connect/doit_pollution/Pollution/Home/functions. Retrieved on 4-5-2017.*
- *committee of Experts on New DMC Act (2011).*
- *montangero, A. and Strauss, M. (2002): Faecal Sludge Treatment. Eawag/Sandec. IHE, Delft.www.eawag.ch/organisation/abteilungen/sandec/publikationen/publi-cations_ewm/downloads_ewm/IHE_lec-ture_notes. pdf Pescod.*
- *Bolomey, S. (2003): Amélioration de la ges-tion des boues de vidange par le renforce-ment du secteurprivé local. Eawag/San-dec.*
- *Strauss, M. et al. (2003): Co-composting of Faecal Sludge and Municipal Organic Waste. IWMI and Sandec. www.eawag.ch/organisation/abteilungen/sandec/pub-likationen/publications_ewm/downloads_ewm/cocomp_review.*
- *Klingel, F. (2001): Nam Dinh Urban Development Project – Septage Management Study. Eawag/Sandec and Colenco. NDUDP. www.eawag.ch/organisation/abteilungen/sandec/publikationen/publications_ewm/downloads_ewm/ND_septage_management_study.*
- *Klingel, F., Montangero, A. and Strauss, M. (2001): Nam Dinh – Planning for Improved Faecal Sludge Management and Treatment. Eawag/*Sandec. *www.eawag.ch/organisation/abteilungen/sandec/publikationen/publications_ewm/downloads_ewm/WSA_paper_Klingel.*
- *WHO (Ed.) (2006): Safe Use of Wastewater, Excreta and Greywater. Volume IV. Excreta and Grey water Use in Agriculture. WHO Guidelines. WHO, IV, Geneva, 182 p.*
- *up.gov.in/department of urban development.*
- *up.gov.in/department of housing and urban planning.*
- *jn.upsdc.gov.in, retrieved on 24-09-2019.*
- *www.cblucknow.org.in, retrieved on 23-09-2019.*
- *The Uttar Pradesh Municipal Corporation Act, 1959.*
- *The Uttar Pradesh Municipalities Act, 1916.*
- *The Uttar Pradesh Development & Planning Act, 1973.*
- *The Uttar Pradesh Water Supply & Sewerage Act, 1965.*
- *www.up.gov.in/department portal/forest retrieved on 6-11-2019.*

5

Faecal Sludge and Septage Management

Introduction

In India, the great majority of urban dwellers, especially poor people, rely for their sanitation on non-sewered systems that generate a mix of solid and liquid wastes generally termed "faecal sludge." In most inner poorly built area and parapheral outer area of rapidly expanding cities, faecal sludge management (FSM) represents a growing challenge, generating significant negative public health and environmental risks. In addition, construction of crores and crores of pit-based individual household toilets and community toilets (under *Swachh Bharat* Mission) has added complexities to the already deteriorated sanitary situation in cities. Without proper management, faecal sludge is often allowed to accumulate in poorly designed pits, is discharged into storm drains and open water, or is dumped into waterways, wasteland, and unsanitary dumping sites.

Faecal Sludge and Septage: How is it Different from Sewage?

Sewage is untreated wastewater which contains faeces and urine, this wastewater gets conveyed through the sewerage system. Generally, grey water from the kitchen and bath room also becomes part of sewage. (The Biochemical Oxygen Demand (BOD) of sewage ranges from 150–350 mg/l and all sewage treatment plants are designed for this load). Faecal sludge and septage is emptied out of pits or septic tanks and is much more concentrated than sewage; (for example, BOD of septage ranges from 1,000–20,000 mg/l). There appears to be a very thin line between septage and faecal sludge. Septage is limited to septic tanks, and has already undergone partial digestion, whereas faecal sludge includes contents from other on-site technologies, including septic tanks, and may or may not be digested.

What is Faecal Sludge and/or Septage Management (FSSM)?

Sanitation often focuses only on provisioning of physical infrastructure–toilets or latrines. In order to provide tangible and sustainable sanitation, there is a need to focus on the entire value chain also known as 'sanitation chain'. It sets out interlinked steps vital to manage faecal sludge and septage and effluent from generation to disposal or end use, there by summarizing the city-level outcomes and current status of the same. Faecal Sludge Management (FSM) refers to the containment, collection/emptying, transport, treatment and disposal or reuse of human waste generated by on-site sanitation systems. When managed appropriately, FSM is an environmentally safe and cost-effective approach to the management of human waste. This has proven to be true in high-, middle- and low-income countries for households not connected to a sewerage network. The faecal sludge chain can be understood as involving many key steps (as shown Figure-5.1), from its initial containment after defecation until its final disposal. This chain is a service chain, in the sense that intermediate steps make up a service delivered to those who are responsible for the maintenance of latrines. Often the chain can also be said to be a value chain, where treatment allows value to be created from sludge for reuse in some way, e.g. biogas or compost.

- *On-Site- Sanitation*—User Interface, Containment.
- *Service Chain*—Containment, Emptying/Collection, Transportation.
- *Value Chain*— Transport, Treatment, Reuse/Disposal.
- *Faecal Sludge/Septage Management*—Containment, Emptying/Collection, Transportation, Treatment, Disposal/Reuse.

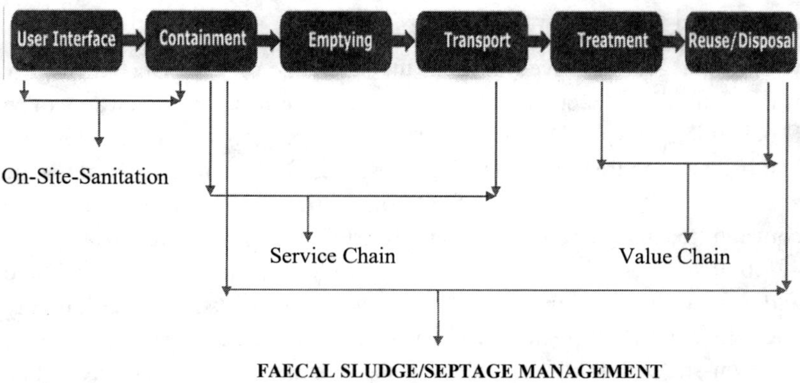

Figure-5.1: Sanitation Chain

Common Technology Options

Variations in housing type, density and settlement layout; poverty status; and access to networked services (especially water supply) mean that different solutions may be needed in different parts of the city or even within the same neighborhood. Rarely is a single option (for example, sewerage) viable for an entire town.

I- HOUSEHOLD SANITATION TECHNOLOGY

Since, the households are first and primary unit of sanitary latrine system therefore, the importance of household sanitation becomes important part of any sanitation drive in order to ensure proper disposal of excreta waste as well prevent open defecation.

It is important to give several technological options or informed choices to the user to choose and own and maintain a sanitary latrine without much external support. These options must help user to select the most suitable to them in terms of cost as well as design without compromising the criteria of sanitary latrine.

As far as toilet technology is concerned, water seal is more prevalent in India due to the practice of anal cleansing with water. But with many other successful experiments, we now have several sanitary technological options for rural India which can be used depending upon the soil conditions, water availability and affordability of the user. Some of the key technological options are:

(i) Simple Pit Toilet

(ii) Ventilated Improved Pit (VIP) Toilet

(iii) Pour Flush Toilet

(iv) Eco-san Toilet

Conventional Pit Latrine with cover

Conventional pit latrine is a non-water dependent latrine, which does not require water for functioning, though a small amount of water can be used to clean the squat plate occasionally. This type of latrine is suitable in water scarce areas or where community uses dry cleansing materials. Therefore, the introduction of an unlined or lined pit with a squat plate with or without a super structure can be the second option. This will be particularly applicable for those communities who have open defecation practice.

Advantages

- Affordable
- Simple technology

- Helps to develop practice use latrine
- Appropriate for low-income group who wants to use latrine initially

Disadvantages

- Not fully sanitary latrine
- Fly breeding
- Odour
- Risk of falling into the pit
- Risk of ground water pollution

The conventional pit can also be upgraded by adding vent pipe, superstructure and lid for covering hole and lining pit with locally available materials. This modified and improved version is called **Lid Cover Toilet**. This is also a non-water dependent latrine which doesn't require water for functioning, though a small amount of water can be used to clean the squat plate occasionally.

Ventilated Improved Pit (VIP) Latrine

A VIP latrine is a non-water dependent latrine, which doesn't require water for functioning, though a small amount of water can be used to clean the squat plate occasionally. These groups of latrines are suitable for water-scarce areas. A ventilated improved pit latrine is an improved conventional pit latrine, slightly offset from the pit and having a tall vertical (gradually tapered towards the pit) vent pipe with a fly-screen fitted outside the superstructure to trap flies and reduce odour nuisance.

Advantages

- Little odour
- Less chances for transmission of excreta related disease than lid or cover latrine
- Good health and hygiene practice
- Can be used as fertilizer after one year of composting
- Better life and environment
- Suitable for water scarce area, no need for water except occasional cleaning of the squat plate
- Suitable for communities using dry cleansing materials
- Can be built with local materials
- Affordable
- Construction and maintenance are easy

- Can be upgraded to pour flush latrine
- Suitable for less densely populated area where space is available for relocating the latrine when it is full

Disadvantages

- Technical support required when installed as proper construction is crucial
- Risk of groundwater and surface water contamination
- Once filled the latrine has to be moved to another location
- Odour nuisance is not fully controlled.

VIP Toilet Model

Twin Pit VIP Model

VIP toilets can also be constructed with a double pit system. This model of toilet has two shallow pits, each with their own vent pipe but only one superstructure. The cover slab has two drop holes, one over each pit. Only one pit is used at a time. When one is full, its drop hole is covered and the second pit is used. After a period of at least one-year, the contents of the first pit can be removed safely and used as soil conditioner. The pit can be used again when the second pit is filled up.

Pour flush latrine

This is water dependent latrine that relies mainly on the usage of water. Without water, these latrines fail to operate. The water dependent latrines can be further categorized on the basis of Flushing (pour flush or mechanical flush). Pour flush, though, is more operational and suitable to the conditions of rural areas.

The pour flush latrine is a specially designed water-sealed bowl, which requires 1-2 liters of water for flushing the excreta. Some water always remains at the bottom of the pan after it has been used. This water seal latrine eliminates the entry of odour and prevents rodents to the latrine room from pit through the bowl. This pour flush latrine consists of a single pit either just below the bowl (onset type) or may be offset from the bowl (offset type) using the pour flush type bowl (pan and trap).

Advantages

- Odour free
- Privacy
- Little chance for transmission of excreta related disease

- Good health and hygiene practice
- Appropriate where water is available
- Long lifetime and no need to move for many years
- Water requirements for flushing is low (1-2 liters)
- Construction and maintenance are cheap and easy
- Offset type can be adjusted in any type of dwelling without causing any foul smell
- Suitable for less populated areas where space is available for relocating the latrine
- Possible to upgrade it into twin pit pour flush system (for offset type)

Disadvantages

- Water necessary for flushing, 1-2 liters
- Risk of groundwater and surface water contamination
- Not appropriate where water is not available
- Dislodging of toilet required every 3-5 years
- Locally manufactured bowls are often of bad quality due to lack of proper moulds
- Difficult to construct in high ground water table area

Options in Pour flush/Water Seal Technology

Direct Pit Water Seal Toilet

This unit consists of a squatting slab monolithically cast with a cement pan having an in-built water seal. The slab (reinforced cement concrete (RCC) or ferro-cement (FC)) can be of either a circular or a rectangular shape.

A pit is dug in the ground and the squatting slab is placed over it. Normally no pit lining is required in the case of hard and compact soil. However, in case of loose soil, the pit is to be lined in order to prevent the side from collapsing. The size of the pit should be such that it takes two years to get filled up. A superstructure may be built over it for privacy and protection.

After defecation, 1-2 liters of water is poured to flush the excreta out of the pan, which accumulates in the pit where decomposition takes place. The gas formed during decomposition escapes through the joints/ openings of the pit lining and is absorbed by the surrounding soil. The effluent is leached out and absorbed by the soil while the solid part (sludge) accumulates in the pit. Thus, on prolonged use, the pit gets filled up. When this happens, a second pit is constructed and the squatting slab and superstructure are shifted over it. The filled up pit is covered with a thick layer of soil and allowed to be stabilized for about two years. During this time the contents of the filled-up pit will have become organic humus and safe for handling. When the second pit also gets filled up, after two years or so, the first pit is cleaned.

Twin Pit Water Seal Toilet

The 'Twin Pit Water Seal Toilet' is a complete excreta disposal system which, on one hand fulfills all the sanitary requirements and on the other hand, provides continuous operation with minimal effort. The squatting platform is a raised *pucca* floor constructed with appropriate plinth and foundation. The pan has a steep bottom slope which allows easy flushing of excreta. The outlet of the pan is connected with a P-trap. On flushing, some water always remains in the trap and forms a 'water seal'. The water seal prevents the bad odour coming from (and the insects reaching the) excreta. The outlet of the trap is connected with a junction chamber either by using a pipe or by constructing a covered brick drains. The junction chamber has one inlet (connected to the P-trap) and two outlets (connected to the leach pits) which are for alternate use.

For making a twin-pit toilet operational, one of the outlets of the Y-junction in the junction chamber is blocked while the other outlet is kept open to the corresponding pit. The disposal process of the excreta is the same as in a 'direct pit toilet'. In this case, when the first pit gets filled up, the flow of excreta has to be diverted to the stand-by second pit. For doing this, one has to remove the cover of the junction chamber, open the outlet connected to the second pit, block the outlet connected to the first filled up pit and replace the junction chamber cover. The contents of the filled pit will become organic humus and safe for manual cleaning in about two years.

Single Offset Pit Water Seal Toilet

A 'Single Offset Pit Water Seal Toilet' consists of water seal pan, a squatting platform, a junction chamber, a temporary/ permanent superstructure and a single pit instead of two pits as described above. The pit is constructed away from the squatting platform and connected to the same by a pipe through a junction chamber. A single offset pit toilet functions in the same manner as a twin-pit one.

Eco-San toilet

Ecological sanitation (Double Vault Compost Latrine) is based on recycling principles. In this approach, the excreta and urine are separated for disposal. The eco-san model consist the double-vault compost latrine consists of two water-tight chambers (vaults) to collect faeces. Urine is collected separately as the contents of the vault have to be kept relatively dry. Initially, a layer of absorbent organic material is put in the vault and after each use, the faeces is covered with ash (or saw-dust, shredded leaves or vegetable matter) to deodorise the faeces, soak-up excessive moisture and improve carbon/nitrogen ratio, which ensures that sufficient nitrogen is retained to make a good fertilizer. When the first vault is three quarters full, it is completely filled with dry powdered earth and sealed so that the components can decompose anaerobically. The second vault is used until it is also three quarters full and the first vault is emptied by hand, the contents are used as a fertilizer.

Ecological Sanitation or Eco-San toilet is based on the principle of minimizing the loss of nutrients in human wastes and using such wastes, including urine for agriculture purposes. It is a closed-loop system, which treats human excreta as a resource. In this system, excreta are processed on-site until it is free of pathogenic organisms. In the system, faeces and urine are collected separately in containers. Urine is used in agriculture land directly, whereas faeces are stored for 6 months or so, to degrade it and its use in agriculture. In this system, water is not used for cleaning purpose. To prevent foul smell, dry ash is put after each use of toilet, in the container. Degraded human waste is directly used for agriculture purposes.

Advantage

- It is most ideal for areas where water is scarce and pour-flushing implies water to be carried from source, or areas where water table is high such as flood plains or coastal areas and densely populated areas where risks of ground water pollution from pits to drinking water sources is assessed high.

Disadvantage

- Proper operation needs full understanding of the concept, lack of which makes the system dysfunctional.
- Where people are eager to use the contents as fertilizer, they may not allow sufficient time for the contents to become pathogen free.

- This system is only to be used where people are motivated to use human excreta as a fertilizer.
- Inadequate number of trained masons impacts the quality of construction.

Limitations: Eco-san toilet is more suitable where people don't use water for cleaning and instead, papers, napkins etc. are used for such purpose. In Indian conditions, cultural aspect does not appear suitable for such Eco-san system in most of the communities. Moreover, cost of the Eco-san toilet is much higher than the pit toilets. More awareness and motivation is required to make Eco-san toilet acceptable at community level in rural areas.

Biogas Toilet

Generation and utilization of biogas from human excreta and other wastes has three major advantages-- it improves sanitation, gives bio energy at low cost and provides better quality of manure for agriculture purposes. It is suitable for all hydro geological conditions and where people use water for ablution. However, household biogas plant solely based on human waste for a family is not economically viable as the biogas produced per family is not adequate for any useful purpose. In a family having 5 users of toilet, only around five cubic feet (cft) of biogas would be produced per day and minimum requirement of biogas is about 40 cft for cooking for two meals in a day for a small family. Therefore, biogas can't meet cooking requirement of a small family, if produced from human waste of a family. However, it can be made viable, when mixed with cattle dung along with human wastes. Biogas from dung of at least 2 nos. of cattle when mixed with human wastes can cater to the need of cooking for a small family.

Design of Biogas Plant

For family size biogas plant, there are basically two designs: (i) Floating Drum Type, popularly known as KVIC Model, and (ii) Fixed Dome Type, popularly known as Deenbandhu Model.

In the **KVIC Model** gas holder is made up of iron sheet (mild steel). During winter season when temperature falls down to about 10^{0}C or so, this model ceases to function as the iron sheet gas holder acts as good conductor of heat and inner temperature of the digester also attains the same temperature. Secondly, this gas holder requires regular care and maintenance to prevent from getting worn out because of corrosion and has short working life. Manufacturing of gas holder requires sophisticated workshop facility which is rarely found in rural areas. Therefore, in rural areas, success rate of this model of biogas plant is far below the level of satisfaction.

Quantity of Biogas production from different feed material:

(i) From animal dung, Around 10 kg dung is available per animal per day. Biogas production rate from dung is about 1.5 cft per kg, i.e., per animal per day 15 cft of biogas is produced.

(ii) From human waste, per person per day, 0.35 kg of waste is produced and gas production from per kg of human wastes is 3.6 cft. Per day per person only one cft biogas is produced.

(iii) A total amount of biogas of one cum can be produced per day from a family having 5 members and 2 cattle heads.

Utilizations of Biogas

One cum of biogas per day can be utilized in a family as follows:

- Cooking of 5 family members for two times a day
- Mantle lamps (2nos.) can be used for 6 hours per night. Such mantle lamps give illumination equivalent to 40 Watt bulb at 220 volts of electricity.
- Can run an engine of one Horse Power for 2 hours

Manure Value of Sludge from Biogas Plant

Besides biogas, the manure of the plant has good plant nutrient value. It is directly used for agriculture purpose.

Deenbandhu Model

Deenbandhu Model of family size biogas plant is predominately used in India. It is a complete brick structure, having very negligible operation and maintenance costs. There is no separate gas holder; biogas is stored inside the plant, through liquid displacement chamber. The cost of Deenbandhu Plant is lesser than the KVIC Model. It has least affect on biogas production during extreme low or high atmospheric temperature, as the soil cover over the top of the dome acts as an insulator. In a small family, biogas plant of 2 cum and 4 cum capacities are normally used, depending upon the number of family members and cattle heads.

Balram Model

This model is more suitable for areas where people use water for ablution. The system consists of 2nos. of chambers connected at the middle. It may be a brick-cement or ferro-cement structure. Cost of a ferro-cement structure is cheaper than the brick-cement structure. Bottom of both the chambers are sealed with P.C.C. (Plane Cement Concrete). During the use of the toilets human waste comes into first chamber and after settlement, it flows to the second chamber. From this second chamber, it flows through the covered drain to its outlet. Toilet seat with pan and trap in the design remains the same as discussed under two pit pour flush toilet.

This model of toilet is useful also in low water table and coastal areas. This is also useful in rocky areas where water of leaching pit may not be absorbed by the ground. The detention period of the soak will increase to a great extent and for a family of 5 members, the detention period will be about 20-25 days and so the B.O.D of the effluent will also be less.

Advantages

- It is suitable even for high water table without any chance of ground water pollution, as the bottom of human waste collecting chamber is kept sealed
- There is no chance of odour with this toilet
- In rocky areas also this type of toilet is suitable

Limitations

- Cost of this toilet is higher than leach pit toilet
- Cleaning of chambers is cumbersome when they are filled. Chambers are to be emptied only through mechanical devices.

Toilet for Physically Handicapped and Old Age People

For physically challenged persons, squatting toilet is not suitable. It needs a suitably modified commode toilet to suit their needs. Such toilet is also useful to elderly people or people having knee / joint pain. For physically challenged people using wheel chair, they need a proper space to move with such wheel chair inside the toilet. A grab bar is needed to provide support to such persons while using the toilet. Taking all these factors in consideration following should be the elements of a toilet for disabled persons:

- One special W.C. should be provided for the use of handicapped persons with essential provision of wash basin near the entrance
- A normal toilet has an average height of around 32-40 cms while handicap toilets have an average height of about 42-48cms. Many people who have no disabilities also find this toilet more comfortable, while it is a necessity for people with back and leg problems

- The minimum size of toilet cubicle should be 1500 mm x 1750 mm
- Minimum clear opening of the door shall be 900 mm. and the door shall swing out
- Suitable arrangement of vertical/horizontal handrails with 50 mm. clearance from wall shall be made in the toilet
- Toilet floor shall have a non-slippery surface
- Guiding block near the entry should have a textural difference
- Light-weight PVC door shutter should be provided as a sliding door
- Provision of vertical and horizontal rail as 40 mm steel pipe
- The rear wall grab bar shall be 36 inches long minimum and shall extend from the center-line of the toilet 12 inches minimum on one side and 24 inches minimum on the other side
- Additional options for handicap toilets include adding a handicap bidet to wash the backside. Some people are unable to reach that area with toilet paper or have trouble in wiping

II- HISTORY OF SEWAGE MANAGEMENT

Basic sewer systems were used for waste removal in ancient Mesopotamia, where vertical shafts carried the waste away into cesspools. Similar systems existed in the Indus Valley civilization in modern-day India and in Ancient Crete and Greece. In the Middle Ages the sewer systems built by the Romans fell into disuse and waste was collected into cesspools that were periodically emptied by workers known as 'rakers' who would often sell it as fertilizer to farmers outside the city.

But, modern sewerage systems were first built in the mid-nineteenth century as a reaction to the exacerbation of sanitary conditions brought on by heavy industrialization and urbanization. Due to the contaminated water supply, cholera outbreaks occurred in 1832, 1849 and 1855 in London, killing tens of thousands of people. This, combined with the Great Stink of 1858, when the smell of untreated human waste in the River Thames became overpowering, and the report into sanitation reform of the Royal Commissioner Edwin Chadwick, led to the Metropolitan Commission of Sewers appointing Sir Joseph Bazalgette to construct a vast underground sewerage system for the safe removal of waste.

One of the first attempts at diverting sewage for use as a fertilizer in the farm was made by the cotton mill owner James Smith in the 1840s. He experimented with a piped distribution system initially proposed by James

Vetch that collected sewage from his factory and pumped it into the outlying farms. The precursor to the modern septic tank was the cesspool in which the water was sealed off to prevent contamination and the solid waste was slowly liquified due to anaerobic action; it was invented by L.H Mouras in France in the 1860s which he called a 'septic tank'; septic having the meaning of 'bacterial'.

Sir Edward Frankland conducted experiments at the Sewage Farm in Croydon, England, during the 1870s and was able to demonstrate that filtration of sewage through porous gravel produced a nitrified effluent (the ammonia was converted into nitrate) and that the filter remained unclogged over long periods of time.

From 1885 to 1891 filters working on this principle were constructed throughout the UK and the idea was also taken up in the US at the Lawrence Experiment Station in Massachusetts, where Frankland's work was confirmed. In 1890 the LES developed a 'trickling filter' that gave a much more reliable performance. The Great Stink of 1858 stimulated research into the problem of sewage treatment.

The idea was officially adopted by the Health of Towns Commission, and various schemes (known as sewage farms) were trialed by different municipalities over the next 50 years. At first, the heavier solids were channeled into ditches on the side of the farm and were covered over when full, but soon flat-bottomed tanks were employed as reservoirs for the sewage; the earliest patent was taken out by William Higgs in 1846 for "tanks or reservoirs in which the contents of sewers and drains from cities, towns and villages are to be collected and the solid animal or vegetable matters therein contained, solidified and dried. Improvements to the design of the tanks included the introduction of the horizontal-flow tank in the 1850s and the radial-flow tank in 1905. These tanks had to be manually de-sludged periodically, until the introduction of automatic mechanical de-sludgers in the early 1900s. Sir Edward Frankland, a distinguished chemist, who demonstrated the possibility of chemically treating sewage in the 1870s.

It was not until the late 19th century that it became possible to treat the sewage by chemically breaking it down through the use of microorganisms and removing the pollutants. Land treatment was also steadily becoming less feasible, as cities grew and the volume of sewage produced could no longer be absorbed by the farmland on the outskirts.

Contact beds were developed in Salford, Lancashire and by scientists working for the London City Council in the early 1890s. According to Christopher Hamlin, this was part of a conceptual revolution that replaced the philosophy that saw "sewage purification as the prevention of decomposition with one that tried to facilitate the biological processes that destroy sewage naturally."

Contact beds were tanks containing the inert substance, such as stones or slate that maximized the surface area available for the microbial growth to break down the sewage. The sewage was held in the tank until it was fully decomposed and it was then filtered out into the ground. This method quickly became widespread, especially in the UK, where it was used in Leicester, Sheffield, Manchester and Leeds. The bacterial bed was simultaneously developed by Joseph Corbett as Borough Engineer in Salford and experiments in 1905 showed that his method was superior in those greater volumes of sewage could be purified better for longer periods of time than could be achieved by the contact bed.

The Royal Commission on Sewage Disposal published its eighth report in 1912 that set what became the international standard for sewage discharge into rivers; the 20:30 standard', which allowed 20 mg biochemical oxygen demand and 30 mg suspended solid per litre.

III-FAECAL SLUDGE AND/OR SEPTAGE MANAGEMENT (FSSM)

FSSM: How to Start?

Faecal sludge and/or septage management is a process and requires attention in every stage of the entire sanitation chain. It needs to be comprehensive and requires step wise approach beginning from systematic planning to ensuring infrastructure and human resource for transportation and treatment of faecal sludge and septage. It has to be sustainable and requires consideration of socio-economic aspects of region. The safe disposal/reuse of faecal sludge, septage and effluent in scientific manner for pollution abatement is the main goal of the FSSM.

Steps in FSSM Planning

- Define the issue
- Identify the key stakeholders
- Stakeholders engagement
- Collect baseline information
- Analyze collected data
- Design strategy for each stage
- Implement
- Monitor

The section focuses on technology but takes into account the full range of factors that affect the outcome of sanitation investments.

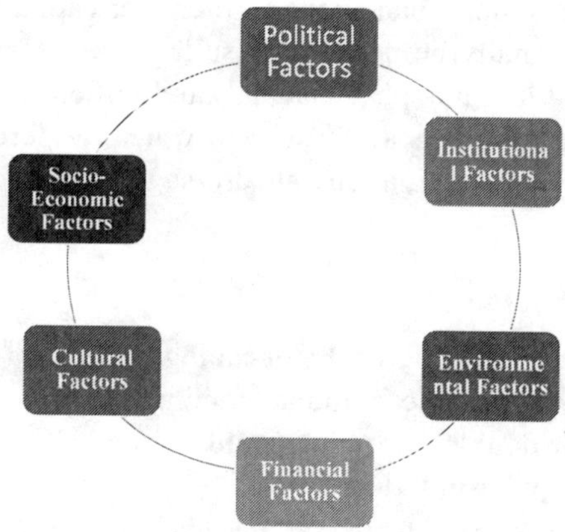

Figure 5.2: Factors Affecting Sanitation

In many situations, on-site facilities may provide a more appropriate, cost-effective technology and, in some cases, an inexpensive option. This book therefore pays particular attention to on-site options, including the removal and treatment of faecal sludge and septage.

Municipal planners should also recognize that the worst sanitary conditions tend to be found in poor areas. Construction of a toilet is generally regarded as the householder's responsibility but, for poor households, investments in sanitation are often constrained by issues relating to:

- Affordability, including the cost of connecting to sewer networks;
- Uncertainty over land tenure (fear of eviction);
- Space constraints; and
- The low priority given to sanitation (people may not appreciate its importance).

Special measures may therefore be needed to support service improvements for the poorest sections of the community. This does not just mean subsidies and awareness campaigns; technology options are also needed that suit the physical conditions in poor communities.

On-Site- Sanitation systems may be either wet or dry. If properly designed and managed, both wet and dry on-site systems can provide a service that is as hygienic and convenient as sewerage. Indeed, if water use is low, on-site- sanitation may provide a better service than a poorly functioning sewerage system.

All on-site systems that are feasible in Indian conditions—whether wet or dry—require a pit, vault or tank to hold faecal sludge. All wet on-site systems are dependent on percolation of wastewater into the ground. Where water use is more than about 30 liters per capita per day, separate provision will normally be needed for sullage and storm water run-off. Where water use is low, the subsoil is sandy and sufficient space is available, it may be possible to dispose of sullage water by percolation into the ground. Normally, however, a separate drainage system for sullage will be required.

Dry (Eco-san) Systems

As already indicated, all the dry or ecological toilets (eco-san) systems that are likely to be feasible in Indian conditions will also are on-site. In theory a single or double pit latrine could be used although these are not widely used or popular in Indian cities.

Some NGOs have installed eco-san toilets on a pilot basis in urban and peri-urban areas. Most of these use a double vault design with excreta stored in the first vault while the second is filling up and vice versa. The advantage of this system is that faecal material is stored for a period of about 12 months before it is removed, giving time for natural processes to break down the material and destroy pathogens and parasites.

Urine is separated and should ideally be stored and used as a fertilizer. Anal cleansing is carried out away from the latrine hole to ensure that the vault contents remain dry. In order to prevent smells and nuisance caused by flies, fine ash is kept in a container in the latrine superstructure and sprinkled over the contents of the vault every time the latrine is used.

Eco-san has yet to be implemented on anything other than a pilot scale in India. It is too early to say whether it will prove to be acceptable to users and technically viable, though compost toilets are prevalent in the mountainous regions of India. Therefore, before deciding to use eco-san, it would be important to ensure that the intended users understood and accepted what was expected of them; also that potential problems had been identified and systems put into place to deal with them.

Wet Systems

Wet on-site systems incorporate some form of water-flushed toilet from which faeces and flush water are discharged into a pit or tank. The toilet is normally a pour flush pan. In some designs, the pit or tank is located directly under the toilet, but the normal arrangement is to provide a short length of pipe to connect the toilet to one or more offset pits or tanks. Having the pit(s) or tank offset makes it easier to desludge them.

Of these, the single leach pit option requires the least space, but the contents—including fresh faeces—must be removed at intervals, creating the need for a hygienic pit emptying system. Similar systems will be required for septic tanks. The twin-pit system is designed so that (as with double vault dry systems) the pit contents are stored for a minimum period before they are removed, during which time the waste decomposes and pathogens die off.

This means that treated wastes can be disposed of or reused without the health risks associated with handling undigested excreta. The main drawback with this system is that it will not work properly if users do not understand, or are not interested in, the way in which the system should function.

Septic tanks consist of a chamber or series of chambers into which wastewater is discharged and contained. Sediment and solids settle to the bottom of the tank and organic wastes are decomposed by the action of bacteria. The effluent from septic tanks may contain pathogens and should be discharged into a soakaway (or drain field). In practice, many septic tanks in India discharge effluent to the nearest open drain. Where drain fields do exist, they may not function effectively due to poor design and lack of maintenance.

Where ground conditions do not permit infiltration of treated wastewater, additional treatment in the form of a constructed wetland or anaerobic filter could be provided prior to discharge into a drain or watercourse. This option should only be considered if management systems for the treatment facilities can be guaranteed, a condition that very often cannot be met.

Containment

The containment aims at removing the wastewater and excreta from households' dwellings. It will either combine a technology for collecting excreta only (simple toilets, VIP latrines, urine diverting dry toilets, flush toilets), with a technology for wastewater collection (soak-away, infiltration trenches, settled sewerage system); or opt for technologies that collect and treat all wastewater and excreta (septic tank, conventional sewerage system).

Individuals generate one liter per day of faecal waste (Kone and Strauss: 2004), that will be temporarily stored (and the case of some technology be partially treated) in some kind of pit when there is no sewerage system. A fundamental distinction in comparing pits is whether the FS is contained in a water-tight containment (as in the case of a properly constructed pit latrine or septic tank), or whether faecal sludge is able to spread into the surrounding ground and cause soil pollution (such pits are referred to as sumps).

Collection / Emptying

At this step the wastewater and excreta is evacuated from the place of defecation and containment and transported for disposal, ideally via final treatment, or treatment and reuse. In absence of a sewerage system, the sludge must be emptied manually (using a bucket or a hand-pump) or mechanically (using a motorized pump of some kind, usually a vacuum) and transported discretely to the treatment plant.

At that stage, the FS can already be considered as a product owned by the pit emptying service providers who start adding value (or strictly, removing the negative value of the potential environmental polluting and damaging health and hygiene effects) by moving the sludge away from the place where users defecate.

On-site sanitation technologies are dependent on the periodic removal of faecal sludge from vaults, pits, and tanks. The most common practice is for households to pay sweepers to empty pits manually, though this carries health risks and is banned by the Constitution of India.

Transportation

Sanitary pit emptying options exist, all incorporating some form of vacuum desludging equipment and its transportation. These have a variety of tank sizes and pumping capacities, each appropriate for a different type of on-site service or settlement type. While some municipalities and private service providers offer a vacuum service, it is more expensive than manual pit-emptying and this tends to restrict its use to institutions and more affluent households. Shortcomings in emptying, removal, and disposal services lead to the widespread dumping of untreated wastes into open drains, fields and watercourses. This causes pollution and is a serious public health concern.

It is important to understand that simply collecting faecal sludge is insufficient; the sludge must also be treated.

Treatment and Reuse/Disposal

Sewage treatment is the process of removing contaminants from wastewater, primarily from household sewage. It includes physical, chemical, and biological processes to remove these contaminants and produce environmentally safe treated wastewater (or treated effluent). A by-product of sewage treatment is usually a semi-solid waste or slurry, called sewage sludge, that has to undergo further treatment before being suitable for disposal or land application.

Sewage can be treated close to where the sewage is created, which may be called a "decentralized" system or even an "on-site" system (in septic tanks, bio-filters or aerobic treatment systems). Alternatively, sewage can be collected and transported by a network of pipes and pump stations to a municipal treatment plant. This is called a "centralized" system.

Sewage is generated by residential, institutional, commercial and industrial establishments. It includes household waste liquid from toilets, baths, showers, kitchens, and sinks draining into sewers. In many areas, sewage also includes liquid waste from industry and commerce. The separation and draining of household waste into grey water and black water is becoming more common in the developed world, with treated grey water being permitted to be used for watering plants or recycled for flushing toilets.

For conventional sewage treatment plants, around 30 percent of the annual operating cost is usually required for energy. The energy requirements vary with type of treatment process as well as wastewater load. For example, constructed wetlands have a lower energy requirement than activated sludge plants, as less energy is required for the aeration step. Sewage treatment plants that produce biogas in their sewage sludge treatment process with anaerobic digestion can produce enough energy to meet most of the energy needs of the sewage treatment plant itself.

Sludge treatment depends on the amount of solids generated and other site-specific conditions. Composting is most often applied to small-scale plants with aerobic digestion for mid-sized operations, and anaerobic digestion for the larger-scale operations.

With suitable technology, it is possible to reuse sewage effluent for drinking water, although this is usually only done in places with limited water supplies. In Israel, about 50 percent of agricultural water use (total use was 1 billion cubic metres in 2008) is provided through reclaimed sewer water. Future plans call for increased use of treated sewer water as well as more desalination plants.

At these steps potential polluting effect of sludge is reduced by physio-chemical and / or biological treatment. Different technologies are used to dispose of wastewater, excreta and sludge, and, if feasible, utilization of the end-product (for compost or bio energy). Treatment plants can be extensive (and require large surface areas, such as solar drying beds combined with composting or planted drying beds) or intensive (facilities that have small footprint -- relatively compact but with relatively high investment costs).

The level of treatment achieved by these technologies depends on a number of different factors, including the composition of the effluent or the quality of management of the facilities.

The treated sludge can then be buried underground where final stabilization of the original sludge matter removes any residual pathogenic bacteria or be utilized as a form of highly effective organic soil enrichment for agricultural purposes or as the basis of bio-energy creation. All sludge treatment produces not only treated sludge, but also residual water. This effluent often needs to undergo secondary treatment in order to let it filter safely into the soil or be reused as irrigation water.

Treatment of Wastewater and Faecal Sludge

A global estimate by UNDP and UN-Habitat is that 90 percent of all wastewater generated is released into the environment untreated. Treatment of wastewater and faecal sludge is required prior to discharge into the environment. This is especially important in situations where sources of drinking water are at risk from contamination or where local residents use rivers or drainage channels for bathing or washing and where the wastewater is reused for irrigating vegetables or horticultural crops.

The purpose of treatment is to reduce the concentration of potentially harmful materials to levels that will not cause harm to either the environment or the people that might come into contact with wastewater. The treatment required to achieve this objective will be influenced by the concentrations of pollutants and pathogens contained in the waste.

While some degradation of waste material may occur on-site in vaults, leach pits and septic tanks, there will almost always be a need for further treatment of faecal sludge, septage, and wastewater. While it is possible to provide this additional treatment on-site, the more common arrangement is to provide it *off-site or 'end-of-pipe'* (at the end of a sewerage system) or where faecal sludge cartage vehicles discharge wastes. Because of their high concentration of pollutants and pathogens and relatively low volume, faecal sludge and septage should normally be dealt with separately from wastewater. For this reason, treatment processes for faecal sludge and septage are considered separately from those for wastewater below. Sullage is less polluting and less potentially harmful than sewage and blackwater, and will normally require a much lower level of treatment.

Treatment Standards

Treatment requirements depend largely on the proposed use of the effluent, but may also be governed by discharge consents if the waste is to be discharged into a natural water course. The purpose of discharge contents is to prevent unacceptable levels of pollution and risks to public health. In most towns little, if any, sewage is actually treated and standards set out in discharge contents are rarely met, even in cases where a treatment plant has been installed. The implication for regulatory bodies is that standards should be set at realistic levels in the light of local circumstances and tightened incrementally as local capacity for wastewater management increases.

Wastewater Treatment

Most waste water treatment technologies use a combination of physical and microbiological processes to remove or degrade pollutants. Preliminary treatment normally includes coarse screening and grit removal while primary treatment is provided in settlement tanks. In both cases, the predominant mechanism is physical. Secondary treatment processes, whether in trickling filters or by activated sludge, is predominantly biological. Where there is a need for further reduction in pathogens or nutrients, a tertiary treatment stage may be added to conventional aerobic processes. Most tertiary treatment processes are designed to remove nitrogen, phosphorus, and industrial pollutants such as heavy metals.

There are two broad alternatives to conventional treatment: extended treatment processes based on natural processes; and anaerobic treatment. The term 'natural' is used here to denote processes that represent managed versions of processes that can occur in more or less the same form in nature, The main treatment options in this category are waste stabilization ponds and constructed wetlands, which are also referred to as reed beds.

Anaerobic treatment processes include upward flow anaerobic sludge blanket (UASB) systems, baffled reactors and upward flow anaerobic filters. Conventional treatment processes produce sludges that contain high concentrations of pollutants and excreted pathogens. Providing for the safe management of these sludges is an integral component of wastewater treatment but is often overlooked.

Faecal Sludge and Septage Treatment

It is normally advisable to treat faecal sludge and wastewater separately, though they can be combined in a wastewater treatment plant if the sludge loads are relatively small.

Options for separate sludge treatment include:

- Solids-liquid separation in batch-operated settling-thickening tanks
- Primary sedimentation/anaerobic stabilization ponds
- Sludge drying beds (unplanted; planted)
- Combined composting with organic solid waste (co-composting) and
- Anaerobic digestion (potentially with biogas utilization)

Treatment results in two components: a solids and a liquid fraction. The solids fraction (bio-solids) is of variable consistency—additional drying or treatment might be required for land filling reuse in agriculture as a soil-conditioner and fertilizer.

Polishing treatment might be necessary for the liquid fraction too, to satisfy criteria for discharge into surface waters or to avoid long-term impacts on groundwater quality, where effluents will be allowed to infiltrate.

Reuse of Treated Wastewater and Sludge

Waste water is used for irrigation in many parts of India, nearly always without pre-treatment. Similarly, untreated faecal sludge is often used on fields or in fishponds. These practices bring financial benefits to farmers but can harm the health of both farm workers and consumers of products produced using the waste. While this may be difficult to stop in the short term, pretreatment should be introduced in the longer term, possibly as part of the resource recovery process.

In the case of reuse, health risks from enteric pathogens must be reduced as much as possible. This is especially important where wastewater is used to irrigate parks and other public places, or food crops that may be eaten raw. Long retention in a waste stabilization pond system is recommended.

Where it is not possible to provide the required level of treatment (due, for example, to a shortage of land) then other strategies are needed to reduce health risks. These could include restricting the types of crops that can be irrigated with wastewater; using drip irrigation rather than spray irrigation; and providing farm workers with boots and gloves.

Stabilized bio-solids make a good soil conditioner as they contain valuable nutrients and minerals. Wastewater is not usually suitable, however, due to a high concentration of dissolved salts.

Nutrients can also be reused as fertilizer for aquaculture, that is, for the cultivation of fish or aquatic plants such as duckweed.

IV-SANITATION COMPONENTS

Pits/Tanks

The function of the pit or tank is to isolate and store human excreta in such a way that no harmful bacteria are carried to new host. Though there is marked difference between pit technology and tank technology as there is practically 'nil' daily maintenance in pit technology for disposing of sewage (water mixed with excreta) as it percolates into the soil every day, continuously. The digested solid removal needs to be attended to once in two to three years only and not daily. The dirty solid excreta are rendered harmless as humus which can be used as beneficial manure.

Leach Pit

According to this technology, the water and gas of the excreta gets absorbed through the pores of the pit and the solid gets decomposed into manure. This technology maintains the system under hygienic condition that is free from odour and insect nuisance. Pits may be circular, square or rectangular and squatting slabs may be circular or rectangular. For circular pits, the minimum distance between the two pits should not be less than the depth pit while for rectangular pits; both the pits can be clubbed together with common partition wall plastered on both the sides.

Selection of Pit

In India, according to published data, the amount of human waste is 400 gram faeces and 2200 gram urine per person per day. For selecting a type of pit, an amount of 1kg of wet weight per person per day is taken into account for calculating the pit design. Based on this, for effective depth or capacity of wet latrines a provision of 37 liters (1.3 cu.ft) per person per year should be sufficient. For dry type (where if mud/soil stones are used as cleansing material), 50 liters (2 cu.ft) per person per year is acceptable.

The pit may be single or double depending upon the need and choice. The pit may be direct or direct with connected with pipes or lined and unlined.

Use of Vent Pipe

In case of pit latrines (single or double pit) vent pipe is not required. Gases produced during decomposition of wastes are diffused in surrounding soil through honeycombs of the walls of pit. Further, if the height of vent pipe is lower-- 4-5 feet (that has been observed in most of the cases), there is sometimes foul smell in the surrounding, resulting in avoidance of construction of a toilet. People are normally unaware of the function of vent pipe, they simply take it as status symbol.

Chart-5.1: Difference Between Leach Pit And Septic Tank

Leach Pit	*Septic Tank*
• Low cost less space • Needs little water • Sludge handling easy- manure • No recurring cost • Pit emptying easy • No mosquitoes	• High in cost • More space • Needs more water for flushing • Sludge handling difficult • Recurrent costs for emptying • Same disposal of effluents- pollution • Mosquito menace

Insufficient Honey Combs

In case of pit toilets constructed with bricks, honey combs are normally provided. It has been observed that honey combs are not provided in the ring channel toilets. Some part of the water leaches out through joints of the channel and through bottom of the pit. Most of the water remains in pit resulting in frequent filling of the pit. Under such condition taking out manure from the pit is quite difficult as the content of the pit remains wet for longer time. In sandy areas, large size of honey combs is not required. In such case, sand falls in the pit through honeycombs. In such cases honeycomb of 1" is sufficient for leaching of water.

Improper Junction Chamber/Inspection Chamber/ Y Chamber

In case of double pit toilet proper junction chamber is essential. It is required to change over pit when one pit is filled. Junction chamber should be suitable enough to block the pit after it is filled. Such blocking is done normally by putting a piece of brick at the opening of the pipe connecting to the pit. In some cases it has been observed that junction chamber/ Y Chamber is not properly designed to block human wastes completely. It results in flow of wastes in both the pits. In such case, contents of the pit remains wet and becomes difficult to take out. In case of single pit toilet also there should be proper junction chamber. It will be required when second pit will be constructed.

Ground Water Contamination

One of the limitations with pit toilet is that there should be a safe distance of 10 meters from drinking water source to the toilet pit. However, not much attention is given by the beneficiaries to this aspect. Due to lack of adequate awareness, people sometimes construct toilet very close to hand pump/ well. A community may face severe water born diseases due to contamination of ground water if safe distance of toilet with drinking water source is not maintained properly.

Faecal Sludge Management: Review of Practices, Problems and Initiatives

While substantial progress has been made in the field of wastewater treatment in developing countries over the past decades, the management and treatment of sludge from on-site-sanitation systems has been addressed, neither by problem holders nor by researchers. This is surprising as the absence or insufficiency of adequate excreta management in many cities of developing countries, particularly so in low-income areas, continuously leads to serious health and environmental hazards. A reason for this backlog in dealing with excreta in urban areas is, among others, the paucity of appropriate managerial and technical measures.

Faecal sludge and wastewater management stand side-by-side in urban environmental sanitation and how they might technically be interlinked. Faecal Sludge Management (FSM) deals with the management of sludge from on-site- sanitation systems, while wastewater management deals with sewered sanitation. FSM may be treated in separate treatment works or co-treated with sludge produced in wastewater treatment plants. Ideally, responsibilities at municipal level for both sectors should be borne by the same authority, which deals with excreta management in an integral manner, i.e. encompassing the aspects of sanitation choices at household level, excreta or wastewater collection, treatment and use or disposal.

The situation and problems associated with FSM are of a nature that – for achieving sustainable improvements – the need for decentralised management imposes itself almost without saying. In urban areas of developing countries; the excreta disposal situation is dramatic. Every day, world around, several hundred thousand tons of faecal matter from either open defecation or collected from on-site-sanitation (OSS) installations (un-sewered family and public toilets, aqua privies and septic tanks) are disposed of into the urban and peri-urban environment. The "waste" are either used in agriculture or aquaculture or discharged indiscriminately into lanes, drainage ditches, onto open urban spaces and into inland waters, estuaries and the sea, causing serious health impacts, water pollution and eye and nose sores.

The problems and challenges in FS management rest with all the components of the faecal sludge stream – viz. pit/vault emptying, haulage, storage or treatment, and use or disposal. All aspects are involved, viz. institutional/managerial, financial/economic, socio-cultural, and technical.

Pit emptying constitutes a major problem in many places, both technically and managerially. In many countries and cities, both mechanised and manual pit emptying services are being offered. Mechanised services are rendered by municipal authorities or medium to large-size entrepreneurs. Individuals, small groups of individuals or micro-entreprises, offer manual emptying. It is traditionally done with buckets. Emptiers step into the vault or pit to evacuate the sludge, which has turned too solid to be scooped. Hence, the traditional manual emptying is associated with considerable health risks – for the emptiers in the first place. The general public is at risk, too, as the emptied sludge is usually deposited into nearby surface drains or into lanes. Manual emptying is often done at night and is associated with clandestineness. It is common that families have or want to rely on such a service, either because services for mechanical emptying are not reliable, too costly, solidified deposits are not removable by suction, or because the pit is not accessible by emptying vehicles. Suitable sites for treatment and use or for final disposal may be found at the outskirts of cities only. Vacuum tankers discharge their load at shortest possible distance from the points of collection to save time and cost. In many cities, dumping sites for FS are close to squatter or formally inhabited low-income areas where they threaten the health of this ever-growing segment of population. Children, in particular, are at greatest risk of getting into contact with indiscriminately disposed excreta.

Current FS management has resulted from the historical development in excreta handling (which, often, is linked to agricultural practices), general socio-economic developments and purposeful planning efforts, which indirectly or directly affect the choice of sanitation systems. Improving on and finding appropriate strategies and solutions in FS management must, thus, be dealt with in conjunction with both unplanned and planned urban and peri-urban development, institutional settings, jurisdictional conditions, and expected future sanitation infrastructure and service provision.

In short, an FS management concept should be based on the assessment of (Klingel 2001; Klingel et al. 2002):

- existing sanitary infrastructure and trends
- current FS management practices and their shortcomings
- stakeholders customs, needs and perceptions regarding FS management and use
- environmental sanitation strategy

- prevailing socio-economic, institutional, legal and technical conditions, and
- the general urban development concept

The Challenges In FS Management

- Institutional and regulatory measures
- Financial/economic measures
- Technical measures, and
- Training in on-site sanitation and FS management in academic institutions and on all professional levels

There is a novel development in Mali where public entities have remained completely uninvolved in FS management, leaving its challenges to the households and private entrepreneurs. Stakeholders, including public authorities, have now become aware, though, that public entities should be made responsible for FS management given the eminent importance of improving people's livelihood by reducing the health risks of current practices.

Approaches and Tools for Improved FS Management

Involving the Stakeholders in Planning

Planning for FS management must form an integral part of long-term urban sanitation planning. Identification, continuous involvement, and definition of the specific roles of all actors as well as sustained concertation among them constitute the single most important set of measures in devising and maintaining improved FS management.

The approach comprises effective stakeholder involvement, assessing families' willingness-to-improve the neighbourhood hygiene, and the strengthening of small entrepreneurs. The success of process of involving stakeholders depends on the motivation and perseverance of stakeholders and their representatives, on the commitment of the municipal authorities, on the political and institutional stability, and on a sustained support by a facilitator. For the scalingup of the method for larger cities, it is recommended to divide the city into smaller zones and to develop to the extent feasible zone-specific strategic-technical-managerial solutions.

Effective and Enforceable Regulations for FSM

Clear local regulations (bye-laws or ordinances), which are both enforceable and enforced, are the logical and necessary extension of institutional responsibilities. Resulting institutional frameworks and bye-laws for FSM should ideally be incorporated into broader Integrated Urban Water Management approaches, to achieve credibility and maximum results, but should be developed in any case. Regulations need not be overly complex to start with, especially when transitioning from informal services.

At the most, basic level the regulations should ensure clean and safe operation (such as by ensuring correct designs and well-constructed containment infrastructure with regular and effective desludging by registered operators), that all faecal waste is safely disposed at designated treatment works, that sanctions are applied for disposal elsewhere, and that workers use protective clothing and undergo health checks. The responsible agency should be required to keep complete records and account for its operations and income, and manage the private sector operators in a fair and transparent manner.

Incentives to improve Disposal Practices

This is a relatively new area, with limited experience gained or documented. However, promising approaches include:

- Providing credits to tankers discharging at the authorized sites instead of charging them a tipping fee;
- Provision of cheap loans, possibly by way of a guarantee fund, to operators to allow them access to modern, efficient and reliable equipment;
- Reducing haulage costs (the biggest ingredient of FSM costs) by building more treatment and/or transfer facilities, thus reducing distances;
- Branding and promotion of improved services to wean customers away from unhygienic FSM practices;
- Reducing prices through promoting competition, as with a customer call center established in Dakar which allows for competitive bidding between operators;
- Teaming up with micro-finance institutions to enable facilitated payment for emptying, which is typically a major cost for a poor household, possibly as much as an entire month's income.

Adequate Containment and Building Regulations

In most cases, especially in economically poor localities, poorly constructed pits and septic tanks contribute to inadequate FSM, as well as to inadequate hygienic conditions for users. Typically, only septic tanks have regulated designs or design parameters, and in informal settlements, where the bulk of FSM services are typically though not only required, such regulations are, more or less by definition, not enforced. The question therefore arises as to how to persuade residents of informal settlements to adopt adequate sanitation infrastructure.

Planning and Budgeting Processes for FSM

Even where FSM is identified in policies, the associated planning and budgeting required for implementation are identified as key weaknesses in the FSM City Service Delivery Assessments. FSM service targets in city development plans, viable service funding arrangements and a clear FSM component in any comprehensive, city-wide sanitation investment plan are crucial – but usually missing. Well-designed national/state/city plans, funding windows and reporting mechanisms can also be critical to achieving success at scale.

Monitor FSM Service Outcomes

The key outcome when considering only the containment stage of the service chain is use of an adequate sanitation facility. Considering FSM as a complete end-to- end system, the key outcome is that people do not interact with faecal sludge in the environment, but this is difficult to monitor. An important proxy outcome indicator to monitor is the proportion of faecal sludge discharged to a proper treatment and/or safe disposal facility, as the intended endpoint of faecal waste flows.

Equity in Subsidizing the Sanitation Chain

Although it is normal worldwide practice that households pay for their water closet and household plumbing, sewerage is extensively subsidized on the basis of providing public health and environmental benefits. Many of the beneficiaries are businesses and richer residential customers, whilst many customers who continue to depend on non-networked sanitation cannot afford the full market cost of mechanical emptying, which is mostly not subsidized. The public good element is a clear argument for subsidizing urban sanitation and there is a real need for smart, targeted subsidies for poor FSM customers, especially when those better able to pay already enjoy significant subsidies through access to sewers. Sustainable subsidization of an on-going service provided by the private sector is much harder than subsidizing major public investment in sewerage systems. Innovative subsidy mechanisms will therefore need to be developed, that target specific cost elements through the entire service chain (not necessarily limited to conveyance, as in the case of sewerage), without compromising the sustainability and inclusiveness of the services.

Smart subsidies for household on-site sanitation may be justified by the externalities resulting from a poorly covered pit or one that requires manual emptying. Output-based aid mechanisms, together with improved faecal sludge management, are being tried in a number of countries. (e.g. Sri Lanka, Indonesia) to improve the quality of on-site sanitation and in the process ensure that the facilities are suitable for regular emptying. A mechanism used in a number of countries is a cross-subsidy from water supply, which can be managed in-house by a utility, or take the form of a transfer to local government if they are responsible for FSM. Whatever mechanism is selected, national government and/or the sector regulator will need to be involved, either to agree on an increased water tariff, or to provide another funding window.

Knowledge Gaps

Knowledge gaps on city-wide urban sanitation and specifically FSM include:

(a) *The need for inclusive delivery of effective sanitation facilities to specific user groups* such as: for tenants of low-cost rental accommodation; sanitation in challenging environments such as high water table and flood-prone areas, rocky ground and steep hillsides, settlements over water, cold climates, etc; upgrading on-site facilities at scale to improve emptiability and user hygiene; modalities and timing for effective urban sanitation and hygiene promotional campaigns; and ensuring that the institutions responsible for health centers, schools, etc. provide adequate sanitation for users.

(b) *Institutional issues* such as developing the community engagement capability of utilities (or other responsible authorities) to enable effective planning and community mobilization for both sewerage and non-networked sanitation; complementary roles and collaboration modalities for utilities, local government and the private sector in diverse governance environments; financing of capital and operating costs, including subsidies where appropriate; the design of institutional incentives; and the development of better political economy analysis tools.

(c) *Clear institutional roles are needed for FSM at local level:* While there is no 'one model fits all', the utility, together with the private sector, may be best placed to manage FSM services where piped water access is substantial. Where local government has responsibility for FSM, the municipality will often be a service provider, which also provides capacity to deal with public emergencies and sends price signals into the market through a limited service for paying customers.

(d) *FSM services are an essential component of urban sanitation:* On-site sanitation systems are the norm for both rich and poor in cities and towns of many developing countries, and are often the only form of sanitation available to poor people. However, they have been largely neglected by the institutions responsible for sanitation, and the construction and servicing of on-site facilities is typically left to an unregulated informal sector. This is compounded in many cases by outdated legislation that may outlaw pit latrines or other non-sewered sanitation options.

(e) *FSM services need to be included in national sanitation policies:* In order to manage on-site-sanitation and FSM effectively, they must be included in national policy and funding arrangements, and any assessment of sanitation services needs to include a focus on how the poorest communities can best be served. This must be complemented with state-level sanitation strategy and further with city-level sanitation planning systems, and bye-laws that allow the authorities to oblige both households and service providers to play their part in delivering a full sanitation service chain.

(f) *The private sector needs incentives* to stimulate and meet demand for affordable FSM services, while also ensuring safe practices, and requires access to safe disposal sites at economical distances from collection areas.

(g) *Financial flow Household (Emptying fee) Private Enterprises-(Discharge fee)—Public utility—(Purchase price) from- End users:* Sanitation taxes, applied most equitably as a function of water usage, can help cover the cost of FSM. The money collected should be used to support the FSTP O&M, assist in regularly scheduling collection or maintenance of household sanitation technologies, offset the discharge fee or generate a fund for discharge incentives.

Licensing, in combination with genuine rights granted to licensees, and enforcement of fines when rights are abused would help to reduce corruption and illegal discharge.

References

- *Government of India (Ministry of Urban Development) and WSP; (2008):Guide to Decision Making: Technology Options for Urban Sanitation in India.*
- *ADB (Asian Development Bank) (2006): Model Terms of Reference: Planning Urban Sanitation and Wastewater Management Improvements. www.adb.org/Water/tools/Planning-Urban-Sanitation-TOR.*
- *Alaerts, G. J., S. Veenstra, M. Bentvelsen, L. A. van Duijl, et al. (1991): 'Feasibility of Anaerobic Sewage Treatment in Sanitation Strategies in Developing Countries'.*
- *IHE Report Series 20, International Institute for Hydraulic and Environmental Engineering, Delft.*
- *Cotton, A. P., and D. L. Saywell (1998): On-Plot Sanitation in Low-Income Urban Communities: Guidelines for Selection. WEDC. Loughborough University, Loughborough.*
- *Department for International Development (1999): DFID Guidance Manual on Water Supply and Sanitation Programmes. WELL Resource Centre, Loughborough University, UK.*
- *Feachem, R. G., J. B. David, G. Hemda, and D. D. Mara (1983): Sanitation and Disease: Health Aspects of Excreta and Wastewater Management. World Bank, Washington, D. C.*
- *Franceys, R. (1997): 'Private Sector Participation in the Water and Sanitation Sector'; Water Resources Occasional Papers No 3. DfID WELL Task paper. WEDC, Loughborough University and IHE, Delft.*
- *Franceys, R., J. Pickford, and R. Reed (1992): Guide to the Development of On-Site Sanitation. World Health Organization.*
- *Government of India (Ministry of Rural Development in the Department of Drinking Water and Sanitation) and UNICEF(2005): Technology Options for Household Sanitation.*
- *Government of India (Department of Drinking Water and Sanitation) (2005):School and Aganwadi Toilets Designs.*
- *Government of India (Department of Drinking Water and Sanitation) (2005-6): Communication Tools.*
- *Heinss, U., S. A. Larmie, and M. Strauss (1997): Solids Separation and Pond Systems for the Treatment of Faecal Sludges in the Tropics. SANDEC Report No. 5/97. Dübendorf, Switzerland.*
- *IETC (International Environmental Technology Centre)(2002): International Source Book on Environmentally Sound Technologies for Wastewater and Stormwater Management.*
- *Iqbal, S. (1999): Duckweed Aquaculture Potentials, Possibilities and Limitations for Combined Wastewater Treatment and Animal Feed Production in Developing Countries. SANDEC Report No. 6/99. EAWAG, Switzerland.*
- *IRC. (1997): Operation and Maintenance of Sanitation Systems in Urban Low-Income Areas in India and Thailand. Report on a joint research programme, 1989-1993. Project and Programme Papers 6-E, International Research Centre (IRC), Netherlands.*

- *IRC Technical Paper Series 39 [School Sanitation and Hygiene Education – India].*
- *Khouri, N., J. M. Kalbermatten, and C. Bartone (1994): The Reuse of Wastewater in Agriculture: A Guide for Planners. UNDP–World Bank Water and Sanitation Program. World Bank, Washington, D. C.*
- *Ludwig, H. F., H. Fennerty, K. L. Sow, and K. Mohit (2005): Textbook of Appropriate Sewerage Technology for Developing Countries. New Delhi: South Asian Publishers Pvt Ltd.*
- *Mara, D., and S. Cairncross (1989): Guidelines for the Safe Use of Wastewater and Excreta in Agriculture and Aquaculture. Geneva: United Nations Environmental Programme/World Health Organization.*
- *Mara, D. D. (1985): The Design of Pour-Flush Latrines. TAG Technical Note No. 15. Washington, D. C.: World Bank.*
- *Mara, D. D. (1996): Low-Cost Urban Sanitation. England, Chichester: John Wiley and Sons.*
- *Mara, D. D. (1997): Design Manual for Waste Stabilization Ponds in India. National River Conservation Directorate, Ministry of Environment and Forest, Government of India, and Department for International Development, UK.*
- *Mara, D. D. (1998): Low-Cost Sewerage. England, Chichester: John Wiley and Sons.*
- *Mara, D. D., A. Sleigh, and K. Tayler. 2000. PC-Based Simplified Sewer Design. Leeds: University of Leeds (School of Civil Engineering).*
- *Ministry of Urban Development (1995): Manual on Sewerage and Sewage Treatment, 2nd edition. New Delhi: Government of India Press. http:// urbanindia.nic.in/ moud/ publicinfo/ manual_sewage.htm*
- *Morel, A., and S. Diener (2006): Greywater Management in Low and Middle-Income Countries—A Review of Different Treatment Systems for Households or Neighbourhoods, SANDEC, Switzerland.*
- *Otis, R.J., and D. D. Mara (1985): The Design of Small Bore Sewer Systems. TAG Technical Note No. 14. Washington, D. C.: World Bank.*
- *Roy, A. K., et al. (1984): Manual on the Design, Construction and Maintenance of Low-Cost Pour-Flush Waterseal Latrines in India. TAG Technical Note No. 10. Washington, D. C.: World Bank.*
- *Sansom, K., R. Franceys, Cyrus Njiru, and J. Morales-Reyes (2003): Contracting out Water and Sanitation Services: Volume 1. Guidance Notes for Service and Management Contracts in Developing Countries. WEDC, Loughborough University, UK.*
- *Sasse, L. (1998): DEWATS Decentralised Wastewater Treatment in Developing Countries. BORDA (Bremen Overseas Research and Development Association), Bremen.*
- *Sinnatamby, G. S. (1986): The Design of Shallow Sewer Systems. Nairobi: United Nations Centre for Human Settlements.*
- *Tayler, K., J. Parkinson, and J. Colin (2003): Urban Sanitation: A Guide to Strategic Planning. UK: Practical Action Publications.*

- *Government of India (2004): TSC Guidelines.*
- *UNEP (United Nations Environment Programme) (2004): Guidelines on Municipal Wastewater Management. Version 3. UNEP; WHO; UN-HABITAT and WSSCC (2004). The Hague, The Netherlands, UNEP GPA.*
- *UNICEF (2003-4): School and Anganwadi Sanitation, Handbook for Technology Options and Design.*
- *UNICEF(1990): Low cost sanitation Facilities, New Delhi.*
- *US-EPA (United States–Environmental Protection Agency) (2002): Onsite Wastewater Treatment Systems Manual. www.epa.gov/nrmrl/ pubs /625r00008 /html / 625R00008.*
- *WHO (1958):Excreta disposal for small communities.*
- *Website: www.ddws.nic.in*
- *Government of India, Ministry of Drinking Water and Sanitation (2002): Handbook on Technical Options for On-Site Sanitation.*
- *Bhaskaran, T.R. (1962): A decade of research in environmental sanitation. New Delhi, Indian Council of Medical Research (Special Report Series No. 40).*
- *Cairn Cross, S., Feachem. R (1993): Environmental Health Engineering in the* Tropic: An Introduction Text, 2nd edition, John Wiley, London, pp. 231-290.
- *Ministry of Drinking Water and Sanitation, Government of India (2011): Ecological Sanitation Practitioner's Book.*
- *Faechem, R G, et al (1983): Sanitation and disease: health aspects of human excreta and waste water management. Cichester, Wiley.*
- *Franceys, R. Pickford j. & Reed, R. (1992): A guide to the development of on-site sanitation, World Health Organization, (WHO), Geneva.*
- *Mara, D.D. (1985b): The design of pour flush latrines. Washington, D.C, World Bank (TAG Technical Note No. 15).*
- *Mara D.D. & Cairn Cross, S. (1989): Guidelines for the safe use of waste water and* excreta in agriculture and aquaculture. Geneva, World Health Organisation.
- *Roy, A.K. et al. (1984): Manual on the design, construction and maintenance of low* cost pour flush water seal latrines in India. Washington, D.C, World Bank.
- *Wagner, e.g. & Lanoix, J.N. (1958): Excreta disposal in rural areas and small communities. Geneva, World Health Organization (WHO Monograph Series No. 39).*
- *WHO(2006): Guidelines for the Safe Use of Waste Water, Excreta and Grey Water.*
- *Klingel, F. (2001): Nam Dinh Urban Development Project. Septage Management Study.*
- *Nam Dinh, Vietnam, November 1, 2001. EAWAG/SANDEC and Colenco (Vietnam).*
- *Klingel, F., Montangero, A., Strauss, M. (2001). Nam Dinh (Vietnam) – Planning forImproved Faecal Sludge Management and Treatment. Paper presented at the Annual Conference of the Water Supply & Sewerage Association of Vietnam, Dec. 6-7, 2001.*

- *Klingel, F., Montangero, A.., Strauss, M. (2002). Guide on Faecal Sludge ManagementPlanning. EAWAG/SANDEC, drafted.Koottatep, T. and Surinkul, N. (1997-2000), AIT.*
- *How to select appropriate technical solutions for sanitation, Methodological Guide no.4, Ps-Eau, 2010.*
- *United Nations (2013) Sustainable Urbanization, thematic think piece prepared for the 2030 development agenda, New York.*
- *Logan, B.; Regan, J. (2006). "Microbial Fuel Cells—Challenges and Applications". Environmental Science & Technology. 40 (17): 5172–5180.*
- *Lienert, J.; Bürki, T.; Escher, B.I. (2007). "Reducing micropollutants with source control: Substance flow analysis of 212 pharmaceuticals in faeces and urine". Water Science & Technology, 56 (5): pp. 87–96.*
- *Harshman, Vaughan; Barnette, Tony (2000): "Wastewater Odor Control: An Evaluation of Technologies". Water Engineering & Management.*
- *Walker, James D. and Welles Products Corporation (1976): "Tower for removing odors from gases." U.S. Patent No. 4421534.*
- *Tchobanoglous, George; Burton, Franklin L.; Stensel, H. David; Metcalf & Eddy, Inc. (2003): Wastewater Engineering: Treatment and Reuse (4th ed.). McGraw-Hill.*
- *Metcalf & Eddy, Inc. (1972): Wastewater Engineering. New York: McGraw-Hill.*
- *Burrian, Steven J., et al. (1999): "The Historical Development of Wet-Weather Flow Management." US Environmental Protection Agency (EPA). National Risk Management Research Laboratory, Cincinnati, OH.*
- *Burton, Jr., G. Allen; Pitt, Robert E. (2001): "Chapter 2. Receiving Water Uses, Impairments, and Sources of Stormwater Pollutants". Stormwater Effects Handbook: A Toolbox for Watershed Managers, Scientists, and Engineers, New York.*
- *Khopkar, S. M. (2004): Environmental Pollution Monitoring and Control. New Delhi: New Age International. p.* 299.
- *Water and Environmental Health at London and Loughborough (1999): "Waste water Treatment Options." Technical brief no. 64. London School of Hygiene & Tropical Medicine and Loughborough University.*
- *EPA. Washington, DC (2004): "Primer for Municipal Waste water Treatment Systems".*
- *"Chapter 3. Flow Equalization". Process Design Manual for Upgrading Existing Wastewater Treatment Plants Report). EPA. October 1971.*
- *Huber Company, Berching, Germany (2012): "Sedimentation Tanks".*
- *Barwal, Anjali; Chaudhary, Rubina (2014): "To study the performance of biocarriers in moving bed biofilm reactor (MBBR) technology and kinetics of biofilm for retrofitting the existing aerobic treatment systems: a review". Reviews in Environmental Science and Bio/Technology. Springer. 13 (3): pp. 285–299.*
- *Randall, Clifford W.; Sen, Dipankar (1996): "Full-scale evaluation of an integrated fixed-film activated sludge (IFAS) process for enhanced nitrogen removal". Water Science and Technology. Elsevier. 33 (12): pp. 155–162.*

- *Black & Veatch Inc. (2009):"IFAS/MBBR Sustainable Waste water Treatment Solutions" (PDF). Archived from the original (PDF) on 2010-12-14, Brochure*
- *EPA. Washington, DC (2000): "Package Plants." Wastewater Technology Fact Sheet.*
- *http://www.wefnet.org/mopnew/Operation_of_Municipal_Wastewater_Treatment_Plants/Chapter%2022%20Revised_6th Edition.*
- *EPA (2013):"Chapter 3. Biological Treatment Processes". Emerging Technologies for Wastewater Treatment and In-Plant Wet Weather Management (Report).*
- *B. Kartal, G.J. Kuenen and M.C.M van Loosdrecht(2010): Sewage Treatment with Anammox, Science, vol. 328 pp. 702-3.*
- *http://news.nationalgeographic.com/news/2005/11/1109_051109_rocketfuel.html*
- *Harhangi, H. R.; Le Roy, M; Van Alen, T; Hu, B. L.; Groen, J; Kartal, B; Tringe, S. G.; Quan, Z. X.; Jetten, M. S.; Op Den Camp, H. J. (2012): "Hydrazine synthase, a unique phylomarker with which to study the presence and biodiversity of anammox bacteria", Appl. Environ. Microbiol. 78 (3): pp. 752–8.*
- *EPA (1976): Process Design Manual for Phosphorus Removal (Report). pp. 2–1.*
- *Das, Tapas K. (2001): "Ultraviolet disinfection application to a wastewater treatment plant", Clean Technologies and Environmental Policy. Springer Berlin/ Heidelberg, 3 (2): pp. 69–80.*
- *Florida Department of Environmental Protection. Tallahassee, FL.(2010): "Ultraviolet Disinfection for Domestic Waste water".*
- *Hernández Leal, L. (2010): Removal of micropollutants from grey water – Combining biological and physical/chemical processes. PhD thesis, Wageningen University.*
- *Ternes, T. (2009): Challenges for the future: emerging micropollutants in urban water cycle. BFG, Koblenz, Germany (presentation for a seminar at UNESCO-IHE, Delft).*
- *Margot, J.; et al. (2013): "Bacterial versus fungal laccase: potential for micropollutant degradation". AMB Express. 3: p. 63.*
- *Crude mushroom solution to degrade micropollutants and increase the performance of biofuel cells: https://www.biooekonomie-bw.de/en/articles/news/crude-mushroom-solution-to-degrade-micropollutants-and-increase-the-performance-of-biofuel-cells.*
- *Hoffmann, H., Platzer, C., von Münch, E., Winker, M. (2011): Technology review of constructed wetlands – Subsurface flow constructed wetlands for greywater and domestic wastewater treatment. Deutsche GesellschaftfürInternationale Zusammenarbeit (GIZ) GmbH, Eschborn, Germany, p. 11.*
- *IPEC Consultants, Ltd., Burnaby, BC, Canada. "IFT – Internally-fed – rotary thickener." Accessed 2012-06-16.*
- *Mine-engineer.com, Long Beach, CA. "Belt Filter Press, How Does It Work?" Accessed 2012-06-16.*

- *GlobalSpec, Inc., East Greenbush, NY and Eco tubes.*
- *"How to Select Dewatering Equipment." Accessed 2012-06-12.*
- *Environment Agency (archive) – Persistent, bioaccumulative and toxic PBT substances at the Wayback Machine (archived August 4, 2006, environment-agency.gov.uk. Retrieved on 2012-12-19.*
- *Natural Environmental Research Council – River sewage pollution found to be disrupting fish hormones. Planetearth.nerc.ac.uk. Retrieved on 2012-12-19.*
- *Endocrine Disruption Found in Fish Exposed to Municipal Wastewater at the Wayback Machine (archived October 15, 2011), USGS.*
- *Haughey, A. (1968): "The Planktonic Algae of Auckland Sewage Treatment Ponds". New Zealand Journal of Marine and Freshwater Research, 2 (4): pp. 721–766.*
- *Edmondson, W.T. (1972): "Nutrients and Phytoplankton in Lake Washington." in Nutrients and Eutrophication: The Limiting Nutrient Controversy. American Society of Limnology and Oceanography, Special Symposia. Vol. 1.*
- *Caperon, J.; Cattell, S. A. &Krasnick, G. (1971): "Phytoplankton Kinetics in a Subtropical Estuary: Eutrophication" (PDF), Limnology and Oceanography. 16 (4): pp. 599–607.*
- *Monfort, P; Baleux, B (1990): "Dynamics of Aeromonashydrophila, Aeromonassobria, and Aeromonascaviae in a sewage treatment pond", Applied and Environmental Microbiology, 56 (7): 1999–2006.*
- *PUB (Singapore National Water Agency)(2011): "NEWater: History".*
- *Martin, Andrew (2008): "Farming in Israel, without a drop to spare". New York Times.*
- *Corcoran, E., C. Nellemann, E. Baker, R. Bos, D. Osborn, H. Savelli (eds) (2010): Sick water? : the central role of wastewater management in sustainable development : a rapid response assessment (PDF). Arendal, Norway: UNEP/GRID-Arendal CS1 maint: Multiple names: authors list (link).*
- *Caribbean Environment Programme (1998): Appropriate Technology for Sewage Pollution Control in the Wider Caribbean Region (PDF). Kingston, Jamaica: United Nations Environment Programme. Retrieved 2009-10-12, Technical Report No. 40.*
- *MassoudTajrishy and Ahmad Abrishamchi (2005): "Integrated Approach to Water and Wastewater Management for Tehran, Iran." Water Conservation, Reuse, and Recycling: Proceedings of the Iranian-American Workshop. Washington, D.C.: National Academies Press.*
- *Zimbabwe: Water and Sanitation Crisis, Human Rights Watch, https://www.hrw.org/news/2013/11/19/zimbabwe-water-and-sanitation-crisis.*
- *Chowdhry, S., Koné, D. (2012): Business Analysis of Fecal Sludge Management: Emptying and Transportation Services in Africa and Asia – Draft final report. Bill & Melinda Gates Foundation, Seattle, USA.*
- *Ashton, John; Ubido, Janet (1991): "The Healthy City and the Ecological Idea" (PDF). Journal of the Society for the Social History of Medicine. 4 (1): 173–181. doi:10.1093/shm/4.1.173. Retrieved 8 July 2013.*

- *Lewis Dunbar B. Gordon (1851): A short description of the plans of Captain James Vetch for the sewerage of the metropolis.*
- *H. H. Stanbridge (1976): History of Sewage Treatment in Britain. Institute of Water Pollution Control.*
- *P. F. Cooper. "Historical aspects of wastewater treatment" (PDF). Retrieved 2013-12-21.*
- *Martin V. Melosi (2010): The Sanitary City: Environmental Services in Urban America from Colonial Times to the Present. University of Pittsburgh Press. p. 110.*
- *Colin A. Russell (2003): Edward Frankland: Chemistry, Controversy and Conspiracy in Victorian England. Cambridge University Press. pp. 372–380.*
- *Sharma, Sanjay Kumar; Sanghi, Rashmi (2012): Advances in Water Treatment and Pollution Prevention. Springer. Retrieved 2013-02-07.*
- *Epidemics, demonstration effects, and municipal investment in sanitation capital.*
- *"Edwin Chadwick and the Engineers, 1842–1854: Systems and Antisystems in the Pipe-and-Brick Sewers War Technology and Culture" (PDF). 1992.*
- *Tilley, David F. (2011): Aerobic Wastewater Treatment Processes: History and Development. IWA Publishing. Retrieved 2013-02-07.*
- *Final report of the commissioners appointed to inquire and report what methods of treating and disposing of sewage (1912). us.archive.org*
- *Sunita Narain* (2017):*Do it differently: Toilets are not enough to achieve sanitation, India must reinvent the waste business; February 11 in TOI Edit Page, Environment, India, population | TOI.*
- *World Fecal Sludge Management: Diagnostics and Guidelines for Service Delivery in Poor Urban Areas.*
- *The World Bank, WSP(2016): Summary Report GWASP OTHER.*
- *Martin Strauss; Agnes Montangero: Feacal Sludge Management: Review of Practices, Problems and Initiatives; EAWAG/SANDEC.*

ANNEXURES

Annexure - I

CASE STUDIES

INLAND

STANDARD OPERATING PROCEDURE FOR INTEGRATED FAECAL SLUDGE MANAGEMENT IN GUJARAT

Existing Faecal Sludge Management Practices

Like in other cities of India, faecal sludge management has been a neglected area in ULBs of Gujarat as well. The sector has not received any attention because of poor understanding of O&M requirements, lack of guidance, inadequate resources and skills, shortage of manpower and finance. Currently out of the 167 ULBs, only 62 have a partial sewer system. Most cities from the Saurashtra region do not have any underground drainage system and are dependent on on-site sanitation systems. The toilets are connected to septic tanks/ pits and the sullage/effluent is often discharged into road side storm water drains which are covered or open. Faecal sludge generated in small cities often ends up in garbage dumps, storm water drains, water bodies or is used for agriculture. In cities that have sewerage network and functional STPs, sludge is emptied in manholes or transported to STPs and treated along with the sewage conveyed through the underground network.

Cities in Gujarat also do not have any reliable data on number of households dependent on each of these above mentioned systems. Anecdotal evidence suggests that cities are moderately aware of the functioning and difference between these systems. The Prohibition of Employment as Manual Scavengers (and their rehabilitation) Act, 2013, prohibits manual cleaning of pit toilets and septic tanks. Adopting mechanical processes for cleaning of septic tanks such as suction emptiers is seen as the only way to eliminate manual scavenging. Regrettably, part of septic tank/pit cleaning in some cities is carried out manually. Based on PAS-SLB data of 2013, 85cities in the state provide mechanized septic tank/single pit cleaning as a municipal service. However, currently there is no infrastructure in any of the Municipalities in Gujarat for adequate faecal sludge treatment. GMFB has provided sludge sucking machines to the ULBs but sometimes these are inadequate and not functioning. Septic tank cleaning hence is often addressed by the private sector with little monitoring and regulation from the ULB. It is feared that the new Act may drive the already secretive business of faecal sludge emptying underground, and drive up the cost of emptying. Hence, it becomes essential that the ULBs recognize and register sludge emptying services as legitimate business, regulate their operations and enforce the use of mechanized suction machines. Simultaneously, ULBs need to augment their infrastructure and resources directly or through contracting out emptying, transport and treatment of sludge. For improving the coverage of safe sanitation in the State, the Government of Gujarat is providing financial assistance for underground drainage projects and for establishing sewage treatment plants. This assistance is under the Swarnim Jayanti Mukhya Mantri Shaheri Vikas Yojana for all 159 Municipalities. GUDM, GUDC and GWSSB have been identified as implementing agencies. But to achieve well functional sewerage, cities need to reach water supply levels of135 lpcd, which is also going to take efforts and time. Till then faecal sludge management is of prime importance to ensure total sanitation. The septic tank combined with soak pit provides good sanitation and can work well with lesser (70-100 lpcd) level of water supply than that needed for conventional sewerage. Therefore it makes both economic and sanitation sense to manage sludge efficiently till sewerage becomes feasible and affordable.

Standard Operating Procedure for Integrated Faecal Sludge Management

An integrated faecal sludge management plan would cover aspects across the value chain of on-site sanitation including safe collection, conveyance, treatment and disposal/reuse of the treated fecal sludge.

***Conduct an Audit of On-Site-Sanitation systems Technologies that Collect and Treat Faecal Sludge*:** A ULB should conduct a comprehensive audit of on-site sanitation systems that provides the city officials with a base line of the existing situation in the city. The audit should cover the following areas:

- Number of toilets connected to various types of on-site sanitation systems (single pits, twin pits septic tanks, others)
- Assessment of local construction standards, methods and technology

- Existing issues with on-site sanitation systems
- Routine O&M by property owners
- Cleaning and emptying frequency

Provide Guidance to Property Owners on Construction of accepted OSS: Toilet and septic tank construction are regulated by the National Building Code of India, 1983. The section on drainage and sewerage specifies sizing and design of toilet, septic tank and other sanitation infrastructure.

***Conversion of Single Pit Systems into On-Site Primary Treatment System*:** The ULBs should take proactive steps towards encouraging households to convert their exiting single pit systems to more advanced systems that include collection and primary treatment. The addition of a septic tank or other treatment system before the single pit can enable households to convert the single pits into a soak pit (if the pit adheres to construction standards and has absorption capacity). The ULBs should also ensure that the disposal system of all existing public and community toilets in the city is improved to an onsite treatment system.

Construction of Twin Pits: Twin pits system consists of two underground chambers (pits) to hold and treat faecal sludge. These are normally offset from the toilet and should be at least 1 meter apart. A single pipe leads from the toilet to a small diversion chamber, from which separate pipes lead to the two underground chambers. The pits should be lined with open-jointed brickwork. Each pit should be designed to hold at least twelfth months accumulation of faecal sludge. Wastewater is discharged to one pit until it is full. Discharge is then switched to the second chamber. The filled up pit can be conveniently emptied after 1.5 to 2 years, when most of the pathogens die off. The sludge can safely be used as manure. Thus the two pits can be used alternately and perpetually.

***Construction of Septic Tank based Systems*:** CPHEEO prescribes septic tanks as double chambered with specified sizes. Septic tanks need to be watertight and are built of bricks, stones or concrete. The sizes of septic tanks and soak pits (used in Gujarat cities to serve dual function of storage & digestion of solids and infiltration of liquids) are as recommended by CPHEEO manual on Sewerage and Sewage Treatment Systems Engineering. Cities can adopt their own innovative techniques for septic tank construction by using locally available material and skills.

The process of design and construction should be done very carefully; otherwise, problems may occur due to poor design and workmanship of septic tank and soak pit. A possible solution to this can be provision of standard designs of septic tanks to the citizens by the ULB and adoption of a simple process of construction, verification and approval which can be clubbed with the house completion report. Effluent from the septic tanks should ideally be disposed using soak pits or leach fields which allow the absorption of liquids in the ground or should be conveyed using a solids-free/ settled sewer.

***Disposal of Effluents using Soak Pits*:** A soak pit is a porous-covered chamber that allows effluent from septic tanks to soak into the ground. It is also known as a soak-away or leach pit. The soak pit should be connected to the septic tank by an extension pipe with a T-junction to receive the over flow from the tank. The diameter of soak pit is generally 900 mm with depth varying from 2400 to 4000 mm. The soak pit is filled with bricks or broken stones and is covered with stone or RCC slab. A vent pipe should be provided to release the gases produced in the soak pit.

***Conveyance of Effluent to an Off-Site-Treatment Facility*:** In cities where discharging effluent into drains is a common practice, it is recommended that ULBs include alternative solutions in their long-term plans. ULBs can explore systems like settled or solids-free sewer system which is designed as a network of small-diameter pipes that transport pre-treated and solids-free wastewater (such as septic tank effluent). This system is economical than the conventional underground drainage system. It can be installed at a shallow depth and does not require a minimum waste water flow or slope to function.

***Provide Guidance to Property Owners on Routine O&M of OSS*:** Routine operations and maintenance of the complete on-site sanitation system is critical to ensuring safe and efficient sludge management practices. ULBs should educate and inform property owners about the proper functioning and maintenance requirements of these systems and encourage them to clean them often. The on-site O&M responsibilities of sanitation infrastructure (private) for which property owners are responsible include:

- Repair and maintenance of toilets, septic tank, soak pit and piping
- Clearing pipe blocks
- Getting fecal sludge emptied from private or municipal vacuum emptier at an interval of 2-3 years.

Prepare a Service Plan for Scheduled Emptying of Septic Tanks: All ULBs should ensure safe emptying of on-site treatment units at regular intervals. Currently most households get their septic tanks cleaned once in 8-10 years. It is evident that there is not enough awareness among households to get their septic tanks cleaned at regular intervals of maximum 2-3 years.

The ULB should initiate scheduled septic tank desludging services and carry out extensive awareness campaigns to ensure that the septic tanks are cleaned at least once in three years. The scheduled emptying services should be provided on a rotating, three to five year cycle.

In order to comply with The Prohibition of Employment as Manual Scavengers (and their rehabilitation) Act, 2013, ULBs need to ensure that all septic tanks and pit systems in the city are cleaned mechanically. The ULBs should either provide the emptying services themselves or enter into service contracts with private agencies. The contracts could also include construction and operation of treatment options like sludge drying beds. If the private players are providing the service, ULB should monitor their services. Suggestive criteria for selecting private emptiers should include:

- Provision of safety and protective gear to the cleaners
- Availability of mechanical cleaning equipment (Vacuum emptiers)
- Availability of a doctor on call
- Adequate number of trained staff
- Agreement to follow procedures listed in SOP

Since the households will be unlikely to pay for the scheduled services, the ULBs can consider raising their local taxes or charge a fixed amount as user charges for sanitation every year. The private service providers could then be compensated by the ULB. ULBs can also procure dedicated small footprint (1500 – 3000 liter capacity) vacuum emptiers to service slums and other areas where access is narrow. For areas with wide roads (>9m), vacuum emptiers of capacity 5000-9000 liters can be deployed.

Construction of Sludge Drying Beds: The ULB needs to construct sludge drying beds to appropriately treat the faecal sludge. As the sludge is partially treated in the septic tank, it requires appropriate treatment before the usage. Drying of the sludge in the drying beds is considered as one of the septage treatment system.

Establish Customer Service Protocols: Once the ULB has procured the vacuum emptiers or made required arrangements with private contractors, the ULB should establish customer service protocols and convey it to the citizens by publishing in the local newspaper, holding meetings and displaying the information at citizen service centers. The ULB should also establish a helpline number and publicize it widely.

Follow operating procedure for cleaning septic tank/ soak pit

Daily Preparation for the ULB / Emptying and Transport service

- Receive work orders for the day

- Check the functioning of vacuum emptier and equipment
- Check personal protective equipment – All employees should be responsible for maintaining their own personal protective equipment (such as gloves, boots, hat, face mask, Davy's lamp) in good condition
- Check Disinfecting and spill control equipment – Operators should be trained on identifying spills and proper methods of disinfecting. Sprinkle lime over spilled area, wait 15 minutes, then wash with water
- Check Hoses – inspect hoses for cracks and wear– discard or repair worn and broken hoses. Connecting the Hose in the correct manner using the clamp style fitting ensures a tight and leak proof connection. Use of twine and plastic for making connections causes leaks and require cleanup.

***Operating the Vacuum Emptier*:** Operators should become familiar with the proper operation of the equipment in use for each operation. This includes the physical operation of the truck, and all valves, piping, power take-offs and ancillary equipment for the vacuum emptier (including the tank, valves, hoses, and fittings). Reach the first site and meet the building owner.

- Before pumping, check the tank to look for obvious damage to the structure and to verify proper piping is in place.
- Check the water level to get clues as to tank condition: high levels (above outlet level) indicate a clogged outlet; low levels (below outlet level) indicate a leaking tank (or tank not in use).
- Check for back flow into tank during pumping and when pumping is complete. Flow back may indicate a problem with plumbing in the house or clogged disposal.
- Open the access covers, inspect the interior and exterior of the tank. If more than one, locate and remove lids (for at least 2 hours) from all compartments.
- Each compartment will require pumping after ventilating. Probe the tank with the last length of hose. This will provide an indication on the volume of sludge to pump.
- Start the pump or vacuum equipment. The operator will make sure there is suction and that the pump is operating.
- Volume in the tank should start decreasing rapidly. Use hose to break up sludge and scum to the extent possible. After pumping is complete, check the tank for remaining sludge. If there are accumulated solids remaining, initiate the pump-back procedure,

which is to send the pumped faecal sludge under pressure back into the tank and direct this flow toward the sludge mass. This will break up the mass, making it possible to pump out. When pump-back is complete, pump out the tank again (suction). When pumping is complete, wash the hoses and replace the tank lids. Clean up any spills and disinfect with lime or bleach solution.

***Septic Tank/Single Pit Emptying*:** The process of septic tank emptying can be broken down into the following three simple steps:

From septic tanks firstly as all quantity of scum in the vicinity of the sunction pipe is withdrawn

↓

Liquid septage is extracted until sludge at the bottom is reached

↓

Sludge comes off last and is fully sucked out only if there is bottom slope in the septic tank towards outlet

It is important to empty the tank completely including sludge. If tanks are emptied partially, they become more and more filled with hardened sludge, washout of solids occurs and quality of effluent deteriorates. Septic tanks must be emptied once in 2-3 years or even earlier intervals when they are overloaded. If the single pits are not dug very deep and cleaned regularly at an interval of 2 to 3 years, the sludge from the pits can be emptied mechanically. If the hardened sludge is to be mechanically removed, the pit should be back washed and the sludge should be diluted and then emptied.

Soak Pit Cleaning: In most cities septic tanks are not cleaned regularly due to which sludge enters soak pits and gets accumulated resulting in diminishing the capacity of soil. In high water table or in stony, gravely soils where percolation capacity of soil is limited, the soak pits get filled and hence need to be cleaned. Soak pits up to 3.5m depth can be fully emptied by the vacuum emptier. Hence it is essential that ULBs and State do not permit soak pits deeper than 3m. Following image shows a typical example of soak pit emptying in Anklav city. For emptying typical soak pits in Gujarat cities the following steps can be followed:

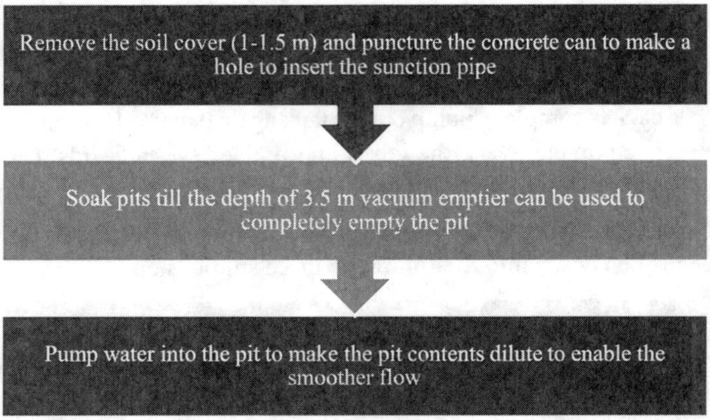

However in the long term, it is recommend that in areas where the percolation capacity has reduced ULBs should consider alternate systems like settled sewerage system or connect to open drain system as an intermediate solution.

Cleaning Twin Pits: Once a pit is full in a twin pit system, it should be closed and the wastewater should be channelized to the second pit. The full pit should be emptied only after one to two years after the contents of the pit have transformed into a partially sanitized, soil-like material called pit humus. Pit humus can be manually excavated.

Safely Transport Faecal Sludge to Sludge Treatment Site

If cities have an oxidation pond or a Sewage Treatment Plant (STP), the emptier should dispose fecal sludge into STP inlet chamber or into the manhole on the outfall sewer or in the sludge drying beds. In case of partial sewerage, it is not advisable to dispose these in the sewers since it will end up as sludge in open drains and make the situation worse.

If the ULB do not have any provision of the treatment system, ULB can select the suitable treatment and the following actions at fecal sludge receiving site are summarized below:

- Plan the trip so as to arrive at the disposal site within the specified disposal site operating hours
- Report equipment malfunctions or required repairs immediately to supervisors
- At the Disposal Facility position the truck so that the fecal sludge may be directed to the receiving chamber with only one length of hose

- Open the valve and allow the sludge to flow via gravity into the receiving chamber
- When the tank is empty, disconnect hose and clean tank and hose with water
- Use all safety precautions at disposal site and keep site clean

Treat and Dispose Faecal Sludge

Sludge is the black water from toilets mixed with grey water from bathrooms whereas septic tank effluent is the liquid part which flows out from septic tank (since solids are trapped in septic tank). Sludge has a much higher concentration of pollutants than the septic tank effluent. Biological Oxygen Demand (BOD) and Total Suspended Solids (TSS) are two common measurements of the strength of wastewater. Sludge may have BOD concentrations between 440to78, 600 mg/l and TSS values in excess of 90,000 mg/l, where septic tank effluent has values averaging 200 mg/l BOD and 300 mg/l TSS. As septic tanks fill with sludge, the effluent begins to resemble fecal sludge with higher pollution values. Therefore, regular desludging provides dramatic improvements in effluent quality. Detailed sludge characterization (BOD, TSS &other microbial characteristics) as well as its dewatering characteristics (specific resistance etc.) should be done prior to the design of any fecal sludge management facility. Treatment of sludge can be of two types, treatment at sewage treatment plants and at independent septage treatment plants. The details of these two types of treatment are given in the section below:

Treatment of Fecal Sludge at Sewage Treatment Plants

Co-treatment of faecal sludge along with municipal sewage at a STP, if available in the city is the most desirable option. Though sludge is more concentrated in its strength than domestic sewage, its constituents are similar to municipal wastewater. The sewage treatment plants should have adequate capacity to accept the sludge without hampering the functioning of the sewage treatment plant. Another possible way (needs checking for STP shock load or overload) is to dispose fecal sludge into easily accessible manholes at steep gradient sections on outfall sewers. Sludge could be added to sewage immediately upstream of the screening and grit removal processes. Faecal sludge could be processed with the sludge processing units of STP. If faecal sludge is to be co-treated with sewage, it will be necessary to construct a faecal sludge receiving chamber. Chemicals such as lime or chlorine can also be added to the faecal sludge in the storage tank to neutralize it, to render it more treatable, or to reduce odours.

Treatment at Independent Faecal Sludge Treatment Plants

When a city does not have a sewage treatment plant, a treatment plant specially meant for sludge treatment becomes the option to consider. These include:

(a) *Lime stabilisation* – odor control, conditioning and stabilization of the sludge.

(b) *Dewatering* – sludge drying beds or mechanical dewatering.

(c) *Anaerobic/aerobic wastewater treatment* – liquid from the sludge drying beds and mechanical dewatering systems.

(d) *Co-composting* with organic solid waste.

***Lime Stabilisation*:** Lime stabilisation is practiced to stabilize, control odour, vector and pathogen destruction. Lime stabilisation involves adding and thoroughly mixing lime (lime powder slaked with water in 1:3 proportions, 15 litres of slaked lime for 4000 litres of septage) with each load of septage to ensure that the pH is raised to at least 12. Lime addition could be done at any of these three points: (i) In the septage emptier, (ii) In a septage receiving tank where septage is discharged (iii) Spread septage in a pit and apply lime every time septage is dumped.

***Sludge Drying Bed*:** An unplanted drying bed is a simple, permeable bed that, when loaded with sludge, collects percolated leachate and allows the sludge to dry by evaporation. Approximately 50-80 percent of the sludge volume drains off as liquid or evaporates. The sludge, however, is not effectively stabilized or sanitized.

***Planted Sludge Drying Bed*:** A planted drying bed is similar to an Unplanted Drying Bed, but has the added benefit of transpiration and enhanced sludge treatment due to the plants. The key improvement of the planted bed over the unplanted bed is that the filters do not need to be desludged after each feeding/drying cycle. Fresh sludge can be directly applied onto the previous layer; the plants and their root systems maintain the porosity of the filter.

***Septage Dewatering*:** The septage after lime dosing is pumped to screw press or any other mechanical dewatering machine. Polyelectrolyte (a chemical commercially available for use as a coagulant in water supply and sewage treatment) is added to improve the dewatering efficiency. The liquid residual/filtrate from dewatering machine needs to be further treated before disposal. The dewatered sludge needs to be dried or composted prior to reuse as soil conditioner/organic fertilizer. Instead of Screw Press the other options could be to use Centrifuge or Belt Press or a Filter Press. Many companies in India are manufacturing sludge dewatering machines.

Composting of Septage: Composting is a popular method of treating septage. During the composting process organic material undergoes biological degradation to a stable end product. Approximately 20 percent to 30 percent of the organic solids are converted to carbon dioxide and water. As the organic material in the septage decomposes, the compost heats temperatures in the range of 50 to 70 degrees Centigrade and harmful pathogens are destroyed. The resulting humus-like material is suitable as a soil conditioner and source of nitrogen and phosphorus. The basic procedure for composting is as follows:

- Septage is mixed with a bulking agent (e.g. agricultural residue, cow dung, organic part of municipal solid waste) to decrease moisture content of the mixture, increase porosity, and assure aerobic conditions during composting.
- The mixture is aerated by mechanical turning ("agitated") for about 28 days. The most common "agitated" method is windrow composting: the mixture of septage or wastewater solids and bulking agent is pushed into long parallel rows called "windrows", about 1 to 2 meters high and about 2 to 4.5 meters at the base. The cross-section is either trapezoidal or triangular. Several times a week the mixture is turned over using a front-end loader to move, push, and turn the mixture. Factors affecting the composting process (USEPA 1984) include moisture content (40 percent to 60 percent); oxygen (5 percent to 15 percent); temperature (must reach 55 to 650 C); pH (6 to 9); and carbon-to-nitrogen ratio (30:1).
- Pit composting is simple, does not need any equipment and has been practiced in Gujarat before. The process involves digging many pits (1.2m wide, 1.5m deep and 4m long) and covering with soil (2-3 inches) every time septage is dumped until it gets filled. Contents of the pit are emptied and can be used for soil enrichment after 6 months, by this time most pathogens die off and composting is complete. Treated septage is safe for agricultural use.

Full Cost Recovery

To be sustainable, the septage management programs should be funded from the users in the form of user fees. This fee can be added to either the property tax or it can also be used as a pay and use system. This fee should include cost of staff, transportation, treatment, disposal and operation and maintenance. An example of cost recovery is Marikina City, Philippines. Manila Water Company, the service provider, will purchase eight new septage pumping trucks and fund a mechanized treatment facility in exchange for a 10% surcharge added to the monthly water bill. The program will fund septage pumping of 55,547 septic tanks every 5.25 years.

Social Marketing

This includes initiating programmes for educating the citizens at large. Dedicated Information, Education and Communication (IEC) programmes need to be undertaken to inculcate education on sanitation for school children, youth and women in the city. The social marketing system has different steps, these can include surveying the existing perceptions, conducting meetings with stakeholders, developing technical committees and outreach tools for media outlets, pre testing the tools, performing final surveys and deploying the messages to gauge results. In Muntinlupa, the city and the technical team developed a campaign plan with target audiences and messages and then developed a mascot, fliers, posters, newspaper ads and a video about the market treatment facility that was aired on a local cable TV station.

Recording and Reporting

Keeping accurate records regarding tanks and volume pumped is important for billing and compliance. Recordkeeping is an integral part of a comprehensive septage management program. The “manifest system” is a tracking and compliance tool. It helps ensure that all of the septage pumped arrives at the disposal site and minimizes the opportunity for illegal discharge. It is also a record that some septage programs may choose to use for paying septage hauling subcontractors.

Manifest forms are simple receipts that specify:

- the location or address of the pumped septic tank
- septage characteristics (residential or commercial)
- the name and address of the property owner or occupier
- the volume of septage pumped
- any notes regarding tank deficiencies, missing pipes or fittings, improper manholes or access ports, cracks or damage observed

All ULBs should keep a manifest form record for each septic tank/ soak pit emptied. Once completed, a copy of the manifest is given to the property owner as a receipt. When the septage load is delivered to the disposal site, the disposal site operator:

- accepts the load
- verifies the volume

- takes a sample if needed
- signs the manifest proving receipt of the volume of septage disposed off

It may be advantageous for the operator (ULB or private) to pump out multiple tanks before going to the disposal site. In this case, a multiple-load manifest form should be completed as well as in addition to individual manifest/receipt forms. The completed document or documents should be given to the ULB for their records. Cities with more than one lakh population should maintain the records at ward level for onsite sanitation system cleaning.

Ensure Safe Practices

Never enter a septic tank / soak pit which has not been well ventilated. Check for gas levels before entering septic tanks, manholes and closed chambers. Following steps should be followed as safety measures for septage management:

- Always keep first aid kit, gas detection lamp and fire extinguisher in the septage emptier vehicle
- Provide training to workers handling septage on safety and hygiene practices
- Provide fencing or compound around septage treatment facility premises
- Train staff and compel them to wear helmets, gum boots and gloves while on work.
- Ventilate covered tanks/pits by keeping them open for sufficient period before entering
- Paste list of emergency numbers on septage emptier and at a prominent place in septage treatment / disposal unit.

Source: *Urban Management Centre*: *Standard Operating Procedure for Integrated Faecal Sludge Management in Gujarat*

A TALE OF CLEAN CITIES: INSIGHTS FOR PLANNING URBAN SANITATION FROM VISAKHAPATNAM

The Influence of City Sanitation Planning

The past 50 years have seen successive efforts towards a systematic development of Visakhapatnam. In 1970, an Initial Development Plan, carried out as part of the General Town Planning Scheme, promoted balanced physical and social development across different parts of the city. In 1989, the growing economic activity and demographic growth fuelled by the mega steel plant and ancillary units pushed Vishakhapatnam Urban Development Authority to develop a master plan, which was revised in 2004 with greater emphasis on sustainable and equitable development.

In 2005, a city development plan was prepared under the Government programme Jawaharlal Nehru National Urban Renewal Mission. It focused on basic service delivery and citywide slum upgrading. Through the National Urban Sanitation Policy (NUSP), each state must develop a State Sanitation Strategy, and cities are tasked with creating a City Sanitation Plan. In 2014, the Dutch Royal Haskoning group was commissioned by the Ministry of Housing, Urban Development and Poverty Alleviation to prepare a city sanitation plan covering all of Visakhapatnam. This project, affected by the considerable shock caused by the Hudhud cyclone in October 2014, did not progress as expected.

So far, much of the development of sanitation has resulted from planning efforts embedded in national flagship programmes, such as Jawaharlal Nehru National Urban Renewal Mission, Andhra Pradesh Urban Services for the Poor programme, or Swachh Bharat Mission. The performance on the Smart Cities contest has allowed Visakhapatnam to increase its planning capacities, and city sanitation planning is thus being reframed in the broader Smart City Plan. The outputs of the city sanitation planning process, in combination with the sanitation strategy design with the support of the WSUP Advisory Cell, are likely to provide very helpful guidance to the city for the next ten years at least.

The Contribution of Development Partners

Visakhapatnam's sanitation development trajectory has been supported by many partnerships involving various national, bilateral, and multilateral organisations. This section focuses on the contribution that such partners made in the recent acceleration of progress, and notably in relation to sanitation planning efforts. From this perspective, the partnerships forged between Visakhapatnam and USAID are very relevant.

USAID previously made investments to support Visakhapatnam's urban development, and provided financial and technical support to the city in the aftermath of the 2014 Hudhud cyclone. The sanitation assessment carried out in early 2015 by Tetratech, with support from WSUP and USAID funding, came in response to the signing of a memorandum of understanding (MoU) between USAID, the Bill & Melinda Gates Foundation, and the national Ministry of Urban Development to advance the Swachh Bharat Mission.

The MoU specifies that the technical assistance component shall focus on Visakhapatnam. The WSUP Advisory Cell is the instrument put in place to achieve this objective, and its support to the GVMC is planned to last three years, ending in May 2018. After less than one year of activity, the contribution of the WSUP Advisory Cell is already significant – WSUP supported the preparation of Visakhapatnam's Swachh Bharat agenda, and notably the development of a draft behaviour change communication strategy and ODF strategy. It helped the city form a sanitation task force to monitor the deliverables and gave much impetus to the training of officials at various levels.

The WSUP Advisory Cell brings considerable urban WASH expertise through a structure well embedded in the GVMC. The team operates as part of the administration, yet it can tap into local knowledge and coordinate technical inputs from national and international sources. It represents a key learning instrument – a valuable asset when considering the observation by senior officials that their time is fully spent in action, leaving hardly any space for learning and sharing.

In February 2016, the United States Trade and Development Agency signed an MoU with India's Department of Municipal Administration to bring support to Visakhapatnam on the Smart Cities Mission. As part of this, a consortium of three US companies (IBM, KPMG and AECOM) have partnered with the city to prepare a master plan. Synergies have already been created and are likely to expand between the support provided by USAID on Swachh Bharat through WSUP and on Smart Cities through this consortium.

Thanks to these very timely partnerships, Visakhapatnam can leverage a rich pool of skill sets and significant national, state and bilateral financial resources to boost its development and become the model sanitation city it aspires to be.

Source: USAID: A Tale of Clean Cities: Insights for Planning Urban Sanitation from Visakhapatnam

FAECAL SLUDGE AND SULLAGE MANAGEMENT IN URBAN MAHARASHTRA

Urban Sanitation Context

Maharashtra is a highly urbanised state, with nearly 50 percent of its population living in urban centres. In economic terms, Maharashtra is one of the leading states in India and contributes about 13 percent to the national GDP with a per capita income of US$ 1600 in 2014. With higher economic performance, better levels of water and sanitation services are expected. However in Maharashtra, this is not the case. Nearly 36 percent of urban population lives in slums, and nearly one-fourth of urban population depend on public or community shared toilets. The full sanitation service chain that consists of five key activities, viz appropriate user interface, safe collection/ containment of faecal matter, safe conveyance, safe treatment and disposal and/or reuse, is not given due attention.

As per the Census 2011, 69 percent of households in urban Maharashtra have access to improved household latrines, about 21 percent use public latrines, and about 8 percent resort to open defecation. The situation in slum areas is worse. Only 39 percent of slum residents have access to improved latrines, while 49 percent population use public shared sanitary facilities, and 10 percent resort to open defecation. Only 33 cities in Maharashtra have underground sewerage network and even in these cities sewerage coverage is only 42 percent, and only about 35 percent of sewage is treated. Of these cities, only 22 have functioning sewage treatment facilities and these treat 35 percent of the collected sewage. On-site-sanitation is the predominant mode with 32 percent of households using such options including septic tanks. Most public facilities, which serve nearly 22 percent of households, are also connected to septic tanks. Most cities do provide septic tank emptying service but treat this as consumer grievance redressal, rather than as a regular service by the local government. None of the cities have a functioning septage treatment facility, and hence dump the collected septage in open dumpyards, along with the municipal solid waste.

Policy and Regulatory Framework

The Government of Maharashtra adopted the guiding principles of NUSP in their Sujal Nirrmal Abhiyan (SNA), a vision statement for the Urban Water Supply and Sanitation Sector. SNA prescribes measures that address provision of community/ public latrines but falls short of addressing septage management related issues. Slum sanitation, is governed by the regulations provided in the Maharashtra Slum Areas (Improvement,

Clearance and Redevelopment) Act, 1971. The rules do not encourage building of household latrines and thus force them to depend on community toilets. This is despite the fact that community toilets (or shared toilets) are not considered as "improved sanitation" by the UN agencies monitoring the progress on MDGs.

Policies and regulations related to 'conveyance' part of the FSM cycle are also listed in the Municipal Acts but are not clearly defined Implicit in this is the fact that ULBs should construct drains and also provide for cleaning/emptying septic tanks. Treatment and disposal of waste water, the last segment of the FSM cycle, are not 'mandatory functions' of ULBs in Maharashtra. They fall under 'discretionary functions' of ULB. As of date only 31 of the 254 cities in the State have partial sewerage systems. Of these, only 15 cities have secondary treatment capacity.

WHAT MAHARASHTRA CAN DO

Short Term Actions (3-6 months)	***Medium Term Actions (1-2 years)***
State Level Actions	
Develop a shared understanding of the definition/ scope of sanitation as the entire FSM cycle, across all the key actors in the state.	Strengthen ULB capacity –more staff, funds, facilities (septic tank empting trucks, sludge treatment etc).
Publish guidelines on septage management processes. Establish regulatory mechanisms for FSM activities along with appropriate IEC activities	Incentivize ULBs for introducing sanitation tax through matching grants for a year
Develop guidelines for covering residents of slums with improved sanitation facilities	Guidelines and tools for private sector engagement for FSM
City Level Actions	
Build a data base on properties with septic tanks, link with building permissions and property tax database to ensure monitoring and regular updates	Implement a scheduled desludging program and monitor through GIS based monitoring systems
Develop holistic FSM plans, expanding the current City Sanitation Plans	Develop adequate septage treatment facilities, if needed through appropriate private sector participation
Adopt policies for scheduled cleaning of septic tank, impose sanitation tax	Universal coverage of scheduled septage management services for all properties

Source: Dinesh Mehta and Meera Mehta; CEPT University Ahamedabad and PAS:Faecal Sludge and Sullage Management in Urban Maharashtra.

INTERNATIONAL

Scheduled Emptying of Septic Tank, Experience from Marikina City, Philippines

To achieve its goal of desludging all septic tanks in the city by 2011, Marikina City is implementing the "Oplan Todo Sipsip" program with Manila Water Company, Inc. (MWCI). Developed with support from the ECO Asia program, the initiative mobilizes local barangay leaders to educate communities about desludging septic tanks. As a result, Marikina City has increased the percentage of households using desludging services from 40 to 55 percent. Cooperative actions include the following:

- Community meetings are held to explain the program in advance of the desludging;
- A sound truck and fliers advertise desludging in a community the day before it is done;
- Local barangay staff accompany MWCI desludging crews to encourage homeowners to cooperate and open inaccessible septic tanks;
- MWCI places stickers on houses that have been desludged, so a second visit can be made later to the homes without stickers;
- Promotion campaigns are conducted that include distributing informative calendars, art contests, and hand washing events.

The project aims to desludge all 90,000 septic tanks in Marikina City on a rotating five-year cycle. At the time of writing, however, MWCI had only desludged 5,400 septic tanks.

Source: A Rapid Assessment of Septage Management in Asia, Policies and Practices in India, Indonesia, Malaysia, the Philippines, Sri Lanka, Thailand, and Vietnam, January 2010, USAID.

CLEAN LEANING UP THE BUSINESS OF SEPTAGE MANAGEMENT: PHILIPINES & MALYASIA

Inadequate Investment in Sanitation

Despite the enormity of the estimated economic losses associated with poor sanitation, investments in sewerage and sanitation have been noticeably minimal compared to other infrastructure subsectors (e.g., energy, transportation, etc.). In the Philippines, it has been reported that a meager 3 percent of public investments in water supply are actually used for sanitation. Several factors contributed to this condition. These include:

(i) Low priority accorded to sewerage and sanitation subsectors;

(ii) Lack of technical capacity to plan, implement, operate and maintain wastewater management facilities both at the national and local levels;

(iii) Low level of awareness and buy-in from the public; and

(iv) Lack of enforcement of regulations.

Low priority accorded to sewerage and sanitation. There exists in the sanitation sector a glaring disparity between capital investment requirements vis-à-vis capital expenditures made. Low priority is often accorded for the provision of sewerage and sanitation services in the order of priorities of the national and local developmental undertakings. For many local officials, preference is mostly focused on the provision of infrastructure wherein the impact is more tangible among their constituents (e.g., roads, school buildings, and bridges). This may indicate low appreciation for proper sanitation services and practices.

A strong indicator for the low priority accorded to sewerage and sanitation is limited service coverage. In the Philippines, nationwide coverage is estimated to be only 4 percent with the existence of sewerage systems confined to a few select cities.

In Malaysia, prior to 1994, only about 25 percent of households are connected to a sewerage system, and about 40 percent of the population connected to septic tanks. Large-scale sewerage systems were only implemented in large cities (having over 100,000 people). Aside from being capital-intensive, the expected returns in sewerage and sanitation interventions are low and the benefits generated are indirect at best. Ideally, in order to achieve full cost recovery, sewerage and sanitation services should be linked to water service provision. However, in some cases, tariff setting is subjected to and highly influenced by political interference from local administrators. Under the veil of water being a social good, tariff levels are kept to a minimum to make it affordable and accessible to their constituents, thereby affecting the flow of funds (through tariffs) necessary for the provision of services such as water supply and wastewater as well as service expansion.

This particular problem is highlighted in Malaysia's case where Indah Water Konsortium (IWK), the private concessionaire tasked to operate, maintain, and develop sewerage services for the entire country, had to be bailed out from bankruptcy by the Federal Government [with an accumulated debt of about RM700 million ($227 million)14], just 6 years in the concession period. The citizens' refusal to pay the intended tariff for sewerage and sanitation services has resulted in a tariff reduction set too low to cover operating expenses, thus, severely undermining the company's financial sustainability.

Lack of Necessary Technical Capacity

Ensuring the technical capacities of service providers, regulators and local operators is crucial in increasing the sewerage infrastructure and sanitation programs' efficiency and sustainability. In reality, however, local operators and professionals are found to be wanting in terms of the numbers and capacities to properly conduct a rapid situational assessment of an area's wastewater needs.

The information gathered from such undertaking would then be used to firm-up baseline conditions, which are important in crafting localized sanitation strategies and plans reflective of the needs of the populace. Likewise, their working knowledge of available technological options for wastewater management treatment and disposal is mostly limited to previously known methods, without much incentive to keep abreast with new and cost effective solutions more responsive to the community's needs. Much is to be desired when it comes to establishing a critical mass of professionals needed to be able to keep pace with the sanitation demands of an ever-growing populace and increased urbanization.

Low Level of Awareness and Buy-In from the Public

The low level of public awareness on the environmental, health (i.e., potential exposure to water-borne diseases) and economic risks associated with poor sanitation has been cited in various literatures as a major factor in the poor willingness by the public to avail and pay for sanitation services offered by the government and service providers. The prevailing lack of understanding and appreciation of the value of proper sanitation makes it difficult to generate public interest and support for sanitation programs (e.g., acceptance of septage user fees), thereby severely affecting efforts to ensure and/or scale-up sustainability.

Creating Awareness among Stakeholders Achieves a Two-Fold Effect

(i) Awareness on the potential adverse effects of poor sanitation provides a strong driver for behavioral change and motivates people to a certain course of action.

(ii) Significant contribution in generating communities' willingness to pay and partake (through household sewer connections) in government and service providers' sewerage and sanitation programmes.

Lack of Enforcement of Regulations

While there exists a whole plethora of legal instruments and design codes (e.g., Building, Sanitation, and Plumbing Codes) to regulate wastewater management, it is the enforcement of such that has appeared to be the weakest link. From the national down to the local levels of governance, weak enforcement of regulations and standards has contributed to the pervasiveness of substandard and poorly maintained septic tanks functioning at less than optimal operational efficiency. It has also contributed to continuous disposal of untreated wastewater (sewage and septage) in drainage canals and other water bodies, threatening sustainability of sources of water and the ecosystem.

Local government units (LGUs) that develop their own sanitation ordinances to enforce regulations is a step in the right direction. Examples from the cities of Dumaguete and Marikina in the Philippines would attest that enactment of local ordinances enables easier imposition of user fees and penalties for non-compliance. Ordinances may likewise cover the enforcement of design standards and maintenance activities for sanitation facilities confined within the political boundaries of a particular locality.

In Malaysia's case, septage management was not done on a regular basis. In 1993, it was estimated that only 1 percent of the total number of individual septic tanks have been desludged, with no dedicated sludge treatment facility to facilitate treatment and safe disposal of sludge.

Presence of Demand for Septage Services from the Populace

This covers aspects such as:

- aconsumer demand;
- socio-demographic conditions of households on sanitation;
- level of public awareness on the ill-effects of poor sanitation and the benefits derived from proper wastewater management;
- willingness to partake in any septage management programs; and
- willingness and ability to pay by consumers on proposed user septage fees.

Financial Viability of Septage Systems and Facilities

This pertains to the cost accounting within a septage management system, which includes capital expenditures, operation and maintenance (O&M) costs, and revenue generation.

Governance Framework

This covers the enactment of legislative instruments, establishment of coordination mechanisms and platforms among stakeholders, delineation of functions and responsibilities, and defining clear cut regulations and standards.

AN OVERVIEW OF THE SYSTEM (TECHNOLOGY OPTIONS) PHILIPPINES

The Metro Manila concessionaires employ a three-pronged approach in addressing wastewater management in Metro Manila, as illustrated here under:

(i) ***Separate Sewer Systems***, whereby dedicated sewer pipes would connect households in the service area to collect wastewater and then direct it toward sewage treatment plants. While this option is most ideal, the expected construction and social costs needed in building the system makes this approach prohibitive, given that the majority of the portions of the metropolis are densely populated.

(ii) ***Combined Sewer-Drainage Systems***, where interceptor systems would be constructed near the outlets of the drainage canals to capture and redirect the flow of wastewater toward the sewage treatment plants, prior to discharge to aparticular body of water.

(iii) ***Septage Management***, which involves maintaining a fleet of vacuum trucks that go around the metropolis to conduct desludging of septic tanks, and then transporting the septage collected to treatment facilities. This approach is ideal particularly for those areas that are currently non-sewered and rely on individual or communal septic tanks to deal with domestic wastewater.

The current septage management program of Manila Water Company, Inc. (MWCI) hinges on the operation of two septage treatment plants situated in Taguig (southern portion of Metro Manila) and San Mateo, Rizal (northeastern portion). Both plants utilize a state-of the-art, small footprint mechanized septage dewatering screw press machines with activated sludge treatment. Capacities for each plant are 814 cubic meters per day (m3/day) for Taguig and 586 m3/day for San Mateo. The Taguig plant was specifically designed to handle not only septage but also sewage coming from an adjacent industrial park.

Considering that these plants currently operate at 35 percent of their capacities, there is still plenty of room for handling a bigger volume of septage to maximize their operational capacities. Collection and transportation of septage to the facilities is done through the use of its fleet consisting of seventy eight vacuum trucks.

Maynilad Water Services, Inc. (MWSI), on the other hand, previously operated a single septage treatment plant located in the northwestern part of the metropolis. The treatment plant is a semi-mechanized treatment system carrying a larger footprint due to the treatment processes utilizing lagoons and wetlands. The plant has a design capacity of 250m3/day, at 8 hours of operation per day. A new septage plant was inaugurated in 2013 to augment existing treatment capacity. Situated in Quezon City, the treatment facility has an estimated capacity of about 250 m3/day.21 A fleet of 25 vacuum tankers carries out collection and conveyance of septage to its treatment facilities.

As for mobile dewatering units (MDUs), MWSI has seven of them. Considered as an in-situ method of septage treatment, MDUs are used primarily to perform desludging of septic tanks as well as separate solids from the septage collected. The liquid collected after separation can then be reverted to the septic tank.

In the case of Dumaguete City, its septage management system can be segregated into three main components:

(i) ***Administration*** – The City Septage Management Administration (CSMA) has overall supervision of the septage management system.

(ii) ***Mobile Component*** – The Dumaguete City Water District (DCWD) manages the mobile component and organizes the septage collection and transport system. There are eight vacuum trucks (previously owned) that collect and transport septage from residences, businesses and institutions, to the septage treatment facility. The capacities of the septage vacuum trucks range from approximately 2–4 m3. A motor pool has been built for the repair and maintenance of the vacuum trucks.

(iii) ***Septage Treatment Facility*** – The treatment facility, handling a daily load of about 80 m3, is located on a two-hectare plot of public land in Barangay Camanjac. The treatment system is composed of a series of grit chamber, anaerobic ponds, facultative lagoon, and maturation ponds. Effluent coming from the maturation ponds flows through a planted gravel filter before eventually discharged to a wetland.

In terms of the operational efficiency of the facility, from a septage with an influent biochemical oxygen demand (BOD) ranging from 1,000 mg/l to 3,000 mg/l, the resulting effluent BOD is reduced to less than 10 mg/l.22 Sludge drying beds are also constructed for the dewatering of accumulated biosolids.

The choice of appropriate technology to adopt was based on (i) affordability (capital and operating cost requirements), (ii) technical and maintenance staff needed to operate the system, and (iii) ability to meet the effluent standards of the Department of Environment and Natural Resources (DENR). Mechanized systems were not considered due to the high costs associated with acquisition and operation, electricity, and maintenance. As a result, non-mechanized natural processes using stabilization ponds were selected despite the sizable amount of land required. A two-hectare piece of public land was made available wherein the septage treatment facility was constructed. The same luxury of having a large footprint is, however, not available for Metro Manila operators, which directly affects the technology adopted and costs.

MALAYSIA

Although sewerage coverage has greatly increased since the privatization of sewerage services in 1994, private developers have played a central role in the diffusion of sanitation systems throughout Malaysia. This has resulted in a vast diffusion of systems of various sizes and types, including ISTs, CSTs, and private STPs. In 2011, more than 7 million population equivalent (PE) users were served by both ISTs and CSTs; and more than 2.4 million PE users were connected to private STPs, representing about 28% of the existing sanitation facilities.

The trend is increasing as new systems are still being implemented in new development areas. In these areas, private developers are required to choose a sewage treatment system approved by the National Water Services Commission (SPAN) – the national regulator of water and sanitation services – and follow its construction guidelines.

Among the simplest forms of wastewater treatment are ISTs, which, in the case of Malaysia, treat grey and black water (or only black water for the tanks built before the 1980s). The materials used for constructing ISTs include polyethylene (PE) or fiber-reinforced plastic (FRP). The FRP is the most popular type among the septic tanks installed.

To tackle the issue of sludge disposal, IWK developed short-term and long-term strategies from non-mechanized to mechanized treatment and disposal systems. As an immediate solution, IWK used the existing sludge treatment facilities available in STPs with excess capacities. For the short-term, covering the period between 2–5 years, IWK constructed sludge trenches and dedicated sludge drying beds. The long-term strategy included the construction of few mechanized sludge treatment facilities through official development assistance (ODA).

Mechanized dewatering units (MDUs) were installed in strategic locations in the country where the sludge from septic tanks and small STPs is transported through tankers and dewatered to reduce volume before disposal. Integrated sludge reception facilities were also added in STPs to enable the discharge of sludge from vacuum tankers. With the increase of sludge production, IWK is currently looking for means to reduce the volume as well as recycle sludge rather than disposing it outright.

The sludge management strategy aims to provide at least one disposal site for each local authority located in the area of operation of IWK. The management of sludge removed from the septic tanks and small STPs not equipped with sludge treatment facilities, as well as septage collected from pour-flush systems, is disposed in identified trenching sites spread throughout the rural areas. Other disposal sites include dedicated dumpsites and landfills of IWK that are managed mainly by local authorities or private companies.

Sludge dewatering (e.g., Geotube) are also tested and considered for application. Likewise, the government is continuously exploring innovative ways to recycle sludge as indicated in research conducted by public universities. These options include composting, land reclamation, reforestation, power generation, and building materials. On its own, IWK has also been conducting joint research for green technology applications, which covers energy recovery systems, reuse of biosolids as soil conditioners, and reuse of bio-effluent with reclaimed waste water.

ESTABLISHING PARTNERSHIPS PHILIPPINES

Metro Manila Concession

The Metropolitan Waterworks and Sewerage System (MWSS) is a government corporation mandated to provide water supply, sewerage, and sanitation services within Metro Manila and some cities of Rizal and Cavite provinces. The passage of Republic Act (RA) No. 8041 (National Water Crisis Act) in 1995 paved the way for the privatization of MWSS.26 The National Water Crisis Act made it possible for the newly privatized MWSS to achieve the following objectives:

(i) increase operational efficiency;

(ii) raise financial resources to finance capital expenditure programs and service expansion; and

(iii) minimize the impact of tariffs on the consuming public.

The type of contractual agreement entered into by the Philippine Government and the service providers (MWCI and MWSI) is referred to as a concession. Under such contractual arrangement, the private operators are given full responsibility of operating, maintaining and managing the water supply and sewerage systems in their respective zones. These include the operation and maintenance of all treatment and distribution facilities as well as undertaking capital investment programs, as necessary, to improve and expand water supply and sewerage services within the agreed upon performance standards and coverage targets.

Originally envisioned as a 25-year concession arrangement (1997–2022), the contract was extended to 2037 by the Department of Finance (DOF) in 2009 to allow the concessionaires to accelerate investments in the wastewater sector in compliance with the Supreme Court mandamus of cleaning up the Manila Bay.

The entire MWSS service area was divided into two zones: the east and west zones. The concession for the east zone was awarded to MWCI, while MWSI was awarded the west zone. The decision to divide the metropolis into two distinct zones is aimed to promote competition between the two private service providers for more effective regulation.

According to the concession agreement, the concessionaires have the following obligations:

(i) service expansion of water supply, sewerage and sanitation to include the marginalized sectors of society;
(ii) provision of a continuous supply of water with the right operating pressure; and
(iii) ensure compliance with national health and environmental standards on drinking water quality, wastewater discharge, and industrial effluents.

Regulatory Office (RO)

A residual MWSS Corporate Office is retained to facilitate the exercise by the concessionaires of its agency powers, carry out accounting and notification functions, administer domestic and foreign loans related to existing projects, as well as manage and dispose retained assets and other big-ticket water supply expansion projects. To ensure that the provisions of the concession agreement between the government and the concessionaires are enforced, a Regulatory Office (RO) was established. With the objective of balancing the interests of the consuming public vis-a-vis protecting the business interests of the private entities through full cost recovery, the

RO was created to monitor and enforce compliance by the concessionaires of their contractual obligations under the concession agreement.

Key Performance Indicators-Business Efficiency Measures (KPI-BEM)

A monitoring system was put in place, collectively referred to as Key Performance Indicators-Business Efficiency Measures (KPI-BEM). Table five shows the parameters comprising the KPI-BEM. The monitoring system provides concrete measures with which the concessionaires are checked against defined service standards. The tool also serves as basis for the allowance (or otherwise) of rate adjustments in each rate rebasing exercise, which is conducted every five years Local Government Unit (LGU) Citywide Septage Management Programme.

In the case of Dumaguete City, its septage management program was borne out of the collaboration between the city government and the water district. Touted as the country's first LGU-financed, citywide septage management program, the city government entered and signed a Memorandum of Agreement (MOA) with the DCWD in 2009. Among the salient features of the MOA include: (i) equal sharing of capital and operating costs as well as income earned between the city government and DCWD; and (ii) clear delineation of duties and responsibilities between the project partners. The city government shall be in charge of operating and maintaining the septage treatment plant, which includes treatment, disposal, and reuse of sludge. DCWD, on the other hand, shall be responsible for collecting and transporting septage to the treatment plant through the procurement of vacuum trucks and collection of septage user fees, as well as maintaining the financial records.

The City Septage Management Authority (CSMA) shall manage the city's septage management program. Composed of representatives from the city government, selected non-government organization (NGO), DCWD, and technical advisers (as the need arises), the CSMA has the following functions:

(i) Conduct of survey on the actual number of septic tanks;

(ii) Inspection of the construction of septic tanks;

(iii) Issuance of the certificates of compliance;

(iv) Conduct of education and information campaigns on septage management;

(v) Supervision of the operation of the septage treatment plant; and

(vi) Conduct of the day-to-day operations of the septage facility.

MALAYSIA

WATER SECTOR REFORMS

With the passage of the Sewerage Services Act (SSA) in 1993, which federalized nationwide sewerage assets and transferred them to IWK for operation, maintenance and development, Malaysia made a consequential step forward for the development of sewerage services and the improvement of sanitation conditions and services. The Act provided the fundamental policies for regular desludging and required septic tank owners or users to properly operate and maintain them. Nonetheless, it was the responsibility of IWK to conduct scheduled desludging and ensure that ISTs are desludged every 2 years.

At the start of IWK's work as a national concessionaire in 1994, sewerage charges for individuals and businesses were imposed for services rendered. However, this has triggered complaints and unrest from the populace, prompting IWK to reduce the tariff at a level that was too low to cover operational expenditures. As the company was heading for bankruptcy with an estimated debt of RM700 million ($227 million), the Federal Government took control of IWK in 2000. IWK became a government-owned company under the Ministry of Finance.

In 2006, another important reform of the water sector was made with the passage of the Water Service Industry Act (WSIA) and the National Water Services Commission (SPAN) Act. WSIA outlines the roles, functions and scope of work to be undertaken by SPAN; while the SPAN Act covers economic, technical, and social regulations, as well as the protection of consumer interests. The WSIA widely restructured the water sector by facilitating the merger of water and sanitation services under the same operator in each state.

Nevertheless, the general application of existing laws on environmental quality, land matters and existing state powers over the water resource remain unchanged (i.e., declaration and regulation of water resources, water catchment areas, and river basins). In this system, the performance of water and wastewater operators is monitored according to key performance indicators defined by SPAN.

For septage management, the WSIA provided the legal basis for the transfer of responsibility of desludging and maintenance of CSTs and ISTs from IWK to the individual owners and residents of each locality. This means that the owners of establishments need to engage the services of IWK (service licensee) or a licence permit holder – both regulated by SPAN – to operate, maintain, and desludge their respective ISTs or CSTs. This policy has been put in place in response to the gradual refusal of septic tank owners to avail of desludging services and the charges associated with it.

Scheduled desludging would no longer be provided by IWK except for government offices, while desludging services for the public are by demand only. This resulted in a noticeable drop in the number of desludging activities in 2008.

In addition, desludging services for septic tanks are conducted at a much longer interval (2–3 years) and penalties for noncompliance are imposed under the new arrangement.

Fines of up to RM50,000 ($16,200) have been enforced, which is quite expensive compared to the usual monthly tariff of RM6 ($2.00) for desludging.

Private developers are still allowed to install small-scale sewerage facilities and septic tanks for new buildings. CSTs fall under the same category as ISTs and are not systematically managed by IWK. Despite the efforts of IWK to gradually take over private STPs for operation and maintenance (O&M), many are still managed by private developers or private contractors.

STAKEHOLDER PARTICIPATION

To foster community participation in septage management, engaging the community through a stakeholder-driven, bottom-up planning process is shown to be effective. Establishing institutional linkages and close coordination among relevant stakeholders provide the venue for collective and collaborative learning. This serves as a platform to engage stakeholders in identifying emerging challenges and needs, and agree on realistic and workable solutions, without unnecessarily compromising one's needs over the other.

Extensive information and awareness campaigns are conducted either through the efforts of LGUs, private operators or service providers, or both, to ensure that all relevant stakeholders attain a better appreciation and understanding on the urgency of the problem as well as the long-term challenges septage management presents.

A case in point would be the implementation of the septage management program in Dumaguete City, where a technical working group (TWG) was specifically established to conduct decision-making and promotions outreach programs targeting awareness-raising and generating buy-in for the new desludging fee. Activities included information dissemination using various media options, launching of sanitation events in schools, and discussion of program benefits during regular city-run meetings.

Evidence points to the fact that promotional activities helped generate the willingness to participate in the program among the residents, which covers the payment of an additional fee for septage management on top of their existing water bills. When the promotional campaigns ceased in 2011, there was a significant decrease in community participation, dropping to as low as 40 percent.

Similarly, in the case of Malaysia, emphasis is put forth in building strong communication and dialogue with stakeholders. This is in recognition of the value of such undertaking in changing people's perception and mindset particularly on the importance of proper sanitation. Such undertaking is also significant in enhancing the willingness to pay for sanitation services by showing how the associated charges are used to improve the living standards of the stakeholders and the environment they live in. Efforts to disseminate information on the activities of IWK to relevant stakeholders include printing of annual reports that detail the company's corporate activities and performance within its area of operation. Likewise, use of every available medium (e.g., bulletins, internet, seminars, radio, and public cable television programs, etc.) is maximized by IWK to get as much coverage and information farmed out as possible.

CAPITAL FINANCING

The investments made by the Metro Manila concessionaires are financed either through debt, equity (issuance of bonds for the case of MWCI), and retained earnings. In the case of Dumaguete City, the city government appropriated its own funds to facilitate the site development and eventual construction of the septage treatment facility in its area. On the other hand, the city government's partner, DCWD, obtained a loan from LWUA to provide additional funds for the construction of the said treatment facility as well as procure the vacuum trucks for the collection and transport of septage.

In Malaysia, investments in the sanitation sector come from three primary sources:

(i) the government, which provides funding investments to build new systems and treatment plants or upgrade and expand existing systems, as identified in its five-year National Plans;

(ii) IWK, which provides funds particularly for the refurbishing and upgrading of existing systems; and

(iii) private developers, which are responsible for building ISTs, sewers and STPs using their own resources, prior to the handover of these facilities to IWK for O&M.

Construction of centralized and/or regional sludge and public sewage treatment facilities is fully subsidized by the Federal Government; while SSD controls the planning and construction aspects. Additional funding for the construction of modern centralized mechanized treatment plants has been provided through ODA. Dependence on funds from international funding agencies, however, is steadily being reduced in light of the improving economy of Malaysia. Operation and maintenance cost financing.

The concession agreement was crafted to ensure full cost recovery for the concessionaires, with an allowance for cross subsidization between water and sewerage and/or sanitation services. Capital investments for operational efficiency and service expansion as well as O&M costs can be recovered through a tariff mechanism.

Likewise, the concession agreement allows for revisiting of performance standards and targets, review of concessionaires' business plans, and renegotiation of tariffs every 5 years during the rate rebasing exercise.

Future expenditures relative to wastewater collection, treatment, and disposal have already been factored in during the previous rate rebasing exercise. The projected tariffs are expected to already cover both water supply and wastewater services offered in terms of O&M.

For Dumaguete City's case, a user fee is charged to consumers in lieu of septage management services being offered. With a user fee of P2.00 ($0.05) per cubic meter (m3) of water consumed, the city expects to cover both capital and operating expenses, as well as generate funds to finance other developmental undertakings in the area. These may include the construction of a new health center and scholarship programs to poor but deserving college students.

Based on the income statement provided by the city government for budget year 2012, the septage management program netted a total income of about P15.4 million ($0.39 million), with the bulk coming from the imposed septage user fee – P14.7 million ($0.37 million).42 Actual O&M expenses were estimated to be about

P11.2 million ($0.28 million) covering salaries, fuel, taxes, supplies, etc. Net income, which is to be equally divided between the city government and DCWD, amounted to P4.1 million ($0.10 million), with the share of the local government set aside for environmental programs and projects.

For Malaysia, although the budget for O&M has been augmented gradually to reach RM553 million ($179 million) in 2011 [from RM455 million ($147 million) in 2008 and RM494 million ($160 million) in 2010)], operating costs have consistently increased at a much faster pace. The continuous expansion of operational coverage and takeover of unprofitable plants or small plants with additional operating costs are the significant contributory factors impeding efforts to cut down on operating costs. Another major issue concerns the implementation of tariffs, where the fees collected are insufficient to achieve full cost recovery.

With IWK's nationalization in 2000, the payment rate for sewerage charges and desludging saw a considerable increase. With the enactment of WSIA, the restructuring of the water industry facilitated the establishment of stronger regulation (imposition of penalties for non-compliance) as well as addressed areas such as system management efficiency and financing issues. Under said legislation, all the water infrastructure assets (and associated borrowings) are transferred to the government. It also mandated service providers of both water supply and sewerage and/or sanitation services to focus solely on the O&M of systems and facilities and how efficiency can be further enhanced.

For desludging activities, all O&M costs are to be borne by the house owner and/or tenant through charges made by IWK or other authorized desludging operators. The current tariff imposed is usually RM6 ($2.00) monthly that is too low to cover O&M associated costs given that no subsidy from the government is provided.

For the sewerage charge, the proposed new tariff is around RM230 ($74) for 2 m3, covering O&M costs and would most likely be implemented after the conduct of general elections and extensive consultations with all the relevant stakeholders.

TARIFF SETTING, REGULATION, AND SUBSIDIES

As of December 2012, all customer types (residential, commercial, and industrial) in Metro Manila pay a 20 percent environmental charge from the basic water charge. For MWSI, a sewerage charge is levied (as high as 20 percent of the basic water charge) on commercial and industrial customers who are currently connected to sewer lines. MWCI, meanwhile, is pegged at 30 percent of the basic water charge.

Although both concessionaires are expected to build, operate and maintain septage treatment plants, and own a fleet of desludging trucks, as part of their program expansion for sewerage and sanitation, both operators carry out actual desludging operations differently. For the case of MWCI, the company procures the services of local firms to perform the desludging of septic tanks within their respective service areas, with their role limited to performing routine checks to verify if targets and schedules are met and in accordance with all necessary procedures. For MWSI, a special team from the company's pool of personnel carries out the desludging activities (coordination, scheduling, and desludging).

In Dumaguete City, the septage user fee was computed based on an estimated capital and projected operating expense of the septage system, with no subsidies extended to the program. Said amount was approved by the City Council as part of the 2006 septage ordinance on the assumption that the septage system would be fully owned and operated by the city government. Approval on the imposition of the new water rates, inclusive of the septage user fee, was subsequently applied for by DCWD and granted by LWUA.

Comparing the city-imposed user septage fee with that of prevailing commercial rates of private desludgers, for an average monthly household water consumption of 15 m3, the estimated total user fee in 3–5 years (regular desludging schedule) ranges from P1,080 ($27) to P1,800 ($45). For private desludgers, rates vary from P3,000 ($75) to P10,000 ($250) for residential customers, and more than P10,000 for commercial ones. Clearly, residents are better off paying the city-imposed septage user fee considering that aside from being considerably more affordable, services provided include both collection and treatment of septage; whereas private sludgers offer only septage collection.

For Malaysia, the tariffs for the desludging of septic tanks located within IWK's service area vary from RM2 ($0.65) to RM6 ($2.00) per house per month. The cheapest tariff is accorded to low-income households with annual revenue of less than RM600 ($195), as well as certain categories of government quarters. Under this system, septic tank owners are required to pay their bill every 6 months, similar to that of households connected to the sewerage system. For industrial customers, the charged tariff is set at RM2 ($0.65) per person per month.

For desludging of septic tanks located outside IWK's service area and pour-flush users located within and outside IWK's service area, responsive desludging is provided. Advance payment is required before the service. Different tariffs are applied depending on the size of ISTs, CSTs, and private STPs. For residential pour-flush users, a unique tariff is imposed–RM48 ($15.53) per 2.5 m3. IWK conducts responsive desludging within 48 hours after the request has been made.

Public awareness and involvement. Prior to the scheduled desludging by barangay in its business area, MWCI, through its management teams, typically holds an event within the barangay to inform residents about the service being offered. Sanitation officers establish close coordination with barangay officials in conducting the survey of the target area and organize house-to-house campaign of said service. The resulting job order is then forwarded to the desludging contractor, who then coordinates their schedule with the target barangay.

On the other hand, MWSI, in implementing its desludging program, coordinates with different barangays and subdivisions to select prospective program areas for massive desludging. A community briefing is undertaken prior to the actual desludging to provide information on the services being provided to the customers. A survey is then conducted in the prospective areas to determine the number of interested customers. Activity scheduling and job orders are then accomplished before the in-house Septage Management Team of the company carries out actual desludging operations.

However, availment rate for the desludging services offered by the concessionaires is rather low (estimated to be around 50 percent only). Factors such as the inconvenience experienced by the public as well as the inaccessibility of the septic tanks contribute significantly to the lack of customer interest in such activity. Such scenario eventually leads to a higher incidence of 'non-programmed' (emergency) desludging call-outs, which, despite the customer paying an additional fee for such service, is highly inefficient, as septage operators would need to divert trucks from other scheduled routes and areas.

In order to create and foster the enabling environment necessary to stimulate not only awareness but also active involvement of the populace in sound sanitation practices, the local government administrators were engaged. As in the case of Marikina City, in addition to carrying out a promotional campaign, a sanitation ordinance was passed requiring the mandatory desludging of septic tanks within the city with the imposition of hefty fines for violators.47 Fostering community pride as a strong motivator to engage stakeholder participation and drive behavioral change coupled with the strict enforcement of regulations, have proven effective in terms of jacking-up availment rates to as high as 95 percent.

Similarly, in Dumaguete City, prior to the development of the city's septage management program, a septage ordinance was drafted to provide the legal framework for such undertaking. Through the technical assistance extended by the United States Agency for International Development's (USAID) Local Initiatives for Affordable Wastewater Treatment (LINAW) program, a TWG was established to draft said legal instrument. The TWG was composed of representatives from the city government offices, members of the Environment Committee of the City Council, and the private sector.

Prior to adoption by the City Council of said ordinance, an intensive social marketing and information campaign was carried out involving discussions with village officials, consultations with media, as well as the conduct of public hearings to ensure public awareness and generate support and interest from relevant stakeholders.

In Malaysia, efforts to educate the public and generate awareness on the importance of sewerage and/or sanitation services are carried out through various activities. These include:

(i) provision of an educational programme targeting students of secondary schools, higher learning institutions and the National Service Training Programme (PLKN);

(ii) conduct of an aggressive information dissemination through mass media, educational trips, etc.; and

(iii) conduct of desludging carnivals specifically for areas where septage collection demand and willingness-to-pay for desludging services are low.

IMPACTS ON THE POOR

A flagship program of MWCI, the 'Tubig Para sa Barangay' (TPSB) or Water for Low- Income Communities, offers water services for considerably lower costs and less stringent requirements to the residents of marginalized communities. Since the first TPSB in 1998, more than 1.7 million people from low-income groups have benefitted from this programme.

Aside from having access to safe water supply, poor communities connected with MWCI are automatically entitled to desludging services free of charge. Under the septage tariff mechanism being implemented in Dumaguete City, the flat fee imposed for every m3 of water consumed is beneficial particularly for the marginalized sector of society. Residents from the poorer sections of the city, who, more often than not, consumes less water, end up paying less for the sanitation services availed. Particularly for those consuming 10 m3 or less, the fee collected is only P20 (about $0.50) per month.

Aside from its impact on the poor, the existing tariff structure has a strong incentivizing effect in promoting water conservation considering the direct correlation between water consumption and the impact on the user fees paid by the consumers.

Likewise, a portion of the septage user fees collected is used to fund the construction of communal sanitation facilities for indigent households, who have no access to sanitation infrastructure and facilities (i.e., toilets).

In Malaysia's case, a special tariff for desludging is applied to low-income households with annual revenue of less than RM600 ($195). In addition, IWK also conducts free desludging services to all non-profitable (tax-exempted) organizations, such as religious centers and welfare homes.

SUSTAINABILITY FOR SUCCESS

Metro Manila Concessions

Aside from drastically improving on sanitation-related statistics in the metropolis reckoned from the start of water and wastewater services privatization in 1997, the two concessionaires have already crafted a roadmap to achieve the ambitious goal of providing 100 percent sewerage coverage in the entire Metro Manila by the end of their concession period in 2037. The total estimated capital investment required is around $3.4 billion.

For a government with scarce resources to fund various developmental undertakings, engaging the private sector in the provision of public services has proven to be a prudent move considering the massive capital expenditure requirement to achieve full sewerage and sanitation coverage for Metro Manila. The efficiency gains achieved in terms of fast tracking sewerage and sanitation services have resulted not only in improving the quality of life for residents, but also provided a substantial contribution in terms of the efforts put forth in enhancing environmental sustainability in the region.

Dumaguete City

With the successful operation of the city's septage management program, the undertaking created the desired momentum for other LGUs to replicate the system within their own localities. Local administrators who have visited the city's septage system (Baliuag, Bulacan; Isabela, Basilan; Lucena, Quezon Province; Metro Cebu and Davao City) are encouraged to pursue their own septage facilities, noting the advantages from both an environmental and economic point of view. Likewise, it has spurred adjacent LGUs to forge partnerships with the government of Dumaguete City to utilize the city's septage facility for their local septage treatment needs. This is particularly of significant importance when considering the lofty goal of establishing septage management systems for all LGUs by 2020, as embodied in the NSSMP.

The programme has also facilitated the regulation of private desludging service providers. While before, private operators would ply their business without permit and indiscriminately dispose septage. Under the current set-up, permits to operate are issued by DENR to private desludging companies with an explicit condition that collected septage would be discharged to the city's septage treatment plant. This has been the major contributory factor leading to the decrease in cases of illegal disposal of septage in the city.

MALAYSIA

The Malaysian government's strong commitment to modernize its country and infrastructure facilitated the implementation of sector reforms in the water industry. Clear-cut regulatory guidelines as well as the sustained infusion of government funding are seen as the major factors in transforming the country's sewerage and sanitation sectors. With IWK's nationalization, investments for the sector saw a dramatic increase, with majority of the funds infused by MOF and the Ministry of Energy, Green Technology and Water. Estimates reveal that, for the period from 2001 to 2011, the Ministry of Energy, Green Technology and Water expended a total of RM4.48 billion ($1.5 billion), with the MOF contributing between RM406 million ($132 million) and RM736 million ($239 million).

Likewise, the engagement of the private sector has largely contributed to the expeditious provision of wastewater and/or sanitation facilities and services nationwide, resulting in substantial health and environmental benefits for its populace. In addition to beefing-up sewerage and sanitation infrastructure compliant with government-approved regulations, IWK has also standardized its operating procedures in sludge collection to improve operational efficiency with the use of a computerized database (households connected to a septic tank) and a geographical information system (GIS)-based vehicle tracking system.

Likewise, the conduct of training programmes and courses for capacity development has been organized and institutionalized in IWK to further enhance the competencies of its workforce. The conduct of a continuous and sustained information, education, and communication (IEC) campaign is still being carried out by IWK involving all relevant stakeholders. The IEC campaign helps to further increase the willingness to pay among consumers for desludging or sewerage charges and to develop people's understanding on the value of good sanitation.

To date, Malaysia holds the distinction of being one of the select countries in the region that provides water, sanitation, and wastewater services to almost all its populace. With widespread wastewater treatment, there has been a drastic reduction in cases related to waterborne diseases as well as the noticeable improvement in river quality in the country.

NO "ONE-SIZE-FITS-ALL"

The cases presented in this study confirm that there are more ways to skin a cat in order to come up with an efficient sanitation solution that will be sustainable. This is just one of the lessons learned from the Philippines' and Malaysia's septage management programmes.

An appropriate sanitation solution tailor fit to the locality. There is no "one-size-fits-all" sanitation solution. Finding a workable and most responsive solution depends on a host of factors, which may differ from one local setting to another. These determinants could be based on:

(i) government needs and priorities,
(ii) site conditions (land availability, population density, and topography),
(iii) prevailing regulatory environment,
(iv) availability of funding and technological options available, and
(v) life-cycle costs of technologies.

As seen from the examples cited in this case study, the problem associated with septage management can be dealt with successfully under various implementation arrangements (e.g., concessions, joint venture, and O&M contract). The examples and experiences highlighted the importance of having a governance framework where priorities in the sanitation subsector have the following qualities:

(i) clearly defined;
(ii) relevant stakeholders with their roles and responsibilities clearly identified and delineated; and
(iii) a robust regulatory regime in place to ensure that public interest is protected through the provision of quality services.

Likewise, in an ideal regulatory environment, service providers are allowed to recover costs incurred through a tariff mechanism. Controls are implemented to promote consistency and accountability without necessarily curtailing flexibility and innovation of the service providers.

In addition, in cases where a government cannot sufficiently allocate funds to meet the capital requirements of establishing sanitation facilities and systems given their capital-intensive nature, forging partnerships [e.g, city government and water district, public-private partnerships (PPPs)] should be explored as a means to address the financing deficiency hampering delivery of a public good. For PPPs in particular, engaging the private sector in the provision of public goods and services does not, in any way, relieve the government of its duty of ensuring the best interests of the public. Institutional and policy reforms must still be aggressively pursued in addressing issues such as public expenditure deficits, structural limitations in areas of regulation, and corruption. This is to assure the public that the government is willing and able to perform its best in safeguarding public welfare.

It is also emphasized that the use of a particular technology for septage treatment and disposal should be complemented with the necessary enabling instruments to ensure program sustainability in the long-term.

Sanitation Options Incorporating Phased Development Strategy

A stepwise strategy in scaling-up investments in the sanitation subsector is a prudent approach in addressing the challenge of wastewater management. A stepwise approach enables government and/or service providers to identify measures, which are implementable given a specific timeline as well as adaptive to the prevailing social and economic conditions of the area. Similarly, a phased approach affords the implementing agencies to commit available resources (e.g., funding and manpower) to achieve the targets. It also establishes key performance indicators to quantitatively measure the progress (or otherwise) of any undertaking. Both IWK and the Metro Manila concessionaires are currently applying said strategy. IWK utilizes existing sewage treatment facilities with excess capacities to handle collected sludge as interim measures before pursuing the construction of mechanized sludge treatment facilities as part of its long-term strategy. The Metro Manila concessionaires, on the other hand, are currently implementing septage management and the use of combined sewer-drainage systems to handle wastewater prior to shifting toward the construction of separate sewer systems for the entire metropolis.

Enabling Conditions, Instruments, and a Robust Regulatory Environment that Lead to Success

The enactment of pertinent laws (Water Crisis Act, Clean Water Act, WSIA and SPAN Act) and other legal instruments (e.g., local ordinances, mandamus from the Supreme Court) provided the impetus needed for government to move forward with its agenda for the development of the sanitation subsector. Said instrumentalities laid the groundwork for which regulatory regimes were established where the rules, regulations and standards are identified for compliance (with corresponding penalties for non-compliance) and the administrative apparatus enforcing the rules and sanctions is created.

In particular, these enabling instruments helped initiatives in septage management gain traction both at the national and local levels. These instrumentalities helped ensure: (i) compliance to standards (e.g., conduct of scheduled desludging with imposition of penalties for violators); (ii) flow of investments (e.g., establishment of partnerships with the private sector and/or government entities or through government appropriations); and (iii) regulation of private service providers (e.g., licensing of private desludgers and standardization of design of sanitation equipment and systems to ensure quality and performance of the same).

It cannot be overemphasized that strong political will and commitment of both national and local administrators are crucial elements in not only enforcing regulations and compliance but also in ensuring that financial support is sustained. This also ensures and that cost recovery mechanisms are implemented and insulated from political intrusion.

Conduct of Aggressive Social Marketing and Public Awareness Campaigns

In implementing septage management programs, it is imperative for both the government and service providers to engage all stakeholders and enhance their awareness and understanding of the potential risks (e.g., health, environmental, and economic) brought about by poor sanitation habits. Enhanced public awareness helps facilitate behavior change within the community as well as assist the same in making informed decisions in terms of the technological options to adopt, the acceptable amount of fee to impose, etc.

Willingness-to-pay and participate in any sanitation program by the community hinges on the level and extent of understanding and appreciation of the populace on said undertaking. Public awareness campaigns and consultations likewise open up the communication lines between the public and the government and/or service provider to solicit feedback from the community. These campaigns also help gauge public sensitivity on issues such as the imposition of septage user fees. Consultations also provide a platform to generate consensus on the most responsive sanitation solution acceptable and tailor-fit to the local needs of the community. Engaging the stakeholders to actively participate in a local septage management program also cultivates their sense of ownership on said activity, which, hopefully, would translate to them extending their full support (e.g., acceptance of user fees) toward successful implementation of the undertaking.

IEC campaigns are at the forefront of awareness-building activities. These include engaging the various forms of media (e.g., television, radio, internet, and print), scaling up social media and school activities, engaging civil society organizations (CSOs) to do advocacy campaigns, and the conduct of public hearings and consultations with targeted constituents.

Aside from making use of traditional media options to reach out to the public, government and service providers are encouraged to use innovative methods in carrying out said activity. Citing the case of Dumaguete City, it made use of an effective approach to promotions by following the USAID 10-Step Promotion Program Toolkit (www.waterlinks.org/promotion), which included forming a promotions team, doing audience research, developing a plan, and pretesting information materials.

Pro-Poor Policy to Facilitate Access to Sanitation

In as much as the ultimate goal of the water resources sector is to provide access to safe water to all, including those marginalized in society, the same approach should likewise be adopted for the sanitation subsector. Subsidies and pro-poor financing mechanisms should be explored to entice those living below the poverty line to avail of sanitation services considering that the same are the most vulnerable to the potential health and environmental risks associated with poor sanitation practices. These mechanisms include reduced tariffs and/or flat rates for low-income households, as well as free desludging services to non-profitable (tax-exempted) organizations such as religious centers and welfare homes.

Institutional Strengthening and Capacity Development Activities

The demand for more sanitation and/or environmental experts is more pronounced now given the expected increase of volume of wastewater resulting from population growth and rapid urbanization. There has to be a concerted effort from the government, private sector, and learning institutions to develop the critical mass of professionals to be more responsive to the growing sanitation needs of society. Curriculums, training programs, and capacity building activities should not only be continuously updated to be in tune with the latest information and technologies available. These should also be made available to the lowest levels of governance to ensure that people on the ground (those involved in project and/or program implementation) are sufficiently equipped with sound and updated engineering practices, theories, and technologies to perform their duties competently.

Sustainable Biosolids Reuse

Extensive research and development (R&D) activities are needed to find alternative uses for the sludge generated as well as enhance its value. Research activities can be done through collaborative arrangements with learning institutions, focusing on ensuring the high quality and consistency of the biosolids produced. Likewise, government intervention can be sought to provide incentives and develop markets promoting the use of biosolids for agricultural productivity.

While biosolids are currently being used as soil conditioners in both countries, more so in the Philippines, promotional activities should be undertaken to target farmers and generate their interest to pay for and use them in their farming activities.

Source: wastewaterinfo.asia: Clean Leaning Up the Business of Septage Management.

SEPTAGE MANAGEMENT IN METRO MANILA

Metro Manila, with a population of 12 million population is comparable to that of Kolkatta. Manila has two water utilities. These utilities also provide sanitation related services. In the city's East Zone, Manila Water Company, Inc. (MWCI) provides water and sanitation services for 5.6 million people. It has initiated septage management projects to provide regular septic tank desludging services. Although the original MWCI concession planned to phase out the use of septic tanks in favor of centralized sewerage systems, this plan proved too difficult due to low willingness of consumer to pay for sewerage services and lack of available land for treatment facilities. Instead, MWCI has shifted its emphasis towards septage management and smaller, localized treatment plants. At present, MWCI maintains a fleet of over 90 vacuum trucks. Since 2005, MWCI has desludged more than 400,000 septic tanks and aims to desludge all tanks in its service area on a rotating, five-to-seven-year cycle. MWCI has three dedicated septage treatment facilities with a total treatment capacity of over 1,540 cubic meters per day. Though a good start, the current total treatment volume provides for only five percent of the capacity required if all household tanks in Metro Manila were to be regularly desludged.

Institutional and Regulatory Framework for Faecal Sludge Management (FSM): Paurashavas, Bangladesh

Proper Design and Construction of Sanitation Facilities and Disposal of Sewage/Wastewater/ Garbage

Although the term "faecal sludge" is not specifically mentioned in the Paurashava Act 2009 (primarily because this term was not widely used at that time), it is clear that the responsibility of management of "faecal sludge" [referred to in the Paurashava Act as "refuse" accumulated in "public toilets, urinals, drains and all buildings and land"] lies with the Municipality.

New Construction

(1) While approving design of buildings, the Paurashava shall check the design of the sanitation facilities (e.g., septic tank, pit latrine), as well as its location/layout (to make sure that it is accessible for manual/mechanical desludging)

(2) The provisions of Bangladesh National Building Code shall be followed for checking design of septic tank system (i.e., septic tank and soakage pit). For pit latrines, where conditions (e.g., availability of adequate land) permit, the Paurashava shall promote use of twin off-set pit pour-flush toilets (or other technologies) that provide a long-term solution to the faecal sludge management problem.

(3) LGD/ Paurashava shall formulate necessary rules/ regulations/ by-laws for preventing misuse of the provision related to "automatic approval of building application" (after expiry of 60 days from the date of registration of approval).

(4) In accordance with Clauses 95 and 96 of Paurashava Act 2009, the Paurashava may engage the private sector/non-government sector (e.g., outsourcing) in carrying out activity (1) above (i.e., checking design, layout of sanitation facilities).

Existing/ Completed Buildings

(5) While inspecting a building during or after completion of its construction/ reconstruction, the Paurashava shall check that the sanitation facilities have been sited and constructed according to the approved design. In case of non-compliance, the Paurashava shall instruct the owner to re-construct the sanitation facilities following the approved design.

(6) In accordance with the provisions of Paurashava Act 2009, the Paurashava shall serve notice to owners of premises where there is no sanitation facility, or inadequate sanitation facility, or sanitation facility in inappropriate locations to arrange proper sanitation facilities or remove inappropriate sanitation facilities.

(7) In accordance with the Paurashava Act 2009, the Paurashava may engage the private sector/non-government sector (e.g., outsourcing) in carrying out inspection of existing/completed buildings for assessment of sanitation facilities.

Disposal of Sewage/ Wastewater/Garbage

(8) The Paurashava shall carry out inspection and make sure that domestic sewage/ wastewater, and discharge from house-drain are not connected to storm sewer/drain or irrigation canal, and that "refuse" (which included fecal sludge) is not thrown/disposed or stored on street or open place (not designated for disposal of "refuse"); these activities are treated as punishable offence.

(9) The Paurashava shall execute punishment for such offences according to the Paurashava Act 2009. The Paurashava shall ask owners of buildings/premises, that are in such violation, to discharge domestic sewage/ wastewater into a septic tank system (consisting of adequately designed septic tank and soakage pit); the effluent from septic tank system (i.e., overflow, if any) may be discharged into storm drains/sewers. Until treatment facility for faecal sludge are built, emptied fecal sludge shall be disposed in a land/area designated by the Paurashava by digging pits/trenches in the ground, and covering the pits/trenches with soil after it is filled with sludge.

(10) In accordance with the Paurashava Act 2009, the Paurashava may engage the private sector/non-government organization (e.g., outsourcing) in carrying out inspection/ survey for identifying illegal practices of sewage/ wastewater/ "garbage" disposal, as service procurement.

(11) The LGD/Paurashava shall work with the Ministry of Railways and the Ministry of Shipping to device appropriate plans/programs to make sure that fecal matters/sludge from trains and water vessels are not discharged directly into the environment.

Faecal Sludge Collection and Transport

(1) The Paurashava shall be responsible for proper execution of the entire FSM service chain, including collection (emptying) and transportation. The Paurashava shall carry out and/or oversee the collection (emptying) and transportation, making sure that these operations are carried out in a hygienic manner without adversely affecting health and safety of emptiers, the public and the environment.

(2) The pit emptying service shall include "transportation of the collected fecal sludge to the designated site for treatment and disposal". The Paurashava shall make sure that the collected fecal sludge is transported to the designated site(s) for treatment and

disposal, and that the collected fecal sludge is never disposed in open space or water bodies or storm drains or sewers.

(3) The Paurashava shall execute punishment for unauthorized disposal of collected fecal sludge (e.g., in open space, water bodies, storm sewers/ drains).

(4) In accordance with Paurashava Act 2009, the Paurashava may engage the private sector/non-government organization (e.g., outsourcing) for collection and transportation of fecal sludge from onsite sanitation facilities.

(5) The Paurashava shall introduce and promote mechanical pit emptying (desludging) services for ensuring health and safety of emptiers and protection of the public health and environment. The Paurashava shall make sure that the manual emptier (traditional pit emptier/cleaner) communities are integrated into the modern FSM services through proper training and support, without adversely affecting their income.

(6) The process of pit emptying involves significant hazard, and the Paurashava shall follow/enforce appropriate health and safety guidelines for emptying services. Until such a health and safety guideline is prepared and approved (by the LGD), the Paurashava shall follow available guidelines being practiced/promoted in some Paurashava.

(7) In accordance with the Paurashava Act 2009, the Paurashava may fix fees/charges for collection and transportation of fecal sludge from sanitation facilities. If faecal sludge treatment facilities are operational in the Paurashava and the collected faecal sludge is transported to such facilities for treatment, the Paurashava may consider the entire service chain (i.e., from collection to treatment) while fixing such fees/charges. The Standing Committees on "Tax and Levy" and "Health, Water and Sanitation" shall facilitate fixation of fees/charges for FSM services.

(8) In order to ensure proper and timely emptying of onsite sanitation facilities, the Paurashava shall gradually develop a database of all sanitation facilities within areas of its jurisdiction, along with probable emptying frequency of these facilities. Once the entire FSM service chain (i.e., from collection to treatment/disposal) is in place, this database would be used for efficient and timely emptying of all on-site sanitation facilities. The Paurashava shall also develop a database of households/ institutions availing the FSM (e.g., emptying) services.

Faecal Sludge Treatment, Disposal and End-use

(1) The Paurashava shall be responsible for proper execution of the entire FSM service chain, including faecal sludge treatment, disposal and end-use. The Paurashava shall carry out and/or oversee these operations, making sure that these are carried out in compliance with existing rules and regulations (e.g., with regard to disposal of liquid effluent, and quality of end products such as compost), and without adversely affecting public health and the environment.

(2) Until treatment facility for faecal sludge are built, faecal sludge (e.g., those desludged from onsite sanitation facilities) shall be disposed in a land/area designated by the Paurashava by digging pits/trenches in the ground, and burying the pits/trenches with soil after it is filled with sludge.

(3) The Paurashava may collaborate with the Department of Public Health Engineering (DPHE) and the Local Government Engineering Department (DPHE) in development and O&M of faecal sludge treatment facilities.

(4) In accordance with the Paurashava Act 2009, the Paurashava may engage the private sector/non-government organization (e.g., outsourcing) for treatment and disposal of faecal sludge, and use/marketing of end-products, as service procurement.

(5) The Paurashava may fix fees/charges for treatment of faecal sludge separately, or together with the collection and transportation fees/charges.

(6) The Paurashava shall seek assistance of the Department of Environment (DoE), and the Institute of Epidemiology, Disease and Research (IEDCR) (or any competent/accredited national/international institution) in fulfilling compliance with the existing rules and regulations with regard to installation and operation of fecal sludge treatment facilities.

(7) The Paurashava shall seek assistance of the Department of Agriculture Extension (DAE) under the Ministry of Agriculture with regard to simplifying the procedure for securing license for using/ marketing of compost/ organic fertilizer produced (if any) at fecal sludge treatment facilities.

(8) The Paurashava shall work with the Ministry of Agriculture to ensure safe use of treatment end products (compost/ organic fertilizer) in agriculture, landscaping and other purposes.

"Environmental Police" for Field Compliance

(1) The Ministry of Environment and Forest (MoEF) shall ensure that all relevant environmental laws, regulations and principles are strictly followed by all concerned throughout the FSM service chain.

(2) The MoLGRDC and MoEF, in consultation with all stakeholders shall initiate development of standards/ guidelines for enduse or disposal of treated sludge.

(3) The MoLGRDC in consultation with MoEF, MoHA, Ministry of Law, Justice and Parliamentary Affairs, and other concerned stakeholders shall take initiative to make a legal provision to develop well-trained, skilled contingents of environmental force styled as "Environmental Police" for ensuring field compliance of laws, regulations, safety standards and policy guidelines with provisions of instant penalties to be decided by the ministries concerned.

Capacity Building, Training and Research

(1) The institutions identified, participating institutions for capacity building would provide support to fill the knowledge gaps, technical assistance, training, quality assurance of process and products (e.g., compost) in the FSM service chain.

(2) The Ministry of LGRD&C would take steps for setting up Unit/ Division for FSM in the Paurashavas organogram, for effective delivery of FSM services.

(3) The Ministries and line organizations, research and training institutions, development partners, and I/NGOs would provide support to develop/enhance skills of personnel of Paurashava and other stakeholders, and to fill the knowledge gaps with regard to FSM.

(4) National level research and training organizations would collaborate with relevant international research/ training organizations/ institutions/ universities, I/NGOs and the private sector in capacity building, training and research on FSM. The Ministries of the GoB and the development partners shall support such initiatives.

(5) The LGD of the MoLGRDC shall coordinate, and develop guidelines for capacity building, research and training initiatives on FSM, and facilitate sharing and dissemination of knowledge/ information on FSM among Paurashavas.

Awareness Building

(1) The institutions identified as participating institutions for awareness building to support awareness campaign, promote private sector participation, demonstration of FSM business The relevant Ministries and line organizations would support awareness building campaigns on FSM.

(2) Local, national and international NGOs/CBOs, with support from the Government Ministries, research organizations and development partners shall play the key role in raising public awareness on FSM and facilitating partnership among key stakeholders including the private sector.

(3) The civil society organizations would also work with I/NGOs and research organizations (for support on technical issues) in sensitizing the public on FSM through use of print, electronic and social media.

Technical Assistance and Funding Support

(1) The GoB will increase funding support and provide other assistance (e.g., secring land for construction of treatment facility) for development of FSM infrastructure in the Paurashavas.

(2) Development partners, multilateral or bilateral, may provide technical assistance and funding support to the Paurashavas for establishing FSM services.

(3) The MoLGRDC through its line organizations (DPHE and LGED) would provide technical and other relevant support directly or on project-basis in planning and implementation of FSM service infrastructure (e.g., faecal sludge treatment plant).

(4) The LGD shall take initiative to develop standards/guidelines for emptying, transportation, and treatment of faecal sludge; operation and maintenance (O&M) of faecal sludge treatment plant; disposal of effluent from faecal sludge treatment facilities, quality control/ standardization of treated products/by-products; and protocol for securing license for using/ marketing of compost/ organic fertilizer produced (if any) at faecal sludge treatment facilities.

Cost of FSM Services

Faecal sludge management system involves different activities e.g. emptying, transport, treatment, and disposal and/or end use and therefore there is cost involvement at each step of activities. Some FSM infrastructure, such as treatment plant and vacutugs require considerable investment; therefore support from the Government would be required for these facilities. Other expenses, including emptying and transportation of fecal sludge, and regular operation and maintenance should be supported from fees/charges from service recipients. Paurashavas shall collaborate with the LGD for establishment of major FSM infrastructure (e.g., treatment plant, vacutugs), and develop appropriate "business models" for delivery of FSM services with contribution/ fees/ charges from service recipients in due course.

A Proposition of Fund Flow for FSM Services

Flow of funds from one step to another has to be considered carefully so that the FSM services are sustained. Considering the existing situation of faecal sludge management in Paurashava, and the level of awareness among different stakeholders of the importance of FSM, the fund flow starts from HH/Community/Institution (both public and private), the collection points of faecal sludge. Payment by HH/Community/Institution is divided into two channels – to the Collection and Transportation Operators (CTOs) as septic tank/ pit emptying fee, and to the Paurashava as sanitation tax/charge along with holding tax to cover all other expenses including FS treatment. The emptying fee will be determined based on volumetric pumping rate, and other considerations as my be determined by the Paurashava; sanitation tax/charge can be determined based on water use or more conveniently on flat rate proportionate to holding tax and should be worked out through consultation by the Paurashava, MoLGRDC and concerned stakeholders. This two-channel payment mode will help support the low income people in slums, as in most cases sanitation tax/charge will be subsidized or fully waived and will be covered by government funds to Paurashava to cover FS treatment and other expenses.

An important feature of the above fund flow approach is the direction of the fund transfer to the private operators. Treatment Facilities Operator (TFO) will pay the Collection and Transportation Operator (CTO) a discharge incentive to dump collected sludge at the FS treatment plant. The financial incentive here is used to encourage socially desirable behavior i.e., to encourage sludge collection and discharge at the treatment plant and reduce illegal discharge. With this approach the CTO would only have to recover a portion of the total operating costs from the emptying fee and the remaining portion would be made up by the discharge incentive from the TFO. As a result, the collection service would be more affordable for poorer households, more sludge would be collected, less sludge would be discharged to the environment and the community as a whole would benefit.

TFO will receive funds from the Paurashava, part of the sanitation taxes/charges collected, to cover treatment plant operation and management expenses. The Paurashava will cha/rge fee for permits/ licenses from the CTO, payable annually. TFO may also receive price of end products from private enterprises or NGOs engaged in marketing and selling of the end product.

However, substantial government support will be needed to fill the budget gaps of the Paurashava, particularly to cover some of the major capital expenditures. This financial flow approach is based on present FSM status and expected to have positive changes in the future with the gaps minimized and FSM services turned out as a viable business.

Source: Working Committee formed by the Local Government Division,Ministry of Local Government, Rural Development and Cooperatives; November 2015: Institutional and Regulatory Framework for Fecal Sludge Management (FSM): Paurashavas, Bangladesh.

SEPTAGE MANAGEMENT IN HAIPHONG CITY, VIETNAM

Haiphong city is the 3rd largest city in Vietnam located 200 km from Hanoi City. The Haiphong Sanitation and Sewerage Company (SADCo) operates the sewer network, drainage channels, regulating lakes and tidal gates in the urban centre of Haiphong. Septage management has been the responsibility of Haiphong

SADCo since July 1998. The septic tanks are emptied on a scheduled basis at an interval of three years. For such type of schedule emptying they have divided the cities into regions, where one region is emptied in a year and then they move to the next region in next year. For faster emptying of septic tanks special type of access covers are provided or else they use a special drill so that they do not have to break the septic tank top. For emergency cleaning of septic tanks in other regions help of external agencies is sought for providing. One cycle of emptying has been completed for the entire city. The collected septage is treated at Trang Cat septage treatment facility, where sludge drying bed and composting technology are used for treatment of faecal sludge and the treated compost is used in industrial plants. The citizens are provided free septic tank emptying service once every three years and in lieu of this a tax of around 15 percent of the water bill (as a part of water bill) is levied on the properties.

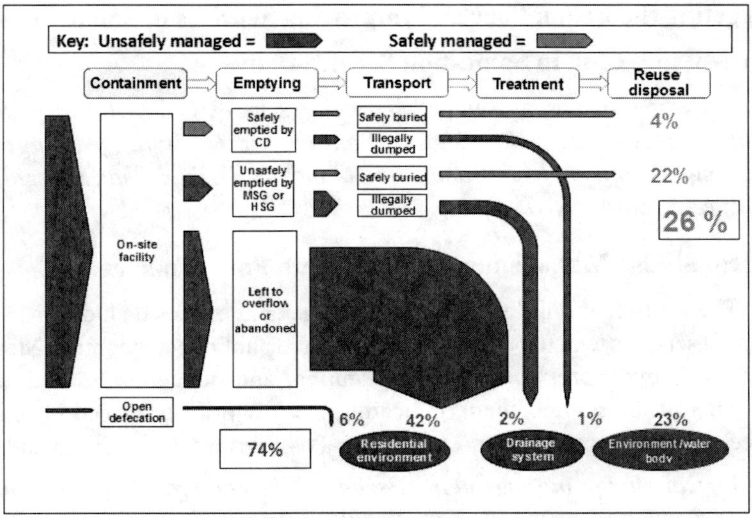

Figure: Faecal Sluge Chain in Faridpur, Bangladesh

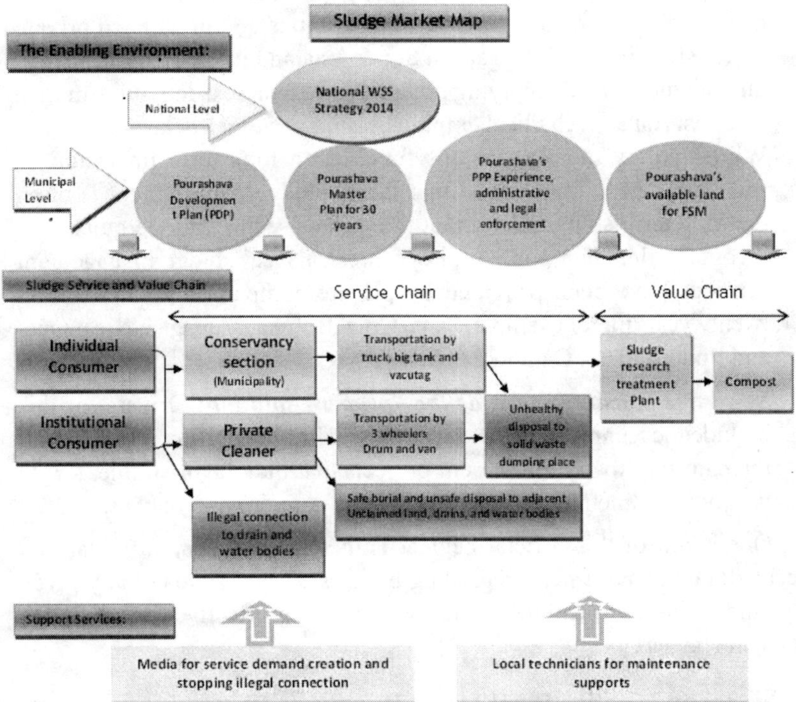

Source: www.practicalaction.org; retrieved on 9-9-2019; Public Private Partnerships for Sustainable Sludge Management Services in Faridpur, Bangladesh;Situation Analysis Report on Faecal Sludge Management in Faridpur Municipality, Bangladesh, June 2014.

Figure: Faecal Sludge MANAgement in Faridpur, Bangladesh

Targeting the Urban Poor and Improving Services in Small Towns

The Missing Link in Sanitation Service Delivery

A Review of Faecal Sludge Management in 12 Cities *(Dumaguete, Palu, Kampala, Manila, Dhaka, Santa Cruz (Bolivia), Managua (Nicaragua), Phnom Penh (Cambodia), Managua, Delhi, Dakar, Senegal);* WSP: April 2014; www.wsp.org

Faecal Sludge Management is Invisible to Policymakers

The study found little systematic management of faecal sludge. Most existing services tend to be informal and outside public sector control. Most cities had low scores for policies, planning, and budgeting around all elements of the service chain, indicating the low priority placed on this aspect of urban sanitation in most countries. Possible reasons for this include:

***Faecal sludge management is seen as a "temporary" or stop-gap solution and primarily for illegal or informal settlements*:** For example, although some city authorities provide limited services with a small fleet of vacuum trucks, in most cities an unregulated private sector steps in to fill the gap. In South Asia and particularly in Africa, unhygienic manual emptying predominates, whereas in Latin America and East Asia, mechanical emptying using vacuum trucks is the norm. Whilst policy mostly remains focused on long-term provision of sewerage, the study showed that faecal sludge management is often the long term solution, and that the private sector may be quicker to recognize this than public policymakers. Faecal sludge management services have been provided by private companies for more than twenty years in, for example, Santa Cruz, Bolivia; Managua, Nicaragua; and Phnom Penh, Cambodia.

***Sewerage is usually seen as the "proper" solution*:** Drivers for this include the technical bias often imparted during engineer training, and the nature of many investment projects that may favor simple, single lumpy investments over ongoing service delivery approaches.

One result of this official neglect is that there is very little data on faecal sludge management, regarding both its current status in any given city, and field-based technical data on delivering effective faecal sludge management services.

Technical and Institutional Issues Requiring Resolution

The data collected and made available by city authorities is weak, often contradictory, and rarely disaggregated in a useful way. However, it is clear that faecal sludge management services are generally highly unsatisfactory. The following significant observations stand out:

- ***Illegal dumping*** by private manual and mechanical pit emptiers into the sea, rivers, wasteland, and landfill sites is common in all but two cities: Dumaguete and Palu. Faecal sludge management services are mostly unregulated, and no specific regulatory framework for these services was encountered.
- The ***quality of household containment is generally inadequate*** and adversely affects owners' ability to have their units emptied. Poor-quality pits are often abandoned unsafely with risks to the environment and public health.

This situation was reported in all but two cities. However, in a few cases where space allows, mostly on the urban fringes rather than in dense slums, the faecal sludge may remain safely buried, with the user covering the pit once it is full.

- There is a ***lack of treatment facilities for faecal sludge***. Usually faecal sludge is dumped into the existing wastewater treatment plant, which may jeopardize sewage treatment. Dedicated sludge treatment facilities exist in only five of the twelve cities.
- Only two cities had any ***mechanism for formal reuse of treated sludge*** (Dumaguete and Manila in the Philippines). However, in neither city is reuse well developed or profitable.
- ***Sludge accumulation rates vary widely***, and it is almost impossible to generate norms that could be used to determine requirements for emptying and transport (in terms of both capacity and the nature of the faecal sludge to be emptied and transported), which in turn has implications for the types of transport and treatment required.

Scorecards and a Typology for City Faecal Sludge Management Services

Based on a review of their faecal sludge management scorecards and faecal waste flow diagrams, the 12 cities were grouped according to the effectiveness of the service delivery framework and the level of service being achieved. Three city types were identified among the 12 case studies:

- ***Poor faecal sludge management***, with no framework for service delivery and almost no services, which could be termed "institutionalized open defecation." These include Managua, Delhi, Phnom Penh, and Dhaka.

- ***Basic fecal sludge management,*** where some of the service delivery framework is in place and there is limited service provision. This category includes Manila and Kampala.
- ***Improving fecal sludge management,*** where most of the framework is in place and services exist, but there is still room for improvement. These include Dumaguete and Palu.

What Else do we Need to Know?

As the challenge of faecal sludge management is generally over-simplified and underestimated, tools to help practitioners make rapid assessments could significantly improve the scale and impact of interventions. This could be achieved by further developing the scorecard, and by systematically assessing the volume of fecal sludge generated and the various pathways it takes from containment to disposal. The faecal waste flow analysis developed here provides a building block for developing the assessments further.

A number of knowledge gaps need to be addressed in order to design effective and sustainable interventions. These include:

(i) The extent and economic value of public health, environmental, and financial benefits arising from effective containment of faecal sludge within the sanitation service chain, from containment to reuse;

(ii) The development of viable market and business models along the faecal sludge management service chain, from toilet construction, to emptying and transport, to reuse;

(iii) The establishment of innovative institutional and management arrangements that allow for clear responsibility for faecal sludge management, and also tie this into the broader local government, utility, and community systems of governance, participation, and feedback;

(iv) How most effectively to fit the range of faecal sludge management technologies to the potential market opportunities, and how to link these with innovative and effective financial arrangements;

(v) The range of regulatory approaches and instruments across the service chain that could best incentivize optimum behaviours by users of faecal sludge management services, service providers, and managers, and effectively link the elements of the service chain together.

ANNEXURE - II

FAECAL SLUDGE MANAGEMENT POLICIES AND STRATEGIES

National Policy on Faecal Sludge and Septage Management (FSSM), 2017

National Declaration on FSSM

MoUD recognizes that the end objectives and corresponding benefits of SBM cannot be achieved without proper management of faecal sludge and septage across the sanitation service chain. Further, it is well understood that sewerage coverage will not meet the complete sanitation needs in all areas, and a strategy which is a combination of OSS and off-site (decentralized and centralised) must co-exist in all cities and must be given equal attention. Over time the relative proportions of coverage by OSS and offsite systems may change but both will need to be managed well. However, the current policies are not explicit enough and also do not provide an outcome-focused direction on this issue. As a first step, MoUD and a host of research and civil society organisations jointly drafted and signed a National Declaration on Faecal sludge and Septage management (FSSM) on 9th September, 2016. Pursuant to the Declaration, this FSSM Policy is being promulgated to address the gaps and provide the necessary directions to diverse stakeholders engaged in provision of FSSM services.

FSSM International Perspective

Globally, around 2.7 billion people are served by onsite sanitation technologies and it is expected that the number is going to get doubled by 2030. On Site Sanitation (OSS) is not only used to fulfill the needs of rural population but also the needs of around one billion people in urban areas. In developing countries OSS, have much wider coverage than sewer systems. For example, in Sub-Saharan Africa, 65-100 percent of sanitation access in urban areas is provided through onsite technologies. Though OSS is used widely the management of FSSM is inadequate and needs critical attention.

- With the fast urbanization the conventional sewerage systems are not likely to keep pace with the growing demand in the developing countries
- Most of the sewerage systems that have been constructed in low-income countries have failed because of high O & M costs.

- For more than a decade, there is a shift in approach among the practitioners globally and they have started to acknowledge and consider decentralized technologies and FSSM services as long-term and sustainable options.

Vision

The vision for Faecal Sludge and Septage Management in urban India is: All Indian cities and towns become totally sanitized, healthy and liveable and ensure sustenance of good sanitation practices with improved Onsite Sanitation Services together with faecal sludge and septage management to achieve optimum public health status and maintain clean environment with special focus on the poor.

Objectives

The key objective of the urban FSSM Policy is to set the context, priorities, and direction for, and to facilitate, nationwide implementation of FSSM services in all ULBs such that safe and sustainable sanitation becomes a reality for all in each and every household, street, town and city. More specifically, the Policy will:

(i) Move India on the path of mainstreaming FSSM in urban India by the year 2019, and ensure that all benefits of wide access to safe sanitation accrue to all citizens across the sanitation value chain with containment, extraction, transportation, treatment, and disposal/re-use of all faecal sludge, septage and other liquid waste and their by-products and end-products.

(ii) Suggest and identify ways and means, including the methods and resources, towards creation of an enabling environment for realising safe and sustainable FSSM in India.

(iii) Define the roles and responsibilities of various government entities and agencies, and of other key stakeholders such as the private sector, civil society organisations and citizens for effective implementation of FSSM services throughout the country.

(iv) Enable and support synergies among relevant Central Government programmes such as SBM, AMRUT and the Smart Cities Mission to realize safe and sustainable sanitation for all at the earliest, possibly by the year 2019.

(v) While not compromising the eventual compliance to the strict environmental discharge standards already set, recognising the constraints in achieving these standards, adopt an appropriate, affordable and incremental approach towards achieving these standards.

(vi) Mitigate gender-based sanitation insecurity directly related to FSSM, reducing the experience of health burdens, structural violence, and promote involvement of both genders in the planning for and design of sanitation infrastructure.

Specific Milestones

(i) Leveraging FSSM to achieve 100 percent access to safe sanitation

- Promoting access for households to safe faecal sludge and septage management facilities (including proper disposal arrangements).
- Promoting community-planned and managed faecal sludge and septage management wherever necessary, for groups of households.
- Adequate availability and 100 percent upkeep and management of Public Sanitation facilities in all Urban Areas, to rid them of open defecation and environmental hazards and to safely manage their faecal sludge and septage.

(ii) Achieving Integrated Citywide Sanitation: Mainstreaming Sanitation

- Mainstream thinking, planning and implementing measures related to faecal sludge and septage management in all sectors and departmental domains as a cross-cutting issue, especially in all urban management endeavours.
- Strengthening national, state, city and local institutions (public, private and community) to accord priority to sanitation provision, including planning, implementation and O&M management.
- Extending access to proper faecal sludge and septage management facilities for poor communities and other disadvantaged settlements.

(iii) Sanitary and Safe Disposal

- Promoting proper functioning of faecal sludge and septage management systems and ensuring proper collection and disposal of the faecal sludge.
- Promoting recycle and reuse of treated sewage for non-potable applications wherever possible.
- Promoting proper design and construction of OSS facilities.

(iv) Awareness Generation and Behaviour Change

- Generating awareness about faecal sludge and septage management and its linkages with public and environmental health amongst communities and institutions including hazards from OSS liquid overflow.
- Promoting mechanisms to bring about and sustain behavioural changes aimed at adoption of healthy sanitation designs and practices, including the responsibility to ensure safe containment and management of faecal sludge and septage by urban households including liquid effluent.

Scope

Only on-site sanitation facilities and areas served by such facilities would fall under the purview of this FSSM Policy. It does not seek to cover network or conventional sewerage system (including treatment plants) of wastewater/sewage management. However it will address synergies between FSSM and sewerage systems or municipal solid waste (MSW) management, e.g., co-treatment of faecal sludge and septage at sewage treatment plants or co-treatment and management of faecal sludge and septage, and MSW. Unless otherwise specified, the scope of this Policy extends to all the projects, programmes and schemes of the Central Government that facilitate and support sanitation services, urban development and improved delivery of services in urban and peri-urban areas of India. It also covers the initiatives undertaken and/or supported by all Central Government Ministries, Departments, Agencies, Authorities and Public Sector Undertakings that have a bearing on sanitation services in urban and peri-urban areas. Further, the Policy applies to every urban local body, outgrowths in urban agglomerations, census towns as declared by the Registrar General and Census Commissioner of India, notified areas, notified industrial townships, areas under the control of Indian Railways, airports, airbases, Ports and harbours, defence establishments, special economic zones, State and Central Government organisations, places of pilgrimage, religious and historical importance as may be notified by respective State Government from time to time.

The State Governments, ULBs, and relevant public and private utilities should take necessary steps to ensure that this Policy covers all the projects, programmes and schemes related to provision of onsite sanitation services in their respective jurisdictions, irrespective of the source(s) of funding for these projects, programmes and schemes.

Central Laws and Rules

The legal context for FSSM includes municipal building byelaws, environment laws, laws for the legal prohibition of "manual scavenging" and institutional laws that provide for the establishment, powers and functions of local authorities. The first category, which includes the Municipal Law, the Environment (Protection) Act, 1986 and the Water (Prevention and Control of Pollution) Act, 1974 provide a framework for control of effluent, sewage and septage discharge. Further, the Solid Waste Management (SWM) Rules, 2016 under the Environment (Protection) Act apply to the final and safe disposal of post-processed residual faecal sludge and septage to prevent contamination of ground water, surface water and ambient air.

Further, the SWM Rules 2016 will also apply for disposal and treatment of faecal sludge and septage, before or after processing, at landfills and for use as compost. The provisions of the National Building Code of India published by the Bureau of Indian Standards (BIS) as applicable for Septic tanks, soak pits, cess pools, leach pits, drainage fields etc. also need to be examined and taken into account while framing the FSSM policy. The Model Building Bye-Laws (MBBLs), 2016 framed by the Town and Country Planning Organisation can also be referred.

The Employment of Manual Scavengers and Construction of Dry Latrines (Prohibition) Act, 1993 put a ban on dry latrines, i.e., latrines with no water-seal or flushing mechanism, and the employment of persons for manually carrying human excreta. This was supplemented in 2013 with the Prohibition of Employment as Manual Scavengers and their Rehabilitation Act, 2013 by which "hazardous cleaning" in relation to sewers and septic tanks was also banned. The law now provides that manual cleaning of sewers and septic tanks, if necessary, may be carried out only in highly controlled situations, with adequate safety precautions, and in accordance with specific rules and protocols for the purpose.

Roles and Responsibilty

The Ministry of Urban Development (MoUD), Government of India (GoI) will be responsible for the overall guidance, coordination and interpretation of this Policy. It will disseminate the Policy among the State and ULB governments as well as dovetail it with the Ministry's urban development programmes and schemes. It will provide the necessary technical and planning support to the States and ULBs and will also design, lead and implement a national awareness campaign on this issue.

GoI recognizes that sanitation is a State subject and on-ground implementation and sustenance of public health and environmental outcomes requires strong city level institutions and stakeholders. Although there are some common elements across urban areas of India, there are a number of factors, constraints and opportunities that are peculiar to specific situation of States and cities with respect to sanitation, climate, physiographic factors, economic, social and political parameters, and institutional variables. Therefore, each state and city needs to formulate its own FSSM strategy and integrate the same in their respective State and city sanitation plans in overall conformity to the National Policy. Several other stakeholders such as households, civil society organisations, the private sector (small, medium and large), research organisations, too have a critical role to play in achievement of safe and sustainable FSSM services for all.

Summary of Roles and Responsibilities

Ministry	*Lead Role*	*Supportive Role*
Ministry of Urban Development	-Technical and planning support to States and ULBs -Training and capacity building of State level officials and those from select ULBs -Funding through specific schemes and plans -National level awareness and behaviour change campaign plans	-Support Research and Capacity Building in the sector -Create enabling environment for participation of the private sector, NGOs and CSOs in provision of FSSM services including to the poor and marginalized households and areas -National level monitoring and evaluation -Formulation of State and City level FSSM strategies and implementation
Ministry of Environment, Forest and Climate Change	-Enforce compliance of the relevant environmental laws and rules during the collection, transport, treatment and disposal of faecal sludge and septage	-Support and build capacity of State Pollution Control towards enforcement of relevant laws and rules
Ministry of Social Justice and Empowerment	-Strive towards elimination of manual scavenging and rehabilitation of manual scavengers -Monitor and evaluate progress at the National Level -National level awareness campaign	-Help States and ULBs eliminate manual scavenging and rehabilitate manual scavengers

(Contd...)

Ministry of Women and Child Development		-Gender mainstreaming of IEC material for FSSM across the country
State Governments	• Develop State level FSSM Strategy and Implementation Plan • Develop Operative Guidelines on FSSM • Training and capacity building of ULB officials and others engaged in provision of FSSM services • State level awareness and behaviour change campaign • Create enabling environment for participation of the private sector, NGOs and CSOs in provision of FSSM services including to the poor and marginalized households and areas • Funding through specific schemes and plans • Support Research and Capacity Building in the sector • State level monitoring and evaluation	• Technical, financial and administrative support to ULBs • Encourage coordination and cooperation among ULBs • Regulate and help ULBs set up systems to ensure financial sustainability in provision of FSSM services -Implement Municipal Byelaws
Urban Local Bodies	Design, develop, plan and implement ULB level FSSM strategy • Set up and ensure operation of systems for 100% safe and sustainable collection, transport, treatment and disposal of faecal sludge & septage • Develop expertise, in-house and outsourced, to provide safe and effective FSSM services • Awareness and behaviour change campaign to engage diverse stakeholders • Develop training programmes for masons to build requisite skills in construction of quality septic tanks as per BIS / NBC norms • Set up systems to ensure financial sustainability in provision of FSSM services • Achieve objectives of FSSM Policy in a time-bound manner • Design and implement plans to eliminate manual scavenging and rehabilitate manual scavengers • Funding through specific schemes and plans • Monitor and evaluate FSSM strategy and implementation plan • Implement Municipal Byelaws	-Create enabling environment for NGOs and private initiatives to achieve safe and sustainable FSSM
Households	-Timely and regular cleaning of septic tanks through approved entities • Regular maintenance and monitoring of septic tanks • Timely payment of user fee and/or charges, if any, towards FSSM services • Practice Building Byelaws for construction of OSS.	-Engage with decision-makers at State and ULB level to ensure that they receive good quality FSSM services

Implementation Strategy

It is envisaged that State-specific FSSM Policy, Strategy and Guidelines conforming to the National Policy will be developed by each State.

State-level Implementation Strategy

In line with the National FSSM Policy each state is expected to develop and issue an FSSM Implementation Strategy and Plan Guideline. In accordance with State Policy and Plan, the Guidelines should provide an overall state level framework, objectives, timelines and implementation plans to the ULBs. States such as Maharashtra, Odisha and Tamil Nadu have already put in place such guidelines. They could be modified, if required, in the context of this FSSM Policy. These existing State-level guidelines provide good examples for other States to prepare their own set of guidelines. FSSM services are provided by a mix of formal public service providers, contractual operators and informal local service providers, but with very little supervision and control to ensure compliance with environment, health, safety and laws prohibiting manual scavenging. Rules, Byelaws, regulations and operative guidelines for faecal sludge and septage management will address:

- Design of septic tanks, pits etc. (adapted to local conditions), including siting, and methods of approval of building plans, or retro-fitting existing installations to comply with rules and byelaws.
- Delineation of private (individual houses, groups housing, institutions etc.) and public responsibilities (urban local bodies and other local authorities) in relation of faecal sludge and septage management.
- Details of the planning and implementation process for carrying out safe and sustainable management of all faecal sludge and septage.

This may be integrated with overall city land use planning, with the timelines for holistically addressing waste water management via on-site, decentralised or centralised systems.

- Special provisions for medium and large format real estate developments
- Frequency of desludging, and O&M of installations and the responsibilities of householders (owner/occupant)
- Operating procedures for desludging including safety procedures with an emphasis on the safety, health and dignity of sanitation workers (abiding by the Prohibition of Employment as Manual Scavengers and their Rehabilitation Act, 2013)

- Licensing, record-keeping, monitoring and reporting arrangements for faecal sludge and septage service providers
- Methods and locations of transport (conveyance), treatment and safe disposal
- Tariffs or cess/tax etc. for septage management in the city
- Penalty clauses for untreated discharge for households as well as desludging agents and unsafe emptying and handling of faecal waste.
- Regular monitoring and evaluation of the entire process of FSSM
- Training, accreditation, education and awareness programmes

All public and private sector staff should adhere to safety norms as provided in the Manual on Sewerage and Sewage Treatment published by the Ministry of Urban Development and such other safeguards under the Prohibition of Employment as Manual Scavengers and their Rehabilitation Act, 2013 and that the ULB may provide under its own rules. For disposal of septage, the ULB will need to follow the standards set out in the Environment (Protection) Act, 1986, and SWM Rules 2016 depending on the mode of disposal.

It is important that all ULBs make provision of land and other infrastructure facilities required for safe treatment and disposal /reuse of human waste generated in their areas. This should go hand in hand with strict enforcement of disposal by desludgers, as well as recognition and partnership with such providers of service. Desludging should be carried out in an organised manner by taking into account of each and every septic tank and its cleaning frequency through a registered agency. Desludgers should be asked to register with the municipal bodies and there should be a strong partnership and dis-incentive to unsafe disposal.

An important part of work on FSSM involves constant and deep engagement with communities, so that they understand and support activities that ULBs will take up. It has been found that communities are reluctant to have faecal sludge treatment facilities close to their vicinity, but is not as sensitive to faecal sludge that is dumped untreated close to their homes. Households should also be encouraged to have a regular desludging schedule and this too, should be monitored by the municipal / urban local bodies through a systematic monitoring system. Some good examples are in setting up call centres, and formalizing associations of desludgers and ensuring that households are regularly desludged. A system of incentives (for example, discounts on taxes) and disincentives (penalties) should be set up.

ULB level Implementation Plan

Each ULB is expected to develop a detailed FSSM plan in conformity to the National FSSM policy and respective State guidelines on FSSM. Citywide assessment of FSSM is the key step for FSSM process planning. Such plan should be technically appropriate and financially feasible. Assessment in each area entails review of available information at city level, identifying information gaps, and conducting field studies where necessary.

In addition, adequate attention and focus has to be paid to public outreach and behaviour change communications to ensure timely and necessary participation of all the key stakeholders. The range of stakeholders may include on-site sanitation. Each FSSM plan will have a specific monitoring and evaluation framework to continuously gauge implementation progress and document lessons for constant improvement. It is very important that cities work systematically with each group of stakeholders to ensure alignment of goals and adoption. The ownership for all activity relating to FSSM must be driven by the Municipal /ULB Chairperson and Chief Executive concerned.

FSSM plans need to be backed by enabling regulatory and institutional framework. Enforcement of all regulations should be strict, to ensure compliance and also provide the right disincentives. At the same time, timely rewards and incentives should be given to both communities and service providers to encourage positive behaviour.

Technology Options

The write-up below provides a brief outline about various technological options practiced in the urban setting.

Septic Tank

A septic tank is a combined sedimentation and digestion tank where the sewage is held for one to two days. During this period, the suspended solids settle down to the bottom. This is accomplished by anaerobic digestion of settled solids (sludge) and liquid, resulting in reasonable reduction in the volume of sludge, reduction in biodegradable organic matter and release of gases like carbon dioxide, methane and hydrogen sulphide. The effluent although clarified to a large extent, will still contain appreciable amount of dissolved and suspended putrescible organic solids and pathogens.

Septic Tank with Drain field

In this modification of septic tank, treatment of sewage effluent occurs in the soil beneath the drain-field, which consists of long underground perforated pipes or tiles connected to the septic tank. The network of pipes is laid filled in gravel trench or beds in the soil. A drain-field trench is generally 18 to 36 inches wide and up to 100 feet long. Liquid waste flows out of the tank into the drain-field through the piping system and the soil below provides the final treatment and disposal of the effluent. After the effluent has passed into the soil, most of it percolates downward and outward.

The soil filters the effluent as it passes through the pore spaces. Chemical and biological processes treat the effluent before it reaches groundwater, or a restrictive layer, such as hardpan, bedrock, or clay soils. These processes work best where the soil is somewhat dry and permeable, and contains sufficient oxygen for several feet below the drain field.

Septic Tank with Soak Pit

Soak pits are cheaper to construct and are extensively used. They need no media when lined or filled with rubble or brick bats. The pits may be of any regular shape, circular or square being more common. When water table is sufficiently below ground level, soak pits should be preferred only when land is limited or when a porous layer underlies an impervious layer at the top, which permits easier vertical downward flow than horizontal spread out as in the case of dispersion trenches.

Minimum horizontal dimension of soak pit should be 1m, the depth below the invert level or inlet pipe being at 1m. The pit should be covered and the top raised above the adjacent ground to prevent damage by flooding.

Septic Tank with Small Bore System

An in-house toilet discharging to a septic tank (or on-site digester) with liquids disposal via a small diameter sewer to a central collection sump oexisting sewer system.

Septic Tank with Baffles

An anaerobic baffled reactor (ABR) is an improved septic tank, which, after a primary settling chamber, uses a series of baffles to force sewage to flow under and over them as it passes from the inlet to the outlet. The sewage is introduced into the chamber at the bottom, leading to an enhanced contact with the active biomass which results in an increased retention and anaerobic degradation of suspended and dissolved organic pollutants. ABRs are robust and can treat a wide range of sewage, but both remaining sludge and effluents still need further treatment in order to be reused or discharged properly.

Twin Pit Pour Flush Latrine

Pour-flush leaching pit latrines were first developed in India in mid-forties with a single leach pit and squatting pan placed over it. When the pit in use gets filed up another pit is dug and the squatting slab is removed and placed over the new pit. The fist pit is covered with earth and the excreta is allowed to digest. After one or two years, the digested excreta is used as manure. To overcome this shortcoming, the Twin Pit Water Seal Toilet design was introduced and in this case when one pit is full, the excreta is diverted to the second pit. Both pits are connected with a junction chamber at one end. Pit walls have a honeycomb structure. The bottom of the pit is not plastered and is earthen. Depending on the number of users of toilet, size of the pit varies. The filled up pit can be conveniently emptied after 1.5 to 2 years, when most of the pathogens die off. The sludge can safely be used as manure. Thus the two pits can be used alternately and perpetually.

This is a suitable on-site sanitation measure for houses where the water table is sufficiently deep to avoid ground water pollution. Leach pits serve a dual function of (a) storage and digestion of excreted solids and (b) infiltration of the waste liquids and are therefore, to be designed on the basis of the following parameters:

- Sludge accumulation rate
- Long term infiltration rate of the liquid fraction across the pit soil interface
- Hydraulic loading on the pit
- Minimum period required for effective pathogen destruction
- Optimal pit emptying frequency.
- FSTP to FSM - a Case Study

Faecal Sludge Treatment Plant (FSTP)

Where there is no sewerage / underground drainage (UGD) system, most of the households depend on septic tanks for sewerage disposal. The collected faecal sludge from these septic tanks / pit latrines can be treated by using "Faecal Sludge Treatment Plant". FSTP is designed to be aesthetically pleasing with no odor so that it could be located close to the town, hence keeping distances low for desludging operators to dispose.

The plant runs on gravity (No electricity) with very little mechanical equipment that does not require skilled operators thus keeping operational expenditure low. These features enable the FSTP to be financially sustained through their own funds.

Financing Plan

The Government of India may provide assistance for funding projects proposed as part of FSM Plans through its ongoing urban development schemes and programmes. However, the emphasis will be on improving the efficiency of existing sanitation infrastructure and service delivery. State Governments should prioritize funds to implement the FSSM plan at City level. They should promote engagement of private sector participation across sanitation service chain and should encourage ULBs to start levying sanitation tax/user charges to meet the O&M cost for effective FSSM operations at city level. They should also facilitate the involvement of private sector participation through an easy and amenable PPP relationship framework, to ensure adequate financing and sustainability of FSSM projects.

Monitoring & Evaluation

At the national level, the Government of India is adopting Sanitation Benchmark framework of revised service level benchmarks for sanitation that assess performance of citywide sanitation, capturing on-site sanitation systems and sewage management. State Government will be responsible for Monitoring and Evaluation of its Cities' performance, and hence needs to devise data collection and reporting systems using indicator framework developed for Sanitation Benchmark. ULBs in turn need to develop database, registry of certified on-site sanitation system, robust reporting format to track compliance of households (establishments, etc.) with outcomes and process standards.

Training And Capacity Building

Government of India will help formulate a strategy on capacity building and training on FSSM to support States and Cities to build their personnel capacities and organizational systems for delivery of sanitation services. Government of India will make effort to integrate the FSSM components in ongoing capacity building programme.

The State Government needs to identify agencies that will train its State level and ULB personnel and orientation of elected representatives on aspects related to FSSM. The States and ULBs need to set up and develop strategies for citizen engagement through city sanitation task forces. These agencies could be specialist agencies of the State Government, academic institutions and private sector organizations. They also need to focus on capacity building, i.e. not just training but also development of systems and capacities of ULBs in sanitation, in line with the Urban Sector Reforms that the State may be implementing. ULBs will need to provide training on sanitation to their own staff – using the specialized agency selected by State Government. They will need to utilize ongoing Govt. of India and State Government Schemes for training and capacity building in order to achieve this. Training will also need to be imparted to private sector players and NGOs to help them engage and deliver effectively in the provision of FSSM services.

Expected Outcomes

As this Policy is implemented across the country, it is expected to yield significant benefits in terms of improved public health indicators, reduced pollution of water bodies and groundwater from human waste, and resource recovery leading to reuse of treated waste and other end products. Some key projected outcomes are:

- Containment of all human waste in 100 percent of the towns and cities
- Safe collection and conveyance of human waste to treatment and disposal sites
- Cost-effective solution for management of human waste through integrated network sewerage, small bore sewerage, and faecal sludge and septage management.
- Clarity among different stakeholders on identifying and implementing best and economically viable sanitation solutions
- Technical capability among ULBs to effectively implement FSSM
- Scheduled emptying of septic tanks or other containment systems at an interval of 2-3 years as recommended by CPHEEO Sewerage & Sewage Treatment Manual and the MoUD Advisory on Septage Management (2013)
- Safe disposal of all collected faecal sludge and septage at designated sites (sewage treatment plants, faecal sludge treatment facilities for safe and scientific disposal, etc.)
- Continuous improvements in efficiency and effectiveness in the entire FSSM chain: containment, collection, conveyance, treatment and disposal
- Preventing Contamination of water bodies and groundwater from human waste (faecal matter) in all the towns and cities across India
- Nuisance from faecal sludge reduced to minimum levels, resulting in nuisance-free living space in urban India

- Maximum reuse of treated sludge as fertilizer in farmlands, parks, gardens and other such avenues, reuse of treated sewage, as source of energy where feasible, and any other productive uses.
- Drastic reduction in incidences of diseases due to safe & sustainable FSSM services.

RAJASTHAN

FAECAL SLUDGE & SEPTAGE MANAGEMENT POLICY (FSSM), 2017

Policy Goals

The primary aim of this policy is to establish FSSM as a central component in delivery of safe sanitation service in Rajasthan by creating a favourable environment for its effective implementation across all urban areas in a pragmatic, sustainable and participatory manner. The Policy will strive for:

- ***Ensuring Timely and Safe Collection and Transport of Faecal Sludge and Septage:*** Encouraging a shift towards scheduled desludging of septic tanks, pit latrines, etc. (periodically within 2 – 3 years) in all ULBs, while generating awareness and incentivizing households for the same. The process would ensure complete containment of waste with no direct human contact with the waste under any circumstance.
- ***Complete Treatment of all Collected Waste****:* All collected faecal sludge should reach the treatment facility (without arbitrary and illegal disposal) and treated as per standards for safe disposal/ reuse. System of incentives and vis-à-vis imposition of penalties will be tool to monitor desludging operators and to ensure disposal at designated locations. There will be greater use of technologies that consume very less power and use biological processes.
- ***Ensuring Resource Recovery***: The treatment facility would maximize reuse of treated wastewater and sludge for various public and commercial purposes. This will contribute in part towards cost recovery and even profit generation.
- ***Create Enabling Institutional Environment and Strengthening Regulatory Framework****:* The mandate, roles & responsibilities of all government departments and other stakeholders would be clearly defined and necessary steps taken for augmenting their

capacities. Appropriate institutions, management & monitoring systems and standard procedures would be in place at state and city level that incrementally strengthen FSSM operations in urban areas. Necessary steps would be taken to augment capacities at state, city and community level for government officials, service providers, residents, etc. The institutional framework would also enable an environment conducive for greater participation of private sector.

- ***Standardized Infrastructure and Professionalized Operations***: Standards and norms documented and adequately disseminated for design, construction and O&M of FSSM infrastructure such as On-Site Sanitation Facilities (Septic Tanks, Soak pits/Soak fields, Lined Pit Latrines, Digestion Tanks, etc.), Suction Emptier trucks & equipment, Treatment technologies (Sludge Drying Beds, DEWATS, FSTPs, Co-Treatment with STPs, etc.) and criteria for end-product disposal/reuse. Moreover, the services provided by various public and private players should be professionalized with standard operating procedures, operating and monitoring guidelines, etc. through appropriate training and capacity building of relevant service providers and regulators.
- ***Innovation in Service Delivery and Management:*** Improving service delivery, management and monitoring by introducing technological interventions such as I.T. enabled single window system, GIS/GPS aided planning and operations, custom MIS modules, etc. and greater emphasis on private participation in service delivery.
- ***Setting up an Urban Sanitation Fund***: This will be a dedicated fund for sanitation and FSSM, which would consolidate resources and funds from multiple sources – various central schemes and programs, state govt. grants, ULB funds, CSR, URIF, Donor fund, Bilateral/multilateral grants & loans; and through innovative instruments such as Social & Development Impact Bonds, Category – I Alternative Investment Funds, etc. which would be managed by the state government (through a designated nodal agency) and provided to ULBs/service providers/ other relevant stakeholders based on a transparent and flexible criteria, linked to performance and need. Similarly, ULBs with sufficient capacities can set-up city sanitation funds (linked to the state sanitation fund) for implementation of city-level FSSM strategy, plan and projects.

- ***Greater Awareness and Participation***: The residents would become active participants in the planning, implementation and monitoring process, while all stakeholders would be sensitized and sufficiently made aware of the processes, procedures, components, etc. of FSSM. Multiple channels (digital, broadcast, print, physical, etc.) for communication, learning and stakeholder engagement would be used.
- ***Promoting Mechanisms to Bring about and Sustain Behavioural Changes*** aimed at adoption of healthy sanitation designs and practices, including the responsibility to ensure safe containment and management of faecal sludge and septage by urban households including liquid effluent.
- ***Developing a Strong Partnership Network***: Multi-sector partnership of government agencies/ULBs with other public/private organisations, groups and institutions for collaborating on knowledge improvement, funding, improved services, business opportunities, research & innovation, stakeholder engagement, peer learning, etc. Formal and Informal platforms would be established for networking among various ULBs, service providers, associations, etc. for learning, knowledge sharing and partnership building.

Intervention Areas for FSSM

In towns without a centralized Sewerage Network (existing or proposed), full Scale FSSM would be implemented across the town including a dedicated Faecal Sludge Treatment Plant.

- Class – III, IV & V towns
- Towns and Cities that are partially covered by a centralized Sewerage Network – un-sewered areas which could not be connected to organised sewerage system, would be served by FSSM services operations and treatment shall be at dedicated centralized Sewage Treatment Plant
- Un-sewered areas within cities where desludging is not possible, provision for Decentralized Treatment of Wastewater & Faecal Sludge shall be made.

Strategic Policy Actions

The strategic points on Policy Actions would outline the broad provision to address the aforementioned issues and lay out a roadmap for effective implementation of FSSM in urban areas across the state. The provisions of the policy are broad-based and a detailed State FSSM Guidelines shall be formulated that will elaborates upon the provisions of this policy and aid relevant stakeholders in planning, design, implementation, management, monitoring and capacity building of various components under FSSM in urban areas of Rajasthan. The Strategic Policy Actions have been classified under the following categories:

IEC & Stakeholder Participation: A rigorous awareness campaign should be undertaken to educate various stakeholders about Faecal Sludge and Septage Management. ULBs can be tasked with spreading awareness among residents about govt. schemes, benefits of scheduled desludging, various incentives for the same, good sanitation practices and monitoring of FSSM operations. This would be done with the involvement of ward councillors, community leaders, CBOs, etc. Special campaigns can be undertaken for making communities and households aware about the importance of scheduled desludging and the incentives to be given for households that participate in scheduled desludging services. Various neighbourhood and city level institutions such as schools, colleges, CBOs, etc. would be actively engaged as volunteers in these campaigns.

A dedicated FSSM Cell & Committee can be set-up within Directorate of Local Bodies, LSG to manage FSSM related initiatives such as projects, city FSSM plans, awareness campaigns, single-window systems, etc. along with the State Sanitation Fund. Various external agencies can be engaged for different initiatives and functions.

State-level FSSM rules and guidelines would be formulated that will include Standard Operating Procedures and training material for ULBs, Manuals for service providers, models drawings/DPRs/Bid Documents, model eptage Management rules for ULBs, technological options, etc. The State level Guidelines and Standard Operating Manual shall include –

- *Format for City level Strategy and Contents for City FSSM plans.*
- *Advisory on selection of suitable FSSM interventions* – Number, Type and Capacity of Vehicles, Transfer Station, Treatment Option, Disposal/Reuse option, etc.
- *Model Septic Tank design/construction/maintenance,*
- *Model for desludging vehicles, cleaning machines, equipment and safety gear*

    - *Options and broad Specifications for Treatment Technologies* – Co-Treatment with STP, DEWATS, FSTP, etc.
    - *Steps for Capacity building at State and City level for government. officials.*
    - *Operative Manual for Desludging and Treatment Plant Operators.*
    - *Model Criteria for Licensing of Desludging Operators.*
    - *Steps for Implementing Scheduled Desludging Services at city level.*
    - *Format for Assessing Financial Requirements for FSSM by ULBs* – Capital and O&M.

- All informal FSSM operations (by masons, desludging operators, cleaners, etc.) would be formalized and professionalized through appropriate channels, such as licensing by ULBs, MIS – based reporting of operations, formal trainings, access to formal finance, etc.
- For Licensing of desludging operators and other service providers by the ULBs, a model eligibility criteria shall be framed. It would allow licensed desludging operators to avail various incentives and benefits. All private desludging operators shall be required to obtain a licence from the respective ULB to operate in the city.
- Roles of various stakeholders including State government departments, ULBs, residents, service providers and private sector partners shall be clearly defined for reducing ambiguities and overlap of functions. The roles and responsibilities have been briefly provided in the subsequent section.
- Various steps would be taken by the state government and ULBs to enable greater private sector participation in FSSM service delivery. Greater thrust would be given to PPP projects in FSSM, VGF (viability Gap Funding) from Central and State government wherever FSSM projects are not completely feasible. Incentives and concessions in various state and ULB taxes/charges for setting up Faecal Sludge treatment plants, setting up guarantee funds to provide financial assistance for purchase of desludging vehicles or capacity building, etc.

Strategic Policy Actions

Agency	*Roles and Responsibilities*
Department of Local Self Governance	Nodal Agency for managing FSSM operations
	Implementation of State level FSSM initiatives
	Overall supervision and coordination of FSSM operations
	Formulating a roadmap for realisation of the State FSSM Policy
	Responsible for preparation of the State FSSM Guidelines, Standard Operating Procedures, User Manuals, Model FSSM rules for ULBs, drafting state acts and policies related to urban sanitation and FSSM, etc.
	Guiding all Urban Local Bodies for implementing city level FSSM strategy, plans and projects during planning, operation and monitoring stages
	Coordinating networking among various stakeholders Responsible for building partnerships
	Prepare a Training Calendar to conduct trainings and workshops across the state, customized to target various stakeholders such as ULB officials, service providers, NGOs, CBOs, Corporates and Public. Coordinate with the ULBs and engage Professionals to provide trainings on FSSM
Rajasthan State Pollution Control Board	Ensure compliance of FSSM operations through inspections, environmental monitoring, etc.
	Address grievance related to environmental hazards due to FSSM operations
	Assist in formulation of relevant advisories, guidelines, manuals, etc. to ensure environmental compliance for FSSM operations
Social Justice and Empowerment Department	Ensuring compliance of provisions under the "The Prohibition of Employment as Manual Scavengers and their Rehabilitation Act, 2013"
Rajasthan Urban Drinking Water , Sewerage & Infrastructure Corporation	Ensure coverage all non-sewer pockets and areas in their project towns through appropriate FSM interventions
Other State Government Departments	Sufficiently incorporating the provision of this policy in their projects, schemes, programs, policies, plans, guidelines, activities, etc.
Urban Local Bodies	Devise a system of appropriate incentives and penalties for residents and service providers to induce desirable behaviour
	Ensuring capacity building and training – manpower, financial, equipment, exposure visits, etc.
	Overall Monitoring and Evaluation of FSSM operations – benchmarking, ensuring compliance, performance monitoring of desludging operators, etc.
	Provide NOC for Licensing of Desludging trucks and Location of treatment plants

(Contd...)

Ward Councillors	Lead the Ward-level awareness generation and behaviour change campaigns
Households	Periodic cleaning and desludging of Septic Tanks as per Schedule
Desludging Operators	Timely collection of waste from households as per schedule and disposing waste at designated locations only
Service Providers – Masons, Designers	Acquire requisite skills through training and capacity building to design and construct quality septic tanks as per ISO norms
Private Sector	Active participation in service delivery of FSSM at state and city level
Financial Institutions	Providing financial assistance to desludging operators for purchasing new vehicles or upgrading existing equipment

Partnership Building

A strong network of partners in various sectors and of various backgrounds would be established, including renowned specialists/experts, Corporates, Research/Academic Institutions, Civil Society groups/CBOs/ NGOs, private service providers, Donor agencies, Bilateral/Multilateral agencies, etc. for bolstering capacities and knowledge in the sector.

There is an increased need to encourage greater private participation in service delivery and financing of FSSM activities by creating an enabling regulatory environment and creating opportunities.

Backward and Forward linkages shall be established with private players, other government departments, trade and farmer associations, etc. for optimum reuse of treated sludge and wastewater. Possibility shall be explored on whether treated and stabilized sludge can be used as organic fertilizer for farming and gardening, biogas recovered can be locally distributed for cooking or production of electricity, while treated wastewater could be reused by industries/power plants/irrigation, etc.

Necessary platforms shall be established such as periodic conferences, workshops, summits, meetings, events, formal groups/associations, and others for regular interaction among various stakeholders and partners for knowledge sharing, peer-learning, progress review, information dissemination, etc.

RUDSICO will be the nodal agency for channelling and utilizing funds (loans and grants) from external sources for sanitation and FSSM projects.

An agreements (such as MoUs) will be drawn which may be signed with prominent partners outlining a common agenda for development and provision of FSSM services in Rajasthan. Various agencies can be designated with specific charge for providing their inputs, such as 'Knowledge Partner',

'Sanitation Technology Partner', 'Media Partner', 'Campaign Partner', 'Capacity Building Partner', etc.

Funding and Financing

New and Innovative modalities for financing FSSM would be explored by ULBs and State government, with involvement of knowledge and funding partners, which may include – PPP, CSR funds, Guarantee funds, Crowdfunding, Donor grants, Social and Development Impact Bonds, ULB Incentive Fund, UPIF, etc.

A State Sanitation Fund should be set-up that will consolidate funds and resources from these aforementioned sources, in addition to central government schemes and programmes, Finance Commission, state funds, etc. It would be managed by the state government (through a designated nodal agency) and provided to ULBs/ service providers/ other relevant stakeholders based on a transparent and flexible criteria, linked to performance and need.

Preference would be given to FSSM models that ensure maximum cost recovery and even profit generation in the O&M stage, partly through reuse of treated end product (wastewater and sludge) in the form of biogas, electricity, water reuse, fertilizer/manure, compost, etc. especially since O&M costs of FSTPs is usually much lower than conventional STPs for smaller towns (Class III, IV & V towns).

ULBs would be empowered to structure their tariff and revenue models, which may include collection of service charges or sanitation taxes from users, tipping fees from licensed operators, etc. in order to maintain a steady revenue stream for O&M of FSSM assets and services.

Synergy would be ensured between funds and goals of various Central government programs such as AMRUT, SBM, Smart Cities, etc. and state government programmes such as RUSDP Phase-III, etc.

The City-level FSSM strategy and plans would duly assess cost requirements during the perspective period, including capital and O&M costs, and accordingly structure their financial model to make the system more feasible and sustainable.

Implementation and Service Delivery

State government will play a facilitating role in implementing of FSSM at state and city level. Necessary support will be given to ULBs for timely preparation and implementation of city level FSSM plans, strategy and rules.

The State governments may explore possibility to link the ULBs with suitable partners (consulting, public outreach, funding, capacity building, etc.) as per the city's requirement for various FSSM related activities.

A system of incentives and penalties may be devised to encourage greater participation among residents, compliance by service providers (heavy penalties for illegal waste disposal, while monetary incentives for disposal at designated site), and better performance of ULBs.

Desludging and Treatment Plant operators shall use requisite safety gear during operations. There should be absolutely no direct human contact with the waste.

Intervention Approach

Sanitaltion and FSSM is a dynamic subject and varies with the context in urban areas, such as the population size and type of predominant sanitation system. Thus a single approach will not be applicable for all towns and need to be disaggregated accordingly. The basic logic is that in urban areas with higher number of OSSFs, FSSM is more feasible and gains prominence, while as the population of the town increases, FSSM is less efficient and centralized sewerage is more suitable where FSSM provides supplementary coverage to un-served areas. The matrix is suggestive and final sanitation approach shall be decided based on local conditions, availability of funds and consultation between ULB and State government.

For urban pockets where both sewerage system and desludging services are not possible, such as compact inner city areas and congested slums, on-site and decentralized waste water and faecal sludge treatment solutions such as DEWATS, Bio-digester toilets, etc. would be explored. A more detailed set of techno-economic criteria shall be developed and provided in the State FSSM Guidelines for the same.

Residents who get their septic tanks cleaned as per schedule or in a timely manner can be given a rebate in the service charge/municipal taxes, while others would have to pay a higher amount for the same.

Licensed service providers can be eligible for accessing financial assistance (through available instruments) for upgrading capacities, equipment, safety gears, etc. Desludging operators who dispose collected waste at designated locations would be given direct/indirect benefits, while others would be penalized - applying the principle of 'polluter pays'.

To ensure regular supply of faecal sludge to the plant, steady flow of revenue and implementing Scheduled Desludging service, a robust database needs to be constructed (ideally linked with Property Tax database) of household/ community/ward level sanitation assets and practices by the ULBs (type of toilet system, Number/Capacity of Septic Tanks or pit latrines, waste water outlets, adjacent road widths, etc.). The database would help in scheduling desludging services, planning FSSM infrastructure, regulate tariff collection, facilitate appropriate incentives or impose penalties on households and operators, maintain up-to-date records and manifests, etc. The database should preferably be digitized on a GIS and MIS based platform

An MIS and GIS-based single-window system can be operationalized which coordinates and facilitates the FSSM services in Rajasthan, including:

- Call-centre for on-call desludging services,
- Schedule for Periodic desludging for ULBs and Desludging operators
- Forms for NOCs, applications & guidelines for licencing of operators,
- Repository of all registered service providers and licensed desludging operators, along with a platform to connect with suitable partners (knowledge, funding, capacity building, etc.)
- Mobile and e-mail reminders of scheduled desludging to households,
- GPS-monitoring panel for desludging trucks,
- Inventory of all FSSM assets in the city and throughout the state,
- Service level benchmarking of all ULBs,
- Capabilities of producing auto-generated and custom updates/ reports/ dashboards for various state government departments, residents, ULBs, etc.

Monitoring and Evaluation

The state will evaluate FSSM operations through dedicated service level benchmarks for all ULBs. A Benchmarking system shall be established for state, similar San-Benchmark Framework suggested in Draft National FSSM Policy. Each ULB will set a yearly target in their City-level FSSM plan on progress and service improvement with respect to these benchmarks, with the goal of achieving the benchmarks by the end of the perspective period.

A performance-linked system of incentives and penalties may be devised for rewarding high performing ULBs and encouraging ULBs with poor performance to improve, as they will be scored annually as per the service level benchmarks for FSSM. A mechanism on performance evaluation tool shall be framed up by the authority.

Local Communities and local groups would be involved in monitoring and compliance of FSSM operations, with encouragement by the ward councillors. The communities would be encouraged to be active and vigilant in reporting incidences of mismanagement by desludging operators, unsafe sanitation practices in neighbouring households, poor Maintenance at Community Toilets, DEWATS, FSTPs or Transfer Stations, etc.

A comprehensive system of reports and manifests would be designed at the city-level, with record of all desludging activities shall be maintained by all service providers.

A robust Grievance Redressal mechanism would be put in place, to be linked with the single window system, telephone call based system or part of local e-governance platform (MIS-based). Typically complaints by users usually pertain to damages to property or septic tank during desludging, insufficient or poor cleaning by the operator, spillage of septage/sludge during transport, illegal or arbitrary disposal by operator, foul smell from the treatment facility, etc. All user complaints and grievances should be acknowledged swiftly within three days, with each complaint given a unique complaint identification number and the complaint should be addressed and answered within two weeks by the ULB.

Capacity Building

A Capacity assessment should be carried out across state government departments and ULBs (similar to or part of SLIPs), and necessary measures would be taken to fill the gaps on Manpower, expertise, equipment, resources, financial management, etc.

External agencies would be engaged and proper modules would be prepared for training government officials, service providers, ULBs, etc. on relevant FSSM practices, technologies, operating procedures, techniques, financial assessment, etc.

Separate initiation and training Modules shall be prepared for State government officials, ULB representatives, service providers, planners & engineers, prospective partners, etc., each customized for the target audience.

Short courses and workshops can be organized on FSSM operations, and successful participants will be given certification at the end of the program/course. Certified professionals will be given preference for all government works and services related to FSSM.

Educational modules on FSSM can be integrated as part of academic teaching at schools and institution of higher education, to sensitize the upcoming population on the importance of safe sanitation and role of FSSM in the same.

While the state government may assist the ULBs in the short-term for preparation of city-level FSSM plans and strategies, in the long-term, rigorous capacity building initiatives should be taken to ensure the ULBs are self-reliant for implementation of their FSSM plans.

Customized Capacity Building and Training Modules can be designed for ULBs with involvement of various knowledge and capacity building partners based on local site conditions.

Since many FSSM concepts such as an FSTP or Scheduled desludging are quite recent, an important component for capacity building of various government officials and service providers will be planned exposure visits to areas with best practices in FSSM, which will help them get a first-hand experience of such operations and alleviate doubts and misconceptions about its efficiency as a long-term solution.

Expected Outcomes

While the goals set out broad aspirations and intention of the policy, the expected outcomes are tangible end results if the goals are achieved.

- ***Enhancement of Sanitation Coverage*** - No direct contact with waste - Safe handling and complete containment of Faecal Sludge and Septage during collection, conveyance, treatment and disposal.
- ***Scheduled Desludging*** - Greater Progress in transition from reactive on-call service to periodic & scheduled service, along with formalization of service providers (masons, operators, tankers, etc.).
- ***Environmental Improvement*** - Significant reduction in contamination of soil and water (surface and underground) due to human waste.
- ***Safe Waste Handling and Better Public Health*** - Safe handling and complete containment of faecal sludge and septage during collection, conveyance, treatment and disposal. Noticeable improvement in public health indicators including morbidity and mortality rates across urban areas in the state reduced incidences of water-borne diseases is expected as an outcome.

- ***New Opportunities*** – Avenues in sanitation and FSSM services emerge, based on cost recovery and profit generating business models.
- ***Greater Institutional Capacities*** - Augmented capacities across institutions (State and city-level) that could possibly be replicated in other sectors.

BIHAR
OPERATIVE GUIDELINES FOR FAECAL SLUDGE AND SEPTAGE MANAGEMENT, 2018

These guidelines are framed by Urban Development and Housing Department Bihar drawing from provisions and specification, related to faecal sludge and septage, of the National Building Code 2005, Indian standard code of practice for installation of septic tanks (IS: 2470) - Bureau of Indian Standards (1986), National Urban Sanitation Policy 2008, CPHEEO Manual on Sewage and Sewerage Treatment 2013, Advisory note on Septage Management (issued by Ministry in 2013), National FSSM Policy 2017 and 'Septage Management – A Practitioner's guide : Urban India's journey beyond ODF' prepared in 2017 by CSE, New Delhi – a designated Centre of Excellence assisting Ministry in Sustainable Water Management area. The existing Faecal sludge and Septage Management Policies (Maharashtra, Odisha, Tamil Nadu, Jammu & Kashmir, Jharkhand, Rajasthan) and guidelines (Maharashtra, Gujarat, Tamil Nadu) including Septage Management regulations (Delhi and Warangal, Telangana) have been reviewed.

Stakeholder Identification and Engagement

All interested parties, be they individuals, groups, organisations or entities, are stakeholders. Relevant stakeholders like representative from ULBs, PHEDS, Pollution Control Board, sanitary inspector, mason, vacuum truck operator, media, farmers etc. should be identified for the target area. Once identified, stakeholders are supposed to be analyzed based on the interest and influence chart. The analysis includes understanding their profile, their interests, their position (for or against), and their ability to influence FSSM practices. Stakeholders are then engaged through different strategies.

Stakeholder engagement is a key pre-requisite for successful implementation of FSSM. If the city already has a city sanitation task-force, as notified in NUSP, then the same team should deliberate about FSSM starting with collection and analysis of baseline data.

Assessment of Baseline Information

The next stage of FSSM is collection of baseline data from secondary sources like Census, state surveys, Detailed Project Reports (DPRs) of previous projects etc. and primary surveys wherever necessary for spatial information. It is important to understand how many households are using OSS. Spatial distribution of the houses in area should be qualitatively mapped. Preliminary surveys of households that are depended on the onsite sanitation system must be done to prepare comprehensive management plans.

Once the baseline data is in place, next step is assessment of initial situation of target area i.e. community, ward, zone or city. There are several tools available to help the ULBs analyze the collected data. One such tool is called faecal waste flow diagram (also known as SFD). It is an easy to understand advocacy and decision-support tool that summarizes and presents what happens to the excreta of the whole city/town through the sanitation chain. To learn how to make an SFD visit www.sfd.susana.org.

Suggested Institutional Framework

In India, there are few institutions on the city and state level which take care of FSSM. This section enumerates the suggestions under the National Urban FSSM policy, which highlights that each state and city needs to formulate its own FSSM strategy and integrate the same in their respective state and city sanitation plans in overall conformity to the national policy.

Current Economics and Business Model

In the present scenario, the FSSM is majorly in the hands of private operators. The operators charge for emptying service provided to different stakeholders. Emptying points can be from individual households, residential colonies, commercial establishments, institutions, toilet complexes, offices etc. Generally, the operators are called for emptying only when the containment is full. The fee for emptying varies widely. Due to absence of a dedicated disposal sites, private emptiers practice illegal dumping of FS/septage into water bodies, utterly disregarding the threat posed to health and environment. They run their business without paying any fees to government authorities which means that despite high charges collected from customers, no revenue is generated by government authorities from emptying business. Farmers in whose fields the collected septage or faecal sludge is disposed of also pay the private operators.

Business Model

A business model not only depicts the financial spending of the institution towards a better FSSM, but reflects a return on the investment. A business model consists of four interlocking elements:

- *Customer Value Proposition (CVP):* Products that create value for a target customer
- *Cost Structure*: All costs incurred to operate the business model
- *Profit Formula*: Revenue streams from each component of the sanitation
- *Key Resources*: Most critical activities required for the business

For a business model of any institution working in the spectre of FSSM, the four elements should create and provide value to customers. The value propositions can be divided into multiple segments, but in this guideline, we have restricted to 5 types as listed below:

- ***Value Proposition 1*** – Access to toilet and treatment for end-use: Providing an improved sanitation service to communities through access to toilet, and recovery of nutrient or energy through treatment of FS/septage.
- ***Value Proposition 2*** – Emptying and transportation of FS: Providing a timely sanitation service for emptying pits and septic tanks at an appropriate frequency.
- ***Value Proposition 3*** – Treatment of FS/septage for disposal: A healthier and safe environment through appropriate treatment of FS/septage.
- ***Value Proposition 4*** – End-use through nutrient recovery: Producing high-quality compost as a soil conditioner.
- ***Value Proposition 5*** – End-use through energy recovery: Improving access to energy.

Depending on the value proposition offered by the business, its customer segment will vary. For a business providing emptying and transportation services, the customer segment is individual households, community toilet and institutions. A generic business model canvas is described in Appendix 4. Government could charge for following activities by private operators and septic tank owners to generate revenue for sustainably run FSSM programme.

- Permits and their renewal for private operator through registration process

- Charges to repair the faulty design through registered mason/plumbers
- Fine to defaulters (private operator/containment owner) for not following instructions given by government agencies

Monitoring and Grievance Redressal Systems

At each stage of sanitation chain i.e. from containment till end-use, monitoring is essential. Any lapse in monitoring means avoidable delays in achieving the goals of the programme. When any services are offered, there are always some issues and challenges associated with them. Customer satisfaction should be main objective of service provider. In FSSM many stakeholders/beneficiaries are involved. It may not be possible that each beneficiary is satisfied with services. Therefore, for appropriate disposal of the complaints with FSSM, a complaint redressal system must be put in place before services are offered. The mode of the redressal system should vary according to the size of the target area, from simple register to complex information technology-based system. Nodal officers must be appointed to dispose of the complaints for each stage of FSSM. Nodal officer should review the complaint and dispose it. However, in case the complaint is not addressed or user is not satisfied, there should be provision to take the complaint to higher authorities or institutions (e.g. pollution control board) for appropriate action.

Awareness Generation and Capacity Building

Awareness generation activities need to be taken up for successful implementation of faecal sludge management plan and community acceptance and adherence to regulations and service plan set up by the ULBs. Associated training and capacity building of municipal staff as well as private sector contractors also needs to be taken up.

***Awareness Generation for Residents*:** Members of Resident Welfare Associations, community organizers, self-help groups and the general public should be made sensitized periodically regarding the need for a sound faecal sludge management system including a 3-year cycle. The health hazards associated with improper collection and treatment of waste, and the ill-effects of sewage discharge into fresh water/storm water drains should be explained to the residents. Awareness generation activities should be carried out at the beginning of introducing a scheduled service in all wards and then repeated periodically over the three-year cycle.

***Capacity Building for Municipal Staff*:** Municipal Commissioners/Chief Officers, Engineers, Sanitary Inspectors, Health Officers, and Sanitary

Workers should be well trained in safe FSSM and its best practices. This involves regular training sessions on safe collection, treatment and disposal. Information regarding standard septic tank design, the need for periodic inspection and desludging of FS/septage, design of a treatment facility, tender details for engaging licensed transporters, etc. should be disseminated widely to achieve a safe faecal sludge management system. Training should also be provided on safety standards.

***Capacity Building for Service Providers / Private Vendors*:** Local bodies should ensure all safety norms are clearly explained to the FS/septage transporters. Private Operators and Transporters should be well trained in safe collection and transportation of sewage including vehicle design, process of desludging, safety gears and safe disposal at the nearest treatment facility.

Technological Options for FSSM

Containment System

In practice the septic tanks are not constructed according to the IS code and hence the efficiency of the system is not up to the mark, it further affects the emptying frequency and the quality of effluent and FS/septage recovered from these tanks. These systems are constructed by local masons generally based on the space available and financial status of the user. The masons often create bigger systems than required. Often, the bottom of the tank is not lined, to decrease the frequency of emptying.

Emptying and Transportation

Emptying of containment system is done both mechanically and manually. At the end of a fixed time period, ideally two-three years, containment system should be emptied of FS/septage. The scheduled emptying should be done in order to facilitate treatment of faecal matter in the onsite sanitation system. There are many benefits of regular desludging including increased efficiency of OSS and better discharge quality of effluent. The Prohibition of Employment of Manual Scavengers and their Rehabilitation Act, 2013 prohibits employment or engagement of manual scavengers, however many locations which are inaccessible to mechanical emptying continue to employ manual scavengers. Other than manual emptying, mechanised methods include use of vacuum tanker or tractor mounted vacuum tankers, these are used for emptying of containment systems. Mechanised systems are usually accompanied with a driver and a helper (which may be two in some cases). Vehicles that carry FS/ septage act as a mobile sewer network for OSS. Ideally ultimate discharge point of collected FS/septage is STP or faecal sludge treatment facility if it exists. No Personal Protective Equipment (PPE) is used by the operators while emptying the tanks or pits posing risk to health.

The two main types of vehicles used in India are:

- Truck mounted vacuum tanker (Vacuum tanker)
- Tractor mounted tanker

Truck Mounted Vacuum Tankers (Vacuum Trucks)

These trucks have vacuum pumps, whose sizes are based on lift elevation, pumping distance, volume of sludge to be removed, and volume of the tank. Their capacity varies from 3000 liters- 10,000 liters.

Tractor Mounted Vacuum Tankers

These vehicles are locally made across India, but capacity is similar to the vacuum trucks. The motor, the tank and the tractor are joined together according to the complimenting capacity of each module.

Precautions to be Taken During Emptying

- Proper Personal Protective Equipment (PPE) should be used to avoid any transmission of pathogens to the operator providing de-sludging service
- Some amount of septage/sludge should be left in the septic tank to ensure retention of necessary microorganisms responsible for anaerobic digestion in the tank
- Due to anaerobic digestion processes, flammable gases are formed in septic tanks. While opening the chambers for de-sludging they escape into atmosphere. Hence, it is recommended not to light fire nearby it. (e. g. use of match stick for smoking) during that period
- Because of the sensitivity of septic systems due to presence of bacteria that speeds up anaerobic digestion process, care should be taken not to scrub the septic tank, clean using strong chemicals etc. so that bacteria do not die.

Faecal Sludge and Septage Treatment

The characteristics of FS/septage show that it is that FS/septage collected from various points in the city needs to be disposed at an appropriate treatment harmful for environment and health of living beings if it is disposed without treatment. Therefore, it is necessary facility. Both FS/septage and effluent needs to be treated. Small bore systems can be used to convey effluent to small distances and then treat it at decentralized scale. To choose the best combination of technologies the existing scenario of the city has to be discussed among the stakeholders. Things like population density, water usage, type of onsite system prevalent in city, soil strata, ground water table, land available, topography of the city, and characteristics of the FS/ septage, demand of the end product, capital cost and operation cost should be considered before deciding on the technology combination. The treatment can be achieved in three ways:

- Co-treatment with wastewater at sewage treatment plant
- Co-composting with municipal solid waste
- FS/Septage treatment plant

The four main functions of FS/septage treatment are: the solid-liquid separation, stabilization, dewatering or drying, and pathogen reduction. Figure 8 shows the different technologies based on their functions.

End-use and Resource Recovery

End-use of FS/septage refers to the safe, beneficial use of human excreta, i.e. faeces and the wastewater from onsite sanitation technologies. The type of end-use should decide the level of treatment. Considering the

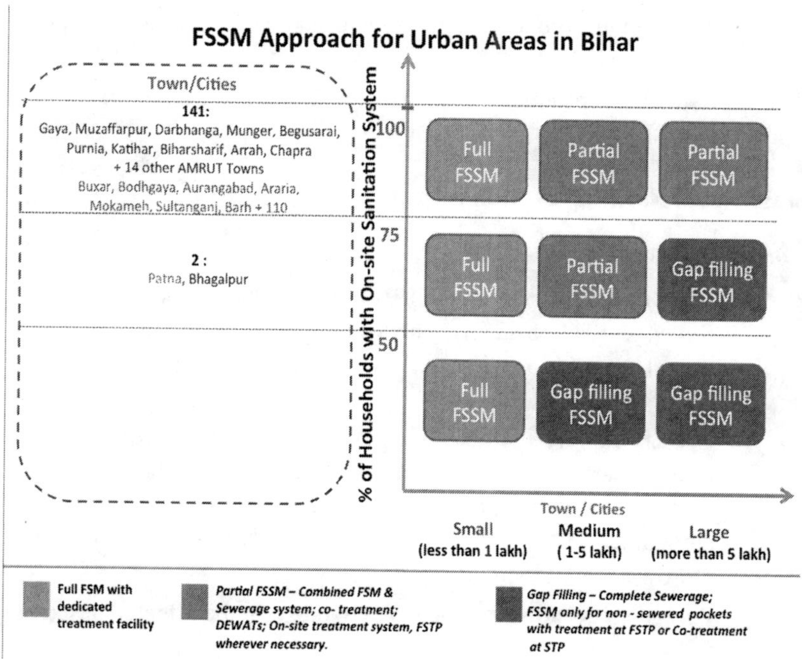

Note: To optimize the cost of implementing FSSM, cluster approach (desludging and treatment services can be shared among two smaller cities or small cities can make use of infrastructure at larger cities) should be adopted.

nutrients, organic matter and energy contained in FS/septage, it can be used as soil conditioner or fertilizer in agriculture, gardening, aquaculture or horticultural activities. Other uses include use as a fuel source, building material or for protein food production. Closing the loop would not only help in reducing fresh water demand and chemical fertilizer demand but also prove to be a source of revenue, in other words can help improve the business model.

Financing Considerations for FSSM

Options for Financing

FSSM when compared with either centralized or decentralized sanitation infrastructure is more cost effective. Most of the initial source of funding across the sanitation value chain will have to be provided by the joint effort of the central and state government primarily through the allied programme funding like Swachh Bharat Mission, Smart City or AMRUT.

Following are the options for sources of revenue for the private service provider:

- Desludging fee paid by user to the desludging service provider
- Fine for faulty containment system construction and illegal disposal of faecal sludge
- Sale of end products (For e.g. dried faecal sludge, water)
- Property tax designated for FSSM

State Level Funding Options

Sources of Revenues for FSSM

- As per the Bihar Municipal Bill, 2007, Chapter XV: Municipal Revenue, Section 128(i), The Municipality has the power to levy user charges for provision of water supply, drainage and sewerage services.
- If ULB explore the possibility of private sector involvement in FSSM, then an **escrow account** can be set up where revenues from the sanitation tax/ charge are transferred. The contractual amount for FSM services to the private party can be paid from this escrow account to avoid delays.
- **Periodic revisions for the taxes/ charges** to be effected based on revisions in costs involved
- To the extent possible, revenues should be generated from **sale of treated FS/septage** for agriculture/horticulture or other purposes

including local reuse of treated water to meet various non-potable requirements

- Funding could be explored through various other central/state schemes- Smart Cities Mission (SCM), HRIDAY, PMAY, NULM, Namami Gange and other state programmes like *Saat Nishchay* etc.
- CSR funding opportunities under Namami Gange, SCM and SBM also are available.

Out of the 199 towns and cities in Bihar, only twenty seven have been selected under the AMRUT scheme. The overall planning and implementation process remains the same. The critical part is the CAPEX and OPEX requirement.

An investment plan suited to the local capacities will be needed by the municipality for asset creation. In order to lower the financial burden on public investments, innovative private sector funding ideas will have to be evolved and a revenue model to determine the user charges will have to be worked out for collection and conveyance.

Other Funding Models

In the absence of any special scheme based funding the towns and cities can resort to either of the financial models:

Table: Alternate Funding Models

Public sector	***Outsourcing***	***Hybrid Annuity Model***	***Private Sector***
CAPEX	State Government / ULB / grant from funding agency (100%)	Government 20-50% Private sector 50-80% Use of land for FSTP on leasehold	Private sector
O&M	ULB operates and maintains the facility	Operation carried out by private sector with service level agreements	Complete private sector with monitoring mechanism
Capital Recovery	Tax from polluters/ cross subsidization/ Expenditure Budget	Tax from polluters, Revenue from services	Revenue from services
Role of ULB	Ownership of assets and operations	Contract management and monitoring	Monitoring for service level agreements

Greater Vishakhapatnam Municipal Corporation Faecal Sludge and Septage Management Policy and Operational Guidelines

Vision

The vision articulated by Visakhapatnam is: "All the inhabitants falling under the GVMC area will live in a city that is free from health hazards, environment pollution and shall be adopting the best practices in sanitation". It provides for a targeted attention desirous for improved onsite sanitation services together with faecal sludge and septage management for benefitting the whole city with focus on the urban poor.

Objectives

Vizag city through this FSSM Policy articulates and set priorities, commitments and direction for city-wide implementation of FSSM services in all the areas of GVMC, such that safe and sustainable sanitation becomes a reality for all households. More specifically, the Policy will:

- Mainstream FSSM in the city by the year 2019. Ensure that all benefits of wide access to safe sanitation accrue to all citizens across the sanitation value chain with containment, extraction, transportation, treatment, and disposal/re-use of all faecal sludge, septage and other liquid waste and their by-products and end-products.
- Suggest and identify ways and means, including the methods and resources, towards creation of an enabling environment for realising safe and sustainable FSSM in the City.
- Define the roles and responsibilities of various government entities and agencies, and of other key stakeholders such as the private sector, civil society organisations and citizens for effective implementation of FSSM services throughout the country.
- Enable and support synergies among relevant Central Government / State Government programs such as SBM, AMRUT and the Smart Cities Mission to realise safe and sustainable sanitation for all at the earliest, possibly by 2019.
- While not compromising on the eventual compliance to the strict environmental discharge standards already set, it shall be recognising the constraints in achieving these standards, it will help in adopting an appropriate, affordable and incremental approach towards achieving these standards.
- Mitigate gender-based sanitation insecurity directly related to FSSM, reducing the experience of health burdens, structural

violence, and promote involvement of both genders in the planning and design of the sanitation infrastructure.

Scope

This policy shall apply to all the areas within GVMC including Anakapalli and Bheemili, whether public or private, residential, commercial, institutional, industrial, proposed/planned or existing.

Policy Outline and Commitments

GVMC intends to foster FSSM, among others, as a means to supporting the achievement of universal and safe environmental sanitation leading up to outcomes on public health and environment. The policy statements not necessarily in any particular order translating the intent to action are as follows:

- GVMC believes in addressing and achieving public health and environmental safety goals through city wide; integrated and life cycle based planning in tandem with complementing sanitation services like sewerage systems, solid waste management, etc. A step by step planning will serve as a basis for all decisions.
- GVMC believes cost-effectiveness and equity (including gender issues) will be two cornerstone principles that will be used while fostering FSSM.
- GVMC understands resource management and loop closure as one of the basic pillars of sustainable development and the nexus between different sectors is recognised. In accordance, GVMC will establish formal institutional and programmatic linkages with other state departments/ agencies whose could be beneficiaries of some of the products and processes, emerging out of this policy, from time to time.
- GVMC will formulate and legalize all rules and regulations required to foster; operationalize the policy as a first step to indicate its intent to providing primacy for operationalizing this policy.
- GVMC will formulate clear roles and responsibilities of various actors in the FSSM ecosystem and strive to formalize them institutionally as personnel / service provider / citizen roles using existing tools and instruments.
- GVMC intends to continually build institutional capacities and of all personnel involved in identifying solutions and implementation

of projects and activities, both within and outside formal delivery process.

- GVMC will or cause to kick start actions across all steps of the value chain in equal measure leading to envisaged outputs and outcomes. Where, integration to other schemes/programs is envisioned, the needs of this policy would be considered in equal standing to other schemes/programs.
- GVMC assures to create an accurate database to support its evidence-based decision-making at every stage, from planning to service provision and user satisfaction.
- GVMC believes a community driven process could provide equal results to conventional processes and use the tenets of the policy to further ward level approaches currently piloted under SBM in Vizag. GVMC also commits to translate increased citizen awareness into quantifiable demand to support the processes at every stage value chain.
- GVMC desires achievement of SDG 2030 goals as a key milestone and institutionalize processes for continued implementation and management of FSSM sector. A critical aspect considered will be renewed emphasis on monitoring and learning to advice time to time the implementation actions.
- GVMC believes in the importance of piloting project(s) and R&D to ensure that best learning's are available for decision-making. These iterative processes on various subjects will be used to achieve the envisioned goals.
- GVMC intends to use best of the range technologies at every stage of project management.
- Primacy will be provided to occupational health & safety at all stages involving human involvement with wastes. Mechanization and automation are approaches to be used for service providers, both internal and external and at the generation and treatment end.
- GVMC intends to follow applicable standards and norms the available from time to time. Where such aspects are not available, GVMC will strive to follow best value for money approaches and principles. In the context of constructing treatment facilities, the focus will be on achieving treatment compliances against national public health & environmental safety standards/norms, prior to working on recycling & reuse.

- Given that GVMC mandate to deliver sustainable sanitation services encompasses more than one sector, and multiple projects/ programs are underway, it will undertake strategic annual review of the progress of the sector and address inter-linkages on a priority basis. When needed, GVMC can choose to update the policy in the light of the benefits derived from the program and any changes to external activities.
- GVMC will and through its awareness creation under SBM linked IEC activities, aim to create an aware and responsive citizenry. The idea is to ensure citizens are at the centre of the overall planning processes, whose needs specific to FSSM are captured and service satisfaction levels are always considered as performance markers.
- GVMC commits to ensure financial sustainability while implementing all activities under this policy.
- Efforts will be made to ensure financial resources for creation of physical infrastructure, institution building, capacity building, improved institutional processes to advance FSSM on par with other infrastructure.
- GVMC intends to foster and formally apply best services management talent from the public and private sector in an appropriate measure, from time to time, best serving to achieve the goals. This intent is to create an enabling environment for the private sector and could include formalization of processes hitherto provided for in an unorganised manner.
- GVMC commits to address last mile connectivity, obviate any barriers to access and include all disadvantaged population into the overall system by way of graded financial subsidies and other financial modes at every stage, as a pre-condition.
- GVMC believes in the use of state of the art IT and mobile applications to manage all activities related to FSSM, from point of generation until its safe disposal with support of continual monitoring, including reporting of outputs and outcomes.
- GVMC will seek institutional support from time to time from established and recognized knowledge platforms and use available support from different projects/programs, to further FSSM sector.

Step by Step Approach: Operationalizing FSSM

Benchmarking the service performance across the sanitation value chain through a city level assessment is the first step in the planning process. It is an important exercise, which provides an initial sense of the state of FSSM facility in the city. It helps in understanding the context and identifying the gaps in key services.

Detailed assessment of the services will need to be carried out across each link in the chain through appropriate field assessments. As policies and regulations already exist ensuring user interface and toilet access, the policy and ensuing operational guidelines focuses on the last four stages of the value chain, i.e. collection & / containment; emptying and conveyance; treatment; reuse and disposal. A snapshot of the aspects covered under critical stages are as follows:

Collect / Containment

The first step in this regard is that GVMC will undertake necessary steps to create a database of all the onsite sanitation facilities that are currently being used in the city. Although current standards provide for comprehensive guidelines regarding construction of septic tank, it is important to understand compliance levels to take corrective measures to support the overall processes in the subsequent steps of the value chain. It is with this view that GVMC will undertake survey of containment system or on-site sanitation system to understand adequacy and address through a robust action plan. It will further strengthen the permitting and inspection process of the septic tank as a vital requirement in the building plan approval for sanctioning of new houses construction. Group housing will be dealt with provisions of having proper onsite sanitation facility within the said complex. In either case, care will be taken to support future migration to sewerage connections when networks are made available.

Emptying and Conveyance

Conveyance describes the movement of sludge from individual septic tanks to treatment facilities, municipal or regional. Currently, these services are largely unregulated across the city of Visakhapatnam. Immediate steps include measured regulation of operators through a system of licensing directed towards enforcement of health and safety standards for prevention of open dumping; and secondly planning for a system of emptying every containment facility with a pre-defined or demanded frequency (typically once every two to three years subject to use levels of households / public accommodations / community or public toilets, and the like). This containment emptying will be contingent on having completed a survey of individual containment facilities to take a fair judgement on the process of emptying.

Treatment

The focus of treatment will primarily be on reaching public health and environmentally safe levels in the first stage and further subject to end use opportunities, suitable reuse treatment mechanisms will be devised. For treatment GVMC will assess the load of septage and assess the requirement of capacity for treatment plant, either exclusively for septage treatment or co-treatment with wastewater or solid waste.

Reuse and Disposal

Reuse/disposal refers to the methods in which products are ultimately returned to the environment, either as useful resources or reduced-risk materials. The treated septage can be used as a soil enricher or as filling material at construction sites. ULB should carry out primary assessment for availability of market and demand for reuse. It is understood that the State FSSM policy recommends co-locating of pure septage associated infrastructure, i.e. building faecal sludge treatment plants next to either sewage treatment plants or solid waste management plants, to gain advantage from synergies in operation and maintenance (effluent from FSTP can go to STP, or output of FSTP can be co-composted with solid waste, etc.). The understanding is that productive value generation from a resource management and financial sustainability perspective will be the last step of the process and dealt with on a case by case basis, at this stage.

Legislative and Regulatory Contexts

State laws, Rules and Regulations

All the stakeholders involved in FSSM in the sanitation value chain should adhere to the requirements of this policy and the State Laws, rules and regulations enacted from time to time and or suitably adapted to Vizag's requirements. The Model Building Bye-Laws (MBBLs), 2016 framed by the Town and Country Planning Organization and as adapted for Andhra Pradesh in 2017 may be referred.

Formation of rules and regulation at GVMC level

GVMC will formulate rules and regulation in the form of septage bye-laws, guidelines for registration and operation of VTOs, DSOs, monitoring frameworks of the overall process etc. within the boundaries of the policy.

These will be complimented and supplemented with regulations from time to time with an intention further the FSSM sector requirements across the value chain. Site selection for sludge use and application by parties (like residential layouts) and GVMC would need a prior consent to operate from the competent authority (like State Pollution Control Board).

Roles and Responsibilities

GVMC and households are the key stakeholders in the overall process of FSSM. They perform different roles given the context and interfaces they are exposed to.

Level	*Lead Roles*	*Supportive Roles*
GVMC	-Design, develop, plan and implement ULB level FSSM strategy -Set up and ensure operation of systems for 100% safe and sustainable collection, transport, treatment and disposal of faecal sludge & septage -Develop expertise, in-house and outsourced, to provide safe and effective FSSM services -Awareness and behaviour change campaign to engage diverse stakeholders -Develop training programmes for masons to build requisite skills for construction of quality septic tanks as per BIS / NBC norms -Set up systems to ensure financial sustainability in provisioning of FSSM services - Achieve the objectives of FSSM Policy in a time bound manner - Design and implement plans to eliminate manual scavenging and rehabilitate the manual scavengers - Funding through specific schemes and plans -Monitor and evaluate FSSM strategy and develop its implementation plan - Implement Municipal Byelaws and Septage Byelaws	-Create enabling environment for the NGOs and private sector to contribute to safe and sustainable FSSM
HOUSEHOLDS	-Timely and regular cleaning of septic tanks through approved entities -Regular maintenance and monitoring of septic tanks - Timely payment of user fee and/or charges, if any, towards FSSM services -Ensure Building Byelaws for construction of OSS are followed - Practice of Septage Byelaws as issued by the GVMC	-Engage with decision makers at GVMC level to ensure that they receive good quality FSSM services

Implementation Strategy

Faecal Sludge and Septage Management (FSSM) for the local bodies includes both residential and nonresidential/ commercial waste (but not including industrial waste). Implementation guidelines are most important as it provides direction, with knowledge, procedure and facilities for the efficient management of FSSM practices. In particular, the City Sanitation Task Forces (CSTFs) shall take up active planning and advisory role in co-operation with the municipal councils in order to dedicate appropriate resources and attention to the challenges of faecal sludge management.

GVMC has planned to address the city and ward wide FSSM issues by looking at the sanitation value chain of FSSM practices in a manner that addresses the technical, financial, institutional, regulatory and social dimensions to the best possible manner to the benefit its inhabitants. It has a comprehensive plan for faecal sludge and septage management with outlined objectives at each step in the value chain. Idea of conceiving an exclusive Septage Management Cell (SMC) is being considered under the Department of Public Health, which will look at all the modalities of FSSM starting from the awareness generation to its capture and reuse.

A Septage Management Committee is being proposed under this policy which will be convened by the Chief Medical Officer Health under the chairmanship of the Commissioner with representative from various line departments to monitor the city-wide implementation programme.

Expected Outcomes

As this Policy is implemented across the city, it is expected to yield significant benefits in terms of improved public health indicators and service level benchmarks, reduced pollution of water bodies and groundwater, and resource recovery leading to reuse of treated waste and other end products. Envisaged outcomes are:

- Safe containment, collection and conveyance of 100 percent human waste to treatment and disposal sites.
- Cost effective solutions for management of human waste through integrated network sewerage and faecal sludge septage management.
- Clarity among different stakeholders on identifying and implementing best and economically viable sanitation solutions.
- Improvement in technical capability among ULB staff to effectively implement city FSSM.
- Scheduled emptying of septic tanks or other containment systems at an interval of three years as recommended by CPHEEO Sewerage and Sewage Treatment Manual and the MoUD Advisory on Septage Management (2013).
- Safe disposal of all collected faecal sludge and septage at designated sites. (Sewage Treatment Plants, Faecal sludge Treatment Facilities for safe and scientific disposal, etc.)
- Continuous improvements in efficiency and effectiveness in the entire FSSM chain: containment, collection, conveyance, treatment and disposal.

- Contamination of water bodies and groundwater from human waste (Faecal matter) reduced to zero levels in all the towns and cities.
- Nuisance from faecal sludge reduced to minimum levels, resulting in nuisance-free living space in the city.
- Maximum reuse of treated sludge as fertilizer in farmlands, parks, gardens and other such venues, reuse of treated sewage, as source of energy where feasible, and any other productive uses.
- Drastic reduction in incidences of diseases due to safe and sustainable FSSM services.

Finance Planning

GVMC will identify suitable location within the city or in its outskirts for disposal of faecal sludge. Possibility of co-treatment with existing sewage treatment plant (STP) will also be looked at considering the quantum of investment involved through CAPEX and OPEX. Where such co-treatment facility is not possible, feasibility of decentralized Faecal Sludge Treatment Plant (FSTP) will be considered. Though services towards sanitation is a one of the basic and foremost duty of the ULB, it is equally important that investment put shall yield returns at least to offset its operating cost and where possible the capital cost.

Given this premise that the reuse market will be surveyed and GVMC will collaborate with Fertilizer Association of India and such other authorities associated with reuse of acceptable by-products for using in farming. The collaboration will also involve sensitization of farmers on the use of sludge as manure in farming, other private and public-sector organizations associated with mineral processing and manufacturing in Visakhapatnam. The possibility of carbon credits from reduced greenhouse gas emissions and capturing high calorific valued methane gas for power generation is also possible avenues of exploration. Sustainability is only possible with efficient and robust recovery of resources as well as finances.

Additional Funding Options

Private Funding Options	*State and Municipal Funding Options*	*Additional Funding Options*
Desludging fee paid by user to the desludging service provider	Conservancy tax under Andhra Pradesh Municipal Corporation Act, 1955	14th Finance Commission funds
Pradesh Municipal Corporation	Periodic revisions for the taxes/ charges	IEC funds under SBM

(Contd...)

Fine for faulty containment system construction and illegal disposal of faecal sludge		National schemes such as Smart City Mission and AMRUT
Sale of end products (For e.g. Dried faecal sludge, water)		Corporate Social Responsibility funds when available
Property tax or septage tax designated for FSSM		

PPP Engagement

The city of Visakhapatnam has sixty eight vacuum trucks owned by private sector operators. They are currently being operated informally and unregulated in operations. To leverage the private sector capability in providing on time services the current policy enables consultation and association with operators'. GVMC will monitor the activities of the VTO with the help of septage bye-laws and will provide training to the operators from time to time. GVMC will further look in to the occupational health and safety requirements of the VTOs by as a welfare measure not only for the person involved in desludging process but also for their family.

GVMC will liaison with the bankers' association and other financial organization existing in the city to help facilitate short term financing towards purchase of new vehicles or modernization, repair and maintenance of the existing vacuum trucks. The private sector operator will be engaged with GVMC under a licensing procedure to carryout necessary work on septage desludging. Option of providing individual license could also be worked out through guidelines, for regularization and registration. To make this service more affordable, an emptying and conveyance business plan will be prepared for the VTOs or the private contractors.

GVMC will also support framing contracts identifying performance level and further to encourage in carrying out ethical practices in sludge disposal. Suitable incentives will be added for the private sector operators.

For effective operationalize of scheduled septic tank emptying service and treatment facilities, GVMC shall also explore the option of private sector participation. The following points should be taken into consideration by the ULB:

- Explore private sector participation for various activities like procurement, operations and maintenance of the suction emptier trucks, construction and operations of septage treatment facility and possible re-users of treated septage within the city as well as in nearby cities.

- Develop performance based contracts such that payment is linked to the performance of private sector for providing the services. Some of the steps that can be taken up to boost the private sector participation are by the means of;
- Tax Incentive and Ease of Doing Business: Business line in sanitation sector especially in faecal sludge management is new in India although the same has been practiced in Western countries and some of the South East Asian countries. Ease of doing business with proper tax incentive to the private operator can increase the possibility of venturing in to the sanitation sector. One stop clearances and active facilitation to the private operators without being propelled in a problematic situation can create a winwin situation for both.

Financing at Low Interest Rate: GVMC will co-ordinate with the Bankers Association of India particularly focusing at Visakhapatnam to come up with loan available at low interest rate particularly for projects in sanitation sector focusing on urban poor. Further funding from bilateral and multilateral agencies in the form of transfer could also be used for financing such projects.

City and Ward FSSM Plan

City and ward level FSSM plan will be developed to identify the gaps through sanitation benchmark as prescribed under the National FSSM policy document. This will be implemented through the ward sanitation committee with the help of community based organization or NGOs and will further be integrated to the City FSSM plan. The development plan for the ward and the city will be considered after finding the gaps, and through a step wise approach by addressing the low-level benchmark first and then further to intermediate level and lastly to the high level. It will be the earnest effort of GVMC to provide hundred percent sewerage coverage and hundred percent sewage connection facility for its citizen in the years to come. Recovery of cost is one of the most important benchmark as suggested by the CPHEEO which has a baseline of at least twenty percent and will try to achieve it through various marketing mix.

It is important to understand the performance of the Sewage Treatment Plant (STP) if at all it is considered for co-treatment. Therefore, the operation and monitoring of the plant shall be taken up on a pilot basis for a month to understand its effect on the plant output parameter, managing sludge lines and addressing the breakdown of the pumps, motors and valves.

GVMC will look in to the intervention tools that are required for successful implementation of such FSSM plan in the city. Some of the important intervention tools that will be considered are as below:

Tool	***Purpose***	***Example/Information***
Capital Investment	Provide new / renewed hardware capacity	Investment can be in upgrading, rehabilitating or new infrastructure (e.g. treatment facilities, IT network, etc.) and / or equipment
Regulation	Ensure public safety and fairness	Regulations are a 'stick' that should be applied only in extreme circumstances when all other 'carrots' have been tried and not proven to be effective enough. For instance, in case behavior change campaigns (BCC), educating and encouraging households to empty their OSS once in every 3 years do not result in improved behaviour, scheduled emptying regulations can be introduced, along with investment in the necessary IT infrastructure and BCC campaigns. Regulation could also be introduced to regulate the price of emptying. Similarly, it is preferable to influence the market (e.g. invest in more disposal points, improve competition, etc.), as enforcement of prices is notoriously difficult.
Experimentation	Trial of innovative approach that may either succeed or fail	Research, design, trial, learning and iteration / or failure of innovative approaches. Experimentation can be undertaken along with any of the other intervention tools. Monitoring, evaluation and learning is a crucial part of experimentation. Failure of the innovation is a possibility that should be expected, however failure due to poor learning from previous mistakes should not be accepted.
Institutional Evolution	Trial of innovative approach that may either succeed or fail	Redesigning of institutional structure and / or incentives to address new challenges. First is, citizens' needs as it relates to FSS management should be assessed. Based on these needs, institutional structures and / or incentives should be re-evaluated and if necessary redesigned to ensure they are responsive.
Information	Improve effectiveness of response to citizen needs	Data on existing sanitation systems, services or citizens' needs is necessary to design solutions. Some information may already be available and needs to be used. Information that is not available needs to be collected (either one-time or regular collection, depending on the requirement).
Behaviour Change and Communication	Inform, motivate, and sustain changes in citizen behaviour	Regular emptying of septic tanks is necessary, even before it starts overflowing. Citizens should be made aware and motivated to regularly empty it by way of behaviour change and communication campaigns (BCC), and the behaviour needs to be sustained through regular reminders (e.g. vacuum tanker operators send targeted reminders every 3 years).
Licensing	Ensure safety of public and operators, ensure competitive market	Licensing is a way for public authorities to ensure service providers (i) have been trained on safe and appropriate ways of service delivery to ensure health and safety of the public and the operators, (ii) are regular and up to date on their training, (iii) their equipment is appropriate and safe, (iv) privileges can be revoked if public health and safety is jeopardized, (v) provide a competitive market – e.g. limited licenses can be provided to avoid oversaturation of market with VTOs.

Form for Application for the License for Collection, Transportation and Disposal of Septage in GVMC

1. Name of the applicant (as per vehicle registration certificate) : Shri/Ms.

2. Details of Employee.

Category of Employee | Name | Aadhar Number

(1) Driver
(2) Assistant
(3) Others (if any)

3. PAN Number of the Applicant

4. GST Number of the Applicant

5. Bank Account No. of Applicant

Place Self-Attested Recent
Passport Size Photograph

6. Savings/ Current

7. Details of Personal Health Insurance

Category of Employee | Name | Number | Validity | Name of Insurance Company

(1) Driver
(2) Assistant
(3) Others (if any)

8. Whether member of NTR Vaidya Sewa Scheme

Category of Employee | Yes | No

(1) Driver
(2) Assistant
(3) Others (if any)

9. Whether covered under PM Chandrana Bhima Yojana

Category of Employee | Yes | No

(1) Driver
(2) Assistant
(3) Others (if any)

10. Medical Fitness Certificate for Employees Available

Category of Employee | Yes | No

(1) Driver
(2) Assistant
(3) Others (if any)

11. Driver License Number

12. Nature of Vehicle for which license is available
13. Address (Regd. Office)
    (Head office)
14. Telephone No. (O) (Mobile No)
15. E-mail id
16. Registration No. of Vehicle
17. Does the Vehicle belong to the applicant?
18. Engine Number Chassis Number
    HCV LCV TW
    License Number
    Yes No
19. Pollution Certificate
20. Vehicle Insurance Certificate
21. Vehicle Fitness Certificate
22. Vehicle fitted with GPS
23. Details of the vehicles indicating model, type, capacity (Document proof of any may be enclosed).
    (a) Model
    (b) Type
    (c) Capacity

ODISHA URBAN SANITATION POLICY, 2017

Vision

All cities and towns in Odisha become totally clean, sanitized, healthy, and liveable, ensuring and sustaining good public health and environmental outcomes for all citizens, in line with the National Urban Sanitation Policy.

Goal

All cities and towns in Odisha become totally clean, sanitized (safe), healthy, and liveable cities / towns that are managed by ULBs with citizen and stakeholder participation.

Principles

The policy will be based on the following principles:

- ***Sanitation will be treated as a basic service***: The State Government shall create opportunities and provide necessary support through which, all citizens can have access to sanitation services as their basic entitlement.

- ***Equity and safety of access and use, particularly to the vulnerable and unserved populations***: The State shall endeavour to ensure that no urban citizen, irrespective of socio-economic status, caste, gender, age, or legal status of land/status of migration is denied access to and the use of sanitation services in Odisha's cities. In the case of residents with no tenure security, the State will make effort to resolve tenure issues in providing individual household sanitation facilities or community sanitation facilities. However, where sanitation services are provided in areas without tenure security, the provision of these services will not entitle the individual/household any legal right to the land.

  In addition to this, the State and ULBs will ensure that access to such facilities (especially community and public) are maintained with an adequate level of cleanliness, and safety of access, especially for women. Adequate arrangements for access for the differently abled will also be made at these facilities (new / upgraded facilities).

- ***Increased awareness of the collective goal of sanitised cities***: The causal linkages of sanitation with public and environmental health need to be made more explicit to citizens, communities and institutions. In addition to the provision of facilities, sustained improvements in the quality of life are possible when supplemented by hygiene and behavior change. The State will aim to generate demand for safe sanitation, especially among the un-served households. Citizens, communities, institutions, and cities as a whole will be encouraged to play an active role in both behavior change towards safe sanitation, and ensuring the adoption and use of safe technology to protect the environment.

- ***Institutional roles, responsibilities and capacity development***: The policy will hinge on progressive articulation in policy and law followed-up by operations that are in line with the spirit of the 74th Constitutional Amendment Act, 1994. Devolution of functions, funds and functionaries will need to be progressively ensured to the ULB with adequate support for building planning, and management capacities. The quality of city sanitation planning will depend upon the vibrancy of sub-city representative institutions that draw on civil society to ensure active citizen engagement.

- ***Emphasis on operations and maintenance of sanitation infrastructure***: One of the key reasons for poor sanitation infrastructure as well as high capital expenditure on sanitation is the lack of operations and maintenance of existing sanitation infrastructure. ULBs will be responsible to ensure that existing sanitation infrastructure is maintained at adequate operational levels, either through official funds, or in partnership with the private sector.

- ***Integrating broader environmental concerns in the provision of urban sanitation service delivery***: The environment (land, air, and water resources) must be considered in all development activities for sanitation provision and management. All planning and implementation will seek to ensure that adverse risks to public health and the environment are adequately minimised at all stages in the sanitation chain – containment, collection, transportation or conveyance, treatment and re-use or disposal. Appropriate protection of the environment shall be applied, including prosecution under the law as required.

  The State Government will prioritise those cities that directly or indirectly affect rivers or river basins in the state due to discharge of untreated domestic wastewater for setting up pollution abatement systems.
- ***Choosing technology and solutions appropriate to the context***: Under the policy, the choice of technology and solutions will be contingent upon the needs of that context. For example, if, in the course of evaluation, decentralized and on-site technologies and solutions are context appropriate, then those should be chosen as opposed to blindly applying the choice of networked sewerage systems.

Outcomes of The Policy

(1) Urban Areas are Open-Defecation and Discharge Free

This shall be a key outcome of the sanitation policy. In addition to infrastructure provision, this outcome requires behaviour change at the individual, household, community, institutional and city levels. It is therefore the most crucial and challenging to achieve. Open defecation free under this policy is understood as the termination of faecal-oral transmission determined by:

- No observed open defecation;
- All city residents have access to and use of household, community, and/or public latrines;
- There is adequate access and use of latrines in all institutions;

- All insanitary latrines (including single pit latrines) are converted to sanitary latrines, and no incidence of Manual Scavenging observed;
- All city residents are engaged in safe hygiene practices, including hand washing;

In addition, open discharge free, under this policy shall be understood to mean an environment free from human waste which shall be determined as follows:

- There is no open discharge of faecal and liquid waste, or raw sewage into the open drains or environment
- There is safe containment, collection, transportation, treatment, and disposal of sewage, septage, and waste water.

(2) Municipal Solid Waste is Safely Managed and Treated

Between March and April, 2016, the Ministry of Environment, Forest and Climate Change, Government of India notified the following rules: (1) Solid Waste Management Rules, 2016; (2) E-Waste (Management) Rules, 2016; (3) Plastic Waste Management Rules, 2016; (4) Construction and Demolition Waste Management Rules, 2016; (5) Bio-Medical Waste Management Rules, 2016; and (6) Hazardous and Other Wastes (Management and Trans boundary Movement) Rules, 2016.

According to the SWM Rules, 2016, solid waste includes solid or semi-solid domestic waste, sanitary waste, commercial waste, institutional waste, catering and market waste, and other non-residential waste, street sweeping, silt removed or collected from surface drains, horticultural waste, agriculture and dairy waste, treated bio-medical waste. This excludes industrial hazardous waste, untreated bio-medical waste and e-waste, battery waste, and radio-active waste.

Municipal Solid Waste Management (MSWM) refers to a systematic process that comprises of waste segregation and storage at source, primary collection, secondary storage, transportation, resource recovery, processing, treatment, and final disposal of solid waste.

Odisha will follow a policy whereby minimal amount of waste is sent to landfills by following the three ₹, namely reduce, reuse, and recycle. The ultimate goal will be to create value out of waste and produce a paradigm shift from garbage as 'disposable' to 'renewable resource'.

The aim of this policy is to ensure cleaner streets and neighbourhoods, improved quality of life by reducing health risks (such as vector vector borne diseases like dengue and malaria) associated with garbage piles, and ensure segregation of waste and doorstep collection at affordable rates. In order to effect this, the state will, in the next 10 years aim to drastically improve the efficiency of waste processed, and eventually move to a decentralised system for processing waste.

(3) Sewage, Septage / Faecal Sludge and Liquid Waste is Safely Managed, Treated, and Disposed

This outcome shall aim to ensure that wherever faecal waste is generated in the urban environment, it is safely confined, regularly collected, safely transported and disposed after adequate treatment; care being taken of persons, machinery, materials and surroundings involved in the process. In Odisha, where the majority of households and institutions have access to on-site sanitation, the focus in the policy will be on Septage/ Faecal Sludge Management (FSM). In the large cities (population of 100,000 or more) with increasing urban density, the state government may, based on context and demand, bring out a separate action plan for sewerage systems in the city. Under this outcome, the entire sanitation chain will be covered.

The State Government will strive to create opportunities and provide necessary support through which all the citizens can have access to septage management services; while enjoining the household to be responsible for maintaining sanitation facilities and ensuring safety as declared by the ULBs.

(4) Safety Standards and Guidelines are Followed in the Physical Handling and Management of Waste

The Prohibition of Employment as Manual Scavengers and their Rehabilitation Act was passed by the Union Government on 19th September, 2013 (MSA 2013). While the list of definitions is exhaustive under the MSA 2013, the following definitions are important for the current Policy and have been reproduced below for ready reference:

(5) Women and Girls have Access to Safe Menstrual Hygiene Management (MHM)

In 2012, the Joint Monitoring Programme (JMP) of the WHO and UNICEF defined Menstrual Hygiene Management as follows: "Women and adolescent girls are using a ***clean menstrual management material*** to absorb or collect menstrual blood, that can be ***changed in privacy as often as necessary*** for the duration of a menstrual period, ***using soap and water for washing*** the body as required, and having ***access to safe and convenient facilities to dispose*** of used menstrual management materials. They ***understand the basic facts*** linked to the menstrual cycle and ***how to manage it with dignity and without discomfort or fear***."

The key challenges faced by women and girls during their periods of menstruation include:

- A lack of sanitary protection materials leading to embarrassment and stress due to leakage and malodour.
- A lack of menstrual hygiene facilities in the home, workplace, and common/community areas, which results in a number of women being unable to change materials in dignity and safety. This results in absence from work and schools.
- A fear of using the latrine due to staining, the lack of privacy, inadequate disposal facilities, or unsafe location of latrine facilities.

To ensure effective and timely action under the policy, the State Government may bring out appropriate instructions for phasing of cities under each outcome on a yearly basis, and the budget for this may be context-specific technologies being proposed/ considered for those cities.

(6) Cities/Towns do not Discharge Untreated Waste (solid, liquid, and faecal waste) into the Water Bodies

The aim of this outcome is the urban pollutants – septage / faecal sludge, and municipal solid waste – into the rivers and river basins of Odisha from urban and peri-urban areas thus ensuring the conservation restoration, regeneration and integrated development of rivers basins in Odisha. At present, cities are disposing septage/sludge directly into water bodies, either though non functional drains, natural drains, or through open defecation. This is compounded by solid waste being disposed into rivers/river basins.

Under this outcome, Odisha will focus on a combination of strengthening the constructed drainage systems, strong FSM / septage management, and/or underground sewerage networks where relevant (including treatment plants), and interception, diversion, and treatment of septage and waste water flowing through natural drains.

Implementation of the Policy

The Housing & Urban Development Department (HUDD) of the Government of Odisha will be responsible for developing a strategy to implement the policy covering all the six outcomes, along with the necessary institutional framework, provisions and guidance for planning, monitoring, evaluation, capacity building and funding.

ODISHA URBAN SANITATION STRATEGY, 2017

The outcome namely **Sewage, Septage / Faecal Sludge and Liquid Waste is Safely Managed, Treated, and Disposed** shall aim to ensure that wherever faecal waste is generated in the urban environment, it is safely confined, regularly collected, safely transported, and disposed after adequate treatment; with due care being taken of persons, machinery, materials and surroundings involved in the process.

The state government and ULBs will undertake the following activities under this outcome:

- ***City sanitation plans (CSPs)*** will include septage management / FSM plans. These CSPs will include elements of the guidelines released by the state government as below, and will cover the entire built environment of the city i.e. both households and non-household institutions within the city.
- The state government will draft ***sewerage and septage management guidelines*** for cities which will cover:
  - (a) ***Safety Standards*** for septic tanks and other on-site systems conforming to Government of India and State Government standards as issued from time-to-time.
  - (b) ***Safe Transportation of sludge***, including a checklist of tools and equipment to be kept with the transportation vehicle, and norms for maintenance of piped underground sewerage systems (including pumping stations) wherever applicable
  - (c) ***Setting Standards and Norms for Safely Treated Septage/ Sewage and Effluent, and Safety and Public Health:*** This will cover environmental standards (not already set by the Government of India) for discharge/disposal of effluent and sludge, post-treatment, into water bodies and land, norms for site selection of treatment facilities, and safety standards for workers involved in safe sanitary disposal and management, including identification of hazards and minimum-worker safety and process standards to be maintained.
  - (d) ***Service Delivery Standards*** for both sewerage and septage management at the city level.
  - (e) ***Engagement of Non-Government Stakeholders*** including the public through IEC campaigns by the ULB, the private sector in infrastructure provision and operations and maintenance (O&M) through public-private-partnerships (PPPs), and the private informal sector in service delivery of FSM at the city/district levels.
  - (f) ***Regulation, Coordination and ULB Primacy***: This will cover strategies for cost recovery (e.g. user charges) of

service delivery, and clear planning and implementation roles for ULBs in this process.

(g) ***O&M and Monitoring & Evaluation (M&E)***: These guidelines must prioritise not just construction of these facilities, but the O&M of these facilities for a minimum of ten years post construction. CSPs must take into consideration the O&M cost, and how these will be met (whether through existing ULB funds, or in partnership with the private sector, NGOs/CBOs or SHGs. The ULBs will ensure close monitoring of the infrastructure creation and O&M thereof; the state government will have a half-yearly review of these facilities and their operationality.

(h) ***IEC and BCC***: This will be expected at three levels – the general public, septic tank masons, and septage transporters and other private operators. At the level of the general public, this includes the need for proper construction of on-site systems, and the public health effects of poor sanitation. Inter alia, targets for this will be resident welfare associations (RWAs), CBOs, SHGs, and schools (with a specific focus on hygiene behaviour and public health impact). The ULBs will identify septic tank masons that are involved in the construction of on-site systems and sensitize them on environmental norms and train them in the guidelines. Wherever feasible, ULBs may consider ground-verification and spot checks on such constructed infrastructure. Finally, IEC campaigns will also cover septage transporters and other private operators to ensure safe handling of septage at the time of desludging and transportation. The state government will develop these IEC campaigns and training programs, train the master trainers in this regard and ensure all urban areas are covered for this.

(i) ***Capacity Building and Training***: The state government will sensitise ULB staff and elected representatives. In order to do this, master trainers will be identified, and training of trainer sessions will be conducted for these master trainers. A calendar of training will then be devised. The ULBs shall ensure that the relevant officials/representatives are mandated to attend these meetings.

- The state through the ULBs, will ensure provision of these services to both household, and non-household facilities – public, community and establishment - where they exist in the city.

- **The District Administration will ensure the following:**
    (a) Provision land for development of sanitation infrastructure for ULBs, either individually, or in a cluster as per the plan for each district.
    (b) Land is to be identified based on technological and environmental considerations. This selection shall be approved by the competent authority identified by the State. The competent authority shall, among other considerations specified under the law, consider quantity of waste generated, and compliance with environmental laws.
    (c) Ensure monitoring and evaluation for septage/sewage management of all ULBs within the district.
- ***ULBs will ensure the following***:
    (a) Nomination of a nodal officer for septage/sewage management in the city
    (b) Extension of full support for capacity building initiatives, including ensuring that the appropriate officials/elected representatives are mandated to attend trainings
    (c) Ensure that all sanitation infrastructure (already created and planned under the CSP) is operated and maintained
    (d) Engagement of the general public under this plan
    (e) Facilitation of engagement of the private and informal sector in infrastructure creation, O&M, and service delivery in the city
    (f) Ensure adequate budgetary provision for city-wide sanitation delivery under the CSP.

As an immediate strategy, and as has been stated above, ***open defecation and insanitary latrines will be eliminated***. Insanitary latrines will be converted to sanitary latrines as per the MSA 2013, households defecating in the open because of a lack of household latrines will be provided access either to an individual household latrine (under SBM, or other relevant programmes of the state or central government), or to a community toilet.

- ULBs will ensure that household, community, public and institutional toilets with on-site sanitation will be provided with and follow ***safe standards of FSM / septage management*** as specified in this Policy.
- ULBs will also ensure that all constructed drains are repaired at vulnerable points to prevent leakages into the environment.

- Wastewater treatment facilities at community and city-levels will be explored to ensure that no wastewater (grey or black) reaches the open environment untreated.
- All MSW dumped into constructed and/or natural drains will be cleaned, and the waste collected will be scientifically treated and disposed as specified above. All new (storm water) drains should be constructed as per approved norms.
- Special care is to be taken with crematoria and other institutions dealing with the disposal of human and/or animal bodies (e.g. slaughter houses). ULBs are to ensure that such disposal is properly monitored, follows set norms, and does not result in pollution of water bodies of the state.
- Eventually the waste management in cities and towns of Odisha must be such that no solid and/or liquid waste is disposed of into the water bodies. Such waste is scientifically processed, and only treated effluent that meets environmental discharge norms may be released into water bodies. The state government will bring out technical guidance notes from time-to time to specify standards, processes and technologies that may be used for this purpose within the context of Odisha. ULBs and the state government will take necessary steps – regulatory or legal – to ensure enforcement of these norms.

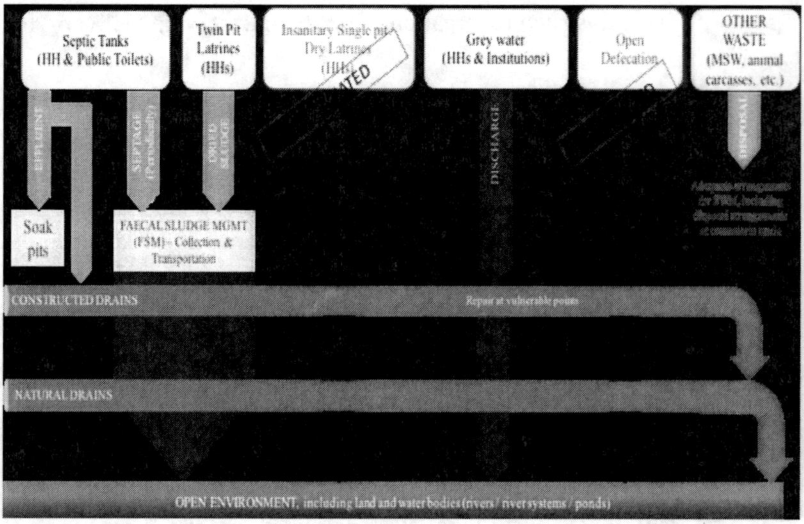

Graph: Intermediate Actions to ensure that cities do not discharge untreated wastewater and septage into the open environment

State Level Institutional Set Up

High Powered Committee (HPC)

The HPC will be the apex body chaired by the Chief Secretary, providing overall guidance and policy direction to urban sanitation initiatives in the state, and overseeing the planning and implementation of the state policy. The Mission will direct all departments and agencies, for the successful implementation of the Odisha Urban Sanitation Policy. It will consist of an inter-departmental-executive setup to ensure successful execution of the state Policy by periodic evaluation of progress across Departments.

The HPC will:

- Guide the actions of the State Sanitation Directorate (SSD) and ensure convergence with other departments for optimising efforts towards successful outcomes.
- Prepare, approve and ensure online publication of the State Sanitation Policy, and City Sanitation Plans (CSP), if not already done so.
- Ensure comprehensive collection of city-wide data on sanitation, covering the whole sanitation service chain – containment, collection, transportation, treatment, reuse/disposal, and wherever possible, link this information to health outcomes in the state.
- Finalise the Concept note on the urban sanitation situation in the state before submission to the SBM National Mission Directorate.
- Empanel consultants of repute and experience for preparation of DPRs for urban sanitation projects, including under SBM(U) and conducting independent reviews and monitoring during execution of projects.
- Empanel reputed institutes like IITs, NITs, State Technical Universities, etc., for the appraisal of DPRs.
- Sanction projects related to urban sanitation service delivery.
- Plan for fund flow in the short, medium and long-terms and plan for additional resource mobilisation as needed.
- Recommend proposals for release of instalments of funds for sanitation projects, including under SBM(U)
- Monitor outcome and O&M arrangements of projects sanctioned and completed.
- Review the progress of capacity building, IEC, public awareness activities and approve annual action plans for these.

- Ensure convergence of action for urban sanitation in the state, and bring about inter-departmental coordination and cooperation for this.
- Ensure timely audits of funds released and review action taken reports on various audit reports and other similar reports.
- Address violation of norms and conditions and review legal issues, if any.

State Sanitation Directorate (SSD)

The SSD is the core HUDD line agency setup to provide implementation support under the policy; and to ensure successful implementation of the state policy by periodic review of progress across line agencies. The SSD shall function as the State Mission Directorate for SBM(U) as well and shall be headed by the Mission Director SBM(U). The Director, SSD shall be supported by a Project Management Unit (PMU) or equivalent with experts and support staff on an outsourced basis covering the verticals of project management, IEC and media, information technology, and monitoring & evaluation. The SSD will:

- Supporting the HPC in the implementation of sanitation programmes and policy in the state.
- Decide the framework for appropriate and effective MIS, HRM, and M&E systems, implementation of the Urban WASH Communication Strategy, engagement with support organisations, and partnerships (PPP or otherwise) required for the sanitation initiatives, especially the SBM(U).
- Set out guidelines for ULBs to operationalise different components of the sanitation policy; including third party roles, etc.
- Provide strategic direction to the State Sanitation Nodal Agency for development, procurement and application of appropriate technology options and service standards for higher environmental and public health outcomes.
- Shall be responsible for the development and deployment of appropriate MIS & M&E systems to monitor progress under the policy.
- Liaise with other line departments and agencies (like Health and Family Welfare Dept., SPCB, etc.) to finalise outcome indicators, enable data capture, etc.
- Create/notify a uniform structure across the state for planning, designing, project preparation, appraisal, sanction and

implementation of sanctioned projects, including under SBM(U) at the ULB level.

- Review and appraise DPRs/project proposals received for urban sanitation under various programmes/schemes, including SBM and recommend them to the HPC. Wherever necessary, the SSD may engage empanelled appraisal agencies for the appraisal of these proposals/DPRs.
- Bring in successful experiences/best practices in other cities, develop collaborations and suitable models for technical options and social mobilisation, including making use of available expertise within government, and disseminate these to other ULBs in the state through the capacity building mechanism.
- Advise the state to strategically implement the best available technology for sanitation service delivery as per the context of the urban sanitation situation in the state.
- Guiding ULBs in the preparation of City Sanitation Plans, channelling financial resources from state, central and externally aided sources and providing technical assistance required by ULBs.
- Examine the need and possibilities of improving and securing (making safe) the work conditions of *Safai Karmacharis*, the sanitation needs of the urban poor, examine the sanitation situation in schools, especially the situation of girl children, with the idea of using this platform also, to trigger behavioural change in the community, design and implement suitable reward schemes that provide incentives to ULB to achieve positive sanitation outcomes, and promote demand-based sanitation while ensuring that suitable protocols for maintenance are set up.
- Advising the state government on necessary modifications/ notifications required by law to affect the sanitation policy, examine the updates made to the Development Control Regulations, and provide other technical know-how for effective management.

District Level Institutional Set Up

In the current devolution scenario, most of the ULBs may have considerable deficits in capacities to plan, implement and monitor urban sanitation programs. While it is expected that ULBs will develop these capacities over the medium term (next three to five years), a district level mechanism will be the appropriate institution for guiding and assisting ULBs in urban sanitation, in coordination with different line departments and their frontline units at the district and the ULB levels. This will also enable leveraging on capacities and programs on-going in the nearby rural areas. Wherever possible and effective, the state government may direct districts to follow a clustering policy where cities within a district are clustered on the basis of geographical proximity to implement the sanitation policy and share relevant sanitation infrastructure.

District-level Review & Monitoring Committee (DLRMC)

The DLRMC will be constituted with a view to fulfil the objective of ensuring satisfactory monitoring of projects under the Chairpersonship of a Member of Parliament. The DLRMC will monitor SBM(U) projects in a given district as per the guidelines issued by the SBM(U) National Mission Directorate. The District Nodal Officer for implementation, monitoring and oversight, will be the District Collector, or an officer nominated by the District Collect. In the event that the District Collector nominates a representative, that representative shall report to the District Collector, who in turn shall report to the State Government in the normal procedure outlined in the institutional framework of the policy.

District Urban Sanitation Committee (DUSC at DUDA)

Chaired by the District Collector, it will be the District-level monitoring and implementing agency for urban sanitation programmes, schemes and strategies with Mayors/Chairpersons and Commissioners/Executive Officers of ULBs, heads of line departments, and representatives from local industries associations, NGOs, etc. The DUSC shall:

- Remain in constant contact with the SSD for implementation of the State Urban Sanitation Policy and coordinate between the ULBs in the District and the State for timely and proper flow of information;
- Direct the Integration of city sanitation planning in the ULBs according to the directions of the State level nodal agency;
- Monitor the progress of preparation of CSPs, and implementation of sanitation promotion, health and environment outcomes, in urban areas of the district and report as required by the SSD;
- Plan for emergency requirements (floods, cyclones, etc.) of sanitation and also seasonal requirements (festivals, fairs, etc.) and approve the arrangement;

- Direct the coordination of the activities of line department frontline personnel towards enabling planned sanitation outcomes;
- Assist the ULBs in carrying out their tasks as provided for in the City Sanitation Task Force (below) in the initial phase;
- Oversee the clustering strategy in the district and its successful implementation;
- Review DPRs for urban sanitation developed by the City PMU under various programmes, including SBM(U). In particular the DUSC shall ensure no duplication of efforts / resources (physical and financial) across clusters wherever applicable;
- All sanitation projects, except for large capital projects on composting, septage/FS Treatment Plants, or STPs, will be approved at the level of the DUSC. The SSD and HPC may amend the limits of these approvals from time-to-time, and issue instructions accordingly.

For this, the DUSC shall be supported by a Project Implementation Unit (PIU).OWSSB and PHEO will nominate representatives for each district to serve as members of the DUSC and attend meetings.

The ULB Level Institutional Set Up

City Sanitation Task Force (CSTF)

This will be created within the ULB under the leadership of the Commissioner/Executive Officer to design, implement and monitor the sanitation promotion programs in the respective ULBs. The CSTF will be responsible for:

- Preparation of baseline database and situation analysis;
- Design of city sanitation plan (CSP) emphasizing participatory approaches;
- Ensuring use of sanitary latrine by all and ensuring safe disposal of sewage and liquid waste;
- Monitoring progress of the campaign and make periodic corrections as needed and regular reporting to district and state coordination agencies;
- Working with support organisations, line departments and civil society formations in setting up systems that enable community level monitoring and management of common sanitary facilities;
- Developing systems that enable community-based monitoring of public health and environmental outcomes;

- Working with the appropriate line departments and civil formations to identify and develop suitable citizen-interaction platforms as a hub for the communication and also monitoring;
- Design and implement incentive schemes for ward or suitable sub-city administrative territory and other identified units – schools, slums, shopping areas; etc.
- Review DPRs for urban sanitation developed by the CMD under various programmes, including SBM(U) and recommend them to the DUSC consideration.
- The CSTF will also make necessary sub-committees (e.g. solid waste, septage, etc.) to ensure ward-level monitoring of the implementation the policy across all wards.

The CSTF will have membership of the relevant elected representatives heading the standing committees and also of women members.

City Project Implementation Unit (PIU)

This will be headed by the Commissioner/Executive Officer to implement the sanitation programmes in the respective ULBs. The SSD will notify the technical support to be provided. The City PIU will be responsible to:

- Conduct the baseline survey
- Provide necessary inputs for the CSP
- Conduct the city-wide communication campaign;
- Work with the community to ensure citizen engagement for sanitation service delivery across all categories, including the vulnerable
- Develop DPRs for urban sanitation under various programmes/ schemes, including SBM(U) for consideration by the state government
- Provide necessary support the CSTF for implementation of sanitation programmes/schemes in the city.

While initially, the PIUs can function as technical cells for the ULBs, eventually, the functions performed by the PIU must be absorbed into the ULB such that it is an essential function performed by the ULB as the local authority for sanitation in the city.

Additionally, the local authority responsible for faecal sludge/septage management in the city will ensure that there is adequate sourcing, organisation, and capacity building of a team of frontline sanitation workers that will deal with on-ground requests for FSM in the city.

Sub-city Level Institutional Set Up

Ward Committees/Area Committees

These will be constituted to be responsible for oversight and implementation of the CSP within the ward and report to CSTF. It will also be responsible for monitoring the progress of the campaign and school sanitation initiatives.

Other Support Organisations

CSTF may involve identified committed NGOs and CBOs by allocating clear roles and outcomes.

Private Sector Engagement is to be encouraged through voluntary efforts, financial contributions or the PPP route.

Planning

ULB Level

City Sanitation Plans (CSPs) will need to be prepared in a participatory manner through consultations with urban citizens, especially the poor and women. The goal of making cities open defecation free and moving towards a safe disposal system for sewage as well as faecal sludge will be the main thrust of CSP. The phasing of the plan, its operational elements, choice of technology options and finances will feature in the plan. This plan will be integrated in to the overall development plan of the ULB and will also be reviewed by the DUSC to dovetail it with other urban infrastructure development initiatives. The CSPs need to be readied within a definite time frame.

State Level

The SSD will consolidate CSPs into a state level plan specifying the time frame, finances, operational components and guideline-sets for these components, to enable the state to earmark resources. The ULB will align to the State plan. Special emphasis will need to be given to urban centres that attract floating population seasonally (tourism) or sporadically (religious/cultural occasions) for planning. Also, appropriate environment-friendly solutions would need to be incorporated for these locations.

A communications strategy evolved at the state level would guide the awareness generation and Behaviour Change Communication components at the ULB level.

Implementation

Setting the Standards

The SSD will draft and issue guidelines for the ULBs in sanitation management covering:

- Environmental standards (like PCB effluent standards for discharge to land and water)
- Technical standards and guidelines for on-site/off-site technologies and its management
- Public Health indicators and standards (like incidence of diarrhoea, ARI, Water Quality standards–faecal coliform)
- Safety standards for workers involved in safe sanitary disposal and management including identification of hazards and minimum worker-safety and process-safety standards to be maintained.

Service Delivery

- The ULB concerned will be accountable with regard to service delivery and for assets created and managed as part of the initiative.
- All service providers will confirm to the SLB standards stipulated by the GoI. & report accordingly.
- All asset-creation that results from the CSP will be clearly inventoried and

ownership made clear. Service delivery could be through agencies contracted by the ULB. However, all non-household assets would be owned by the ULB with clear lease arrangements for users.

Regulation, Coordination &ULB Primacy

Strengthening existing state level institutions that are charged with ensuring compliance of ULBs to environmental standards (e.g. State Pollution Control Boards), health outcomes (e.g. Health Departments), and Service Delivery Standards (e.g. State Urban Departments). Wherever these responsibilities or action on deviance are not spelt out clearly, the SSD would examine and advise the state government on making these clear. The policy also identifies the ULB as having the key regulatory role over all properties and agencies/households in the city in respect of outcomes and stipulated process standards, subject to due cognisance of law.

Planning, Monitoring & Evaluation

The institutional setup at the city-district-state will be responsible for operating the M&E system detailed by the SSD. The outputs of this will be reported and reviewed by the Government of Odisha. The key guiding principles would be:

- SSD will be responsible for M&E of cities' performance through the DUSC;
- ULBs in turn need to track compliance of households (establishments, etc.) with outcomes and process standards that it has adopted;
- Supplementary features like introducing citizens' report cards, citizens' monitoring committees, self-assessment system, inter-city competitions, etc. will be considered as part of the overall State Policy. The roles of third party agencies-NGOs and CBOs - in this process will be made clear.

Incentives for ULBS to Make Progress in Sanitation

The state will institute an assessment scheme to encourage competition and transparency in sanitation actions, amongst the towns/cities in Odisha. HUDD will ensure that all ULBs ensure detailed and timely monitoring of sanitation services and outcomes in their respective cities. HUDD will evolve a monitoring framework for ULBs for this purpose.

The goal of the reward is to encourage ULBs to strive for 100 percent access to sanitation facilities to all residents and hundred percent safe disposal of all waste generated within the urban environs. The assessment and award is based on the premise that improved public health and environmental standards are two outcomes that ULBs must ensure for urban citizens. In doing so, city governments must adopt a holistic, city-wide approach while incorporating processes that help reach outputs pertaining to goals of this policy.

The state reward scheme would be designed in consultation with the ULBs, for incentivising city performance in sanitation aspects. It would consist of an assessment format with weighted indicators (this would enlarge on the ODF/++ framework specified in Annexure I), and would also provide basis for performance based financial incentives for cities making progress on the sanitation front. The cost for this will be borne out of the performance grant available under the 14th Finance Commission, where the state government will include suitable performance indicators for sanitation in the overall performance grant framework.

Capacity Building & Training

It is understood that the capacities of the existing ULB structure – political and executive – are rather limited, to proactively take up and manage the list of activities envisaged under this policy. Suitable institutions that are equipped to build capacities in these local bodies are imminent and a state training institute for urban leaders and managers is urgently recommended. In the interim, the SSD could make use of the training capacities already built up within the state and districts for the rural sanitation campaign and utilise these to create the pool of local trainers necessary for the implementation of the policy with necessary urban adaptations. This pool of master trainers will conduct cascaded training sessions to ensure coverage of all stakeholders, within the ULB. ULBs will need to provide training on sanitation to their own staff – using these identified state level resource agencies. They will need to utilize Govt. of India (including NUSP) and State Government Schemes for training and capacity building in order to achieve this.

Additionally, frontline sanitation workers may be organised by functionality e.g. solid waste workers, sewerage workers, FSM works, and the like, in each ULB to ensure that in addition to planning and monitoring, ULBs ensure adequate staff for service delivery.

The SSD would develop the content-needs document and TNA for this HRD exercise. This will also need to focus on capacity building, i.e. not just training but also development of systems and capacities of ULBs in sanitation (including both internal and external communication), in line with the Urban Sector Reforms that the state may be implementing. This will not be limited to government functionaries, but also to frontline sanitation workers who may or may not be on government payrolls, and will be capacitated for service delivery at the city, ward, and household-levels. Where needed, the SSD would identify, select and engage specialised agencies of the government, and/or NGOs and private sector organizations.

Phasing & Funding The Policy

To ensure effective and timely action under the policy, the state government may bring out appropriate instructions for phasing of cities under each outcome on a yearly basis, and the budget for this may be based on context-specific technologies being proposed / considered for those cities.

The Housing & Urban Development Department (HUDD) of the Government of Odisha will be responsible to ensure that the necessary funds to implement the Policy are made available. This may be through an outlay from the State Government and may be supplemented with funds as applicable from the central government, or other sources such as donor funds. The state government may choose to notify a suitable nodal agency to manage the funds under the supervision of the state government if deemed necessary. The HUDD should specify a minimum five-year time horizon for budgeting under the policy and the expenditure and budgets must be reviewed against outcomes on an annual basis."

In addition to this, Districts and ULBs are free to leverage additional funding for action under the Policy like fees, fines, penalties, user charges, etc.

TAMILNADU

OPERATIVE GUIDELINES FOR LOCAL BODIES FOR EFFECTIVE IMPLEMENTATION OF SEPTAGE MANAGEMENT

Septage Management for the local bodies includes residential and non-residential/commercial waste (excluding industrial waste). These Operative Guidelines seek to empower the local bodies with knowledge, procedures and facilities for effective septage management.

The key elements of Septage Management are:

- Design and Construction of Septic Tanks
- Septic Tank Pumping & De-Sludging
- Septage Transportation
- Treatment & Septage Disposal
- Fees/Charges for Collection, Transportation and Treatment
- Information, Education and Communication
- Record-keeping and Reporting (MIS)

35 clusters of Local Bodies have been identified based on the existing location of STPs. The local bodies have been grouped in such a way that all collections points are situated approximately 18-20 kms of radius of the designated STP. These clusters should be revised after establishing new STPs.

The Operative Guidelines for each of these key elements are as follows:

Design and Construction of Septic Tanks

- Evaluate existing septic tank designs and other storage/treatment systems and modify (in case of variation) based on given design.
- Issue notice to owners of septic tanks that do not meet the standard septic tank design under Tamil Nadu Public Health Act, 1939
- Identify insanitary latrines1 and convert them to sanitary latrines for safe collection and disposal of waste.

Pumping and De-Sludging

- Conduct Periodic and routine De-Sludging based on capacity of septic tank.
- Collection system for cluster Local Bodies: Wherever sewage is currently discharged into fresh water or storm water drains, Local Bodies should ensure proper collection (transportation) system, and treatment of septage at the nearest STP and safe disposal.

Septage Transportation

- Local body clusters have been identified for treatment of collected septage at earmarked STP locations. All Septage Transportation Vehicles should be directed to transport septage to their designated STP.
- Only certified and licensed Septage Operators to de-sludge and transport waste to the designated STP. The operators should be selected in accordance with The Tamil Nadu Transparency in Tenders Act, 1998.
- Septage Transportation Vehicle Operators involved in the process of collection, treatment and disposal of sewage should be well trained and equipped with protective safety gears, uniforms, tools and proper vacuum trucks, to ensure safe handling of sewage. The rules under the Prohibition of Employment as Manual Scavengers and their Rehabilitation Act, 2013 provide for a comprehensive list of safety gear that should be used.
- Insanitary Latrines in households are those where night soil is removed by human, serviced by animals or/and night soil is disposed into open drain or pit into which the excreta is discharged or flushed out, before the excreta fully decomposes.

Treatment & Final Disposal

- Design of Decantation Facility: Decantation facility should be designed based on expected volumes of septage generated in local body clusters with adequate capacity for the next five years based on urbanization trend in the cluster.
- Quality Check: Input quality of the collected septage should be tested at the decant facility for presence of any metal or traces of industrial waste.
- The septage receiving facility should be operational during working hours and a responsible person should be appointed in the facility

to ensure that no industrial waste is unloaded through these facilities.

Information, Education and Communication

- ***IEC for Municipal Staff*:** Municipal Commissioners, Engineers, Sanitary Inspectors, Health Officers, and Sanitary Workers should be well trained in safe septage management and its best practices. This involves regular training sessions on safe collection, treatment and disposal. Information regarding standard septic tank design, the need for periodic inspection and De-Sludging of sewage, design of a decant facility, tender details for engaging licensed operators, etc. should be disseminated widely to achieve a safe septage management system. Training should also be provided on safety standards. In this regard, CMWSSB and CMA will design the course material and draft a calendar for training to ensure complete coverage before December 2014.
- ***IEC for Residents*:** Members of Resident Welfare Associations, community organizers, self help groups and the general public should be sensitized periodically regarding the need for a sound septage management system. The health hazards associated with improper collection and treatment of waste, and the ill-effects of sewage discharge into fresh water/storm water drains should be clearly explained to the residents. CMA will produce sample IEC material and also draft a campaign for residents.
- ***IEC for Septage Operators/Private Vendors*:** Local Bodies should ensure all safety norms are clearly explained to the septage operators. Private Operators and Transporters should be well trained in safe collection and transportation of sewage including vehicle design, process of de- Sludging, safety gears and safe disposal at the nearest STP. CMWSSB and CMA will draft tentative training calendar for septage operators/private vendors.

Fees/Charges for De-Sludging, Transportation and Treatment

- Fees for De-Sludging to be collected from residents by the certified/licensed tanker operators.
- Transport charges should be determined based on market rates while ensuring that residents are not exploited by the tanker operators.
- For treatment, the on-going rate of Rs. 150-200 may be charged for 9000 litres of waste collected.

- Periodic revision for the charges to be effected based on changes in costs involved.

Record Keeping and Reporting through MIS

- *Management Information Systems (MIS)*
  (i) Information related to septage generation from residents and commercial establishments needs to be collected by the Local Bodies.
  (ii) Household level details of insanitary latrines, identification of septic tank location, Operator in-charge for each location, Vehicle Details, Name & Location of STP earmarked for disposal of septage, and decant facility details should be duly collected by all Local Bodies.
- *Geographical Information System (GIS)*

GIS can be used to be plan the route of septage vehicles and tracking these for regular record keeping. Public Grievance Redressal to also form part of local bodies' record keeping. Helpline numbers to be also shared with residents.

Septic Tank Design

Depending on the geography, soil condition, water seepage capacity of the soil the design should be prepared and approved by the Local Bodies. Proper septic tank design consists of the following factors:

- Sized properly with appropriate sludge detention time, volume and hydraulic retention time
- Proper inlet and outlet structures
- At least one baffle separating the tank into multiple compartments
- Water tight
- Access port for each compartment that allows for inspection and pumping

The Draft Septage Management Bye-laws

Reformative measures and Compliances by Owner or the Occupier

The Owner or Occupier of a building or part of it located in the ULB Limits shall from the date of these bye-laws coming into force be liable to perform the following obligations:

- shall within the time specified in the notice issued by the Authority as per these bye-laws, discontinue the usage of insanitary latrines in such building and also close all outlets to common drains or open plot/land or water bodies located nearby and construct, operate and maintain only Sanitary Latrines in the buildings owned or used by him;

- duly inform the officials of the Authority prior to the filling up of the Septic Tanks and ensure that the Septic Tanks are maintained in a proper manner so as to ensure that the Septage does not overflow;
- allow the officials of the Authority inspection at reasonable times with prior notice;
- engage only authorised operators for the collection and transportation of septage from their building.
- pay the fees and charges as notified by the Authority for the collection of Septage

Administrative measures and Enforcement of Bye-laws

The Authority shall from the date of these bye-laws coming into force have the right to perform the following functions:

- undertake the survey and inspection of buildings located within the ULB Limits and issue certificate of compliance to buildings which are in compliance with these bye-laws;
- issue notices to Owners or Occupiers of buildings which are non-compliant to these bye-laws;
- implement and supervise the compliance of the bye-laws;
- conduct information, education and communication campaign with respect to awareness of Septage management;
- conduct competitive bidding for selecting, issuing license to Operators and publish the names of such licensed operators;
- direct, regulate and supervise the collection, transportation and disposal of Septage at the Treatment Facility;
- inspect and regulate the quality and maintenance of the Specified Vehicles;
- direct, regulate and supervise the day-to-day operations of the Treatment Facility;
- inspect the quality of Septage being collected and transported to the Treatment Facility
- undertake investigations and levy penalties on Owners, Occupiers or Operators found to be in violation of these bye-laws.

Appointment and Operation by Operators

- The Authority shall within a reasonable time period from the date of these bye-laws coming into force, conduct competitive bidding for the selection of Operators.
- Upon selection of the successful bidder issue license as per the format attached in Annexure to these bye-laws.
- The Operators shall be responsible for maintaining and operating Specified Vehicles and associated equipment, if any, as per the guidelines issued by the Authority from time to time.
- The Operators shall be responsible for the collection and transportation of Septage from buildings as per the performance standards to be determined and the instructions issued by the Authority from time to time.
- The Operators shall comply with the provisions governing the license and shall not transport industrial or mixed industrial waste of any nature whatsoever.
- The Operators shall comply with all the local legislations and maintain all permits and approvals required for the performance of its activities permitted under the license.
- The Operators shall employ only trained personnel and provide all necessary protective gear to such personnel while performing the collection and transportation of Septage.
- The Operators shall employ adequate number of personnel so as to ensure that the collection and transportation of Septage is performed as per the performance standards notified by the Authority from time to time.
- The Operators shall at all times ensure compliance with the Prohibition of Employment as Manual Scavengers and their Rehabilitation Act, 2013 and rules.
- The Operators shall perform all such protective activities as instructed by the Authority during the occurrence of an accident.
- The Operators shall be responsible for the safe disposal of the Septage at locations notified by the Authority.
- The Operators shall charge fees as notified by the Authority for the collection of Septage.

Penalties for Violation of Bye-laws

The Authority shall take cognizance of any violation of these bye-laws and take the following actions:

- in case of the Owner or Occupier, the Authority shall issue show cause notice and have the right to levy penalties of up to ₹ 5000 for each violation or such other amount as may be notified from time to time. In case the Owner is in continuous violation of these bye-laws the Authority shall have the right to levy penalties not exceeding ₹ 25,000.
- in case of the Operator, the Authority shall issue show cause notice and have the right to levy penalties of up to ₹ 50,000 for each violation or such other amount as may be notified from time to time. In case the operator is in continuous violation of these bye-laws the Authority shall have the right to levy penalties not exceeding ₹ 2,00,000.
- in case the Operator is in violation of para 5 sub-paras (v) and (ix) the Authority shall issue show cause notice and also have the right to cancelthe license issued to the operator.

Appeals

- The ULB shall within a reasonable time period from the date of these bye- laws coming into force constitute an Appellate Body and issue necessary notifications.
- The Owner, Occupier or the Operators shall have the right to appeal to the Appellate Body against a show cause notice issued by the Authority, within 30 days of the receipt of such show cause notice.
- The Appellate Body shall commence hearing an appeal within fifteenth days of it being filed.
- The Authority, Owner and the Operators shall be liable to comply with the decisions made by such Appellate Body

License

- License no :
- Issuing Authority : *[Insert designation and address of the concerned officer]* Photograph of Manager of the licensee
- License holder : *[Insert name and address of the collection agent]*
- Validity of license :
- The licensee shall maintain the Specified Vehicles in good and workable condition so as to avoid any accidents.
- The licensee shall employ only trained personnel for performing the licensed activities and provide protective gears to all such personnel.

- This license is not valid for the collection of industrial waste of any nature whatsoever.
- The Issuing Authority reserves its right to vary any of the conditions of this license or impose further conditions from time to time during the validity of this license.
- Details of Specified Vehicles :
- Activities permitted : This license is hereby granted to the license holder named above for performing the activities stated herein above, to be performed as per the Septage Management Bye-laws for the Municipal Corporation of *[please insert name of the relevant ULB]* and any amendments made there under. This license shall be subject to the compliance by the license holder of the conditions stated overleaf.

Signature and Seal of Issuing Authority

- The Operator is required to maintain adequate and correct records of collection, transportation and disposal of septage as required by the ULB.
- The licensee shall levy fees and charges for licensed activities

Sl. No.	Licensed Activity	Fees/Charges

MADHYA PRADESH

WASTE WATER RECYCLE & REUSE AND FAECAL SLUDGE MANAGEMENT (FSM) POLICY, 2017

Vision, Goals and Purpose

The Policy, envisions, "All MP State cities and towns become totally sanitized, healthy and liveable and ensure and sustain good public health and environmental outcomes for all their citizens, with a special focus on hygienic and affordable sanitation facilities for the urban poor and women".

This Policy is to ensure improved health status of urban population, specially the poor and under privileged, through the provision of sustainable sanitation services and protection of environment. The policy specifically endorses the following core principles:

- To protect public health.
- To protect the environment and the State's water resources.
- To promote proper functioning of network based sewerage systems and ensure connections of household so as to prevent dry weather flow in drains & streets.

- Treatment of sewage and sludge is required prior to discharge into the environment.
- Promote recycling & re-use of treated sewage for non-potable applications.
- To make Sewerage project economical and environmentally sustainable.
- Inclusive and participatory decision making with Experts & Focused Group discussions with stakeholder in the localities.
- Transparent decision making processes to achieve socio-environmental as well as economic & financial objectives.
- Capacity building for enhanced institutional ability to govern the sector effectively.
- Ensuring, protecting and optimizing investments.
- Public Private Partnership (PPP) in the most appropriate manner
- Public outreach for environmental and health related outcomes.
- Establishment of an efficient, effective, affordable and accountable system for managing urban sewerage and septage management.
- Effective monitoring and evaluation of the initiatives intended to improve sewerage and septage management services.
- Coverage of all citizens in the urban areas for service provisioning.
- Adequate sewerage and Septage facility provided to all urban customers
- Equity across geographical as well as demographic fabric of the customer base.
- Ensuring the system's financial sustainability in a progressive manner through improved efficiency, tariff rationalization and corporatized operations there by decreasing dependence on unsustainable resources.
- Improved service levels in a well-defined and phased manner by ensuring interventions in the spheres of infrastructure, institution, autonomy and management, monitoring mechanism and regulatory framework.

On-site Sanitation

The collection and treatment of waste is done where it is deposited. Examples are the use of pit latrines, septic tanks, and imhoff tanks. This is being adopted by almost 80 percent of urban town in MP consisting of some form of toilet that passes waste to leach pits, pits with mechanical removal options and septic tanks. The second on site disposal option being exercised is defecation in open space. This causes passing of the chemical and pathogenic infections to the ground waters, to the drains and water bodies, outside resulting in severe risk to human health. Therefore, followings points has to be considered in this matter:

- The options of the onsite system will depend on the substrata, space availability and social acceptability. These also are dependent upon the water absorption capacity of the soil. Rocky areas and high water table areas are not suitable for this at all as they do not provide any protection against the pathogens. It is generally suggested that the risk factor for pollution is related to the traverse time between polluting point and the water table. A traverse time of 50 days is considered low risk, 25-50 days is to be considered as medium risk area and less than 25 days is considered as high risk areas with the point of view of pollution of the ground water. Finer soils with high clay content have low permeability and thus greater risk reduction in lesser depths whereas coarse sands and rocky fissures provide high permeability and lower reduction. Generally, a minimum distance of two to three m is required for risk reduction.
- The on-site option for solids removal combined with carriage of the sewage through conduits to the general sewerage system can also be considered as a good option in critical areas. Such options could be a combination of small bore/shallow sewers for sewage collected after settling of solids in a tank (e.g. septic tank effluent) and in site disposal systems.
- All in site options must be adopted after full involvement of the local users who know all the feasible options and must have a say in the choice. Assistance of NGOs and dedicated organizations for this option should be encouraged. On Site technologies represent viable and affordable options if collection, transport, treatment and safe end use or disposal is managed properly.
- Bio digester, Pydroid technology based on site solution accompanied by root zone treatment can be suitably used for onsite sanitation. Reed Bed filters, horizontal or vertical, can be deployed before final disposal/Re-use.
- The ULB through its suction machines shall facilitate the clearance of sludge on payment basis. Municipality can also authorize any private person/Agency for clearance of sludge through mechanical means.

Off – Site Sanitation

The ideal mode for sanitation is an off-site system which collects all the waste from within the city and transfers it to a treatment facility outside the city which treats it to acceptable levels of effluent and sludge which is then disposed /reused. The essential pre-requisite to a sustained functioning of the offsite facilities are:

- Adequate sewerage flow (approximately 108 lpcd minimum) which is possible only in town/areas with a minimum supply of 135 lpcd and 100 percent connectivity.
- Availability of Land for Sewage Treatment Plant and Pumping Stations will be ensured while preparing the master plan of sewerage for town. Town planning department shall mandatorily earmark land for Sewerage Treatment Plant and other facilities.
- Where possible, gravity flow shall command the collection and conveyance lines.
- Treatment plants shall be located away from any potential population growth. Location selection shall be coordinated and approved with the concerned governmental agencies. Due consideration shall be given to interact with landowners and adjacent communities.
- It is mandatory to construct decentralized Sewage Treatment Plants (STPs) for the treatment of waste water in high rise buildings, so that sewerage system in that area may function properly and the treated waste water may be utilized in the nearby area. It will also reduce the investment requirement of sewerage system.
- The use of advanced wastewater treatment technologies shall be endorsed and encouraged. However, appropriate wastewater treatment technologies shall be selected with due consideration to operation and maintenance costs and energy savings, in addition to their efficiency in attaining and sustaining quality standards.
- Innovative approaches to wastewater treatment, particularly for the small municipal systems have to be considered. Design criteria, performance specifications and guidelines for such systems shall be adopted and generalized.
- Design and performance specifications of wastewater treatment plants shall be as per guidelines given in the manual on sewerage treatment systems published by CPHEEO. Sufficient room in

tendering for the construction of new plants s hall be provided for competition to take place in both technologies and costs.

Septic Tanks

Septic tanks are one of the most common forms of urban sanitation facilities in MP. Major part of MP has not been connected to municipal sewer system which makes people dependent on the conventional individual septic tanks.

Technical Advisory on Construction of Septic Tanks

A. General

The septic tank is originated in France during the early 1800s where it was developed to deal with human wastes generated in the new towns that expanded rapidly to support the industrial revolution following the regime of Napoleon Bonaparte. Until that time, the wealthy used buckets in an ablution room within their house and the staff emptied the contents when necessary into the same cesspit latrine adjoining the house that they used themselves.

A septic tank has three main functions:

- Separation of sewage solids from liquid (the faecal solids float to form a scum);
- Reduction of scum (stools) and dissolved COD (mostly urine) by anaerobic bacteria (in both chambers); and
- Storage of inorganic solids and minerals (septage) as a fine silt on the floor (to be removed by spade or suction periodically - usually every one-three years).

Natural anaerobic bacteria and associated microorganisms living within the septic tank adapt to degrade human sewage to simple biomasses, water and inorganic radicals (for example, trace minerals in food). Septic tank is a combination of sedimentation and digestion tank having a detention period of 24 to 48 hours on an average daily flow of sewage, where sewage is detained for some time when the suspended solids settle down to the bottom of tank and this is accompanied by anaerobic digestion of sludge and liquid, resulting in appreciable reduction in the volume of sludge and release of gases like carbon dioxide, methane and hydrogen sulphide. But the effluent of the septic tank is very septic and malodorous and it is more objectionable than the liquid that goes into the tank. It is therefore requiring a secondary treatment by disposing the effluent through soak pit (seepage pit), leach pit or dispersion trenches or ST effluent to connect in to public sewers.

Location

- Septic tank should be located in the area, which is having porous soil for the subsurface disposal of effluent as for as possible.
- Big STs should be located away from the residential buildings, to avoid public health hazard and nuisance.
- It should not be located in the swampy area or area prone to flooding.

Design Criteria

- *Sedimentation*: To remove the maximum possible number of suspended solids from the sewage, a minimum depth of 30 cm is necessary, which requires a surface area of 0.92 m2 per 10 lpm of peak flow rate.
- *Sludge Digestion*: Sewage is detained in the tank to undergo anaerobic digestion for destroying the organic matter and converting it into innocuous sludge, which becomes suitable for dewatering and drying. The volume required for digestion of sludge is 0.032 m3/capita.
- *Sludge and Scum Storage:* Adequate provision should be made for the storage of digested sludge and scum in the tank.The volume required for sludge and scum storage is 0.0002 m3/capita/ day.
- *Freeboard:* A minimum free board of 30 cm is required in the tank including the provision for seed sludge.
- *Sewage Flow*: The maximum flow (peak flow) to the tank is calculated on the basis of number of plumbing fixtures discharging simultaneously and not only the number of users or per capita wastewater flow expected to reach the tank.

Recommended Capacities of Septic Tanks

In view of the unsatisfactory quality of the effluent and the difficulty in providing a large area for the final disposal of effluent through sub-soil dispersion system, septic tanks are constructed only for the individual homes and small communities having a total contributory population of 300 persons. For larger communities, provision of septic tanks should be avoided as far as possible, but it may be extended to a population of 500 in the undulating topography.

Construction Details

(i) Length of the tank (L) should be 2 to 4 times the width (B).

(ii) Inlet and outlet should be located as far away as possible (on opposite sides) from each other and at different levels.

(iii) Both inlet and outlet should dip 25 to 30 cm into the liquid and project 15 cm above the liquid.

(iv) First baffle should be placed at a distance one-fifth of the length (L/5) from the mouth of the inlet pipe (For Large ST having designed for population more than 50 persons)

(v) Second baffle should be placed at a distance of 2/3 L from the outlet pipe. (For Large ST having designed for population more than 50 persons)

(vi) The invert level of the outlet pipe should be placed at a level, 5 to 7 cm below the invert level of inlet pipe.

(vii) A bottom slope of 10% (0.10) or more, from all the corners of the tank towards the outlet of desludging chamber should be provided.

(viii) Septic tank should be provided with a ventilating pipe. The height of the ventilating pipe should extend at least 2 m above the top of the highest building within a radius of 20 m.

(ix) Septic tank should be provided with a watertight cover of adequate strength, Access manhole of adequate size should also be provided for the purpose of inspection and desludging of tank.

Secondary Treatment of Effluent

Satisfactory disposal of effluent depends to a great extent on the porosity and percolation characteristic of the soil, level of sub-soil water table and the concentration of suspended solids in the effluent. The disposal of effluent may be either under-ground or over ground. Normally underground disposal either in the form of soak-pit (seepage pit) of dispersion trenches is practiced.

Soak-Pit (Sepage Pit)

Soak pit can be adopted in all type of porous soils where percolation rate is below 25 minutes per cm and the water table is 180 cm or more from the ground level. Soak pits are cheap to construct and are extensively used. They are filled up with rubble or brickbats. The depth of soak pit is usually kept 1 m below the invert level of outlet pipe. The pit is covered and the top is raised above the adjacent ground level to prevent the damage by flooding.

Proposed Septic Tanks

For various Population Load of 5, 10, 50 & 250 (Type-1-2-3-4) are suggested to be constructed:

- Length 'L' should be 2 to 4 times the width 'B'.
- First baffle should be placed at a distance one-fifth of the length (L/5) from the mouth of the inlet pipe.
- Second Baffle should be at 2L/3 from the outlet pipe Invert level of outlet pipe should be 5 to 7 cm below the invert level of inlet pipe.
- Both inlet and outlet pipes should be provided with a 90o bend which should dip in the liquid. Inlet should project at least 15 cm above the liquid.
- Bottom slope from all the corners towards the desludging chamber should be at least 1 in10.
- The length of ventilating pipe should be 2 m more than the highest building within a radius of 20 m.
- In the case of large installations, the depth of septic tank for desludging interval of 1,2 and 3 years should not be less than 1.1, 1.4 and 1.75m.

Construction

- Concrete structures are preferred.
- They should be water tight and multi-chambered.
- Bottomless septic tanks should be prohibited.
- Must be sized so that the volume is at least 1.6 times the daily flow but preferably 2 or 2.5 times the daily flow.
- The bigger the tank, the less frequently it will need to be desludged. Multiple chamber septic tanks should be designed for new installations.
- Must also be accessible (have a removable cover and not be located directly under the house) to pump sludge when sludge level becomes too high.
- Small housing blocks may share a community septic tank to reduce per household costs.

Maintenance

- When the septage occupies two-thirds of the depth of the tank, it needs to be removed; otherwise there is a risk that excreta will pass directly through the tank and overflow into the disposal system.

- Septage should be taken to an approved sludge treatment and disposal site by means of a vacuum tanker.
- Households should be encouraged to minimize their use of water and be careful about what they put into their septic tanks.
- The septic tank should be desludged every 2 to 3 years depending on the capacity and design.
- The desludging schedule should be prepared (preferably computerized) and should be notified to the household about their due date.

Present Status of Septage Management

The adequate facilities and services for collection, transportation, treatment and disposal of urban domestic septage do not exist in most of the cities. Most on-site sanitation systems (OSS) are emptied manually in absence of suitable facilities. Ideally a septic tank system should be desludged every 2-5 years. But ignorance towards maintenance and operational conditions often results in accumulation of organic sludge, reduction in effective volume and hydraulic overloading which ultimately causes the system failure and release of partially treated or untreated septage from the septic tank. Private operators often do not transport and dispose of septage several kilometres away from human settlements and instead dump it in drains, waterways, open land, and agricultural fields.

Technological Options for Septage Management

The septage treatment required depends on the types and sources of domestic waste water and faecal sludge. The domestic waste water and faecal sludge often contains high concentration of organic matter and pathogens. Hence it is important to provide environmentally suitable technological options for collection, transport, treatment and disposal/reuse of faecal sludge/septage.

Current Practices

In MP towns/cities, municipalities/local government bodies are mainly responsible for ensuring the safe handling and disposal of septage generated within its boundaries. They also establish local ordinances or regulations to govern septage handling and to meet all requirements and standards. In most of the cities, only crude and unhygienic septage handling practices exist and there is no proper municipality infrastructure that performs the task of septage management. Most of the septic systems are not well maintained in the country and if they are maintained by individual home owners, many of them do not have the technical know-how for its operation and maintenance. For example, the household garbage disposals and pouring of grease into domestic drains can reduce the effectiveness of the septic tank in the long run. In terms of system operation, as many as 75 percent of all system failures have been attributed to hydraulic overloading.

Desludging of septic tanks is an over burden for many home owners that they postpone until the tanks have reached its capacity and they start overflowing. Untreated septage is often disposed in low lying areas or agriculture farms or even in a water body, which poses serious health and environmental problems.

Stages of Septage Management

The septage management basically consists of collection, treatment and proper disposal of septage.

Septage Collection

An important feature of septage which has to be considered for septage collection is the septage generation rate and sludge withdrawal.

Septage Generation Rate

Septage generation rates vary widely from place to place depending on practices of septic tank use, number of users, water used for flushing, efficient functioning of the tank and level of contamination control. It can be considered that the volume of sludge evacuated from a septic tank corresponds more.

Type Source

- Faecal sludge
- Pit latrines and leach pits
- Decreasing concentration of pollutants and pathogens (topto bottom)
- Septage Septic tanks
- Blackwater Water closets
- Domestic sewage Sullage and black water mixed together
- Sullage (grey water)
- Personal washing, laundary cooking and cleaning or less to the volume of the septic tank, plus some cleansing and rinsing water.

The size of a septic tank in individual houses in MP ranges from 1 to 4 m3, the size of a septic tank in office or apartment buildings from 10 to 100 m3.

Desludging of Septic Tanks

In most of the cases the septic tanks are desludged manually. This is considered as unpleasant and repulsive job since the sludge (including fresh excreta) generally gets spilled around the tank during emptying, and poses a risk of transmission of diseases of faecal origin. Given the safety and health risks of manual desludging, it is critical for cities to take measures to stop this common practice. The most satisfactory method of sludge removal is by vacuum tankers. The faecal sludge needs to be correctly disposed and further treated. For this, the faecal sludge should be separated from the liquid in drying beds or by settling. The separated effluents from these systems should be treated in Waste Stabilization Ponds (WSP) or constructed wetlands.

Septage Transportation

The septage transportation is one of the most important components of septage management. Recognizing a standard method of collection, handling and transportation of septage is an important requirement. Desludging trucks act as a "mobile sewer network" for onsite sanitation systems is used.

Septage Treatment And Disposal

Septage can be treated in a variety of ways, and there is no single best option considering the widely varying conditions of urban areas in MP. The selection of treatment depends upon characteristics of septage to be handled.

Septage Characteristics

The quality and quantity of septage coming out of the tank depends largely on the type of treatment adopted, the frequency of desludging, climate, soil conditions, water usage and household chemicals going in the septic tank. The physical and biological characteristics of septage are highly variable. The anaerobic nature of septage results in the presence of odorous compounds such as hydrogen sulfide, mercaptans, and other organic sulfur compounds. Septage contains constituents that may result in unpleasant odours, risk to public health and serious environmental hazards. Since septage is highly concentrated, if it is discharged into a water body it may cause immediate depletion of oxygen, increased nutrients leading to eutrophication and increased pathogens leading to a risk of health hazards.

Knowledge of septage characteristics and variability is important in determining acceptable disposal methods.

Septage Treatment Options

The treatment and disposal methods of septage can be conventional or non-conventional. The conventional methods are the most widely used and they serve the purpose of treatment of sludge and effluent.

Pre-treatment of Septage

Pre-treatment/stabilization includes physical, chemical, or biological processes. Stabilization is a pretreatment method that decreases odours, the levels of pathogens and further decay of septage. *Stabilization Options* include lime stabilization, aerobic digestion, anaerobic digestion, and composting. In *Alkali (Lime) Stabilization l*ime or other alkaline material is added to liquid septage to raise the pH to 12.0 for a minimum of 30 minutes. Although there is a lot of variation in septage characteristics and lime requirements, mixing is not very difficult, and approximately 20 to 25 pounds of lime is used for every 4,000 litres of septage. Lime addition could be done at any of these three points:

- To the hauler truck before the septage is pumped,
- To the hauler truck while the septage is being pumped, or
- To a septage storage tank where septage is discharged from a pumper truck.

Although there is a lot of variation in septage characteristics and lime requirements, mixing is not very difficult, and approximately 10 kg to 12 kg of lime is used for every 1,000 gallons of septage.

Aerobic Digestion

In this method, septage is aerated for 15 to 20 days in an open tank to achieve biological reduction in organic solids and odour potential. The time requirements increase with lower temperatures. Normally, this is not a cost-effective option.

Anaerobic Digestion

Septage is retained for 15 to 30 days in an enclosed vessel under anaerobic conditions to achieve biological reduction of organic solids. Anaerobic digestion is generally not suggested except for co-treatment with sludge. However, one advantage is that anaerobic digestion produces methane gas, which can be used as fuel.

Composting

Liquid septage or septage solids are mixed with a bulking agent (e.g., wood chips, sawdust) and aerated mechanically or by turning. Biological activity generates temperatures that are high enough to destroy pathogens. The composting process converts septage into a stable, humus material that can be used as a soil amendment. However, there is a possibility of odours.

After the septage is stabilized, it can then be sent for further treatment or disposal.

Land Application

Land application is the most commonly used method to manage the septage after stabilization. There are various application methods to dispose off septage on the land viz. Surface application, sub-surface application and burial.

Surface Application

It is relatively simple and cost effective, uses low energy, and recycles organic material and nutrients to the land. However, it has high odour potential during application and possibility of pathogen dispersal if not lime stabilized. Surface application includes spreading septage from septage hauler trucks, specially designed land application vehicles, or tank wagons onto sites, or using spray irrigation, ridge and furrow irrigation, and overland flow. Septage can also be applied to the land as a fertilizer and soil conditioner. Application rates depend on the slope, soil type, depth of application, drainage class and hydraulic loading. Septage must not be applied before or during rainfall or in the areas where water table is shallow. Thus, an interim storage facility is needed. The various surface application methods are as follows:

- ***Spray irrigation***- Pre-treated septage is pumped at 80 to 100 psi through nozzles and sprayed directly onto the land. Spray irrigation can be used on steep or rough land and minimizes disturbances to the soil by trucks.
- ***Ridge and Furrow Irrigation***- In this disposal method, pre-treated septage is applied directly to furrows or to row crops that will not be directly consumed by humans. This is used for relatively level land, usually for slopes in the range of 0.5 to 1.5 percent.
- ***Hauler Truck Spreading***- Septage is applied to the soil directly from a hauler truck that uses a splash plate to improve distribution.

The same truck that pumps out the septic tank can be used for transporting and disposing the septage.

- Farm tractor and wagon spreading -Liquid septage or septage solids are transferred to farm equipment for spreading. This allows for application of liquid or solid septage. The septage must be incorporated into the soil within 6 hours, if lime stabilisation has not been done.

Subsurface Incorporation

In this method, untreated septage is placed just below the soil surface, reducing odour and health risks while fertilizing and conditioning the soil. Subsurface incorporation allows better odor control than surface spreading and reduce the risk of pathogen dispersal. Septage can only be applied to slopes less than eight percent, and the soil depth to seasonal high water table must be at least 20 inches (or as mandated by local regulations). A holding facility is required during periods of rainfall or wet ground. To prevent soil compaction and allow sufficient infiltration, equipment must not be driven over the site until one to two weeks after application. There are two ways for subsurface application:

- ***Plough and Furrow Cover***— Liquid septage is discharged from a tank into a narrow furrow about 15 to 20 cm deep and is then covered by a second plough.
- ***Subsurface Injection***— Liquid septage is injected in a narrow cavity created by a tillage tool with an opening of about 10 to 15 cm below the surface.

Burial: Major form of septage burial includes disposal in holding lagoons, trenches, and sanitary landfills. High odour potential during septage application is inherent until a final cover is placed on the top. Appropriate site selection is important not only to control odour, but also to minimize potential groundwater pollution.

- ***Holding Lagoons***- These lagoons are a maximum of 6 feet deep and do not allow any soil infiltration. The septage is placed in small incremental lifts of 15 to 30 cm and with multiple lagoons loaded in sequential order for optimum drying. To decrease odours, the lagoon inlet pipe can be placed below liquid level.
- ***Trenches***- Septage is filled sequentially in multiple chambers in small lifts of 15 to 20 cm for optimum drying. Each trench is then covered with soil (2 feet) as a final covering and new trenches are opened. An alternate option is to leave a filled trench uncovered to permit maximum solids to settle and liquids to evaporate and

leach out. The solids, as well as some bottom and side wall material, are then removed and the trench can be reused.

- ***Sanitary landfills***- Production of leachate, treatment, and odour are the primary problems to be considered when septage is added to sanitary landfills. As such, septage must not be added in landfills in areas that have over 90 cm of rainfall, landfills that do not have leachate prevention and control facilities, or those not having isolated underlying rock. A 15 cm of soil cover needs to be applied each day in the landfills where septage is added and 2 feet of final cover within one week after the placement of the final lift. In general, sanitary landfills are not cost-effective disposal options of sludge.

Treatment at Sewage Treatment Plants

Co-treatment of septage along with domestic sewage at a sewage treatment plant (STP) is a feasible and acceptable alternative for septage treatment. Though septage is much concentrated in its strength than the domestic sewage, its constituents are similar to municipal wastewater. Sewage treatment plant should have an adequate capacity in order to accept the septage without hampering the normal functioning of other processes.

- *Septage Addition to nearest Sewer Manhole*- Septage could be added to a sewer upstream of the sewage treatment plant, and substantial dilution of septage occurs prior to it reaching the sewage treatment plant, depending on the volume of sewage flowing in the sewer.
- *Septage Addition to STP*- Septage could be added to sewage immediately upstream of the screening and grit removal processes. It is economical because of the very simple receiving station design and also allows the wastewater treatment plant staff to have control of the septage discharge

Constructed Wetlands (CW)

A septic tank provides only primary treatment and should always be followed by a soakage pit. In the areas where water table is shallow, the effluent from the septic tank/improved septic tank could be connected to constructed wetlands to prevent ground water contamination. Constructed Wetlands (CW) are a biological wastewater treatment technology designed to mimic processes found in natural wetland ecosystems. These systems use wetland plants, soils and their associated micro-organisms to remove contaminants from wastewater. They act as a filter removing sediments and pollutants such as nutrients and other heavy metals from waste water and septage. The bed is filled with porous media and vegetation is planted in the media. These systems require land but offer very effective biological treatment response in a passive manner so that mechanical equipment, energy and skilled operator attention are minimized. Vegetation in a wetland provides a substrate (roots, stems, and leaves) upon which microorganisms can grow as they break down organic materials. Constructed wetlands are of two basic types: horizontal flow constructed wetlands and vertical flow constructed wetlands.

Horizontal flow constructed wetland is suited for secondary treatment of wastewater or liquid component of the septage coming out of improved septic tank/anaerobic baffled reactor. The flow pattern is horizontal in the filter bed. A horizontal planted gravel filter acts through the combined effect of the filter material and plants growing on the filter media. The effluent is odour free. As wastewater flows from one end to the other end through the planted gravel filter, it is resupplied with oxygen. A depth of 30-60cm is maintained in the bed with a slope of 1 percent. The advantage of this system is that it can achieve high treatment efficiency at low-cost and since the flow is sub-surface, there is no odour problem.

Vertical flow constructed wetlands operation is normally used to treat sludge or septage having high solid contents.

To operate in a vertical-flow mode, the septage is uniformly distributed on the surface of the CW units. Vertical flow constructed wetland are usually preceded by some form of primary treatment, although some are built to receive raw sewage/septage. Each bed resembles a trickling filter, except that it has a layer of sand on top where aquatic plants are grown, usually the common reed (*Cana indica*). The septage is introduced to the surface of the bed and it percolates down through the sand and gravel media to the base.

Sludge Disposal/Reuse

The sludge which is generated after the treatment of septage should be disposed appropriately. Even after the sludge is stabilised in the lagoons, additional stabilization or treatment measures may be required to generate final product of acceptable quality.

Septage Management System

The septage management system includes designing, operation and maintenance, desludging, institutional mechanism, monitoring, financial arrangements, legal provisions and administrative procedures. In MP, out of 379 towns, in most of the towns due to absence of organised sewerage scheme, sewerage system is managed on ad-hoc basis in which mostly on-site sanitation facilities like septic tanks are constructed without understanding the efficient mechanism to get waste water treated onsite that to techno-economically. Since the concept of simple mechanism of primary treatment of waste water inside the campus of households or nearby in the form of septic tank is very common practice, perhaps the simplest and longest surviving example of an anaerobic process is septic tank, normally provide 24 hours' detention time and are often built as horizontal flow units with one or two baffle arrangements between the inlet and outlet.

Simultaneously very simplicity in construction and use lead to imperfections in operation, first in the form of short- circuiting and secondly in the form of disturbance to anaerobic activity by some dissolved oxygen always coming in with the inflow. Septic tank effluent has to be soaked, as surface discharge is not allowed. This is done by providing either soak pit or soak trenches. But in MP effluent of septic tank is usually discharged conveniently in nearby roadside storm water drain. Here in the policy MP Govt. emphasis to have construction of septic tanks with technological concept.

Desludging Procedure

There is a widespread promotion of OSS. However, all the programmes and city agencies still do not address adequately the issue of septage that accumulates inside septic tank/OSS. Due to lack or inadequate public services, private service providers have emerged to empty OSS by hand or with vacuum trucks. Operators with mechanized equipment often transport and dispose of septage several kilometres from people's homes in drains, waterways, open land, and agricultural fields. Manual desludging is also done in low-income areas and squatter settlements. They are often inaccessible by truck and hence deposit the septage within the household, into nearby lanes, drains, open land or waterways. Thus, the poorest have the highest health risk both because they are the most likely to provide manual desludging services, and because their homes are closest to the actual dumping grounds.

In carrying out manual desludging all the precautions should be taken to protect the workers as provided under Municipal Solid Waste Rules. The sludge after removal should be transported in a controlled manner to avoid leakages or spillage en-route. Before desludging, if the liquid level in the tank is higher than the outlet pipe, this may indicate clogging in the outlet pipe or in the drain field. The sludge then may be collected through safe containers or pumping. Before pumping, the scum mat is manually broken up to facilitate pumping. Before this is done, the liquid level in the septic tank first is lowered below the invert of the outlet, which prevents grease and scum from being washed into the drain field. After the scum mat is broken up, the contents of the tank are removed. Normally, the vacuum/ suction hose draws air at a point where 1 to 2 in. (2.5 to 5 cm) of sludge remains over the tank bottom; this material should be left in the tank. Washing down the inside of the tank is not required unless leakage is suspected and the inside must be inspected for cracks, if internal inspection is warranted, fresh air should be continuously blown into the tank for at least ten minutes.

Septage Transportation

The sludge after collection should be transported through trucks to the treatment or disposal sites, with proper regulation. In MP there is a comprehensive regulation on transport of solid wastes (municipal solid wastes, biomedical wastes and hazardous wastes), however similar regulation is not existing for transport of septage. The septage transport should be regulated in the same manner as provided under Municipal Wastes (Handling and Management) Rules 2000.

Septage Treatment Facilities

There are number of treatment options available. Treatment using natural processes, including waste stabilization ponds, unplanted sludge drying beds, constructed wetlands, and composting, are considerably cost-effective solutions. Anaerobic digestion (with biogas generation), lime treatment, and mechanized systems, such as activated sludge process, are also widely used technologies in treating septage. Important considerations include the cost of land, the capacity of staff to operate and maintain the system, and the location of the treatment facility with respect to OSS. Digested sludge from OSS is hundred times more concentrated than domestic wastewater flowing in the sewer systems, and therefore should not be treated with wastewater in sewage treatment plants. If the dried sludge meets established standards, it can be used as a soil amendment for reclaimed land, landfill cover, landscaping compost, or fertilizer for non-edible plantations. For use as compost for edible crops, treatment facilities need to ensure that the end product attains standards for agricultural reuse.

Decentralizing Physical Infrastructure

In all the large cities there is difficulty of collecting septage and hauling it across cities to designated disposal and treatment sites. It is important to consider decentralized treatment and reuse of wastewater and nutrients may be the best option. This may significantly reduce collection and haulage costs. Capital, operating and maintenance costs decrease with increasing plant size. However, since larger treatment plants require longer haulage distances between pits and disposal sites, costs escalate for collection companies, which in turn increase the risk of indiscriminate and illegal dumping. The optimum plant size has to be determined on a case-by-case basis as it depends on the local context (e.g., labor cost, land price, treatment plant scale, haulage distance, and site conditions).

Costs and Cost Recovery

Neither local authorities nor water supply authorities in MP have adequate capital or leverage to finance expensive sewer networks or sewage/ septage collection and treatment facilities. Thus, major sanitation improvements are dependent on a mix of government funding, external assistance and increased user charges. Project design should incorporate institutional building and financial viability. Obtaining funds and enacting necessary reforms (e.g., linking revenues with expenditures) requires careful negotiation and cooperation between local stakeholders, especially when elected officials are sensitive to popular concerns regarding tariffs. Multi-sourcing of funds can be used to effectively reduce the funding requirements of ULBs by encouraging project investment and O&M costs.

Operation and maintenance (O&M) expenses for septage management programs typically include the following:

- labour
- overhead (e.g., benefits, employment taxes)
- utilities
- transportation for processed and incoming materials
- vehicles and other equipment maintenance
- taxes
- disposal costs for dried cake
- licenses and permits; insurance
- testing and other monitoring and
- miscellaneous supplies

Revenue Generation Plan

- n: Political approval and effective administration of such taxes and charges have proven to be too difficult. Many cities in the country are increasingly realizing the importance of septage management and trying to introduce the taxes to recover at least the part of the cost with water bill. Charges can be linked to water consumption; disconnection of water supply provides an effective sanction against non-payment.

- The disadvantages are that the water service provider is not always willing (or able) to collect sanitation charges, and, while there are strong synergies in financial management, sanitation services require different skills and resources to those needed for water supply.
- Government funding is also essential, notably for the provision of sanitation services to the urban poor who remain excluded from public sanitation services and unable to develop private alternatives.
- Some cities charge a flat rate (or zero) tariffs, collect revenues lower than their O&M costs and, are dependent on subsidies.
- The other part of the arrangement is between the Sewage Treatment Facilities and ULBs (or the contractor collecting the septage). The tipping fee is perhaps the only variable of the facility's financial system. Calculating the desired tipping fee requires "working backwards." The cost to process the septage is determined by the facility's monthly operating expenses.
- The tipping fee (per unit basis) is determined by dividing the total tipping revenue by cubic meters of incoming septage. Therefore, to determine the tipping fee, the tipping revenue must first be calculated using the following equation:

  Tipping Revenues = Operating Expenses +Profit Margin – Material Revenues.
- In most cities, desludging is done only when requested by households and usually when the septic tank overflows. Costs are paid by the household directly to a private desludging company. To implement a city- wide septage management program, there is a need for the ULB and/or water supply authority to develop a system to ensure that all septic tanks are desludged regularly and that the septage removed is treated. Each ULB should develop a system that works for them. ULB/water supply authority could collect fees from the households and pay the contractor for each truck-full of septage brought to the treatment facility. This would give the contractor an incentive not to simply dump the septage, as is currently being done. This can be a source of revenue generation.

- In case sewage, septage, or sludge is collected, transported, treated & disposed by a third party, the final disposal of the treated sewage, septage or sludge shall comply with relevant MINAS Standards notified under Environment (Protection) Act, 1986.
- Reuse of treated sludge for agriculture application should comply with the standards notified for compost under EPA.

Public Participation

Public awareness and interest on the issues related to the conservation of natural resources have steadily increased and their participation needs to be promoted in the septage management programmes. The effective management of septage is of concern to a broad segment of the population as it affects the day-to-day life of individuals and communities. Communities should become involved in decisions concerning the development and siting of septage disposal point and desludging procedures, handling, transport and treatment methods and possible adverse effects including health effects of septage mis-management. Hence a strong public awareness programme is very important to implement the septgae management policy. The ultimate aim of the public awareness programme is to shape human behavior of all concerns including septic tank users, desludging staff. An education system is to be established in order to achieve effective awareness generation programme and to promote responsible citizenship behaviour. Following four areas need to be focused:

- ***Sensitivity:*** to help citizens and social groups gain a variety of experiences in, and acquire a basic understanding of septage and associated problems.
- ***Attitude:*** to help citizens and social groups acquire a set of values and feelings of concern for septage and motivation for actively participating in septage management.
- ***Skill:*** to help citizens and social groups acquire skills for identifying and solving septage related problems.
- ***Motivation:*** There should be a system to motivate the citizens through various incentives e.g image boosting for better work and rebate in charges on septage collection and disposal.

Awareness Generation

The ULBs may consider creating a Mass Awareness Cell. This cell will be responsible for creating awareness programmes on septage management. The cell should constitute committees at various levels and involve various stakeholders including representatives of citizens, RWAs,

ULBs authorities, NGOs, transporters and others. In organizational aspect, the cell should-

- Assess current practices
- Identify the role of key community members
- Identify the resources available from the authorities and resources to be contributed from the citizens, businessmen, industrial units, dairies etc.
- Highlight personal responsibilities and obligations in keeping septic tanks clean as per schedule
- Inform people about the duties and responsibilities of both individuals and community in cooperating with municipality in septage management
- Inform people about advantages of desludging septic tanks regularly
- Inform people about need of septage treatment before disposal in terms of health and environmental impacts
- Inform people about the need to pay for septage collection and its disposal
- Development of monitoring mechanism for effective implementation of awareness programme

Mechanism of Communication

All the above information will help define a proper strategy for communicating with different stakeholders. To reach out to the community media, group campaigns, video forums, pamphlets, home visits and other outreach formats can be prepared. The various means of public contacts-

- Print media, hoardings, posters, leaflets, publicity materials, radio, TV
- Open forum, signature campaign
- Direct communication, through RWAs, seminars, meetings
- Door-to-door awareness and motivation programme
- School programme
- Involvement of National Cadet Corps, National Social Service, scouts
- Involvement of religious leaders
- Involvement of mahila mandal and women associations

Reuse of Recycled Waste Water/ Effluent

Recycling of wastewater is essentially, reusing treated waste water for beneficial purposes such as agricultural and landscape irrigation, industrial processes, toilet flushing, and replenishing a ground water basin (referred to as ground water recharge). Recycling and reusing are both aimed at conservation and waste reduction, but they are not the same thing. Recycling is a process, while reusing is a practice. Recycled wastewater may be adhered to be used for sewerage schemes based on design years-

- about 15 percent of the sewage generation for base design year,
- 40 percent for intermediate design year (after 15 years) and
- 60 percent for ultimate design year (after 30 years).

Benefits of Reuse of Wastewater

- Helps save water, since it reduce the demand for freshwater for various uses, thus it helps to supplement potable water for non-potable uses
- Helps reduce pollution in the water bodies, since water is being recycled and treated
- Recharges ground water and replenishes surface water bodies
- Provision to develop and use a reliable in-house water source availability
- Reduction in fresh water cost and reduction in disposal cess-pools
- An approach towards zero liquid discharge
- A low-cost method for sanitary disposal of municipal wastewater
- Reduces pollution of rivers and other surface water bodies
- Conserves nutrients, thereby reducing the need for artificial fertilizer
- Provides a reliable water supply to farmers
- Protection of environment and effectively combat the water scarcity

Quality Concerns

Despite a long history of sewage/septage reuse in India, the quality issues linked with safety of sewage/septage reuse still remains an enigma. Public health concern is the most important issue in any type of reuse of sewage/septage, be it for irrigation or non-irrigation use. There is always a difficulty in delineating acceptable health risks and waste water reuse is a serious debate all over the world. The fundamental precondition for water reuse is that its application should not cause unacceptable public health risks. Untreated wastewater poses a serious risk of water-borne diseases, such as cholera, typhoid, dysentery, plague and helminthiasis. Use of untreated waste water for irrigation should be discontinued and replaced with irrigation using treated wastewater that meets public health guidelines in order to minimize the exposure of farm workers and consumers. For agricultural applications, the WHO has published guidelines for wastewater for restricted and unrestricted irrigation (WHO 2006). Governments have also developed more stringent criteria for agricultural applications. For non-agricultural applications, no global water quality standards exist, and various governments have issued their own standards.

Other water quality parameters of concern in sewage/septage reuse are:

- Toxic metal accumulation in soil
- Salinity due to salt present in sewage/septage

The availability of heavy metals to plants, their uptake and their accumulation depend on a number of soil, plant and other factors. The soil factors include, soil pH, organic matter content, cation exchange capacity, moisture, temperature and evaporation. Major plant factors are the species and variety, plant parts used for consumption, plant age and seasonal effects. Dissolved salts causing salinity in sewage/septage exert an osmotic effect on plant growth. An increase in osmotic pressure of the soil solution increases the amount of energy which the plant must expand to take up water from the soil. As a result, respiration is increased and the growth and yield of plants decline. However, it has been found that not all plant species are susceptible. A wide variety of crops normally are tolerant to salinity. Salinity also affects the soil properties such as dispersion of particles, stability of aggregates, soil structure and permeability.

Sewage/Septage Quality Standards in Practice

Although, no specific standards exists for sewage/septage reuse, however General Effluent Standards notified under Environment (Protection) Act, 1986 (Schedule - VI, Part A, GSR 801(E) dt. 3 1.12.93) by Government of India for disposal on land for irrigation are applicable. These standards specify limits on suspended solids, pH, oil and grease, biochemical oxygen demand, arsenic; cyanide, radioactive substances and toxicity. Considering the wide-ranging potential for sewage/septage reuse, it may be difficult to set some common quality standards for all types of reuses.

Recycling, Reuse & of Treated Effluent and Safe Disposal of Sludge

- Treated wastewater effluent is considered a water resource and is added to the water stock for reuse.

- Priority shall be given to agricultural reuse of treated effluent for unrestricted irrigation. Blending of treated wastewater with fresh water shall be made to improve quality where possible. Crops to be irrigated by the treated effluent or blend thereof with freshwater resources shall be selected to suit the irrigation water, soil type and chemistry, and the economics of the reuse operations.
- Crop nutrient requirements shall be determined taking into consideration the prevailing effluent quality. Overuse of nutrients shall be avoided.
- Accumulation of heavy metals and salinity shall be monitored, managed and mitigated. Leaching of soils shall be advocated by the irrigation authorities.
- Farmers shall be encouraged to determine the rate of water application needed for different crops, taking into consideration the value of nutrients in the treated water and other parameters.
- Farmers shall be encouraged to use modern and efficient irrigation technologies. Protection of on-farm workers and of crops against pollution with wastewater shall be ensured.
- Treated effluent quality should be monitored and users alerted to any emergency causing deterioration of the quality so that they will not use such water unless corrective measures are taken.
- Studies should be conducted and projects designed and implemented to store the excess treated wastewater in surface reservoirs but artificial recharge is not permitted . Due attention shall be given to the quality of treated and groundwater and the characteristics of the strata.
- Plans and studies for power generation from sludge, if proven technically, economically and financially feasible, shall be made with due attention to environment impacts.
- Sludge produced from the treatment process would be processed so it may be used as fertilizer and soil conditioner. Care shall be taken to conform to the regulations of public health and environment protection norms.
- Industrial reuse of reclaimed wastewater represents major reuse next only to irrigation in both developed and developing countries. Reclaimed wastewater is ideal for many industrial purposes. Where effluent is to be used in the industrial processes, it should be the responsibility of the industry to treat it to the quality standards required. Pilot scale feasibility studies carried out in

Australia have concluded that it is possible to economically treat the domestic waste water to achieve adequate quality for reuse as cooling water. Based on the conclusions of the feasibility study, a full-scale treatment plant employing cross-flow membrane microfiltration system may be installed. The membrane filtration system can remove all suspended solids, fecal coliforms, and giardia cysts. It could also significantly reduce human enteric viruses such as reovirusand enterovirus. The water reclamation plant at Eraring Power Station demonstrates the potential for reuse of wastewater in power generation and other industrial manufacturing facilities. Industrial uses for reclaimed water include:

- Evaporative cooling water:-
  (a) Once-through cooling system.
  (b) Re-circulating cooling system.
  (c) Cooling water quality requirements.
- Boiler –Feed water- The use of reclaimed water differs little from use of conventional public supplies for boiler-feed water, as both require extensive additional treatment quality requirement for boiler feed make up water are dependent upon pressure at which boiler is operated.

- Industrial process water- Suitability of reclaimed water for use in industrial process depends upon particular use like:
  (a) Pulp and paper.
  (b) Chemical industry.
  (c) Textile industry.
  (d) Petroleum and coal.
- Whenever possible, other end uses of treated effluents; such as recycling, cooling, power generation, etc. shall be considered.
- Re-use Options: The following options for re–use of effluent have been identified: In general, public health concern is the major issue in any type of reuse of wastewater, be it for irrigation or non-irrigation utilization, especially long term impact of reuse practices. It is difficult to delineate acceptable health risks and is a matter that is still hotly debated. Potential reuse of wastewater depends on the hydraulic and biochemical characteristics of wastewater, which determine the methods and degree of treatment required. While agricultural irrigation reuses, in general, require lower

quality levels of treatment, domestic reuse options (direct or indirect potable and non-potable) reuses need the highest treatment level. Level of treatment for other reuse options lie between these two extremes. The reuse options may be (artificial recharge of aquifers is not permitted):

- Irrigation
  (a) Agriculture and forestry
  (b) Landscaping
- Fish – farming
- Industry
- Non-potable Domestic Reuse.

The detailed project report should clearly define the best reuse option particular to town and strategy to obtain it. Action plan with clarity should be the part of Detailed Project Report (DPR), while preparing sewerage projects. Before deciding the reuse of treated waste water, authorities must full fill the water quality norms and its legal implications.

- Governing local body can sell the treated waste water and digested sludge to generate the revenue.

Inflow & Outflow of Funds & Cost Analysis

- In view of increasing marginal cost of wastewater collection and treatment, wastewater charges, connection fees, sewerage taxes and treatment fees shall be set to cover at least the operation and maintenance costs. It is also highly desirable that part of the capital cost of the services shall be recovered. The ultimate aim is for a full cost recovery.
- Appropriate criteria in order to apply the "polluter pays" principle shall be established.
- Different charges for different areas may be applied. This shall be assessed for each geographical area as a function of end users and effluent quality and will be subject to economic and social considerations.
- Because of the limited financial resources available to Government of M.P., setting investment priorities in waste water will be compatible with government investment plans.
- Criteria for prioritizing investments in the wastewater sector shall take into account the current and future needs of the state, needs to expand waste water systems in urban areas and to provide waste water systems to smaller towns and villages.

- Priorities of waste water projects shall not be disconnected from water supply projects and urbanization in general. Decisions will be made concerning them to attain optimum solutions to the need for services, availability of finance and availability of trained manpower.
- Treated effluent shall be priced and sold to end users at a price covering at least the operation and maintenance costs of delivery.
- It is the intention of the Government, through private sector participation, to transfer management of infrastructure and from the public to the private sector, in order toimprove performance and upgrade the level of service.
- The role of the private sector will expand with management contracts, concessions and other forms of private sector participation in wastewater management.
- The concepts of BOO/BOT shall be entertained, and the impact of such concepts on the consumers shall be continually addressed and negative impacts mitigated.
- The private sector role in reuse of treated effluent shall be encouraged and expanded.
- As per urban reforms (under various schemes by MOUD) 100 percent cost of O&M of sewerage system shall be recovered from consumer. The costs will depend on the system/technology adopted for collection of sewerage and treatment and the administration costs. It is important that the full cost of the service is assessed for each urban area instead of adopting a typical cost assessment. The full cost shall cover the following:
    - Institutional aspect of the sanitation service e.g. the management information systems accountancy and finance management, billing and collection, customer services, etc. and oversight activities.
    - Operating, maintaining (on a planned maintenance basis), repairing replacing and extending sanitation service physical infrastructure.
    - Keeping updated infrastructure and customer data on a GIS base.
    - Managers, staff, vehicles, equipment and consumables associated with the above.
    - Consumable like chemicals etc.
    - Power charges.

- Spare Parts.
- Any other O&M contract amount

Standards to be Adhered, Regulations & Quality Assurances

- Particular attention shall be focused on adopting and enforcing effluent and sludge standards for municipal and industrial wastewater treatment plants and for discharges from industries, laboratories, hospitals, slaughterhouses and other businesses.
- Extensive and comprehensive monitoring programs shall be developed. Influent to and effluent from the plants and throughout watercourses shall be measured and monitored against all appropriate parameters to ensure that public health objectives and treatment efficiency goals are attained.
- All crops irrigated with treated or mixed waters shall be analyzed and monitored periodically.
- Observation wells shall be installed near the treatment plants to monitor groundwater quality where necessary, and to mitigate adverse impacts where and when needed.
- Data collected from the monitoring process shall be entered and stored, processed and analyzed through computer software, and results published periodically.
- Roof and storm water connections to public sewers shall be prohibited. Collection of storm water shall be done separately and will be the subject of water harvesting.
- Effluent and sludge standards for the disposal of hazardous liquid wastes shall be defined to ensure the safe disposal of such wastes.
- EPCO/MPPCB/ CPCB regulations for disposal norms shall be mandatory.
- Industrial waste water is not allowed to dispose of in the sewer line. ULB can issue notification for penalties to be imposed on such industrial units.
- Laboratories shall be maintained and properly equipped to provide services and reliable data needed to ensure enforcement of and adherence to standards and regulations.

Legislation and Institutional Framework

- Legislation and institutional arrangements for the development and management of wastewater shall be periodically reviewed. Gaps shall be filled, and updating of the institutional arrangements with parallel legislation shall be made periodically to cope with varying circumstances and for this government shall notify an agency giving full power to take necessary action in this matter.

- The role of the Government shall be fine-tuned and its involvement reduced to be regulatory and supervisory. Involvement of the stakeholders in wastewater management and support shall be introduced and expanded.

Public Awareness and IEC & Priority Issues

- The public shall be educated through various means about the risks associated with the exposure to untreated waste water and the value of treated effluents for the different end uses.
- Programs for public and farmer's awareness shall be designed and conducted to promote the reuse of treated waste water, methods of irrigation and handling of product. Such programs shall concentrate on methods of protection of farmers health, animal and bird health and the environment.
- Public awareness campaigns shall also be waged to educate the public on the importance of domestic hygiene, waste water collection, treatment and disposal.
- It is observed that the system is dependent on the appreciation of the beneficiaries to the advantages and importance of the system to them and thereby working together towards making it successful. The co-operation is vital for following areas:
  (i) Protecting the system from getting choked due to entry of extraneous material in the sewer system. A vigilant public will help prevent this.
  (ii) The sewerage system yields full benefits or disease protection when there is 100 percent connectivity.
  (iii) It is important that the beneficiaries appreciate the benefits and pay for their upkeep. The systems require proper upkeep and the cost associated with maintenance and upkeep should at least be recovered from the beneficiaries. The principle of the polluter pays will be adopted only by an enlightened and participating public.
- A conscious campaign has to precede the planning and implementation of the sewerage systems.ULB, Non-Government Organizations and local neighborhood committees could give the process a thrust.

- A public participation process will not only aid in identifying potential consumers but also serve as a public education program. Potential users will be mainly concerned with the quality of reclaimed water, reliability of its delivery and the constraints in using reclaimed water. Also, connection costs or additional sewerage treatment cost might affect their ability to use the product. Consultations with various stake holders will aid in structuring of tariff and discounts for adopting reuse technologies, awareness on dual piping system, water conservation and safety issues.
- Municipal Bodies should decide and pass resolution regarding sewer connection charges. The provision should be widely publicized. Linkage of fixation & revision of user charges with other services need to be ensured from time to time. Implementation of user charges framework addressing affordability considerations and progressively move to user charges with due consideration to Cost Recovery of O&M System for initial years and progressively to cover debt servicing.
- Series of 'Sewer connection camps' may be organized. The time and venue should be publicized widely to inform residents. The days, time and venue should suit the convenience of public.
- Ensure that all Government offices and schools are connected with Sewer Connections or Safe Sewage disposable facilities.
- Implementation & Monitoring of Consumer Management & grievances redressal system in place with each ULB.

Human Resources & Continued R&D

- Capabilities of human resources in the management of wastewater shall be enhanced through training and continuous education. Work environment shall be improved and incentives provided.
- Establishment of State Water & Waste water Training Center at state level. It will help in training of human resources in this sector.
- Human resources performance will be continually appraised in order to upgrade wastewater treatment technologies, reduction of energy consumption and others will receive adequate support.
- Cooperation with specialized centers in the country and abroad shall be encouraged, and raising of funds for this purpose shall be supported.

- Transfer of appropriate technology suited for local conditions will be a primary target for the development activities and for adaptive research.

Service Level Benchmarking & Implementation Plan

Focus of improvements sewerage is on creation of new assets rather than management of existing assets. In order to bring about improvements in delivery of municipal services, a need has been felt to develop National Benchmarks in respect of basic services for sewerage are given below The Ministry of Urban Development has taken the initiative of bringing out a Handbook of Service Level Benchmarks, in 2008, which provides for standardized framework for performance monitoring in the four sectors. For Sewerage & Sanitation Services SLB are fixed.

The physical Infrastructure required to be planned can be broadly classified as:

- ***A Sewerage System*:** Including the onsite disposals system, network of pipes that collect sewage from domestic, institutional, commercial and industrial premises, the collector and interceptor sewers and pumping stations that convey the sewage to treatment plant. Storm water and industrial waste water shall not be allowed in the Sewerage system. Heavy penalty is to be imposed on the industries discharging industrial waste water in the sewerage system.

Industries should make separate arrangement for treatment of Industrial waste water.

- ***Treatment Plant*:** Where the quality of the sewerage is improved for its safe disposal or reuse. The sludge generated by the sewage treatment process is also normally processed at the plant for safe disposal and reuse. Treatment plants must have disinfection unit. The treated waste water shall not be allowed to discharge/reuse without disinfection to eliminate the pathogens present in the treated waste water. In each STP (proposed and existing) about 100 m- 200 m distance shall be declared as exclusion zone and in this zone thick plantation is to be done and priority is to be given to indigenous plants.
- ***Effluent Disposal Facilities*:** For conveying the treated liquid effluents to the point at which they are either safely disposed of into the ground or to a body of water – a water course or lakor to a point where they are directly reused in agriculture, fish farming, forestry, industry or planned reuse site. The disposal in the water

body shall be taken up only when other options are not feasible / appropriate.

- ***Sludge Disposal*:** By means of which liquid, semi-solid or dried sludge are transported to the point where they are either safely disposed to sanitary landfill or recycled, principally for use in agriculture. It shall be ensured that there shall be no crude dumping of STP sludge as it may create unhygienic and un-aesthetic conditions. Adequate processing of sludge must be carried out before disposal.

The proposed systems should satisfy the following:

(i) Satisfy its purpose based upon appropriate technology.

(ii) Will respond to environment and social concerns.

(iii) Will generate a satisfactory rate of return.

(iv) Be both sustainable and affordable.

The sewerage system is designed for a sufficient design period (generally thirty years) consisting of one or more outfall sewers, trunk sewers and laterals generally operating by gravity, but with force mains and pumping stations where required. The systems are to be designed on separate system to accept the domestic waste including sludge but excluding any rain water and industrial waste as acceptable. The house collection system should be designed to achieve this. Households sludge connectivity should be ensured for smooth functioning of the STP. Awareness program should be planned for households sewer connection.

Both the alternatives (i) centralized system and (ii) decentralized system should be evaluated before deciding type of system. Where funds are restricted or for smaller towns based on possible re-use of treated waste-water, decentralized approach may be adopted.

The system is beneficial when all the premises are connected to the system and there is no waste water flowing in the drains. The service lines to connect the house connections to the sewer system should be laid along with the laying of the sewers up to the boundary of the premise and plugged so that it can be extended by the premise owner within his premise.

The surface drains should not be connected to the sewer systems as they also carry rain water, solid wastes and silt which tend to choke the sewers.

The program of construction of the sewerage systems especially in the existing inhabited colonies should be made very carefully. Any systems that are laid but not commissioned are prone to be filled up by dirt and solid waste. This is likely to make the commissioning very difficult at a later date.

It is desirable to start from the downstream end of the out fall and commission it. The trunk mains should be taken up after this and commissioned as the work progresses. The laterals that get connected to the commissioned sections of outfall/trunk sewers only should be laid.

The construction program for the STP and sewer network should be planned and executed in such a fashion so that both of these get commissioned at the same time.

It is generally not possible to take up work for the whole city at once and the work may have to be prioritized. A method of prioritizing can be:

- Population of area.
- Areas where lack of sewer system is creating unhygienic living conditions or unacceptable odor levels, e.g. areas with a high population density and no drainage system or found with low permeability adversely affecting septic tank soak ways.
- Areas with high groundwater level requiring the use of cess-pools and where frequent emptying of the tanks is either impractical or extremely costly.
- Area where the quality of the ground water is adversely affected by septic tank effluent and ground water is a source of drinking water or discharges in a polluted state to a water course.
- City Centre, Commercial Centre etc.

In general pumping stations should be avoided on the sewerage systems to the extent possible because of the additional costs involved in construction and operation. They have to be installed if the design so requires. A properly designed and constructed pumping system can give trouble free service. The pumping stations can be suitably automated for better operation.

During construction, full care needs to be taken for diverting traffic and for fencing and safety of the excavation sites. The provisions for properly supporting the trenches should be taken. Special care should be taken for ensuring proper backfill and immediate repair of the roads after the work is completed.

The most common form of installing sewer is open excavation of trenches or open cut. This method has limitations on account of depth that can be handled, time taken and the disruption of the services of the concerned street for the work period. Usually this method is not feasible beyond 5-6 m depths.

Alternative techniques of trench less technologies involving tunneling and micro tunneling are used for laying sewers where open cut is not feasible on any of the above counts. This procedure though prevalent in developed countries, is not common in MP, but should be considered as an alternative where the situations warrant. The techniques of thrusting pipes in ground can also be used in specific cases.

Laying sewer and water pipelines & road restoration:

- In case water supply line or sewerage is to be carried out in the same street, the work of water supply line or sewerage should be done first and the road work be done after they are completed to avoid damage to the road once constructed.
- If both the work of sewerage and water supply pipelines is to be carried out in a street, it should be ensured that both the works are carried out at the same time to ensure that the road is not disturbed two times.
- The issue of relative placement of the water line and sewer line in relation to possibilities of pollution should also be paid attention. For that horizontal and vertical separation should be followed with the provision in Manual.
- Where the laying is being completed under a road, backfilling and compaction should be done as per specifications. If excavated area has a road pavement, it should be finished at top with a road pavement of the same standard and specifications as the existing pavement. It is desirable to use mechanical compaction devices for ensuring proper compaction and to avoid sinking of the repaired pavement.

Sewer network has not been utilized/remain under-utilized in the cities where sewerage facility is available. A large number of households are not connected to sewerage network resulting in prevalence of problems of sanitation, health and hygiene. Hence steps have to be taken at local level for utilization of network.

For more effective and quicker utilization of sewerage network created/ under creation, greater participation of residents of the city is required. Following steps may be taken to connect every house hold with sewerage network:

- Information, Education and communication (IEC) activities to be carried out to interact with citizens to convince them to take sewer connection. IEC activities may be taken up using newspapers, cinema slides, Nukkad Natak, Radio, SMS, Facebook, Twitter, Audio-Video clips, Films on local cable network etc.

- NGOs working in this field and volunteers may be engaged to motivate people to take sewer connections. Children and Schools may provide excellent motivation tool. Competition at school/ community level may be held to provide enthusiasm to carry out this activity.
- The plumbers of the city may be enlisted. Workshop of Plumbers must be carried out to train them to carry out sewer connections, without doing any damage to sewer network and connecting waste water of Bathroom, Kitchen and Toilet in proper fashion to avoid any problem of choking.
- A tentative estimate for joining the system of house to sewer line after categorization of houses in different categories such as A, B, C.... based on requirements should be prepared by Municipal Body and must be provided to residents so that there may not be overcharging incidences by the plumbers.
- In order to have proper functioning of sewerage, residents should be educated so that solid waste must not find access to sewerage system. The kitchen and bathroom should be provided with mesh.

Operation & Maintenance of Organised Sewerage System

- Operation and maintenance should be carried out in accordance with the provisions of CPHEEO manual for O&M as amended time to time. It is important to plan for the proper operation and maintenance of the assets created for sewerage disposal. Operation and maintenance should be carried out in accordance with the provision of CPHEEO manual for O&M period of minimum 10 years.

Dedicated fund should be provided/planned for proper operation and maintenance of sewerage system and STP.

- The important inputs for proper upkeep of the systems are a proper institutional arrangement for overseeing the work, appropriate technical back up, adequate funds, and active cooperation of an enlightened beneficiary public. A monitoring committee/vigilance committee should be constituted to monitor the waste water and storm surface water. A toll free number for helpline proposes should be created for public grievances.

- Most often, there will be lack of technical know-how and experience for operating the systems which are fairly sensitive and require professional attention. The O&M component of the contract can be for 10 years. The responsibilities should be clearly defined in the contract.
- Procurement of suitable equipment for ensuring proper maintenance like jetting machines, vacuum tankers, high powersuction machines, sewer rods, bucket cleaning machines, etc.
- Possibilities may be explored for Operation and maintenance on basis of cluster approach of urban bodies for using the facilities jointly and saving on investment.
- Funds for O&M: The cost involved in running the plant, transportation of the raw sewage etc makes the system in loss. The present practice is that the sewage collected at STP is released in natural drains or rivers which make them highly polluted affecting the human health downstream of the point of sewage in river. This makes it necessary to treat the water to extent it can be utilized for irrigation, Industrial or other purpose. Treatment to tertiary level also involved additional cost. Local body will plan to generate funds for O &M.
- The tariff for domestic, industrial and irrigation water may be increased so that the reclaimed water becomes competitive or cheaper than the normal water. Local body may provide information on quarterly basis regarding quantum of treated wastewater available including long term availability especially in areas which have been declared notified/over-exploited by Central Ground Water Authority (CGWA) ,so that interested parties/ Departments can make an application for reservation of treated waste water.

The Municipal Bodies should take into confidence all the stake holders and frame a suitable micro level policy for the sewerage disposal system within the guidelines stipulated in the State Policy and taking into account the local ground level realities. They should take advice from professionals for understanding the options. Such a Policy can include at municipal level:

- Physical Targets for Sanitation Coverage with a view of assigning time schedule and setting priority for covering various parts of the city.

- The standard of the service level that may be targeted and should be achieved by regular efforts.
- Effluent disposal standards can be fixed earmarking sites for sewage treatment facilities. Identification of effluent disposal options and sites.
- If more than one municipality can be gainfully combined for the system, identifying the options and working for such an agreement.
- Identifying and laying down the targeted recycle/reuse option of the effluent and sludge.
- Recognition of the principle of "the polluter pays" i.e. recovery of the financial liabilities being undertaken for the system.
- User to involve in participation for creation of fund for capital work.

References for Design of Sewerage System

The sewerage system and its appurtenances will be designed and implemented as per the guidelines laid out in the "Manual on Sewerage and Sewerage Treatment" latest edition published by the Central Public Health and Environmental Engineering Organization (CPHEEO), Ministry of Urban Development, Government of India following the latest developments in the industry and good engineering practices and National Sanitation Policy by GoI.

O & M Costs: Salaries and wages, electricity expenses, repairs, chemicals and other material purchases, Rents, Fuel, etc.

Capital Costs: Debt service charges, depreciation.

Major Drawbacks in the Existing Tariff Structure System

- Recovery of Capital Cost-Nil, since in most of the towns in the state only partial and temporary Sanitation/Sewerage facilities available. Tariff determined as per existing practices are largely aimed at recovering the historical costs rather meeting the long-term incremental costs and increased investment needs of an expanding system.
- Tariff structure not strictly followed due to political interference.
- Missing attention on the affordability and willingness to pay.
- Not linked with the quality of service.
- Minimum life line rates not defined.

Policy: Suggestive Landmarks

- Delinking of the service charges from the property tax net.
- Two-part tariff structure for -one for access and another for use or services rendered.
- Initially Tariff Structure should be based upon the average incremental costs and willingness to pay of different user groups. Allow for the lower charges to ensure life line rates. Cross subsidy mechanism should be introduced for Pro-Poor.
- Survey of quantity, quality and willingness to pay at regular intervals for various areas by Focused Group Discussions.
- Tariff Indexing keeping in view the rising cost of the service provision be done with reference to RBI WPI.
- Improved efficiency in delivery of service including in billing, collection, etc.

Inter- Departmental Co-ordination for Use of Recycled Effluent

It is necessary to recycle and reuse at least 20 percent of effluent after treatment. This resource should be judicially used after adhering to different requirements/ desired characteristics for end use of the product. Various departments may be given mandatory guidelines to use recycled water wherever possible with in the best usable characteristics achieved. Various department which may be considered for such uses are agriculture, horticulture, Industries, PWD, Rural Development and other which are using huge quantum of water in their day to day activities. For this purpose, it is necessary to have co-ordination between various departments of MP in their reachable activities in techno-economic, best use of available resources.

MAHARASHTRA

GUIDELINES FOR SEPTAGE MANAGEMENT, 2016

Objectives

The objective of this guideline is to facilitate all ULBs in Maharashtra to prepare an integrated faecal sludge management plan and implement a full septage management service in their cities. This would cover aspects across the service chain of on-site sanitation including safe collection, conveyance, treatment and disposal/reuse of the treated faecal sludge for all type of residential and non-residential properties (except industrial properties). These guidelines for seek to provide urban local bodies with knowledge and procedures of preparing a septage management plan. These guidelines also discuss other aspects related to regulation, monitoring and awareness generation that are needed in sustainable implementation of septage management in their cities. The septage management plan would help ULBs improve overall sanitationintheirtowns.

Guideline for ULBs for Effective Implementation of Septage Management Plan

Septage management Plan covers the entire service chain starting from design of septic tank, collection, conveyance, safe treatment and reuse or safe disposal of septage. The objective of these guidelines is to help city achieve improved sanitation situation in the city through implementation of septage managementplan.

Step by step approach: Operationalize of Septage Management Plan

The following is the step by step guide for effective implementation of septage management plan:

Preparation of Plan for Septage Management

(1) Existing situation assessment across sanitation service chain
   - Steps for assessment of existing toilets and septic tanks and creation of database
   - Steps for Scheduled septic tank empting services
   - Steps for Planning of septage treatment facility

(2) Explore private sector participation for septage management activities

(3) Awareness generation and capacity building activities

(4) Record-keeping, reporting (MIS), monitoring and feedback systems

Financial Resource Mobilization Plan

- Sources of revenues for septage management
- Mobilize financial resources to implement septage management plan

Existing Situation Assessment across Sanitation Service Chain

Assessing service performance across the service chain through a city level assessment is the first step in planning process. It is an important exercise, which provides an initial sense of the state of septage facility in the city, help in understanding the context and identifying gaps in key services. Detailed assessment of services will need to be done across each link in the chain through appropriate field assessments:

- ***Access & Collection***: Access describes the type of toilet and captures if the HH uses individual, shared or community facility. The choice of User Interface will depend on the availability of water. At city level it also measures the availability of public toilets. For sullage disposal, it captures access to bathroom facilities and drainage outlets. Collection and Storage/Treatment describes the ways of collecting, storing, and sometimes treating the excreta, grey water generated at the User Interface. The toilet may be connected to sewerage system; onsite systems like septic tank with soak pits, pits or may be functioning as Ecosan/ composting toilets. Similarly for grey water disposal, the HHs may be connected to sewerage system or drains of any kind (Open/covered).

Steps for Assessment of Existing Toilets and Septic Tanks and Creation of Database

(a) City level assessment of coverage of toilet and on-site sanitation facility using the existing database (like property tax module, Census 2011 etc.) or based on recent survey carried out under SBM.

(b) If the ULB do not have database, then ULB shall create database of toilets and septic tanks based on a questionnaire. All ULB shall link the key result related to toilet availability, type of toilet and its connection with waste water outlet with property tax database on e-governance platform.

(c) ULB shall keep updated database related to toilet availability and on-site sanitation through property tax assessment survey carried out at every four years of interval

(d) Evaluate existing septic tank designs and other storage/ treatment systems and modify (in case of variation) based on design.

(e) Notices should be issued to all property owners whose septic tanks do not meet the standard septic tank design.

(f) Identify insanitary toilets1 and convert them to sanitary latrines for safe collection and disposal of waste as per norms set out.

(g) All existing septic tanks should have access covers for each chamber, so that they can be easily opened during emptying process. Where such covers are not available, it should be made compulsory for all property owners to provide proper covers.

(h) The new septic tanks need to be designed and constructed as per the norms suggested in National Building Code, 2005 and CPHEEO Manual, 2013 which takes reference of design norms from IS: 2470 on Code of practice for installation of septic tanks - Part 1: Design and Construction and Part 2: Secondary treatment and disposal of septic tank effluent 1985 (Reaffirmed 1996).

- ***Conveyance*** describes the transport of products across the service chain. ULB should plan for scheduled septic tank emptying services for effective implementation of septage management plan. Prior to plan for the same ULB shall first assess its role and capacity for implementation of septage management plan. ULB should assess various aspects of septic tank empting like how many septic tanks required to be emptied annually as per CPHEEO norm versus how many are emptied in a year, how many vaccum emptying trucks/ capacity of trucks are required if number of septic tank emptied as per CPHEEO norm versus how many trucks are available/working with capacities of emptier trucks, assessing the cost per emptying visit, method of maintaining the register for septic tank emptying services database etc.

If private player is involved in septic tank emptying business in the city, then, ULB shall also review the role of private septic tank emptier and assess their capacity in lines with the number of septic tank empting annually, charges/fees for empting services, location of disposal, registration/licensing with ULB or not etc.

Steps for Scheduled Septic Tank Empting Services

(a) ULBs should initiate pre-determined scheduled septic tank empting services and develop a route plan for the same.

(b) Mobilize or procure adequate number of suction emptier trucks to maintain a three year rotating cycle. Number and type of vehicles to be purchased based on the sizes of septic tanks or septage generation rate for the city, distance from the location of septic tanks to the septage treatment facility, cleaning frequency of septic tanks and available road width for the suction truck operations.

(c) ULBs should either provide the emptying services themselves or enter into appropriate management contracts with private agencies. In case of private sector contract, ULBs should certify and license private septage transporters to de-sludge and transport waste to the designated treatment facility.

(d) All septage transporters need to maintain a collection and transport receipt.This needs to be filled duly by the private/ULB service provider and submitted to ULB office.

Measures to be taken during Desludging of Septic Tanks

(a) While desludging the following norms should be followed:

  (i) The septic tanks should not be fully emptied; small amount of sludge of around 1 to 2 inches should be left in the septic tank to facilitate decomposing of incoming faecal waste.

  (ii) No fire or flame should be used near the septic tanks as there may be inflammable gases inside septic tanks

  (iii) Proper safety gears should be used by the operator while desludging/emptying the septic tanks

(b) Septage transportation vehicle operators (whether from ULB or private sector) should be well trained and equipped with protective safety gears, uniforms, tools and proper vacuum trucks, to ensure safe handling of sewage/septage. The rules under the Prohibition of Employment as Manual Scavengers and their Rehabilitation Act, 2013 provide for a comprehensive list of safety gear that should be used while providing these services.

- ***Treatment and Disposal***

Treatment: ULB must not dispose the septage collected from septic tank without any treatment and ULB must comply with CPCB and MPCB norms before disposal of septage. ULB should assess the load of septage and assess the requirement of capacity for treatment plant. ULB should first try and assess the possibility of setting up septage treatment facility at the solid waste treatment/disposal site and at the STPs within the city or in nearby city.

Reuse/Disposal refers to the methods in which products are ultimately returned to the environment, as either useful resources or reduced-risk materials. The treated septage can be used as a soil enricher or as filling material at construction sites. ULB should carry out primary assessment for availability of market and demand for reuse.

Steps for Planning of Septage Treatment Facility

(a) Septage collected from the septic tanks or pits should not be disposed without any treatment.

(b) ULB should first assess the possibility of septage treatment at existing STP in the city or STP of nearby city through appropriate agreements with STP operators and receiving ULBs.

(c) If STP is not available in the city or nearby that can receive the sludge, then ULB should plan for new septage treatment facility. Such a new septage treatment facility should be designed to cater to expected volumes of septage generated in urban local body and if faecal waste is expected from nearby urban local bodies.

(d) Input quality of the collected septage should be tested at the treatment facility for checking presence of any metal or traces of industrial waste.

(e) The faecal sludge treatment plant should be operational during working hours only and a responsible person should be appointed in the facility to ensure that no commercial or industrial waste is unloaded in these facilities.

(f) Septage should be reused / safely disposed only after it meets the parameters.

Measures to be taken while planning for Septage Treatment Facility

Identification of septage treatment site is crucial for effective implementation of septage management plan. Following parameters to be taken into consideration before finalization of treatment sites:

Distance of Treatment Site: Distance from emptying to delivering and accessibility of the treatment site are major issues. The transport of relatively small fecal sludge volumes (5-10m3 per truck) on congested roads over long distances in large urban areas is financially unfeasible. A site that is too far away implies fewer trips per day, less revenue and more fuel costs to private operators.

Reliability of Electricity: It is also important to assess the availability and reliability of electricity if treatment technology has mechanical operated parts; as in case of fluctuations it will increase treatment time and will affect optimal utilization of treatment capacity.

Neighborhood: A treatment site may generate nuisance, especially bad odors. For this reason it should be located at an appropriate distance from the residential areas.

Land availability: Projects are often delayed because of non-availability or high price of land. ULB should identify the land bank for treatment facility. ULB should also explore the possibility of developing septage treatment facility at solid waste dumping or treatment site.

Geological Parameters: Assessment of existing geological conditions on site like groundwater table, type of soil, prone to flooding is always recommended as it may directly affect selection of technology option.

Explore Private Sector participation for Septage Management Activities

For effective operationalize of scheduled septic tank emptying service and treatment facilities, ULB may also explore the option for private sector participation. Following points to be taken into consideration by ULB:

(a) Explore private sector participation for various activities like procurement, operations and maintenance of the suction emptier trucks, construction and operations of septage treatment facility and possible re-users of treated septage within the city as well as in nearby cities.

(b) Develop performance based contracts such that payment is linked to the performance of private sector for providing the services.

• ***Awareness Generation and Capacity Building Activities***

Awareness generation activities need to be taken up for successful implementation of faecal sludge management plan and community acceptance and adherence to regulations and service plan set up by the ULBs. Associated training and capacity building of municipal staff as well as private sector contractors also needs to be taken up.

Awareness Generation for Residents: Members of Resident Welfare Associations, community organizers, self-help groups and the general public should be made sensitized periodically regarding the need for a sound faecal sludge management system including a 3-year cycle. The health hazards associated with improper collection and treatment of waste, and the ill-effects of sewage discharge into fresh water/storm water drains should be explained to the residents. Awareness generation activities should be carried out at the beginning of introducing a scheduled service in all wards and then repeated periodically over the three year cycle.

Capacity Building for Municipal Staff: Municipal Commissioners/ Chief Officers, Engineers, Sanitary Inspectors, Health Officers, and Sanitary Workers should be well trained in safe septage management and its best practices. This involves regular training sessions on safe collection, treatment and disposal. Information regarding standard septic tank design, the need for periodic inspection and desludging of septage, design of a treatment facility, tender details for engaging licensed transporters, etc. should be disseminated widely to achieve a safe faecal sludge management system. Training should also be provided on safety standards.

Capacity Building for SeptageTransporters /Private Vendors: Local Bodies should ensure all safety norms are clearly explained to the septage transporters. Private Operators and Transporters should be well trained in safe collection and transportation of sewage including vehicle design, process of desludging, safety gears and safe disposal at the nearest treatment facility.

- ***Record-keeping, Reporting (MIS), Monitoring and Feedback Systems***
  (a) **Record keeping and manifest forms** should be an integral part of a comprehensive septage management program. Record keeping requirements should be codified into the law governing the program.
  (b) The completed document or documents with signatures of the household/property, suction truck operator and treatment plant operator should be submitted to the local government for their records. Payment to the suction truck operator should only be made if there are signatures of all the stakeholders.
  (c) An ***MIS system*** such as the one discussed in access and collection will need to be developed and maintained.
  (d) Where possible, **GIS** should be used to be plan the route of suction emptier trucks and tracking these for regular record keeping.
  (e) ***Consumer grievance redressal system*** for faecal sludge management should also be set up as a part of urban local body record keeping systems and helpline numbers to be shared with residents as a part of monitoring and record keeping systems for faecal sludge management.

Sources of Rvenues for Septage Management

(a) ***Sanitation tax/charge*** should be levied on all the properties for sustaining the septage management activities. The tax/charge can be added either as surcharge on property tax or a new sanitation tax/charge can be levied under the Maharashtra Municipal Councils,

Nagar Panchayats and Industrial Townships Act, 1965, Chapter IX: Municipal taxation, Section 108.

(b) If ULB explore the possibility of Private sector involvement in septage management, then an **escrow account** can be set up where revenues from the sanitation tax/charge are transferred. The contractual amount for FSM services to the private party can be paid from this escrow account to avoid delays.

(c) ***Periodic revisions for the taxes/charges*** to be effected based on revisions in costs involved.

(d) To the extent possible, revenues should be generated from ***sale of treated septage*** for agriculture or other purposes.

Mobilize Financial Resources to implement Septage Management Plan

(a) ULB may utilize the funds from 14th FC to implement the various components related to septage management plan. Creation of database for toilets and septic tanks, procurement of suction emptier trucks and construction of septage treatment facilities are the permissible components to utilize the 14th FC funds. The funds would also be provided as preparatory activity like preparing detailed project report and prefeasibility report for septage management.

(b) ***IEC & Capacity building funds*:** IEC funds under SBM shall be utilized for various awareness generation activities undertaken for implementing septage management plan includes capacity building activities for ULB staff, septage transporters, treatment plant operators and residents of city.

(c) Convergence with existing schemes/activity: If any ULB is going to undertake the water audit survey under MSNA or survey under SBM or property tax assessment etc, then ULB should integrate the sanitation survey with the respective activity.

Faecal Sludge / Septage Treatment Options

Septage is the settled solid matter in semi-solid condition usually a mixture of solids and water settled at the bottom of septic tank. It has an offensive odour, appearance and is high in organics and pathogenic microorganisms, whereas septic tank effluent is the liquid part which flows out from septic tank (since solids are trapped in septic tank). Septage has a much higher concentration of pollutants than the septic tank effluent. Biological Oxygen Demand (BOD) and Total Suspended Solids (TSS) are two common measurements of the strength of septage. As per U.S. EPA,

1984 septage in tropical countries may have BOD concentrations between 440 to 78,600 mg/l and TSS values in range of 310 to 93,378 mg/l, where septic tank effluent has values averaging around 200 mg/l BOD and 300 mg/l TSS. As septic tanks fill with septage, the effluent begins to resemble faecal sludge with higher pollution values. Therefore, regular desludging provides dramatic improvements in effluent quality. Detailed septage characterization (BOD, TSS &other microbial characteristics) as well as its dewatering characteristics (specific resistance etc.) should be done prior to the design of any faecal sludge management facility. Treatment of septage / faecal sludge can be of two types, treatment at sewage treatment plants and at independent septage treatment plants. The details of these two types of treatment are given in the section below:

Treatment of Septage/Faecal Sludge at Sewage Treatment Plants

Co-treatment of septage along with domestic sewage at a sewage treatment plant (STP), if available, is the most desirable option. Though septage is more concentrated in its strength than domestic sewage, its constituents are similar to municipal wastewater. But care should be taken that the STP should have adequate capacity to accept the septage without hampering the functioning of the sewage treatment plant. The municipality should monitor the incoming wastewater load to the STP and accept the septage, if the design norms are not violated with the increased load (on account of the septage). The treatment plants that are under-utilized can serve as treatment plants for septage from nearby ULBs and if the STPs are working closeto the design capacity, additional loads due to disposal of septage will necessitate expansion or up-gradation of the STP capacity.

The septage could be added at various locations for treating it along with STP wastewater:

- **Septage Addition at the nearest Sewer Manhole**: Septage could be added to a sewer upstream of the STP, and substantial dilution of septage occurs prior to it reaching the STP, depending on the volume of sewage flowing in the sewer.
- **Septage addition at the STP:** Septage could be added to sewage immediately upstream of the screening and grit removal processes.
- **Septage addition to sludge digesters/sludge drying beds:** Septage could be processed with the sludge processing units of STP.

If septage/faecal sludge are to be co-treated with sewage, it will be necessary to construct a septage /faecal sludge receiving chamber. Chemicals such as lime or chlorine can also be added to the faecal sludge in the storage tank to neutralize it, to render it more treatable, or to reduce odors.

Treatment of Septage/Faecal Sludge at independent Septage Treatment Plants

When an STP does not exist for a city, or the distance or the capacity of the available plant becomes a limiting factor, it is not a feasible option to transport and treat the septage at the sewage treatment facilities. Hence, a treatment plant especially meant for septage treatment becomes the option to consider. Independent septage treatment plants are designed specifically for septage treatment and usually have separate unit processes to handle both the liquid and solid portions of septage. These include:

- Lime stabilization – odor control, conditioning and stabilization of the sludge.
- Dewatering – sludge drying beds or mechanical dewatering.
- Anaerobic/aerobic wastewater treatment – liquid from the sludge drying beds and mechanical dewatering systems.

Co-composting with organic solid waste: The choice of mechanical dewatering or sludge drying beds would be dependent on the land availability, with mechanical dewatering systems being preferred where land is scarce and sludge drying beds being adopted where land availability is not a constraint. The benefit of using these treatment plants is that they could provide a regional solution to septage management. Many septagetreatment plants use lime to provide both conditioning and stabilization before the septage is dewatered, and this dewatered sludge can be used as organic fertilizer after drying and composting. Additionally, lime stabilization also helps to reduce/minimize odour. The common practice is to add lime to raise the pH to 12 and hold it for a period of 30 minutes. The filtrate from the dewatering units needs to be further treated through treatment process such as waste stabilization ponds, anaerobic baffled reactor, constructed wetland or aerobic treatment systems before discharging into the environment. However, the choice of an appropriate septage management system is dependent on land availability, local site conditions, level of treatment requiredhauling distance, technical requirements, costing , requirement of expertise for construction and operation, availability of skilled labour, legal and regulatory requirements. The management option selected should be in conformity with local, state, and central regulations. From review of various options for the Septage treatment, it was observed that treatment options could broadly be divided into two types. One form of technology is to convert faecal sludge/septage to compost and another is to convert septage to energy. These technologies can be grouped as shown in the figure. Details of these technologies are detailed out in section below:

- ***Sedimentation Ponds/Settling Tank/Thickening Ponds***: Sedimentation or Thickening Ponds are simple settling ponds that allow the sludge to thicken and dewater. The effluent is removed and treated, while the thickened sludge can be treated in a subsequent technology. Settling tanks provide a liquid retention time of a few hours (enough to ensure quiescent settling of settle able solids). Here input is faecal sludge and output is dried Septage and effluent, which can be used in agriculture, arboriculture and pastures. This treatment option can be coupled with sludge drying bed or co-composting for treatment of thickened sludge. This technology is affected by seasonal changes and can be efficiently used in hot and temperate climate. The discharging area must be maintainedand kept clean. The thickened sludge must be removed mechanically when the sludge has thickened sufficiently. Septage and effluent may require further treatment.
- ***Sludge Drying Bed / Unplanted Sludge Drying Bed***: An unplanted sludge drying Bed is a simple, permeable bed that, when loaded with sludge, collects percolated leachate and allows the sludge to dry by evaporation. Approximately 50 percent to 80 percent of the sludge volume drains off as liquid. The bottom of the drying bed is lined with perforated pipes that drain away the leachate. On top of the pipes are layers of sand andgravel that support the sludge and allow the liquid to infiltrate and collect in the pipe. In this technique input is faecal sludge and output is treated sludge and effluent, which can be use in agriculture, arboriculture and pastures. Sludge drying bed can be coupled with co-composting for further treatment. This technology is affected by seasonal changes and can be used in hot and temperate climate. Excessive rain may prevent the sludge from proper settling and thickening or this can be avoided by providing transparent sheds over the sludge drying bed. Over most of the year, the septage drying time is expected to be about seven days; however, an average of ten days is considered to accommodate longer drying periods during the rainy season. Dried sludge must be removed every ten to fifteen days. Sand must be replaced when the layer gets thin. Treated Septage and leachate may require further treatment based on output quality.

- ***Planted Sludge Drying Bed***: Planted sludge drying bed is similar to an unplanted drying bed with the benefit of increased transpiration. The key feature is that the filters do not need to be desludged after each feeding/drying cycle. Fresh sludge can be applied directly onto the previous layer; it is the plants and their rootsystems that maintain the porosity of the filter. The roots of the plants create pathways through the thickening sludge to allow water to escape more easily. In this technique input is faecal sludge and output is treated sludge and effluent, which can be use in agriculture, arboriculture, pastures and as cattle fodder. Planted sludge drying bed can be coupled with co-composting for further treatment. It is affected by seasonal changes. The drains must be maintained and the effluent must be properly collected and disposed off. The plants should be periodically thinned and/or harvested. Treated Septage and Leachate may require further treatment based on output quality.
- ***Co-Composting***: Co-Composting is the controlled aerobic degradation of organics using more than one feedstock. Faecal sludge has a high moisture and nitrogen content while biodegradable solid waste is high in organic carbon and has good bulking properties. There are two types of Co-Composting designs: open and in-vessel. A Co-Composting facility is only appropriate when there is an available source of well-sorted biodegradable solid waste. Mixed solid waste with plastics and garbage must first be sorted. In this technique input is faecal sludge and biodegradable organic solid waste and output is compost which can be use in agriculture, arboriculture and pastures. It is affected by seasonal changes and depending on the climate (rainfall, temperature and wind) the Co-Composting facility can be built to accommodate the conditions. At places where there is heavy rainfall covered facilities are especially recommended. Careful monitor of the quality of the input materials & track of the inflows, outflows, turning schedules, and maturing times is required to ensure a high quality product. Turning must be done periodically.
- ***Deep row Entrenchment (Trenching)***: It consists of digging deep trenches, filling them with sludge and covering them with soil. Trees are then planted on top, which benefit from the organic matter and nutrients that are slowly released from the FS. Availability of land is a major constraint & distance to groundwater bodies. This technology is feasible in areas, where the water

supply is not directly obtained from the groundwater and groundwater table is low.

- ***Mechanical Dewatering***: Mechanical dewatering is normally associated with large waste water treatment plants and is used to separate sludge (residual sludge from wastewater treatment plants or faecal sludge from on-site sanitation) into a liquid and a solid parts. These techniques are usually sophisticated and costly for smaller systems to be implemented on community level. The process does not treat the sludge, it only separates solid from liquid parts. Both solid and liquid parts still contain pathogens and pollutants and further treatment is necessary. Mechanical parts need periodical inspection and replacement. In this technique input is faecal sludge and output is black water, organic solid waste, compost/biosolids which can be use in agriculture, arboriculture and pastures. It requires to be coupled with co-composting or incineration treatment technique. This technology is not affected by seasonal changes as it is entirely depends on mechanical process. This technology requires less space.
- **Waste Stabilization Pond (Non - aerated):** WSP comprises pre-treatment units (tanks or ponds) for solid-liquid separation followed by a series of one or more anaerobic ponds and one facultative pond. A number of problems may arise where waste stabilisation ponds are used to treat municipal wastewater and co-treat FS. In many instances, the problems are linked to the fact that the wastewater ponds were not originally designed and equipped to treat any additional FS load. In this technique input is faecal sludge and output is sludge & effluent, which can be use in agriculture, arboriculture, pastures, ground water recharge in deep aquifer and in desert areas. It requires to be coupled with co-composting or sludge drying bed. It can be implemented at neighbourhood level or city level. This technique is affected by seasonal changes. As per sanitation experts and review of various technical documents, it was analysed that waste stabilization pond is good option for treatment of waste water but not a good option for treatment of Septage.

Advanced Nutrient Recovery: Wastewater, municipal sludge or the ash after dried sludge, which is incinerated or disposed of, can be a very rich source for nutrients, in particular phosphorus and nitrogen. There is a wide range of promising technologies emerging which can convert septage to phosphorus and nitrogen. Some of these techniques are still not fully developed. These technologies are expensive and require engineering knowledge to guarantee a sustainable and long-term operation of the facility. In this technique black water, faecal sludge and grey water is converted to fertilizer and treated waste which can be use in agriculture, arboriculture, pastures, ground water recharge in deep aquifer and desert areas. This technology is highly expensive.

Septage to Energy

- ***BIO-METHANATION/ANAEROBIC BIOGAS REACTOR:*** In this treatment technology there is microbes driven anaerobic decomposition of organic components in faecal sludge to biogas. Faecal sludge & organic solid waste is converted to treated sludge, effluent and Biogas. Pretreatment of sludge is required but not compulsory. To start the reactor, active sludge (e.g. from a septic tank) should be used as a seed. The tank is essentially self-mixing, but it should be manually stirred once a week to prevent uneven reactions. However once stable state reached, stirring not essential. Gas equipment should be cleaned carefully and regularly so that corrosion and leaks are prevented. Grit and sand that has settled to the bottom should be removed once every year. Bio-Methanation/Anaerobic biogas reactor option is popularised by Sulabh organization in India.

  Advantages:

  (i) Established and mature technology.

  (ii) Best suitable for wastes with high moisture content.

  (iii) Technology could be optimized for any scale.

  (iv) Considerable reduction in the emission of greenhouse gases like methane is possible.

  Disadvantages:

  (i) There are concerns with odour and pathogen dissemination from the digestate.

  (ii) Issues are there in controlling microbial activity if the digester is beyond a certain size.

  (iii) Affected by temperature less efficient in colder climates

- ***INCINERATION*:** In Incineration treatment option there is oxidation of organics in the sludge under the conditions of complete aeration or oxygenation and requires high temperature. Incinerators are a useful technology to combust household waste, medical waste, slaughter waste, etc. instead of discharging it in a landfill. Furthermore, heat and energy may be recovered and it helps to avoid open burning of municipal waste which creates much more harmful emissions and endanger human health and environment. In this treatment sludge is converted to heat. Drying of sludge is required prior for treatment in incinerators. This technology requires trained operators. There is risk of malfunction if not properly maintained and operated.

***Advantages*:**

(i) Incineration is relatively a simple technology for treating all kinds of wastes.

Disadvantages:

(i) Liberates considerable amounts of emission

(ii) Sludge incineration costs are not attractive to be used in India

(iii) Sludge incineration is not proven in India

- ***GASIFICATION:*** In Gasification treatment technology there is thermal transformation of organic mass under limited supply of air/oxygen to Syngas. In this technology sludge is converted to syngas & biochar. Drying of sludge is required prior for treatment in incinerators. This technology also requires trained operators and there is risk of malfunction if not properly maintained and operated.

***Advantages*:**

(i) Technology best suitable for dry feed stocks. The produced gas can be converted into any type of fuel by FT synthesis.

Disadvantages:

(i) Gasification of faecal sludge is a relatively new concept in India.

(ii) Process is very energy intensive, as wet feedstock cannot be used directly in a gasifier.

(iii) The process is economically less viable.

- ***PYROLYSIS:*** In pyrolysis treatment technology there is thermal conversion of carbonaceous materials in sludge toproduce complex oil in the absence of air/oxygen. In this technology sludge is converted to Bio-oil, Pyrolytic Gas and Bio-char. Here also drying of sludge is required prior for treatment in incinerators. This technology requires trained operators and there is risk of malfunction if not properly maintained and operated.

Advantages:

(i) Energy recovery efficiency is high.

Disadvantages:

(i) Pyrolysis has been attempted only for the treatment of plastic and related feed stocks so far.

(ii) This process is also energy intensive like gasification, as more energy is needed to dry of feedstock.

(iii) High capital and operational costs make the process economically less viable.

Safe Reuse/Disposal of Treated Septage

For dewatered septage/sludge can be used as fertilizer in agriculture application, it should satisfy the following criteria of Class A Bio-solids of US EPA: A faecal coliform density of less than 1000 MPN/g total dry solids, Salmonella sp. density of less than 3 MPN per 4 g of total dry solids. WHO (2006) suggests Helminth egg concentration of < 1/g total solids and E coli of 1000/g total solids in treated septage for use in agriculture MSW Rules (2000) recommended the quality for compost.In the absence of any standards, it is recommended that these be adopted until such time standards are notified by the Central Pollution Control Board. Properly treated sludge can be reused to reclaim parched land by application as soil conditioner, and/or as a fertilizer. Deteriorated land areas, which cannot support the plant vegetation due to lack of nutrients, soil organic matter, low pH and low water holding capacity, can be reclaimed and improved by the application of treated septage. Septage sludge, as a result of lime stabilization has pH buffering capacity that is beneficial for the reclamation of acidic soils. Treated septage contains nutrients in considerable amounts, which supports the growth of a number of plants.

Drip irrigation is the preferred irrigation method for settled septage effluent when irrigation is feasible. Crops which could be safely grown are corn, fodder, cotton, trees including fruit trees, eucalyptus and poplar. Aquaculture can be practiced for settled septage effluent when freshwater is available to achieve dilution to ensure dissolved oxygen is above 4 mg/l. Fish species of tilapia and carp are preferred since they tolerate low dissolved oxygen. Both drip irrigation and aquaculture need land and are feasible at city outskirts.

UTTAR PRADESH
STATE SEPTAGE MANAGEMENT POLICY, 2019

Key Tenets

The policy is being formulated on the following key tenets:

- The households will continue to invest their financial resources in the construction of HH toilets (user interface) and septic tanks as per the prevailing guidelines and scheme requirements. Notwithstanding this private investment, the Government will make all efforts to advocate sound design and construction practices.
- To treat septage management (SM) as a service, beyond infrastructure.
- SM plans at the city level will integrate existing infrastructure besidesnewasset creation and serve as prerequisite for funding.
- "Polluter pays principle" applies to all stakeholders i.e. citizensas waste generators. The payments are mandatory for all recipients of services to ameliorate pollution i.e. septage/sewerage service.
- An efficient and single point payment system irrespective of whether it is through taxation by ULBs or levy of charges/fees by private operators.
- Universal household coverage with septage services on equity principles; while tariff design will account for the true cost of the services, includingsubsidiesand/or top-up incentives to account for all disadvantaged groups.
    (i) Cover 100 percent opex across along the value chain
    (ii) Extended to cover capex (current + depreciation; all value chain elements; payments for ecosystem services) and refinancing of future assets
- The government will financially support and regulate across the value chain until
    (i) A formalized private sector services market is developed for various value chain elements and
    (ii) ULBs become financially self-reliant to invest in infrastructure creation and management.
- Towards achieving environmental and public health safety, the government will invest in asset building (including private assets i.e. IHHL) up to a basic level through different schemes for poor and slum dwellers.

Goal

The goal of the Policy is: "**All ULBs commit to continually adopt sustainable septage services, which is inclusive and equitable; for its citizens to live in an environment free of pollution and health hazards; with the support of public and private sector, under a sector regulator**". The Policy provides for addressing the needs of the urban poor and slum dwellers on priority and those desirous for continued on-site sanitation services; on the same lines as that of the whole city. Also, covered is the aspect of reduction in pollution load in the immediate ecosystem across all ULBs, by managing 5558 MLD of wastewater annually and 13.7 MLD septage treated daily.

Septage Policy Target

This Policy articulates and set priorities, commitments,and direction for ULBs to undertake the city-wide implementation of SM services alongside sewerage services, within its jurisdiction, such that safe and sustainable sanitation becomes a reality for all households.

Scope of the Policy and Applicability

- The policy is valid until the end of 2023. Given that 652 ULBs require to implement the policy, it is expected that changes and modifications would be required in the policy as lessons are learned year on year. The annual and terminal evaluation by the Department will advise the policy amendment(s).
- This policy shall apply to all ULBs, outgrowths in urban agglomerations, census towns as declared by the Registrar General and Census Commissioner of India, notified areas, notified industrial townships, areas under the control of Indian Railways, airports, airbases, defense establishments, special economic zones, State and Central Government organizations, places of pilgrimage, religious and historical importance as may be notified by State Government from time to time.
- The policy shall apply to all newly added geographical areas to the ULBs, between the time of notification and 2023.
- The policy does not address the exclusive need(s) of sewerage systems but envisages a complementary role in ULBs where such systems exist or is currently under implementation.

Service Levels

The criteria of service levels will be as follows:

- Coverage of adequate onsite sanitation system
- Collection efficiency of the sanitation system
- Adequacy of treatment capacity of sanitation system
- Quality of treatment of sanitation system
- Extent of reuse and recycling in the sanitation system

Service Charter

To ensure consistency in operations across all ULBs, a set of permissible codes for key stakeholders will be drawn by the UDD is drawn in Table 3 which will form the basis of engagement with the operators (individuals/ firms). This charter shall be updated once in two years based on compliance levels under different conditions.

Policy Outline and Commitments

The Urban Development Department (UDD) shall support initiatives under septage management to achieve universal and safe environmental sanitation by taking following steps:

PlanningConsideration with City Nomenclature

"Categorization of ULBs to strategize interventions and implementation plans".

Due to huge variation in size of ULBs, spatial distribution and the pace of creation of sewerage systems, auniform sectoral approach will not bear desirable results.It is proposed to adopt a segmented approach to managetheseptage management sector in the state.

The following categorization is outlined:

- **Category A:** Universal septage management coverage through the sewerage system. SM to play a gap filling and complementary role prior to HHs migration to sewered mode. SM sector requiresinvestment and regulatory control to serve the unsewered areas.
- **Category B:** Universal SM coverage through a combination of sewerage and septage solutions. A large number of house sewer connections have been sanctioned under AMRUT, eventually ULBs with STPs will end in this category. SM interventions to be targeted in uncovered areas or until the transition to sewer connections is completed.

- ***Category C*****:** Universal SM coverage through predominantly septage services. Except for pending sewerage projects, all new projects will aim to formalize end-to-end septage services. Investments will be made towards STPs and a viable, regulated emptying &conveyance model.
- ***Category D*****:** For smaller towns the way forward is to establish septage services. Given a small market in such towns and unviable for sewerage services and septage treatment, FSSTPs can be planned on cluster basis as well.

The purpose of this classification is to direct interventions under the policy, towards a particular type of service management to benefit from economies of scale within the city as well as the region.

Accounting for future increase in ULB area: It is well understood that ULBs'geographicalsize and morphology changes with time. The predominant reasons are:

(a) Increase in the administrativearea of ULBs on account of
  (i) Merging, upgradation of ULBs and creation of new ULBs.
  (ii) Addition of surrounding rural areas to the ULB.

(b) Semi-urban areas showing similar characteristics of urban areas that can benefit from economic reasons of service delivery.

Public Health & Environmental Safety Considerations

The outcomes on public health and environment are paramount to the policy deliberations. It is for this reason that the wastewater generated across ULBs require regular monitoring especially for the cities with treatment and disposal mechanisms. The database generated through the monitoring mechanism will be used to establish ULB categorizationas an input and basis for channelizing the resources.

Standardisation of Norms, Design and Specification of SM Infrastructure, Operations and Services

"Universalize septage management services across all ULBs with uniform quality in standards and efficient administration"

In the specific context of the cities and towns of the state of Uttar Pradesh, policy recommends development, dissemination and enforcement septage management norms, design and specification for the infrastructure construction and O&M of SM infrastructure including the aspects of user interface, evacuation trucks & equipments, treatment technologies covering the aspects of criteria for end-product disposal/reuse. The policy is establishing SM services charter and this provision is will assist towards it to ensure that the ULBs render professionalization amongst both public and private players. The SM Service Charter is detailed in Section four for compliance and updated from time to time for continuity in the standardization of SM infrastructure and services.

Rolling Out Septage Policy through ULBs

"ULBs are advised to address and achieve public health and environmental safety outcomes in their cities through integrated and life cycle-based planning in tandem with complementary sanitation services like sewerage systems, solid waste management amongst others"

Under SBM (Urban), ward and city level institutional structures have been establishedto address sanitation issues, create awareness and engage with communities. The Ratings for SWM, ODF+ and ODF++ have become mandatory for ULBs. It is the bottom-up planning through the ward level mechanism that provides the tool for achieving the goals in a sustainable manner. It is with earnest that the ULBs are encouraged to use the tenets of this policy to further the ward level community-based approaches in services provision and its management. It is necessary to increase citizen awareness and demand creation across value chain elements through the ward level interface. For the purposes of ODF++ ratings, the roles of the existing institutions can be extended to complement the planning activities under this policy. The ward, zoneand city level Septage Plans are mandatory to provide the basis of investment for the different elements of the value chain and sustaining SM results.

The policy recommends a development of SM Plan by each ULB with a time frame to match the overall policy milestones and the plan alone shall form the basis for raising funds from different sources. A step by step planning guide for ULBs shall support the SM plan preparation.

IT-Based State-wide Management System for Septage Management

"The Department will introduce and use evidence-based decision-making tools at every stage, from planning to service provision and mapping user satisfaction".

An accurate and real-time database of all related SM components is recommended for establishment by ULBs and its integrationwith existing databases/systemscreated under different Missions. It is also directed that ULBs develop I.T. enabled single window system, GIS/GPS aided planning and operations, custom MIS modules to facilitate acompliant, accountable and transparent ecosystem of SM services provided in association with the private sector, in addition to reporting for different rating exercises such as *Swachh Survekshan* and State initiated *Swachh Ward Pratispardha*.

The Policy recommends to ULBs for assessing the quality of ST/OSS infrastructure (as against standards) using a GIS-basedreal-time CSIS (City Septage Information System) awarded as an innovativepractice for the city of Agra and Mathura as part of *Swachh Ward Pratispardha 2018*. The database generated by CSIS is a useful evidence to support SM plan preparation. The survey results could also be used to identify and support scheduling of cleaning services.

User Interface Management

"The Policy mandates ULBs to ensure urban areas to be open-defecation free through universal access to sanitary toilet. The commitment is backed by continued financial investments and top-up incentives and subsidies".

The SBM – U has been prime mover for improving the household level access to sanitary toilet to ensure safe containment of the human faeces. However, a little purpose is served if no arrangements are in place for safe emptying, disposal and treatment of the accumulated septage. Therefore, to further pursue the objective of public health and environmental outcomes, incentivesfor poor and slum dwellers will continue in ensuring that safety of the containment in the On-Site Sanitation (OSS) systems by way of retrofitting and refurbishment of the faulty septic tanksresponsible for septage leakages. The Policy encourages ULBs to provision for an incentive system for both new structures as well as upgrades and replacement, equivalent to sewerage system connection costs. Given that uniform citywide systems and processes are envisaged, financial support may be provided for poor, slum dwellers and other vulnerable groups such as female headed households. A lack of fuller understanding of the quality of septic tanks in terms of technical design and performance has significantly affected the choice of treatment impacting a proper estimation of cost to services. A following actions are being suggested for follow-up:

- Provision of septic tanks / upgradation of faulty septic tanks or twin pits or OSS
- Shifting of septic tanks those sited below toilets and other inaccessible locations
- Incentives for poor, slum dwellers and vulnerable communities
- Use of prefab systems for easy cleaning & consistency, thereby fostering private sector manufacturing

Scheduled Emptying Services

"The Policy encourages ULBs to ensure safe, timely collection and transport of septage through scheduled emptying services. This shift in processes would ensure complete containment of waste with no direct human contact."

The efficacy of scheduled emptying systems depends on robust database of demand, a reliable and uninterrupted availability of service providers, a good management system for coordinated emptying process end to end (disposal at designated locations for treatment). It is important to compliment newly created real-time database with the existing ones already created under different missions for harnessing the synergies of the data-fields. This database shall guidethe treatment systems in terms plant size determination, technology choice and disposal points for safe emptying, amongst others. This evidence-based decision-making system will help ULBs to undertake reform towards an accountable and transparent ecosystem of services provision, particularly when PPP models are envisaged. This will also support the ULBs' preparedness for different rating processes.

The Policy recommends ULBs to plan for the SM system with a mandatory 5-year cleaning cycle for septic tanks. The state-levele stimated targets to be realizedunder this component is ~ 72 lakh septic tanks / OSS in the State ~ 1750 to 3000 MLD of septage treated annually ~ 14 to 24 lakh emptyingsannually ~ 600 Vacuum trucks operating daily.

Technical Options for Vehicles and Cleaning

"Primacy will be accorded to occupational health & safety of the workforce engaged in the full sanitation value chain especially for the instances of contact with human waste. The mechanization and automation are non-negeotiable requirement from ULBs and service providers across the value chain. The state-of-the-art IT and mobile applications will be deployed to track and monitor septage from point of generation until its safe disposal".

Given an overwhelming magnitude of engagement of the unorganized sector in the delivery of SM services especially emptying and conveyance, it is necessary to accord primacy to occupational health & safety of workforce under different value chain elements. The Government e-market place (GEM) Portal has empaneled vehicles of different sizes to help ULBs in procurement for reference.

- Suction-cum-jetting machines are the higher end of the band for the similar volume
- Most economical vaccum tankers are from six CUM category

- 6 cum (₹ 30 lakh) for large cities and 3 cum (₹ 20 lakh) for small cities proposed

The average size of a septic tank or an OSS is 2m X 2m X 1.5-2m an equivalent volume of ~ 6 to 8 cum [Source: CSIS – Agra & Mathura ~1000 samples].

An estimation of the total truck requirement for the emptying business is 572 to match the current demand. The estimation does not include the current stock of vehicles held by the private sector and rendering services and requires to accounted before finalizing the demand for vaccum trucks.

It is recommended that all ULBs should always have basic minimum number of septage cleaning and conveyance equipments in functioning condition based on their size. This will ensure emergency preparedness with the ULB. It is also understood that risks to private sector participation require to be mitigated through this basic mechanization process, more so when scheduled cleaning is mandated.

Treatment, Resource Recovery and Disposal of Septage

The significant determinant for selection of the treatment option is the characteristics of septage.The treatment facility would maximize the reuse of treated waste water and septage for various public and commercial purposes. This will contribute in part towards nutrient &cost recovery and even profit generation. The major focus must be on:

- Treating the effluent for the disposal or for secondary use
- Reducing the moisture content in the sludge and treating it for secondary use
- Pathogen reduction
- Nutrient recovery
- Operation, maintenance and energy requirements of the treatment technologies

The Municipal Bodies with the presence of STPs are being impressed upon to urgently undertake the feasibility of the treatment options amongst exclusive septage treatment, co-treatment with waste water,co-treatment with solid waste,reuse for energy generation and production of products. Additionally, these Municipal Bodies are required to properly document the lessons learnedduring the implementation process to allow for the knowledge generation that shall be useful in advising on the designing new STPs,disposal points and related STPs processes modification.

As regards the new treatment site, it is advised that the following parameters should be taken into consideration before finalization:

- The land parcel (either government or private) for treatment facility should be explored near existing STP, as the land acquisition could increase thecapex for setting up a treatment plant. A land leasing arrangement could also be explored.
- The location of the treatment site may be explored not very far away from the population served. This helps in offsetting high fuel costsdue to long distance transportation by the vaccum tankers as this may result into higher cost to service. The typical distance to treatment unit shall be factored in the pricing for services.
- A fair assessment of the size and dimensions of the land parcel should be undertaken considering the technology choice of the treatment.
- The treatment plant location needs to be appropriately distanced from the residential area. A Rapid Environment Impact Assessment (REIA) of the potential sites and rehabilitation plan shall be assessed.

The treatment plant will require a reliable power supply and uninterrupted water supply for its efficient functioning if the treatment unit has mechanical parts for its operation.

- The geological parameters such as soil type, depth of groundwater table and low-lying areas.
- An assessment of space for future expansion.
- The cost of the land parcel in terms of the purchase price or lost future revenue for alternative uses.
- Climate resilience and flooding risk for the site.
- Other aspects: The location should maintain a safe distance to surface water sources such as pond/river ordrinking water sources such as open wells/ bore wells etc.

To further promote carbon absorption and mitigate climate change resulting from the treatment of the septage and SM related services, tree plantation will be carried out at the treatment facilities and also encourage the local use of the treated waste in form of compost and other products to offset the carbon generation and mitigate the climate change impact. The state of Uttar Pradesh is already carrying out large scale tree plantation and these efforts will further enhance those goals and also contribute to the sustainable development goals related to carbon absorption and climate change besides generating additional financial resources. 5.9 [B] A long-term plan will be developed with regards to the use of treated waste from STPs and FSSTPs so that the unit receives additional financial benefits as well as to ensure the valuable use of waste generated from the unit.

Tariff Mechanisms

"The Policy recommends a septage tax in line with the sewerage tax currently followed in ULBs. A separate head of tax may be created as part of the property tax collection system. This direction is propounded to enable ULBs an uniform and equivalent payment system for wastewater management systems by ensuring a stable funding source to facilitate operations, maintenance and refinancing for new assets. A single point payment system for users to facilitate easy payments to all stakeholders rendering services".

Different payment methods are available for ULBs to set forth charging for septage services rendered by ULBs or by the private sector. While setting up the process of tariff fixation, the cost to cleaning and payment mechanismsshall be kept in mind.

Financial Sustainability of Septage Services

"The Policy recommends financial sustainability as a critical parameter for septage management while designing activities under this policy and commits to financial support for SM on par with other infrastructure".

(a) On the lines of sewer tax, Urban Development Department, Go UP shall develop a septage tax with a separate accounting head. Currently, 4 percent ARV (Annual Rental Value) for residential houses is being charged as sewer tax. Given that treatment costs are on par, an equivalent amount can be explored as septage tax. The use of the funds shall be provisioned for CAPEX and OMEX of FSTPs/co-treatment as applicable; payment of scheduled emptying and transportation services;subsidies for new/rehabilitation of old septic tanks, offset for incentives for the urban poor, etc.

(b) The part funding can be sourced from different flagship programs (for asset creation/Viability Gap Funding [VGF]), private sector investment through PPP models and CSR funding. Where possible, extending the scope of existing projects to some SM elements can be explored. For example, STPs provided with septage disposal points; HHs provided with additional subsidies to construct STs (prefabricated); health, economic and social benefits extended to for staff working in SM, amongst others. Some of the avenues for fund sourcing are SBM for ODF++, AMRUT, Smart Cities, NamamiGange, NULM, Ayushman Bharat, Deen Dayal Adarsh Yojana, 14th FC devolutions and other State Schemes.

(c) Another source of funding is chargingfines for punitive actions like septage discharge into drains (on households), illegal discharge of septage on VTOs, pollution control board fines. In addition, license/permit fees including renewals; disposal fee at discharge points, additional cleaning requests beyond one-time cleaning; cleanings undertaken for non-residential or commercial customers could also contribute.

(d) Other options include those accruing from PPP arrangements for cleaning, treatment, recycle & reuse and sale proceeds from resource recovery (compost, other products, energy, etc.).

(e) Revenues from other service providers for the use of SM linked elements for advertising, providing telecom services, proceeds from other co-treatment with SWM, amongst others.

Legal Framework for SM

"All ULBs to adopt rules, regulations and legal instruments required to operationalize the policy, prior to planning".

All developmental initiatives need legal backing and moreso when active private sector involvement is envisaged. The upfront endorsement of state policy by the ULBs will provide a frame work for pursuing all improvements and activities identified in the SM Plan.

Enabling Institutional Environment and Capacity Enhancement

"To sustain the SM initiatives, the Policy recommends creation of appropriate institutions, management & monitoring systems and standard procedures at state and city level that will incrementally strengthen SM operations in urban areas".

The mandate, roles & responsibilities of all government departments and other stakeholders would be clearly defined and necessary steps will betaken for augmenting their capacitiesatthe state, city and community level for municipal functionaries, service providers, residents, amongst others. The institutional frame work will be evolved for greater participation of the private sector.

On the lines of *Swachh Survekshan*, all Municipal functionaries working on SM and related themes are expected to benefit from a periodic in-service orientation and training. The certification processes like the MoHUA's e-learning modules will be developed and initiated under this policy. The training will be extended to all stakeholders. Given that SM is in the nascent phase in Uttar Pradesh, a dedicated training facility is established for providing services during the policy period. The existing coordinating structures created under SBM (U) may be used for SM policy roll out.

Role Clarity of Different Stakeholders

A clear guideline on the rolesand responsibilities of different stakeholders are required to issued at the first instance for an effective policy rollout. It is equally important for the seamless coordination and timely action by different agencies. For example, Urban Development Authorities (planning & building sanction for new buildings supports in data generation of septic tanks and property register for data integration), *Jal Kal* (operations of STPs/co-treatment facilities, including record keeping), *Jal Nigam* (technical advice on the different co-treatment options, adopt co-treatment in existing and proposed STPs, monitor performance of STPs), Police Department (monitoring of vacuum truck operators compliance), Labour Department (employee/labour welfare and safety), Health Department and Flagship ProgrammeMissions (livelihoods and rehabilitation, health benefits and monitoring), Urban Development Department (rationalization of user charges in line with property taxes, financing for capex for ULBs), amongst others.

Awareness Creation for enhanced Citizens'engagement in SM

"Awareness on SM and septic tank cleaning requirements among citizens is critical to create demand and solicit their active participation".

It is critical to foster "Polluter Pays Principle" to the point closest to the generation of pollutants. Given this construct, awareness creation is critical to ensure households construct septic tanks as per tehnco-legal requirements, periodically empty septic tanks (or similar infrastructure), pay for cleaning services upon demand. The ward level institutional structures available in form *Ward Swachh Vatavaran Protsahan Samity* will help create awareness within their neighbourhood amongst citizens and consequently trigger demand for cleaning services. On similar lines, awareness is also deemed critical for accountability and transparency in services, from a value for money perspective.

Furthering Empowerment alongside SM Implementation

"The Policy envisions empowerment and equity (including aspects of gender, children, senior citisens, differently abled, vulnerable) as

cornerstone principles while fostering SM in the State. The existing guidelines/policies on women, barrier-free environment, livelihood opportunities shall be followed where applicable under SM roll out".

At the national level, generic guidelines and schemes are already under implementation. A due emphasis is to be given to gender equity, where women are encouragedasan active change agents and participants. This will help to mitigate gender-based sanitation insecurity arising due to lack of safe sanitation facilities and practices by reducing health, nutrition,andcare giving burdens.

Inclusion and Incentives

"The Policy recommends SM sector to address last mile connectivity, obviate any barriers to access and include all disadvantaged population into the overall system by way of graded financial subsidies and other financial modes at every stage".

This is to ensure access to services is universal (including a low income or BPL families and slums). In this regard, different options can be explored like:

- Existing incentive mechanisms for sewer connections and IHHL construction will also be extended for septic tank upgradation / construction.
- While new septic tanks can be integrated with new IHHL constructions, refurbishments/upgradation can be taken up based on the septic tank surveys as provisioned earlier.
- An incentive mechanism may be developed to increase the uptake of septage services. For example,
- Households of RWAs adopting decentralized treatment services could be provided septage tax rebates.

Engagement Models for Different Elements of the SM Value Chain

The role of ULB is predominantly on ownership of assets, contract management & monitoring, cost recovery and sometimes that of a regulator. The engagement models outline the relationships between different entities contractually or otherwise. The service charter will form the basis for engagement. The models will detail costs and return on investments within the designed ecosystem. The returns are not necessarily quantified as money but accounts for benefits accrued out of health improvements, social infrastructure andenvironmental improvements. The typical engagement models also include employment of personnel for specific elements of the value chain, use of private agencies for service contracts (individually elements or end-to-end) or PPP arrangements.

Commitments for SDG and Climate Change Missions

"Resource management and circular economy principles will be considered while planning for SM services. Towards this, Policy recommends formalizing institutional and programmatic arrangements with other departments/agencies with whom products and processes will be jointly developed within the framework of this policy, from time to time".

Standards, Regulations & Quality Assurances

"ULBs to follow standards and norms available from time to time and compliances".

- Attention shall be accorded on adopting and enforcing effluent and sludge standards for municipal wastes.
- Extensive and comprehensive monitoring programs shall be developed ranging from influent, effluent from the plants and subsequently on down stream reuse to ensure that the public health objectives and treatment efficiency goals are attained.
- A periodic monitoring will be followed, if reuse from STPs for agriculture and crops irrigation is undertaken.
- The observation wells shall be installed near STPs to monitor groundwater quality where necessary, and to mitigate adverse impacts where and when needed.
- UPPCB/ CPCB regulations for disposal norms shall be mandatory.
- Industrial wastes shall not be allowed to be disposed of or treated in STPs. ULB can issue notification for penalties to be imposed on such industrial units.
- Laboratories shall be maintained and properly equipped to provide services and reliable data needed to ensure enforcement of and adherence to standards and regulations.
- The compliance to the following provisions by the Septage Treatment Facility/s will be necessary as per the Act, Rules and Guidelines issued by Central Pollution Control Board/UP Pollution Control Board from time to time:
  (i) According to the relevant rules of the Water (Prevention and Control of Pollution) Act, 1974 and Air (Prevention and Control of Pollution) Act, 1981, it will be mandatory for the

Septage Treatment Facility/s to establish prior to establishment/ expansion.

(ii) It will be mandatory for the Septage Treatment Facility/s to operate according to the relevant rules of The Water (Prevention and Control of Pollution) Act, 1974 and The Air (Prevention and Control of Pollution) Act, 1981.

(iii) The compliance of the charter issued by the Central Pollution Control Board (CPCB) will be ensured by the Septage Treatment Facility/s.

(iv) Online Continuous Emissions and Effluent Monitoring System will be installed by the Septage Treatment Facility/sand it will be linked to the Central Board and UP Pollution Control Board servers before the Septage Treatment Facility/scan start operation.

(v) The Pan, Tilt, Zoom (PTZ) rotating camera with open access system at the appropriate locations will be installed at the Septage Treatment Facility/s to carry out online monitoring of the pollution control systems and will be linked to the control room set up at the UP Pollution Control Board headquarters.

(vi) The Septage Treatment Facility/s will ensure compliance with the provisions of the Corporate Environment Responsibility Office Order dated 01.05.2018 issued by the Ministry of Environment, Forest and Climate Change, Government of India.

(vii) The Orders issued by the Central Pollution Control Board/ Uttar Pradesh Pollution Control Board and Ministry of Environment, Forest and Climate Change, Government of India and Government of Uttar Pradesh will be followed by the Septage Treatment Facility/s.

(viii) The following steps will be taken by all Septage Treatment Facility/sto ensure sharing of benefits, facilities and concessions as per the principles of Green Productivity and Green Good Practices, namely:

(a) Encourage 7-R principles, namely proper utilization of resources by refuse, reduce, reuse, recycle, redesign, refurbish and recovery.

(b) Undertake Green productivity measures in the continuous production and its regular audit in accordance with environmental principles.

(c) Certification by Bureau of Energy Efficiency.

(d) Adherence to "Energy Conservation Building Code" in new buildings related to Septage Treatment Facilitys units as per rules.

(e) Increase the use of alternative energy. (f) Reduction in emission of greenhouse gases and carbon offsetting.

- ***Financing Septage Management Interventions***

"To advance the achievement of the policy goals and targets, a dedicated fund named "UP State Septage Management Fund" will be set up".

The Septage Management Fund shall be used to support the creation of public infrastructure, cross-subsidy for ensuring reach of services for disadvantaged groups, conducting pilots and innovations, training and capacity building of personnel, building private markets to support service delivery, procurement/acquisition of land for setting up treatment units; amongst others. This fund shall consolidate resources from multiple sources such as centrally sponsered schemes and programs; national/state government grants; Finance Commission devolutions; CSR; bilateral/ multilateral grants & loans; Social & Development Impact Bonds; alternative Investment Funds, amongst other. To manage this task, a dedicated fund management agency may be designated at the State level. The Project plans and proposals shall be aggregated by this agency and funds will be directed based on performance linked criteria. On similar lines, ULBs are encouraged to set up/pool funds under similar budget heads to supplement city-level project implementation.

- ***Legal and Regulatory Support***

State Laws, Rules and Regulations

All the stakeholders involved in SM across the sanitation value chain hence forth shall adhere to the requirements of this policy and modify the respective rules and regulations to harmonize them in the best interest of public health and environment outcome of this Policy. The Model Building Bye-Laws (MBBLs), 2016 framed by the Town and Country Planning Organization (TCPO), Gol as adapted for Uttar Pradesh,will be updated. The suggested themes of support are:

(a) Advise on enforcement and / or regulation of septage services and promote the policy objectives.

(b) Lead the formulation and amendment of regulations related to different elements of the value chain.

(c) Lead and recommend reforms to further achievement of state vision for SM.

(d) Guidance on the choice of treatment systems for disposal, recycle and reuse.

(e) Further, the building and improvements to the septage services industry, including monitoring of operators' compliance with stipulated standards, contractual obligations,and relevant laws and guidelines.

(f) Lead efforts towards improving the operational efficiency of the SM sector, in particular, occupational health & safety, environmental and public health safety through short-term, medium-term and long-term programmes.

(g) Monitor the collection, treatmentand discharge of Septagein compliance with the requirements including reporting on the quality of treated effluent; impact on the environment and performance of treatment plants (co-treatment with STPs & others).

(h) Towards long-term sustainability of the septage services, strive to identify continued investments in infrastructure development.

(i) To serve as platform and account for all reasonable demands for various stakeholders (including private sector), in consultation with the relevant authorities.

(j) Advise on the VTO permits/licenses and other contracting and / or private sector engagement arrangements across the value chain.

(k) Advise on dispute resolution and pricing of services.

Institutional Structures for Operationalizing Septage Management

Septage Management for cities includes both residential and non-residential/commercial waste, but not industrial waste. The implementation guidelines are to be formulated to provide direction, generate knowledge, procedure and facilities for efficientand effective SM practices.

The ULB is responsible and shall be accountable for delivering the services and results under SM. It will manage the overall implementation, make available funds, enter into contracts with different stakeholders, have oversight as per the implementation plan. The ULB shall also ensure clear understanding is available for all stakeholders and maintain a balance of functions (addressing technical, financial, institutional, regulatory and social dimensions) amongst its staff to the best possible manner. Where technical advice and support is required, the services of the State Level PMU shall be enlisted. To support the rollout of the policy, institutional structures are envisaged at three levels – State, District, and ULB.

(a) **At the State level**, a PMU shall be created to act as a Technical Secretariat and support the statewide rollout and management of policy actions. Periodic meetings to review the progress may be worked out. Review of the progress made shall be undertaken quarterly. In addition, a dedicated State level fund management agency shall be created to identify, acquire and manage funds for implementation of the policy and initiatives thereof.

(b) **At the District level**, under the Chairmanship of the District Collector form a Committee to monitor the progress of achievement policy outputs and coordinate city and regional level activities. The DPMs currently positioned at the districts shall extend technical support and coordinate district-level meetings. The quarterly meetings shall be carried out, the results of which will form the basis of a review of the policy at the State level.

(c) **At the ULB level**, to support the rollout, four support structures are required with clear role definition. Their roles can be extended from time to time depending on the policy needs. These institutions are:

    (i) Create an exclusive **Septage Management Cell** (SMC) within the city or extend the role of such an institution already created under SBM-U to support the overall implementation of activities emerging out of the policy. The Cell will comprise of expertise for different themes and projects.

    (ii) Currently, **Ward *Protsahan* Committee** (WPC) is institutionalizedunder SBM-Uand placed with the responsibility of various themes related to urban sanitation. Their role may be further extended to cover septage related activities and accordingly, their capacities built to support the policy rollout at ward level. Their key roles are to support ward level planning to create demand, awareness, and mobilization. The WPC shall meet on a fortnightly to monthly basis.

    (iii) **Septage Management & Co-ordination Committee** (SMCC), an inter-departmental co-ordination committee constituted under the chairmanship of the Commissioner with a representative from various line departments to coordinate and monitor the city-wide implementation, apart from ensuring linkages with existing schemes/missions. The SMCC shall meet on a monthly basis.

(iv) **City Sanitation Task Force** (CSTFs) shall take up active planning and advisory role in co-operation with an elected council and other city level agencies to dedicate appropriate resources and attention to the challenges of SM. The CSTF shall be convened on a quarterly basis.

Policy Evaluation

This Policy shall come in to force from the date of its issuance. The policy may be reviewed once in a year for assessing its effectiveness and making changes if necessary. A state-level committee under the Chairmanship of The Principal Secretary, Urban Development Department of the GoUP and comprising both Departmental and Mission linked agencies, shall review the progress of the operationalization of the Policy, once every six months. The PMU at the state level shall support the processes of policy evaluation and further reporting to Government from time to time.

Modification or Amendments to the Policy

The Government shall from time to time under the framework of the policy, issue directions in the form of Government Orders (GOs) and/or circulars amongst other for rollout of the supporting activities.

Studies and Research to Advise Policy Roll Out and Implementation

Given the magnitude of the challenge ahead, detailed and continued research is required to finetune the policy and support the roll out to meet the targets set forth under this policy.

Technical Options for Septage Treatment The technical options for Septage Treatment can be broadly divided based on the technologies involved in them, namely - Mechanised and Non-Mechanised Technologies. *Mechanized technology* involves automated handling and dewatering of septage with minimal intervention of operators and is designed to optimize solid-liquid (bio-solids and filtrate) separation and enhance pollutant removal in the downstream process. The preliminary treatment for this process involves removing inert solids using septage acceptance units (screening and grit removal), followed by mechanized de-watering using screw or belt press. The de-watered solids may be used as soil conditioner or landfill cover, while the filtrate is further treated biologically using a high-rate aeration system, which is a process used for sewage treatment prior to disposal into a receiving body of water. *Non-mechanized technology* generally involves pond systems requiring relatively large footprints. The preliminary treatment involves the removal of non-biodegradable inert components of the septage (i.e., mostly plastic materials). The septage is then allowed to stabilize in ponds for 30-45 days to further remove organic contaminants. The accumulated sludge at the bottom of the pond is usually pumped out and dewatered using drying beds. When sufficiently dried, the sludge may be used as soil conditioner or landfill cover. The dewat technology or use of plants, microorganism and drying beds is also a low capex and low opex system. There are obviously pros and cons to the two technical options, most notably the land area required, efficiency and ease in operation. Mechanized plants require smaller footprints compared to non-mechanized systems (for example a plant with a seventy cubic meters capacity per day require a 1,100 square meter lot for a mechanized system and 4,000 square meters for the non-mechanized system). Mechanized plants have more reliable and consistent process in meeting effluent standards but require higher capital outlay for the equipment compared to the mainly civil works component of the non-mechanized system. In terms of ease in operation, mechanized plants require less human handling and intervention but will have higher operating costs (e.g., for power, chemical, spare parts replacement).

Fully Mechanized Septage Plant Components	***Non-mechanized Septage Plant Components***
Septage Accepting Unit: The hose of the desludging truck is hooked to the septage acceptance unit (SAU), where the solid waste and sludge are automatically separated.	The mechanical screens are used to separate the solid waste from the sludge. This is a cheaper alternative to the septage acceptance unit, but will involve manual handling of the solid waste.
Dewatering Unit: The screw press is one example of a de-watering equipment. Other options include centrifuge decanter, belt press or filter press.	**Pond** systems typically comprise a treatment train, which involves a series of ponds: anaerobic – facultative – aerobic – maturation, to achieve BOD and pathogen reduction prior to discharge to the environment.

Index

D

E

F

N